the organizational world

HAROLD J. LEAVITT
STANFORD UNIVERSITY

WILLIAM R. DILL
NEW YORK UNIVERSITY

HENRY B. EYRING
RICKS COLLEGE

HARCOURT BRACE JOVANOVICH, INC.
NEW YORK / CHICAGO / SAN FRANCISCO / ATLANTA

Acknowledgments

Many of our students, colleagues, and executive friends contributed to this book—mostly unknowingly. The bulk of the typing, collating, and backing and filling was handled patiently and with good humor by Mrs. Katherine Bostick.

The book is dedicated to all our children, who have influenced it much more than they realize.

©1973 by Harcourt Brace Jovanovich, Inc.

All rights reserved. No part of this publication may be reproduced or transmitted in any form or by any means, electronic or mechanical, including photocopy, recording, or any information storage and retrieval system, without permission in writing from the publisher.

ISBN: 0-15-567562-1
Library of Congress Catalog Card Number: 73-1243
Printed in the United States of America

Contents

Introduction　　　　　　　　　　　　　　　　　　　　　　xiii

PART 1　　INSIDE THE ORGANIZATION　　　　　1

1　A Systems View of the Organization:
　The Moving Model　　　　　　　　　　　　　　　　　3

　　The Organization as a Dynamic and a Human System
　　Is the Organization Unpredictable?
　　Consider the Organization's Tasks
　　Summary

2　Organizational Task Objective and Goal:
　What Are We Doing Here?　　　　　　　　　　　　15

　　Organizational Tasks: What We Do Determines What We Are
　　What We Are Also Determines What We Do
　　Do Continuously Changing Tasks Guarantee Lively Jobs for All
　　　People?
　　Management by Objective: One Approach to Specifying Middle-
　　　Range Goals
　　Organizational Goals: Why Is It So Hard to Set Them?
　　How Are Goals Set?
　　The High School: An Example of Multiple, Conflicting Objectives
　　　and Goals
　　Summary
　　Notes and References

3 *Organizational Structure:*
   Up the Hierarchy   30

   Formal Authority
   Other Functions of the Hierarchy of Authority: Order, Predictability, and a Long Life
   The Psychology of the Hierarchy of Authority: Some Intended and Unintended By-Products
   Hierarchies Serve Functions Unrelated to Authority
   Trends in the Use of Authority
   Summary
   Notes and References

4 *Organizational Specialization:*
   Little Cogs and Big Wheels   45

   The Scope of Specialization
   The Functions of Specialization
   Forms of Specialization
   Some Costs of Specialization
   Summary
   Notes and References

5 *Information and Control:*
   Maintaining Organizational Law and Order   57

   Information Systems Are Where the Action Is
   Are Elaborate, Formal Information Systems Really Necessary?
   What Are the Important Informational Problems?
   What Sorts of System Are Needed to Help Solve Problems?
   Structure vs. Flexibility: One Major Problem in the Design of Information Systems
   The Problem of Speed in the Design of a Good Information System
   The Problem of Standards in the Design of a Good Information System
   Using Information Systems for Planning
   Getting It All Together
   The Whole Man Strikes Again: Human Problems of Formal Information Systems
   Summary
   Notes and References

6 *Technical Tools for Decision Making:*
   Systems Analysis, Model Building, and Their Relatives   81

   An Early Example of Systems Analysis
   Some Current Examples

Can Systems Analysis Really Deliver?
Is Modeling a Passing Fad?
Glue, Spit, and Bailing Wire: Some Tips on Making Models
What Gives Models Their Power?
Systems Analysis and Discontinuities
Relevant Modeling and the Computer
Summary
Notes and References

7 Computers:
  Brother? Big Brother? Oh, Brother!   99

  Just One More Machine?
  The Newness of It All
  How Do Computers Work?
  Programs: The Things That Make Computers Go
  How Computers Earn Their Keep: The Patient Clerk
  The Decision-Maker's Assistant
  Costs and Capacities
  Computer Speed: The Fastest Gun Is Getting Faster
  The Consequences of Speed
  On Living with the Computer
  Summary
  Notes and References

8 People in Organizations:
  People as People and People as Resources   121

  Two Views of Man-in-Organization
  Men, Groups, and Organizations
  Summary
  Notes and References

9 Work and Motivation:
  You Can't Hire a Hand and You Can't Motivate One   128

  The Hand-Hiring Period
  The "Human-Relations" Period
  The Whole-Man Movement
  Motivation: Is It a Phony Problem?
  Who in the Organization Is Insufficiently Motivated?
  The Worsening Problem
  On Remotivating the Demotivated
  Motivation as a Problem in Coordination and Integration
  Motivation as Imbalance
  A Dilemma: Acceptance vs. Evaluation

Which Model for the Organization? Evaluation or Acceptance?
Summary
Notes and References

10 Groups and the Manager:
   Just the Immediate Family   148

   When Are Groups Useful? And Why?
   Groups That Work and Groups That Don't
   Breaking Groups In
   Group Process
   The Cost of Maintaining a Group
   Up the Ladder to Autonomy?
   Groups and Their Relations with Other Groups
   Summary
   Notes and References

11 Groups, Politics, and Conflict:
   The Many Faces of Organizational Warfare   159

   Some Varieties of Conflict
   How Organizations Handle Conflict
   Some Old and New Tools for Dealing with Conflict
   Summary
   Notes and References

12 Organizational Growth:
   A Reprise   173

   How Growth Changes Structure
   Growth and Its Effects on People
   Growth and Technology
   Task and Growth
   The Differentiated Organization and Its Integration Problems
   The Inaccessible Executive and the Plural Executive
   Why Grow?
   Summary
   Notes and References

        PART 2   OUTSIDE THE ORGANIZATION   191

13 The Organization and Its Environment:
   From the Inside Looking Out and From the Outside
   Looking In   194

      Internal Sources of Change
   People Inside the Organization
   Success and Failure

Organizational Sensors
The Basic Function of the Organization

External Sources of Change

Time and History: Society Fights Back
Social Protest
Technology
The Bright Side?
Summary
Notes and References

14 *Customers, Clients, Consumers, Constituents:
    The Restless Love Life of the Organization*   209

The Customer as Final Authority
The Organization's Stake in Persuading Customers
The American Way of Marketing
Does He Really Love Me?
Putting the Shoe on the Other Foot: Caveat Vendor!
The Morality of Marketing
An Illustration: Population Control and Marketing
Summary
Notes and References

15 *The Money-Go-Round*   227

Money as Social Glue
Money as Oxygen
Das Kapital: Fixed and Working
Clever Accounting and Capital Requirements
Looking for Investors
The Cost of Capital
Money in Motion: The Concept of Cash Flow
Keeping Your Backers with You
Summary
Notes and References

16 *Rulemakers and Referees:
    To Kibbitz or to Control?*   248

Who Owns the Whistles?
The Many Faces of Government
How Regulators Regulate
Bargaining to Get Your Way
Uses of Authority across Organizational Lines
Disunity of Command
Dependence as the Counter to Authority

    Mixing Regulation with Other Roles
    Responding to Regulation
    Summary
    Notes and References

17 *Organizing Society:*
   Pluralism vs. Hierarchy on a Grand Scale   268

    The Failures of Pluralism
    Alternatives to Pluralism
    Life in a State-Organized Society
    Summary
    Notes and References

18 *The Organization Abroad:*
   Good Guy or Bad Guy?   285

    Morality and Propriety
    Summary
    Notes and References

19 *Operating Away from Home*   292

    The Offshoot Squeeze
    Relevant Differences among Cultures
    Factors Affecting Adjustment
    Some Tentative Rules of Thumb
    International Offshoots and Supranationalism
    Summary
    Notes and References

20 *Strategies for Survival:*
   How Organizations Cope with Their Worlds   303

    The Points of Contact
    Sense Organs and Survival
    Internal Communication, Muscle, and Survival
    Some Alternative Designs for Survival
    Organizational Tuning
    Overcentralized and Undercentralized Organizations
    The Strategies of Imperviousness, Adaptation, and Action
    Redesigning Oneself
    Summary
    Notes and References

21 *The Future of the Organization-Environment Relationship: Can This Marriage Last?*   316

    Do Organizations and Societies Blend or Clash?
    Change as a Series of Overlays
    Techniques Bring Change
    The Age of Aquarius?
    And Aquarian Organizations?
    Some Alternative Ways of Organizing for the Future
    Summary
    Notes and References

Name Index   331
Subject Index   333

Introduction: A Rationale for This Book

This book is about organizations in the contemporary world and about the people in them, with particular emphasis on business organizations. It is intended mainly for people who don't know and may not care much about organizations and especially for those who are suspicious of the values and ethics of organizations or their treatment of human beings. We may not eliminate these suspicions; we do hope to put them in perspective.

This is not a how-to-do-it book, but it does try to describe the way organizations work and why they work that way. It points out that they often don't work well and suggests some ways to make them work better. It tries to show how and why organizations do or don't seem to fit their social environments and explores ideas for improving that match. We believe, however, that the work of individuals in serving and shaping organizations is a very particular and personal business. We offer some concepts and viewpoints from which you may develop your own outlook and fashion your own style and technique.

The book is also a propaganda piece: it asserts that organizations are necessary. Under every kind of political and social system that man has conceived so far, they *do* exist, and they *do* serve important needs. In the three most common contemporary political environments—capitalist, socialist, and communist—organizations are growing in size, complexity, and power. They are not going to wither away.

Further, organizations are *the* forces that can change the world and through which imaginative and active young people can magnify their influence. The book suggests to older managers that they owe their organizations more than blind loyalty; that they should acknowledge deficiencies and respond to people with ideas for change. For there is a widely held view, especially among the young, that organizations strap people into straitjackets and force them to spend their lives doing obeisance to false gods; that managers spend their lives selling carcinogenic cigarettes or exploiting Peruvian peasants while ignoring social change; and that the young person who is foolish enough to enter a large organization must become a passive servant of whatever is already there, to be shaped and molded by "Them."

There is, unhappily, much truth in those views, but far less than there used to be and far more than there needs to be. Organizations today are not as sure of themselves as they once were. They are searching for ways to change even as they resist change. And the itch for change is not unique to youth. Though the tactics of used-car salesmen and the blight of industrial air pollution are still with us, large business organizations today do have other sides too. They worry about desalinizing sea water, industrializing Crete, and developing techniques of mass education, crime prevention, population control, and farming (not raping) the sea.

Not that business organizations don't intend to make a profit while they do good. They do. Profit-seeking remains an important discipline when the path to profits lies in serving customers well. Managers have to recover the cost of the capital that has been used to build their business if the business is to survive. Making money remains an ever-present short-run goal.

Most managers, though, realize that they must think beyond profits. They must carefully consider not only the short-run effect of their decisions on company revenues, but also the long-run impact of those decisions on society. Managers have to cope with changing values and with changing knowledge about the long-run effects of business decisions. The "fast buck," they realize, is often a costly one to make. They are having to rethink their methods and, more important, their goals.

But the manager has one thing going for him (and against him too). He has a big, powerful organization. It's awkward and cumbersome, to be sure, but it provides him with a potent tool for social change.

We must remember too that his big cumbersome organization has also changed. It has become much more of a multipurpose tool than it used to be. It is no longer rigidly bound to follow a single track. It can move in many directions at many speeds. The modern indus-

Why Focus on Organizations?

To understand why the workings of organizations must be of greater concern for you than for your great-grandfather, consider these facts of a century ago:

- The average college enrolled fewer than one hundred students and had a faculty of ten.
- There were fewer corporations with $5 million of annual sales than there are with $50 million of sales today.
- The total revenues of the federal government were less than the sales of any of the three hundred largest private companies in 1972.
- It took days, not hours, to travel across the country and weeks to travel to many points overseas; it took hours, not minutes, to exchange messages by telegraph or cable. (Even as late as 1929 the President of the United States did not have a telephone on his desk.)
- Fewer people lived in villages like White Plains, New York, than currently work there for single corporations like IBM or General Foods.
- Your college textbook in business management, if you had one, was more likely to contain advice on how to satisfy customers and keep records in a one-man proprietorship than guidance on how to build an organizational career.
- Except in a few parts of the country, companies could dump waste and towns could dump sewage in rivers without raising complaints from the people who lived downstream.

trial organization, despite its size, is a far more flexible, self-modifying organism than its predecessors. In fact, some new organizations are so flexible that they *cannot* ride on the old track and survive. The choice is not between continuing the old and trying the new. The organization *needs* the new in order to function. It *needs* change to keep its highly trained people happy and to exercise its new technological power.

Such flexible organizations are always searching for new problems. Their appetites are not just large but diverse. Today's manager has to steer the beast through new and unfamiliar terrain, so he must keep worrying about where it ought to go next. He needs new products, new companies to ingest into his own, new problems to overcome, new markets to exploit. The flexible organization will go almost anywhere as long as today's destination is different from yesterday's.

But given the myriad of choices, *how* shall the new manager choose? Perhaps the same way young people seem to choose: uncertainly, but preferring the socially relevant to the irrelevant.

Many organizations are slowly (very slowly) becoming activists—well equipped, eager to break out of the past, and pushed from behind by affluence, by technology, and by their own people.

More than ever before young people can influence the shape and direction of business organizations. The organizational world is passing through what might be called "a decline of experiential power." The length of one's experience is simply not so determining as it used to be. Much more weight is being ascribed to knowledge, intelligence, energy. This is not at all to say that the bright young graduate, fresh out of school, will find himself in the president's chair in three months. But he need not spend five years on the shop floor before he is given some responsibility for initiating action. In tomorrow's organizations, a young person will be more likely to complain that he is in over his head than that he doesn't have enough to do.

That young men and women are being listened to in large organizations is apparent everywhere around us. The demand for talented new people increases from year to year, and the rate at which they move into responsible positions is speeding up too. Most of them, of course, are moving into positions of second-order influence. They are most likely to show up in staff jobs, as organizational thinkers, analysts, planners. These are roles that affect the direction an organization takes, but they are also roles through which people can be coopted into the system.

And that is one of the important dilemmas of organizational life. A good way to change organizations is to join them. But the price of membership in any group is some degree of conformity. By the time one wins enough influence in an organization to change *it* significantly in *his* direction, will the organization have changed *him* in *its* direction so that he will no longer try quite so hard?

One more point: young people are discovering that life in organizations need not be lonely. The typical operational unit is coming to be the small group—several people working closely together on some large problem. Work, these days, is moving much more toward working *with* than *for* others, more toward cooperation than toward competition.

As you make your way through this book, judge for yourself the validity of this basic syllogism:

—Complex organizations have a large potential for changing the world.

—Young people, well educated and well motivated, have a large potential for changing complex organizations.

—Therefore young people, through organizations, have a large potential for changing the world.

PART 1

INSIDE THE ORGANIZATION

"There ain't no free lunch."
—Anonymous

A NOTE ON DESIGN

In the twelve chapters of Part I we try to dissect the organization, looking *inside* to see what makes it tick, and occasionally considering whether it ought to tick that way.

In Chapter 1 we look at the whole internal system. Then, in Chapters 2 through 11, we break the system into four key elements:

1. *Organizational tasks and purposes.* What are the goals of organizations, and how do they go about achieving them?
2. *Internal organizational structure.* What are the building blocks of organizations? Are there different ways of viewing structure? Why?
3. *Tools of organizational administration.* How are changing technologies for information storage, communication, and control being used to perform tasks and hold organizations together?
4. *The organization's people.* How are the ideas and activities of *individuals*—the most critical of all organizational elements—meshed to achieve cooperative ends?

After we have taken the organization apart, we try to put it back together in Chapter 12, with particular emphasis on understanding not only how the organization works but on how it develops and grows.

1

A Systems View of the Organization: The Moving Model

Lift the hood and look inside any large organization — General Motors for instance, or your local hospital. What do you see?

What you may expect to see — but don't — is an animated organization chart — a pyramid of little boxes, each sitting astride seven others, and seven more under each of those seven, and seven more, and so on. Perhaps, too, you expect to see each of the top boxes occupied by a faceless figure in a gray flannel uniform and the lower boxes occupied by figures, also faceless, in overalls. Each figure is busily pushing levers to make other faceless figures turn and jump in unison until the whistle blows, when they all stop together.

But that is not what's inside the organization — not a clean, orderly, noiseless, and synchronized arrangement of people. Things go wrong in organizations. Equipment breaks down. Crises destroy the peace. Competitors do the unexpected. And the people are *real*. They don't move in unison. They have faces. Sometimes they cry. Sometimes they spit.

But perhaps all these events are just deviations from the ideal — imperfections that we should try to refine away.

That is pretty much the view that organization theorists used to hold: the perfect organization would show a completely detailed structure designed flawlessly to perform a specified set of functions. Into that structure one would then plug specially designed tools and machines, and specially designed people — specially selected, specially molded, indeed specially clothed. Each little part would have its own discrete purpose. The whole organization, according to this view, would precisely equal the sum of its parts. But in recent years that ideal structure has come to be seen as neither achievable nor desirable.

The Organization as a Dynamic and a Human System

Consider first what we do find in organizations today, and then whether or not what we find is what we should find. In today's organizations we find just what we find in the rest of the world: that the system needs oil and grease and constant adjustment and that we must pay some price for what we get in performance. We must modify the system when we add new parts or try to put it to new uses. We find that it consumes more fuel at one time than another, that it overheats under certain pressures and temperatures.

The complex organization is more like a modern weapons system than like old-fashioned fixed fortifications, more like a mobile than a static sculpture, more like a computer than an adding machine. In short, the organization is a dynamic system.

After we get used to the noise and complexity of a large organization, we can begin to break it down into at least four basic parts:

1. Tasks — the organization builds things or designs things or provides services, all with certain purposes in mind.
2. Structure — the organization has some broad, more or less permanent framework, some arrangement of processes and material resources and people in some sequence and hierarchy.
3. Tools — the organization incorporates technological advances and provides tools that enable people or other machines to perform tasks. These tools also provide the means for administrative control.
4. People — the organization is populated by these sometimes troublesome, but highly flexible, doers of work.

In this view of the organization as a dynamic structure, the parts themselves are of less significance than the varied and multiple relationships among them. In the older, classical view of organizations, pretty much the same parts were present, but the relationships among them were conceptually simpler. The parts worked in a kind of preordained order. According to the old view, the manager first defined the tasks to be performed, then he collected the tools and the people he needed to get those tasks carried out. Then his job was complete. He had it made, forever and ever.

Structural vs. Systems Views of Organization

A good way to think about the differences between a structural and a systems point of view is to consider the difference in usefulness between an organization chart of a football team and the team's book of plays. The chart will tell you something about authority and function, but not very much about other matters:

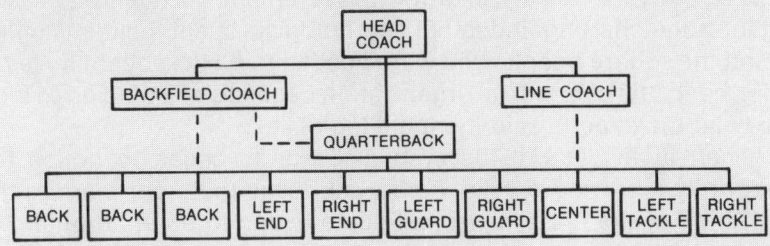

The diagrams of plays, however, tell you a great deal about how a team works together against an opponent to gain yardage and score touchdowns:

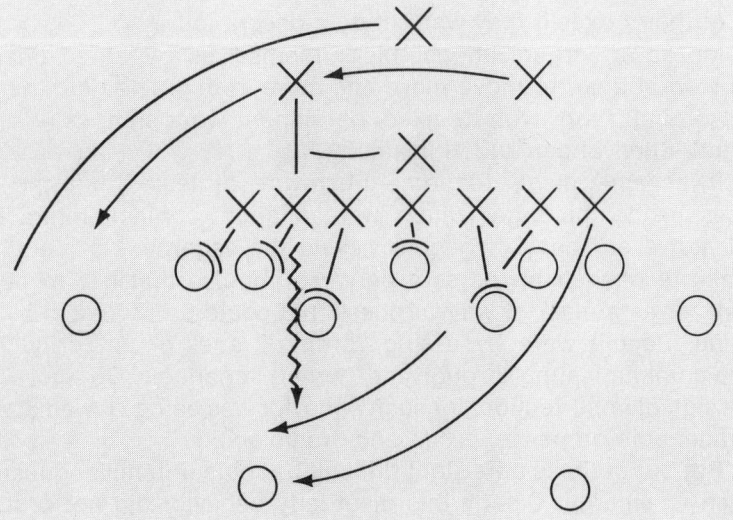

A Systems View of the Organization

Somehow over the years this cold, though seemingly logical, view of what organizations *should* be like became confused with what organizations actually *were* like. This confusion was partly the result of several decades of trying to conform the world to the model, to make the organizations look like organization charts. The classical model served as a goal, as an ideal toward which to strive. Hence it is not surprising that real organizations *did* gradually begin to look more and more like this ideal.

In the 1930s and 1940s, trying to achieve the classical ideal led to a great flurry of activity in work measurement, job definition, and organization charting. Industrial psychologists spent their time trying to find the square people who were needed to fill the square boxes in those neat little charts. The organization began to be tidied up to look like what the experts said it should look like.

Then in the late 1940s even the experts began to notice the stubbornly recurring cracks, holes, and leaks that kept marring the perfection of the classical form. People began to break through the walls defined by organization charts, refusing to suffocate in their tight organizational cells. They began to rebel, partly against the routine and monotony of their constraining jobs, but partly too for the chance to do their jobs right. They were fighting nonsense—boundaries and rules that didn't work, ideal forms that didn't fit the irregularities of real life. Reasonable people, people of good will, not just those radical socialistic "Wobblies," found that they had to break out of their boxes if they were to do a decent job.

Moreover, organizational tasks themselves began to change. The world began to move more and more swiftly. The rigid, permanent organization, with its fixed, permanent work stations, was left behind. Survival demanded flexibility.

It became clear—to some observers at least—that the real forces inside the organization were change, conflict, interaction. Still, however, many managers viewed the eagerness of people to break out of their boxes as a perverse impulse that had to be put down, or as a mark of waywardness that could be corrected by discipline. People were bypassing "proper" lanes of authority. They were communicating through the "wrong" channels. Conflict was a sure sign of imperfection, for such behavior was being viewed against a model built on peace, order, and predictability.

But out of these persistent difficulties some unfamiliar questions began to emerge. Clearly this disorderly behavior did not promote smoothness and clockwork precision. But might it perhaps serve some other function? Was it of any use?

Some of the new questions were humanistic: Could this disorder reflect an effort by the people in the organization to gain needed satisfaction? Was it part of a natural human search for challenge,

> *Havens against Change*
>
> Not all organizations have to change in order to survive. Many organizations stay in business because they offer a shelter against pressure for rapid social or technological change. Many fraternal groups, many societies for preserving ethnic or national traditions, some churches, and some political and educational organizations are frankly dedicated to keeping things the way they used to be. If the Automotive Old Timers, the National Society of Colonial Dames of the Seventeenth Century, and the Ancient Order of Hibernians are too radical for you, you can always apply for membership in the Flat Earth Society.

for variety, during the long workday? Might it even be evidence of *creativity*—the struggle of frustrated people trying to inject new ideas into a rigid system?

But some of the new questions were concerned with the organization as a system: Was the disorder related to adaptiveness? Was it possible that in the rapidly changing world there were new pressures acting on the organization that required new responses— responses that the old structure wasn't flexible enough to accommodate? Could one design—especially given new technology—*self-modifying* organizations that would be more dynamic, less rigid?

And along with these glimmerings of the *functional* character of what had earlier been seen as disorder came new models of what the organization *should* be like: new models shaped by an awareness of the external pressures acting on the organization, by a new view of man, by new technology, by the recognition of new organizational tasks. The several models that emerged, though different from one another, were all dynamic. The organization was more and more being treated as a self-modifying, adaptive, creative organism.

The individual parts of the organization remained pretty much the same even in the newer models. What had changed profoundly, however, were the *relationships* among the parts. According to the old model, *structure* was king. People, tools, even tasks and resources were subordinated to the logic of structure. But one new model was a *systems* model, in which change could take place in *any* part, with all the other parts capable of being modified to adjust to that change. And another new development was a humanistic model, with a built-in assumption that the organization would and should adapt first to *people*—that it should be first an organization of men and women and only after that an organization of tools, tasks, and structures.

Though the proponents of the systems model and of the human-

> ### Contrasting Visions of a Recurring and a Changing World
>
> Stripped of technicalities the method of the modern efficiency engineer is simply this: First, to analyze and study each piece of work before it is performed; second, to decide how it can be done with a minimum of wasted motion and energy; third, to instruct the workman so that he may do the work in the manner selected as most efficient.
> ... It is simply an honest, intelligent effort to arrive at the absolute control in every department; to let tabulated and unimpeachable fact take the place of individual opinion; to develop "team play" to its highest possibility.
>
> —*American Society of Mechanical Engineers,* Ten-Year Progress in Management Report, *1912.*
>
> My argument is that the first assault on bureaucracy arose from its incapacity to manage the tension between individual and management goals. However, this conflict is somewhat mediated by the growth of an ethic of productivity which includes personal growth and/or satisfaction. The second and more major shock to bureaucracy has been caused by the scientific and technological revolution. It is the requirement of adaptability to the environment which leads to the predicted demise of bureaucracy and to the collapse of management as we know it now. . . .
> In these new organizations, participants will be called on to use their minds more than at any other time in history. Fantasy and imagination will be legitimized in ways that today seem strange. Social structures will no longer be instruments of repression . . . but will exist to promote play and freedom on behalf of curiosity and thought.
>
> —*From* Changing Organizations *by Warren G. Bennis, pp. 10, 14. ©1966 by McGraw-Hill Book Company. Used with permission of McGraw-Hill Book Company.*

istic model seldom agree, they at least share the belief that the healthy organization is one that can modify itself in response to changed conditions. So both these newer models point toward less rigid, more open communication. They are more concerned with process than with form.

According to these newer views everything affects (and should affect) everything else in the organization. In practice, this means that the new manager looks at organizational problems differently than the old manager did. The old manager worried endlessly about the relationship between structure and task and tried to fit people and tools into the "appropriate structure." The new manager worries about how a change in *any* part of his system will affect all the other parts. He knows that some of the effects may be helpful, but that others may be harmful. And somehow he must identify the secondary and tertiary consequences of any change as well as its primary effects. If he doesn't, those unforeseen effects may more than cancel the primary effects.

The old model dictated that task and technology determined structure and that structure determined how people should behave. The newer models have the same parts but assume that all relationships run in both directions:

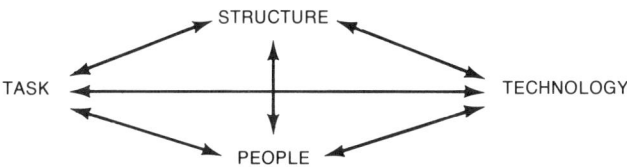

If we introduce something into one part of the system, bells ring and lights flash *all over the system* (often in places we never knew were wired for sound or light).

Is the Organization Unpredictable?

The complexity of organizations does not mean that they are hopelessly unpredictable or ungovernable. Over the last few decades we have learned a great deal about the subtle relationships among the parts of organizations—about structure and people and technology, and about how they are wired to one another. So we now know a good deal more than we used to about what is likely to happen when we throw a particular switch. And at least we know enough to stay alert.

Yet our knowledge is still incomplete. Some observers tend to emphasize the significance of one component and to minimize the significance of the others. There are structuralists and technologists and "people people." Each group may be oversold on its own approach and overly enthusiastic about what can be done by changing structure or technology or people. And each tends to reject the perspectives of the others. How can we find our way through all these complexities?

A Systems View of the Organization

New Interests Are Not Harmful to Your Health

> "What company went from $3 million to $783 million in sales in just six years?" asks a recent newspaper advertisement. Answer: The American Nontobacco Company—the collection of businesses that American Tobacco has bought or developed since 1966 as a hedge against possible declines in cigarette consumption. American Nontobacco includes ventures in foods, beverages, hardware, optical goods, pumps, valves, toiletries, and office supplies.
>
> Now that these new enterprises amount to a third of its total business, American Tobacco has changed its name to American Brands, and can worry less about warnings from the surgeon general. Nor is American Brands either spectacular or unique in its diversity. From a producer of evaporated milk, Pet Incorporated became a diversified food and food service company, even operating Medicare Pharmacies to provide low-cost prescription drugs for those it used to feed as babies many years ago. The Greyhound Corporation operates buses, leases computers, does maintenance on airplanes, and processes meat and poultry products. Even small businesses and nonprofit organizations change directions: a jeweller who escaped his reliance on Christmas sales and profits by starting a potato chip venture; the National Foundation for Infantile Paralysis, which, after perfection of the polio vaccine, switched to raising money for research on birth defects; homes for unwed mothers that are trying to convert themselves into homes for the elderly. The possible varieties of profitable diversification are endless.

Consider the Organization's Tasks

We can start by looking at the *task* component of the organization. What does the organization do? What does it build? What does it sell? As we try to answer these questions, some useful patterns begin to emerge.

First, most large organizations do *many* things at the same time, not just one thing. They do not just make widgets. They build new facilities. They search for new markets. They devise new methods for both production and marketing. They attract new people to keep the operation going. They stave off a wide variety of threats, threats ranging from hurricanes to antitrust suits. Organizations do many things.

Second, these tasks may differ widely, one from another. Some

Rise and Fall of the Railroads

Less than 80 years ago American railroads enjoyed a fierce loyalty among astute Wall Streeters. European monarchs invested in them heavily. Eternal wealth was thought to be the benediction for anybody who could scrape a few thousand dollars together to put into rail stocks. No other form of transportation could compete with the railroads in speed, flexibility, durability, economy, and growth potential. As Jacques Barzun put it, "By the turn of the century it was an institution, an image of man, a tradition, a code of honor, a source of poetry, a nursery of boyhood desires, a sublimest of toys, and the most solemn machine—next to the funeral hearse—that marks the epochs in man's life."

Even after the advent of automobiles, trucks, and airplanes, the railroad tycoons remained imperturbably self-confident. If you had told them 65 years ago that in 30 years they would be flat on their backs, broke, and pleading for government subsidies, they would have thought you totally demented.... The very thought was insane. Yet a lot of insane notions now have matter-of-fact acceptance—for example, the idea of 100-ton tubes of metal moving smoothly through the air 20,000 feet above the earth, loaded with 100 sane and solid citizens casually drinking martinis—and they have dealt cruel blows to the railroads.

—Theodore Levitt, "Marketing Myopia," Harvard Business Review (July–Aug. 1960), 56.

are relatively precise, repetitive, programed tasks. Others are poorly defined, unique, ill-structured tasks.

Third, organizations live through time. Tasks that are critical for a young organization are not necessarily critical for an old one. In their early stages organizations may have to concentrate on the problem of "getting organized"—developing a structure and a set of routines and maintaining enough resources to stay alive. Sometimes, like people, older organizations get set in their ways, and their adult behavior may reflect the ways of their childhood. Organizations that have survived a childhood of near starvation may become rigid, tight, stingy adults, with organizationally "anal" personalities. They may grow incapable of changing in the face of changing times, and yet they may remain highly efficient in getting routine work done. Such rigidified systems have the strength of security and predictability; they go plodding along even when "brighter" organizations would have sense enough to quit. During the Second World War, for example, the French postal system delivered its mail on schedule in Paris on the day the Germans moved in. But the offsetting cost of such single-minded regularity has to be inflexibility.

Fourth, organizations differ in their *attitude* toward particular tasks. Organizations have memories. They learn not only in their heads but in their guts. As they grow from childhood to maturity, they learn how to solve problems and how to structure themselves. And they also learn, as we all do, to be fearful of undertaking certain tasks because they got hurt the last time they tried them. They feel comfortable and secure in doing other tasks because that's where they succeeded in the past. But they may avoid tasks that they now could or should undertake.

So as we try to predict or control an organization's behavior, one good place to start is with an analysis of the nature of the tasks the organization does and might perform.

Summary

Organizations are not just what is represented on organization charts. In recent years they have come to be viewed as more alive, more idiosyncratic, more irrational, and much more human than those neat, charted boxes suggest. Like individual human beings, organizations are dynamic, self-adjusting systems.

The total organizational system includes at least four basic components: the tasks of the organization, its structure, its tools and technology, and its people. Since all four components are closely interrelated, changing any one of them will affect all the others. One important chore of modern management is to predict, and correct for, the widespread effects of what may appear to be only a modest change in any one component.

This more dynamic and more humanistic view of the organization is also a more complicated view. In dealing with any particular organization, one way to simplify the picture is to look first at the organization's tasks. The degree to which those tasks are programable, and their variety, can tell us a good deal about what we should expect by way of structure, managerial technology, and human relations.

In the rest of this first part of the book, we shall examine both the anatomy of organizations and their psychology. We shall look some more at tasks and then at the components of structure, technology, and people. We shall not worry very much about the world that organizations live in — we'll save that for the second part of the book. In looking at each of these components, we shall try first to describe what is, *then consider what ought to be,* and *finally conjecture about how organizations may progress from where they are toward where they might be.*

Notes and References

In the early pages of this chapter we suggested that for many years organization theorists tried to squeeze organizations into idealized, logically structured molds. This attitude was particularly characteristic of organizational theory during the 1930s and 1940s. For a deeper understanding of the rationale behind this type of management philosophy you may want to look at some of the books of that era, such as Alvin Brown, *Organization of Industry* (New York: Prentice-Hall, 1947), or F. W. Taylor, *Scientific Management* (New York: Harper and Bros., 1947, first published in 1911).

In these two thoughtful works you will find not only an emphasis on structure but an underlying belief that men in organizations should do what is prescribed for them by their organizational roles. Brown simply expects that men will do their duty because it *is* their duty and because they have "contracted" to do it. Taylor treats the worker's resistance to the organization as evidence to support his belief that the common working man is not very bright or very rational. Resistance to what is "obviously" good for them "proves" that workers must be made to do what is good for them. Like small children, they are inferior and can't make judgments for themselves.

Starting around 1940 there emerged a new set of criteria for organizational design—criteria based on the novel assumption that management might heighten organizational effectiveness by paying attention to such matters as human need-satisfaction and creativity and adaptiveness.

The major impetus for this new view came from the early work of a group of scholars and researchers at Harvard University. For a historical perspective, you might look at some of their classic works. These works have proved highly influential in contemporary organization theory. Among them are: F. J. Roethlisberger and W. J. Dickson, *Management and the Worker* (Cambridge, Mass.: Harvard University Press, 1939), and Elton Mayo, *The Social Problems of Industrial Civilization* (Boston: Division of Research, Graduate School of Business Administration, Harvard University, 1945).

Out of these early works emerged a view of the organization as a dynamic system whose effectiveness depends on all its many parts. To get a sense of this view of the organization, see also: Chester Barnard, *The Functions of the Executive* (Cambridge, Mass.: Harvard University Press, 1938); H. A. Simon, *Administrative Behavior* (New York: Macmillan, 1954); Douglas McGregor, *The Human Side of Enterprise* (New York: McGraw-Hill, 1960).

While Barnard and Simon are primarily concerned with a more systematic and dynamic view of organizations, McGregor's contribution was chiefly humanistic. It was McGregor, probably more than anyone else in the United States, who was responsible for bringing consideration for *people* to the forefront of management theory.

For a discussion of a model of an organization that stresses the interrelation of the various organizational components, see H. J. Leavitt, "Applied Organizational Change in Industry: Structural, Technological and Humanistic Approaches," in J. G. March, ed., *Handbook of Organizations* (Chicago: Rand McNally, 1965).

Toward the end of this chapter we spoke of the organization as a dynamic organism that learns from experience, somewhat like a person. For a useful discussion of organizational learning from a behavioral systems view, look into R. M. Cyert and J. G. March, *A Behavioral Theory of the Firm* (Englewood Cliffs, N.J.: Prentice-Hall, 1963). For a more humanistic view of management which stresses the executive's role as an educator, see Harry Levinson, *The Exceptional Executive: A Psychological Conception* (Cambridge, Mass.: Harvard University Press, 1968).

2

Organizational Task Objective and Goal: What Are We Doing Here?

"Tell me, young man," asks your prospective father-in-law, "what are your goals in life?" You stammer something about getting a good education and serving humanity and raising a happy family and perhaps getting rich. But you don't feel comfortable about the question, and even less comfortable about your answer.

"Tell me," says the senior consultant to the young new company president, "what are your company's long-range goals?" The president points to a framed document on the wall titled "The Long-Range Objectives of the Cymbeline Company." The document lists several goals: producing more and better widgets at the lowest possible price, providing the best possible service to consumers, acting like responsible citizens, making a reasonable profit in a way that is consonant with the glorious traditions of the American Free Enterprise System, and a lot of other stuff.

And if the president is a bright, sensitive person, he will also feel a little uncomfortable about his answer. Both he and the prospective son-in-law feel, somehow, that their words have a hollow ring. Indeed, it's very difficult for any of us to have a clear and fixed idea of where we're going, of our long-run goals. We suspect that whatever we say today may not be what we will feel tomorrow. We want to hold on to an option to change our minds.

On the other hand, if the prospective father-in-law or the consultant were to ask a couple of different, though closely related, questions, they could be answered much more confidently. Suppose the first question were simply the behavioral one: "What do you do?" Then the young man could answer firmly and proudly that he is a student majoring in social instability. And suppose the second were a short-term question: "What will you do next year?" He could answer that he will graduate, perhaps *cum laude,* at the end of next year; that he hasn't yet made up his mind whether he will go into the Peace Corps, join a commune, or work in his father's fish hatchery. And the company president could answer both questions quite clearly and confidently too: "We produce 900,000 plastic widgets a day in twenty-seven styles, thirty-nine colors. We have 19,000 people on our payroll in seven countries. Next year we will open sales offices in Peking and Murmansk." We can talk easily about what we now do—our tasks; we can talk a little less easily about our short-term objectives; and we usually have a great deal of trouble talking clearly about long-run goals.

In this chapter we shall consider the relationships among the immediate tasks, the short-term objectives, and the long-term goals of an organization, and also the relationships between each of those and its structure, technology, and people. The key issues of the chapter are these: How do particular tasks affect people, and vice versa? What problems do organizations encounter in trying to specify their objectives and their goals? And are clear goals necessary anyway?

Let's first consider tasks, then objectives, and then longer-range goals.

Organizational Tasks:
What We Do Determines What We Are

In organizations, what we *do* tends to be the core around which structure, technology, and people are deployed. An organization that sees its chief task as the production and sale of detergents is likely to be different in all three of these dimensions from one whose chief task is to cure the sick or to move freight.

We don't have a very good taxonomy of organizational tasks. One thing, however, seems clear: to the extent that an organization's tasks are operationally specific, regular, and predictable, the organization is likely to generate a *structure* that is specific, regular, and predictable. If an organization knows not only what it is trying to do, but how and when it must be done, then we should expect its structure to evolve directly from that task, with authority and responsibility carefully allocated, and with pieces of the task carefully cut up and assigned. But if the organization doesn't know exactly what it is trying to do, as may be the case in a research organization—where deadlines, methods, even the problems themselves are ill defined—we should expect the organization to take a different shape. We should expect a more open structure with more autonomy for its people, enabling them to make freer use of their judgment, their initiative, their imagination.

When organizations think they know how to do what they're doing, they can play the tight-structured organizational game. When they aren't sure they know how to do what they're doing, they must rely on their people.

It follows that if an individual wants a hand in shaping what the organization does, he will do well to look for an organization that is unsure of itself! If that description makes an organization sound weak, we can choose words with stronger connotations but with the same fundamental meaning—for example, an organization that is "open to new ideas," that is "searching for new possibilities."

Remember, too, that certainty is in the eye of the beholder, organizationally as well as individually. Many organizations that feel certain they know exactly what they are doing march proudly ahead, with bands blaring, right off the edge of a cliff.

What We Are Also Determines What We Do

The relationship between organizational tasks and each of the other components of organizations is a two-way street. In a real organization, the task that is actually done first is not always the first, logically decided, fixed task of the organization. While it is true that new tasks cause changes in structure, which in turn cause changes in technology and in the ways that people are required to work, it is also true that people, all by themselves, tend to change the ways in which they work, which then changes structure, *and* tasks, and so on.

One important characteristic of people in and out of organizations is their desire to convert chaos into order. We humans are characteristically intolerant of ambiguity. We try to force structure upon things, and so we try to turn ill-defined, unprogramed problems into orderly, programed ones. The first time you play tick-tack-toe, you aren't quite sure what moves to make or when to make them. But after a few experiences with the game you begin to program it, to set up some specific operational rules. Thereby, incidentally, you fence yourself into a tight structure—and thereby, too, you kill most of the fun. But for that very reason you begin to look for new challenges, only to find yourself then converting them from disorder to order, thus making them less challenging, and thereby leading you to search for new challenges, and so it goes.

Satisfaction with having worked something out generates dissatisfaction and starts us searching for something new to work out. The search often leads us not only to set new tasks but to devise new technology. Having identified a new task, we often don't quite know how to perform it. So we put our imagination to work, and we devise not only a set of rules but a set of tools. The function of the tools is to simplify and further program the task. At first we cut out paper dolls with a razor blade, then we discover we can cut several at a time with scissors, and finally we discover that with some simple redesigning we can put a paper-cutter to work. Now we can slice out hundreds of dolls at a time. But our tools often press us toward greater uniformity, less leeway, a tighter system. That's not true of tools in general, of course. It tends, however, to be true of the tools we develop ourselves, if we start from the task and work backward.

But tools that come into the organization by other routes—tools, for example, that were invented outside the organization for other purposes—may have the effect of not only programing existing tasks but of generating brand new tasks. Given a new tool, we can search for new uses for it. Computers are a good example. Until recently, organizations used clerks and business machines and special sets of rules and routines for working out the payroll. Then someone invented a "cheap-enough" computer. Soon countless organizations —large and small—brought the computer in to do the payroll, further routinizing the payroll process and further reducing the role of human judgment in performing that task. But that wasn't the end of it. Next, organizations discovered that the computer, a multipurpose machine, could economically do many other tricks. Once that discovery was made, the arrows began to point in the opposite direction. Computer-aided organizations began to search themselves and the world around them for tasks they could do now that they couldn't do before. In this case the introduction of a new technology served to open things up for people in the organization.

The whole relationship, then, between the tasks of an organization and its structure, its tools, and its people is a dynamic set of exchanges. In most steady, ongoing industrial organizations of the past, the tasks tended to predominate; they were the anchor onto which the structure and the technology and the people were more or less permanently hooked. A shoe factory made shoes. It could plan on making shoes tomorrow too. Tasks shaped organizations.

But now there are counterforces at work that tend to reduce the primacy of tasks in shaping organizations. These counterforces generally lie *outside* the organization—in research and educational processes that keep generating new skills, almost new kinds of people, for the organization to use; in technological innovations that suggest new products or new ways to make old ones; in changed social conditions and preferences that alter the kind of products or services that consumers want. The organization is imbedded not only in a task world but in an educational, technological, and social world. Even if men and women in the organization show no propensity to seek novelty for its own sake, they increasingly face a need to change the task mix so that the organization will survive. Even stodgy organizations are becoming resigned to learning new tricks.

Do Continuously Changing Tasks Guarantee Lively Jobs for All People?

Organizations often earmark particular subsets of tasks to be performed by particular sets of people. While some workers get frequent opportunities to work on the new, the challenging, the different, others are full-time dishwashers. Organizations are almost always *differentiated* in this fashion, with different units performing different kinds of tasks. Typically, the more routine tasks are relegated to the lower levels of the hierarchy. It's no accident that complaints about monotony and boredom generally come from assembly-line people and file clerks and draftsmen. Such complaints come much less frequently from staff people or top managers, or, please note, from private secretaries whose pay and "rank" may be low but whose jobs are often varied and rich.

One great organizational dilemma arises here: as some units of organizations get differentiated according to task, with some dealing almost exclusively with programed tasks and others dealing almost exclusively with unprogramed tasks, the structures of these various units begin to take different shapes. The result of such differentiation is that some employees enjoy the relative freedom and autonomy of fairly loose and open structures while others are required to work within tightly constraining boxes. Organizational life is likely to be varied, challenging, and sometimes even exciting for the first group; but it is likely to be deserving of the apathetic response it often gets from the second group. It's easy to make organizational life fun for the planners, the thinkers, the explorers. It's hard to make it fun for the nut-turners.

One of the traditional solutions to this dilemma, a solution that is becoming less and less viable, is to argue that people are different. Some people like to be nut-turners, so let's find those people. But somehow, these days, such people seem to be getting scarcer and scarcer.

Another "solution" is to try to compensate for stultifying work with higher pay, or incentive schemes, or suggestion systems. While such devices often do serve to distract from the pain, like

*The Benefits of Programing and "Rationalizing" Work:
A View from One Originator*

One of the great task-programers of all time was F. W. Taylor, father of "Scientific Management." Taylor's view of man is reflected in the following excerpts from a letter he wrote to *American Magazine* in February 1911. The letter was a response to an earlier letter by Upton Sinclair criticizing Taylor for his tendency to dehumanize men by routinizing their jobs without paying them all the profit derived from their increased productivity. Parts of Taylor's letter may seem absurd now, but its basic viewpoint is still widely held in certain management circles. Taylor is discussing the case of a pig-iron handler named Schmidt whose job he had timed and programed and whose productivity had greatly increased as a result:

> To return to the case of the pig-iron handler. We must assume then that the larger part of the gain which has come from his great increase in output will in the end go to the people in the form of cheaper pig iron. And before deciding upon how the balance is to be divided between the workman and the employer—namely as to what is just and fair compensation for the man who does the piling and what should be left for the company as profit—we must look at the matter from all sides.
> *First:* . . . The pig-iron handler is not an extraordinary man difficult to find; he is merely a man more or less of the type of the ox, heavy both mentally and physically.

music in the dentist's office, they usually do very little to remove its cause.

Two alternative solutions have found favor recently. One calls for "job-enrichment" programs, which seek to eliminate highly programed tasks and to substitute jobs big enough for whole people. The other solution, which may coexist with job-enrichment programs, is to automate dull jobs, thereby removing them altogether from the human realm. Thermostats probably don't mind spending their time switching the furnace on and off. We'll look at both solutions more closely in later chapters.

*Management by Objective:
One Approach to Specifying Middle-Range Goals*

In the range between short run and middle run, some organizations, like some people, can set and try to reach fairly clear objectives. Indeed in the last decade or two, a whole philosophy of management

> *Second:* The work which this man does tires him no more than any healthy laborer is tired by a proper day's work. (If this man is overtired by his work, then the task has been wrongly set, and this is as far as possible from the object of Scientific Management.)
>
> *Third:* It was not due to this man's initiative or originality that he did his big day's work, but to the knowledge of pig-iron handling developed and taught him by someone else.
>
> *Fourth:* It is just and fair that men of the same general grade (when their all-round capacities are considered) should be paid about the same wages when they are all working to the best of their abilities. (It would be grossly unjust to other laborers, for instance, to pay this man three and six-tenths as high wages as other men of his general grade receive for an honest full day's work.) . . .
>
> And the means which the writer firmly believes will be adopted to bring about, first, efficiency both in employer and employee and then an equitable division of the profits of their joint efforts, will be Scientific Management, which has for its sole aim the attainment of justice for all three parties through impartial scientific investigation of all the elements of the problem. For a time both sides will rebel against this advance. The workers will resent any interference with their old rule-of-thumb methods, and the management will resent being asked to take on new duties and burdens; but in the end the people, through enlightened public opinion, will force the new order of things upon both employer and employee.
>
> Did public opinion (or anything else) force Taylor's new order of things upon both employer and employee?

has been built around the technique of objective-setting by establishing time-limited tasks or targets throughout the organization. The technique is concerned with a kind of middle range of "objectives" which lie somewhere between immediate tasks and long-term goals. If the groups and the individual members who make up an organization can work together to specify realistic short-term objectives, and if all these objectives can be coordinated into a broad scheme, many positive outcomes will emerge: people who are involved in the process of setting objectives and who know what they are trying to accomplish will be likely to work more effectively to accomplish those objectives. The measurement of progress and the evaluation of performance will become easier. The autonomy of individual members will be more readily maintained because it is progress toward objectives, not personal styles of behavior, that can be evaluated. The organization members will become more selective in their response to multiple pressures because they know where they want to go.

But it is no easy matter to devise a set of objectives for the organization as a whole, and subobjectives for subgroups, and

> ### Management by Objectives Comes to Education
>
> Some people see the careful analysis of tasks and objectives as the most promising avenue for increasing the effectiveness and controlling the costs of education. Company training directors, school principals, college presidents, and educational publishers are beginning more and more to use charts like this one to describe the "modern approach" they are taking.
>
> ```
> ┌──────────────┐     ┌──────────────┐
> │ Set          │────▶│ Set behavioral│
> │ general      │     │ objectives for│
> │ training     │     │ course       │
> │ goals        │     └──────────────┘
> └──────────────┘            │ ▲            ┌──────────────────┐
>                             ▼ │            │ Develop course   │
> ┌──────────────┐     ┌──────────────┐      │ materials        │
> │ Test         │────▶│ Measure      │      │                  │
> │ performance  │     │ attainment of│      │ Texts            │
> │              │     │ objectives   │      │ Projects         │
> └──────────────┘     └──────────────┘      │ Laboratories     │
>        ▲                    │              │ Films and tapes  │
>        │                    ▼              │ Lectures         │
>        │             ┌──────────────┐      │ Computer exercises│
>        │             │ Teach        │      │ Etc.             │
>    ( STUDENT )◀──────│ Prescribe self-│◀───└──────────────────┘
>                      │ study        │
>                      │ Guide and advise│
>                      └──────────────┘
> ```
>
> While most people applaud the effort to be clear about setting objectives and careful in designing and assigning lesson materials, critics smell a rebirth of some of the worst aspects of Taylorism. Will the students who experience this new approach be any happier than Schmidt, the pig-iron handler?

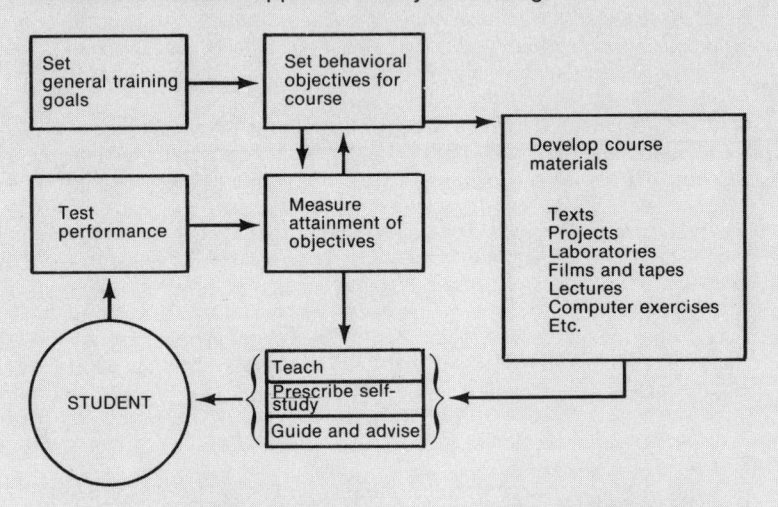

sub-subobjectives for still smaller units. Ideally, the objectives of each unit must be (1) measurable, (2) acceptable to the members, (3) attainable with "reasonable" effort, and (4) coordinated with the objectives of other units. Do you think you could design such a set of objectives for any organization you know? Could you do it for yourself? Could you do it for yourself, but with the concurrence of your immediate boss? Many organizations are trying, with some success, to do just that.

Organizational Goals:
Why Is It So Hard to Set Them?

As we said earlier, it's easier for people to say what they do than to say where they want to go in the long run. The same is true of organizations. But why should it be difficult for a person or an organization to plan ahead? One reason is that thinking about current tasks tends to drive out thinking about long-range goals. We pay attention to the doctor's appointment at 9:00 A.M. tomorrow because it's there, it's scheduled. We work on the theme that's due on Monday. We push aside thinking about the future because we must think, right now, about pressing deadlines. Organizations tend to get caught in the same trap. The president's office is constantly filled with the clanging of firebells. It's easy for him to spend all his time responding to them.

Another reason for the difficulty of planning ahead is that the world out there keeps changing. The rational, parsimonious man buys insurance only to find that inflation has eaten up its benefits before he (or his heirs) can enjoy them. A company tools up to make a new insecticide, and Rachel Carson writes a book that scares off all the customers before the factory can get into production. We say we are determined to spend our first years after college out seeing the world, but at the end of our senior year we decide we can't wait even six months to get married.

Though it is growing more and more difficult to plan for the future in our changing world, planning ahead is not a foolish pastime. Modern organizations are trying to think about the future. Unlike individual people they can do such thinking by specializing, by allocating part of themselves to think about the future *full time.* For the professional planner in the organization, the long-range plan thus becomes the doctor's appointment; it is his *current* task.

How Are Goals Set?

Goal Setting Is a Political Process. Even if long-term goals are immediate and engrossing to a few people at the top, they are hardly so to the rest of the people in the organization. Most of us aren't terribly concerned with the long-term fate of the organization we work for. But we are likely to be vitally interested in the growth of our own department—and even more interested in the growth of ourselves. People in organizations, like people anywhere else, tend to take "local" things more seriously than distant ones.

Moreover, if, as we argue, large organizations are not solid large units but more like patchworks of more or less loosely connected little units, they are likely to have many goals at many levels —individual goals, group goals, suborganizational goals. And these numerous goals are rarely perceived and understood from one unit to another.

The problem wouldn't be very serious if all the discrete little goals meshed together into one big beautiful goal. It would be great if everybody who was trying to get what he wanted caused the organization itself to get what it said it wanted. But in real life individual and departmental goals (which are often only vaguely understood even by those who share them) tend to conflict with one another. In fact, Departments X and Y may have to compete for the same piece of pie in order to achieve their separate goals. Conflict and competition among groups and individuals are characteristic of all complex organizations.

All these conflicts produce a net effect on the direction in which the organization actually moves. Even though we usually think of the organization as setting its goals from the top, pressures from below can turn the rudder. The top managers are supposed to look at the environment in which the organization exists and the resources it has at its command and decide how they want the organization to move and where they want it to be in five years. And when top managers do set such goals, their decisions will usually significantly affect (but not dictate) the organization's movement.

Other forces, however, are also at work. In a very real sense, *the actual goals of an organization are set to a large extent through internal negotiation among organizational subunits.* Think of the organization not as a coordinated body run from the top, but as a political system in which subgroups and individuals are performing different tasks in different ways with different deadlines and, indeed, with different goals, albeit unclear ones. The sales manager wants to put on a costly campaign to push Product X. The production people want to get those six new plants constructed as quickly as possible. The international people want to develop the European market, and they need lots of good people from within the company and lots of money to do it. The management-development people want all the bright young men in the organization sent off for six weeks of advanced training. These more specific goals (almost *tasks*) — each of them crucially important to the group that is promoting it — also move the organization; they move it in a direction that is the resultant of the bargaining and competing and cooperating that take place among all the groups. And as top management goes about the process of trying to plan and set corporate goals, it must explicitly respond to the demands of all its constituencies.

Goal setting, then, is a political process that must take into account the organization's power structure, its history, and the personalities of its members.

Goal Setting Is Limited by Real or Imagined Constraints. Where organizations go is determined in part by where they *can't* go. We go to Corkscrew University because we can't get into Harvard, or we take a job in Elmira because we can't find one in San Francisco.

Each of us is constrained by our history, our commitments, the society we live in, and the opportunities it provides. We can dream impossible dreams, but most of us eventually settle for goals that are within our grasp.

Organizations must be even more realistic than individuals in order to survive. They are fenced in by limited resources, skills, and markets: RCA might still be in the computer business if it had chosen a better competitive strategy and if it could have funded a longer battle against IBM. Organizations can also be fenced in by legal constraints, national borders, and public attitudes. In the spring of 1972, ITT faced renewed antitrust action, expropriation of its properties in Chile, and lawsuits by Ralph Nader's consumer protection forces. The organization is no freer to do anything it likes than is the fifty-year-old accountant who would like to become an astronaut.

Goal Setting Is an Imaginative Human Process. Even though we admit that internal negotiations and internal and external constraints limit goal setting, let us not scorn the executive's dreams. Some constraints can be broken; some dreams can be carried over the barriers of political bickering. To realize that managers must be aware of constraints and the conflicting goals of their constituencies is not to deny them all power of purpose! The greatest determinant of organizational goals is still the vision and determination of far-sighted managers.

Everybody Wants Everybody Else to Set Goals. One of the most common complaints of the middle manager is this one: "Top management doesn't establish and communicate clear goals. If we knew what they wanted and what for, we could clarify our own goals and objectives." But one of the most common complaints of top managers is this one: "Our middle managers aren't imaginative about proposing new goals and objectives. If they told us what they want to shoot for, we could say yes or no and clear the path for them."

Everybody wants more clearly defined goals and objectives. But almost everybody would be miserable if they got them. For they would feel imprisoned by them.

The High School: An Example of Multiple, Conflicting Objectives and Goals

Consider the case of a senior high school in suburban America. What are its goals? How were they set? How are they changed?

In a commencement speech the supervising principal describes the school's goals this way: "Our goal is to provide the best possible educational preparation for life. Our goal is to teach, to help our students learn, to prepare them to become responsible citizens of our society."

But the principal's wife and secretary know that he has other objectives in the back of his mind, objectives one does not mention in commencement speeches. He wants to keep school costs as low as possible; he wants to make the taxpayers happy; he wants to get the teachers' union to ease up on the pressure they're applying. In short, his goals are to a considerable extent defined by the constraints imposed upon him.

Besides, the stated goal of providing the best education isn't very operational. What does "best education" mean? Maybe the principal wants to build the best school system in the state, though even that can be a nebulous goal. But really the principal—and the school board itself, for that matter—actually spend very little time even talking about *basic* goals. They spend their time preparing budgets, reviewing proposals, and dealing with complaints from students, teachers, and other groups in the community. They work on *tasks* rather than goals. Only implicitly, *through their approach to short-term tasks,* do they commit the organization to long-term goals.

In any event, the principal's goals are not the *only* goals of the school. Also at work are the respective goals of teachers, students, parents, and state agencies, all of whom are part-time or full-time participants in the system.

The chief "goal" of many teachers, for example, is to practice their specialties before a student audience. A few may simply want to hold on to their jobs; others truly want an opportunity to work with young people.

For many students the school exists for social as well as educational purposes—it gives them a place to meet. For others the school is a stepping stone to college and thence into a profession. To them, the school's broad educational philosophy matters very little so long as they can get a diploma.

For certain special-interest groups the school is a place to train safe drivers, or loyal, true-blue Americans, or economically sophisticated citizens, or football and basketball players, or revolutionaries. Viewed from all these perspectives the goals of the school turn out to be diverse and operationally vague.

On the other hand, you may argue, schools do educate students. That goal persists despite the welter of divergent interests. And that's usually true of other organizations. Some overriding goals do survive over periods of time. But remember that even those objectives are subject to change. Will education remain the overriding goal of American high schools, or will it take second place to what may come to seem more pressing goals, like racial peace and urban development? Will the production of petroleum products remain an overriding goal of the oil industry? Or will even that goal give way in time to public insistence on the reduction of air pollution and to the availability of fuel cells? Might there one day be a new plaque hanging on the oil company president's wall, one that says, "Our goal is to produce energy to preserve our environment—at a profit"?

Certainly the forces acting on an organization, both from the inside and from the outside, will have a long-term effect on the direction in which the organization moves. But in the shorter run individual people still have a profound and immediate influence on organizational goals. A new supervising principal with vision, and with a good measure of managerial savvy, may just be able to move his school in new directions.

Once we understand the forces shaping the direction of organizations, we are left with these two guides to their behavior: (1) if you want to know where an organization is most likely to go, look not only at its mottoes but at the pressures acting on it, and (2) if you want to *influence* the direction in which it goes, push!

Summary

Organizations, like individuals, usually have a clearer picture of their tasks (what they do) than of their goals (what they want).

In organizations, tasks used to be the primary determinant of organizational structure, the kind of technology the organization used, and the way it handled people. More recently, with new kinds of people, more flexible technology, and a more rapidly changing world, tasks have become less fixed, less permanent organizational anchors. People and technology can now change tasks as well as vice versa.

This more dynamic relationship tends to open things up for people in organizations and to provide new challenges. But the benefits do not extend to all people all the time, because: (1) people themselves tend to convert challenging new tasks to dull routine ones, and (2) organizations tend to differentiate their people, feeding some of them a diet of only routine, fixed tasks and leaving the new and challenging tasks to others.

Organizational goals—longer-term targets—are harder to specify than more pressing immediate tasks. Most organizational goals are operationally vague. Moreover, they are usually organizationally multiple—that is, often different, conflicting subgoals exist in different parts of the organization.

The organization isn't a free agent. Even if it sets clear goals, obstacles in the outside world won't always let it move directly toward them. In fact, goals are partly determined by constraints—by the do-not-enter signs that surround the organization.

Finally, however, even given the conflicting subgroups and the constrained alternatives, there remains a critical, though sometimes small, area of imagination and vision in goal setting. The amount of imagination and vision shown by organizational leaders separates the effective organizations from the others.

Organizations have begun to give new emphasis to the selection of goals. They are seeking ways to assure imaginative proposals and thoughtful resolution of conflicting points of view. One method many organizations use in goal setting is to set up special planning groups whose only job is to worry about where to go and how to get there. Another widely used method for shorter-range goal setting is called "management by objective," which demands that every unit of the organization specify targets in coordination with other units. The first method assures that some very good people will work on setting objectives, but it runs the risk that their proposals will be ignored by people outside the planning group. The second method is more likely to yield consensus than innovative vision.

We'll take a closer look at the problems of planning and goal setting in Chapters 20 and 21.

Notes and References

For an excellent analysis of the relationship between organizational tasks and the other components of the organization, see P. R. Lawrence and J. W. Lorsch, *Organization and Environment: Managing Differentiation and Integration* (Boston: Division of Research, Graduate School of Business Administration, Harvard University, 1967).

Several good empirical studies have been done in the United Kingdom, where the impact of task, technology, and structure on the organization has commanded the attention of researchers for many years. For example:

Joan Woodward, *Industrial Organization: Theory and Practice* (London: Oxford University Press, 1965), relates the technical requirements of jobs to the structure of organization that emerges.

T. Burns and G. M. Stalker, *The Management of Innovation* (Chicago: Quadrangle Books, 1962), contrasts the "mechanistic" and "organic" forms of organization that emerge from different patterns of task design.

E. Trist et al., *Organizational Choice* (London: Tavistock Publications, 1963), describes the negative social and organizational effects produced by the introduction of "long-wall" technology in coal mining and tells how a new organizational form was developed to fit the technology.

On our propensity to structure the unstructured, see H. J. Leavitt, "Unhuman Organizations," in *Harvard Business Review*, July–August 1962.

Whether or not people are *really* different in their preferences for monotonous or challenging jobs depends on how we define *really*. On one side, Robert Dubin argues that people are "really" different—that some people are "satisfied with a monotonous job and that others search for challenging tasks." See those articles written by Dubin in Robert Dubin, *Human Relations in Administration, with Readings,* 3rd ed. (Englewood Cliffs, N.J.: Prentice-Hall, 1968).

On the other side, the human-relations proponents imply that people are "really" all alike in valuing challenge and growth—or that they should be, because growth is a healthy process. This argument is made explicit in Chris Argyris, *Integrating the Individual and the Organization* (New York: John Wiley and Sons, 1964).

For a more empirical statement containing research evidence that sheds light on the question of motivation in the work situation, see V. H. Vroom, *Work and Motivation* (New York: John Wiley and Sons, 1964).

For an analysis of the goal-setting process and a discussion of goals in general, see J. G. March and H. A. Simon, *Organizations* (New York: John Wiley and Sons, 1958); R. M. Cyert and J. G. March, *A Behavioral Theory of the Firm* (Englewood Cliffs, N.J.: Prentice-Hall, 1963); and J. D. Thompson, *Organization in Action* (New York: McGraw-Hill, 1967).

Hard evidence on the role of "vision" in organizational goal setting is scarce. You will find some suggestive passages in books like Alfred P. Sloan, *My Years with General Motors* (Garden City, N.Y.: Doubleday, 1964); Winston Churchill, *The World Crisis* (New York: Charles Scribner's Sons, 1931); and V. Collins and D. G. Moore, *The Organization Makers* (New York: Appleton-Century-Crofts, 1970).

If you are interested in the concept of management by objectives, the classic work is Peter Drucker, *The Practice of Management* (New York: Harper and Bros., 1954).

3

Organizational Structure: Up the Hierarchy

Anyone who has spent time around large organizations knows that the official system does not always reflect the way things are actually done. There is an informal system as well as a formal one. Hospital patients discover that the official rules often have little to do with the way nurses and doctors actually behave. Students discover that the college catalogue doesn't necessarily tell it like it is. In industry there are grapevines, special privileges, politics.

It is dangerous, however, to conclude that the informal system is the only "real" organization, that all the formal rules—who is responsible to whom and who has what duties—are a kind of ritualistic nonsense that has no meaning and serves no purpose. The formal organization is ritualistic all right, but it isn't nonsense. In fact, the formal organization is extremely functional, and it's quite effective in keeping the organization going. This chapter is about that formal organization, especially the most visible and controversial aspect of it—the *hierarchy*.

The hierarchy is the chain of command, the pyramid of authority that narrows at the top. The stars on the general's shoulders *do* affect the way people behave toward him and *do* affect the kinds of decision he can make, though many people object to such differences in rank and feel that they are prisoners of structure. Yet if we eliminated all the paraphernalia of rank and authority in large organizations, we don't really know what we would end up with. There are no

On the Universality of Structure—
Even in Supposedly Informal Organizations

Structure is not just a concern of perverse people who compulsively need to have things spelled out and formalized. It is a requirement for stability, survival, and success in even the most informal of organizations. A picture of how and why formal structure appears in youth communes is given by this excerpt from, would you believe, the *Wall Street Journal:*

> In the heady youth culture of the late 1960s, communes largely ignored worldly considerations. Spontaneity was the watchword; planning was for the stodgy. But communal wreckages have brought, along with disenchantment, a concern for learning from past mistakes. And along these lines, several conferences were held in various states last summer at which dozens of representatives from the nation's communes (2,000 to 3,000 in number) exchanged ideas of effective management and discussed the formation of cooperative buying groups, barter arrangements and communication networks.
>
> One such conference was held at Twin Oaks, a four-year-old, 35-member commune located on 123 acres near Louisa, Va. While Twin Oaks was formed on the precepts of psychologist B. F. Skinner's "utopian" community—a society free of what its adherents term debilitating competition—the commune is nevertheless a corporation and operates with meticulous plans that rival those of many large companies. . . .
>
> For Twin Oaks members, the commune's businesslike methods begin with a contract executed before joining. Under this agreement, members either lend or donate money to Twin Oaks at the time of membership; and after three years, Miss Griebe says, members "are expected to turn over all their assets as outright donations to the community. Everybody is full of idealism and talking money seems grimy work—but it will make nothing but heartache if it isn't done." . . .
>
> Members are paid in "labor credits" for their various chores; the more distasteful the task, the higher its credit rating and the less time needed to earn the weekly quota of 40 credits. (Dishwashing, for example, is thought by most members to be undesirable and rates 1.4 credits an hour; more desirable tasks rate only one credit an hour.) Overseeing the awarding of credits and other administrative tasks are managers—one for every communal sector (including the garden, pets and construction, among others)—who are appointed by a "board of planners" that acts much like a corporate board.
>
> The planners at Twin Oaks consult with the membership as a whole prior to making decisions, but unanimity of opinion isn't required. "Group consensus becomes a silly forum for people fond of their own voices," Miss Griebe says. "My solution: Let them talk—then have experienced and responsible people make decisions."

—Reprinted with permission of the Wall Street Journal.

clear examples of large human organizations that operate without a formal hierarchy. It may even be that some form of hierarchy is *necessary* for organizing a complex set of people and resources.

So let us consider this formal hierarchy, this differentiation of "superiors" from "subordinates," cardinals from bishops, professors from assistant professors, division heads from department heads, commissioned officers from noncoms. And let's ask: Why has it come about? What functions does it serve? What trouble does it cause? What is likely to happen to it in the future?

Formal Authority

When we talk about hierarchy, we usually mean the hierarchy of authority, the authority of A to tell B to do something. It's easy to get bogged down over what we do and don't mean by authority. For present purposes we mean not just power to perform certain acts but power that is bestowed formally by someone on someone else. Sometimes it is bestowed by the strong upon themselves or upon others whom they wish to make strong. Sometimes it is bestowed, as in a democracy, on someone by the total population to legitimize his power. But the purposes of such ranking and titling always seem to be the same: First, to *empower* the holder to control the behavior of other persons and to make certain classes of decisions. Second, to try to guarantee the holder's *acceptance* of certain powers exercised by persons of higher rank. The army makes the young ROTC graduate a second lieutenant so that (1) he can *give* certain orders that sergeants will carry out, and so that (2) he will in turn *take* orders from first lieutenants and himself carry them out.

This formally bestowed power—the power we call *authority*—is not always the strongest form of power. For it is not *only* by virtue of authority that some people manage to control and influence others. Money may help. So may love, intelligence, and special knowledge or the possession of needed skills. So may special information about what's going on. The sergeant with years of experience in the army may be able to exercise more power than the new second lieutenant. And a group of people together may wield combined power that far outweighs the power of a single person of superior rank. There's an old union song that goes:

> The boss won't listen when one guy squawks
> But he's got to listen when the union talks. . . .

But adding a stripe to a man's shoulder usually increases his power and therefore increases the *probability* that he will be able to control the behavior of people of lesser rank.

Notice, too, that authority can be given to an office or a role as well as to a person. Incumbents come and go, but most of the power stays with the office to which authority has been allocated.

*Other Functions of the Hierarchy of Authority:
Order, Predictability, and a Long Life*

One obvious function of hierarchical authority is to provide predictability. It increases the probability of orderly, regular, institutionalized behavior. The organizational world becomes much more predictable when it is set up as a system of offices rather than as a gathering of men. We can salute the office even when the man who fills it changes; we can predict within limits the behavior of the occupant, regardless of his personality. And on the other end, we can be reasonably sure that our own instructions will be carried out, that people will do what they are told.

A formal system of authority serves yet another related function: it is a mechanism that allows men to build institutions that will live beyond their own periods of participation in an organization. Formal authority, as we find it in military and industrial organizations, is assigned to *roles,* not to people. The presidency of the United States is a role, and a role that will continue, with specified kinds of authority and power, well beyond the term of any individual who fills the office. This *institutionalization* of organizations—the fact that they survive even as their members come and go—is made possible in large part by formal systems of authority.

The hierarchy of authority also provides a tool for coping with conflict. Large organizations are characteristically seething with debate and conflict among persons and among groups. An authority structure can set the rules by which the game is refereed. The chancellor of a university settles quarrels between deans, for example. A committee can be given authority to resolve interdepartmental arguments about budgets. Some may be unhappy with the decisions, but they will live with the outcome because it has been handed down through the structure of institutionalized authority.

In childhood we begin to learn the usefulness of authority when we get into disputes with brothers, sisters, or friends. It's good training toward maturity to work out solutions for ourselves, but it's mighty useful to have mother or father around in case the squabble drags on too long. The children don't necessarily love one another after father has made his ruling, but at least the fight stops and the basic relationships stay intact.

In conflicts between some organizations—company versus union, or nation versus nation—there is often no higher authority to

Authority, Democracy, and Progress

One may not admire the way Tammany Hall ran New York City at the turn of the century, but one of the Tammany leaders had this to say about how organizations are run:

> Suppose the city had to depend for the last twenty years on irresponsible concerns like the Citizens' Union, where would it be now? You can make a pretty good guess if you recall the Strong and Low administrations when there was no boss, and the heads of departments were at odds all the time with each other and the Mayor was at odds with the lot of them. They spent so much time in arguin' and makin' grandstand play, that the interests of the city were forgotten. Another administration of that kind would put New York back a quarter of a century.
>
> Then see how beautiful a Tammany city government runs, with a so-called boss directin' the whole shootin' match! The machinery moves so noiseless that you wouldn't think there was any. If there's any differences of opinion, the Tammany leader settles them quietly, and his orders go every time. How nice it is for the people to feel that they can get up in the mornin' without bein' afraid of seein' in the papers that the Commissioner of Water Supply has sandbagged the Dock Commissioner, and that the Mayor and heads of departments have been taken to the police court as witnesses!

—*From the book* Plunkitt of Tammany Hall *by William L. Riordan, 1963, p. 82. Dutton Paperback edition published by E. P. Dutton & Co., Inc. and used with their permission.*

turn to. Ideally, organizations and their leaders will be mature enough to work out a solution that if not good is at least not disastrous. Too often, however, the conflict gets out of control, with strikes or wars that benefit no one. An authority structure can help prevent or limit primitive conflict and is itself an acknowledgment of our nearness to the primitive. Authority can be oppressive, but it usually beats war.

Limiting conflict is not the same thing as resolving conflict. Authority is often not useful for really *working out* a solution. Authority may also be an expensive tool to use. Sometimes those in authority limit conflicts so severely that the protagonists become more dissatisfied with the authority than with one another. And at other times, the protagonists may approach the authority figures like children who, when they know that father and mother are available, begin to play up to them. Distortions in communication creep in. Exaggerated stories get told. In organizations the struggle for a piece of the budget may produce the same sort of distortion. Exaggerations of

Organization Charts

> The following observations on the impractical extremes to which hierarchies of authority can be stretched were made by Clarence Randall, formerly head of Inland Steel and a skeptic about much of American management practice:
>
>> Now, obviously, to know who is to do what and to establish authority and responsibility within an institution are the basic first principles of a good administration, but this is a far cry from handing down immutable tablets of stone from the mountaintop. Not even the Ten Commandments undertook to do more than establish general guidelines of conduct. They contained no fine print and no explanatory notes. Even the Almighty expected us to use our own good judgment in carrying them out. . . .
>>
>> I remember how shocked I was once when I went to call on the Chicago representative of a large corporation whose main office was in the East. I was a vice-president of my company at the time. He was not only a senior vice-president of his company but a director as well. I felt entirely at ease in deciding for my company the question before us without even telling my boss that the problem existed. But when I put it to him, he opened his desk, took out a black book, thumbed the pages for a few minutes, and said, "No dice. Home office!" With complete complacency he simply dumped the matter on the desk of a remote boss, because the book told him to. As a consequence, his company missed out on a matter of importance, for I had no intention whatever of going East to pursue it.
>
> —*Clarence Randall,* The Folklore of Management (*Boston: Atlantic-Little, Brown, 1962*), *pp. 24–25.*

need, overestimations of requirements, and a whole variety of other devices are used to fool that higher-level judge into making a favorable decision. Organizations that traditionally call upon authority to limit conflicts are often plagued by such games, just as parents are who habitually use their authority to adjudicate their children's conflicts.

The formal hierarchy of authority, then, serves several purposes, however imperfectly: (1) It supplements the informal power of individuals, helping even little men to perform big jobs. (2) It provides control, order, and predictability. (3) It helps to institutionalize the organization. (4) It helps to control and limit conflict.

True, some second lieutenants, even with the authority of their office, still can't handle the job. Some presidencies go down with their presidents. Some organizations grow so tyrannical that they are overthrown by their members. But formal authority remains a useful tool for providing order and stability in organizational systems.

The Psychology of the Hierarchy of Authority:
Some Intended and Unintended By-Products

At the beginning of this chapter we said that while one function of authority was to give the holder power, another function was to guarantee that holder's acceptance of higher authority. The lieutenant not only exercises power but must accept authority from captains. We sometimes forget this counterbalancing aspect of organizations when we look at them from outside. We tend to see the hierarchy as made up of two classes of people: those who exercise power and those on whom it is exercised. But at each level of the hierarchy authority that is being exercised downward is also being accepted from above. Formal systems of ranks are good devices for guaranteeing acceptance of higher authority. The lieutenant knows that his promotion depends in large measure on the captain's opinion of him. The whole training process for officers involves *taking* as well as giving orders.

So we must not assume that people on the receiving end of authority *necessarily* abhor the exercise of authority upon them. If successive levels of the hierarchy were not ready to receive as well as give orders, most organizations would have collapsed long ago.

Authority, of course, can look very different when viewed from below than when viewed from above. The subordinate on whom authority is exercised may perceive it as the power to punish. He may see it as a weapon given to the other guy to ensure the other guy's victory. Seen from below, authority thus is often viewed as somehow unjust. The professor's authority to grade and discipline is viewed that way by some students; the boss's authority to fire looks that way to some clerks. This view of authority as unjust stems from the fact that the formal system of authority, by its very nature, divides the pie of power unequally. If one receives a relatively small piece, he may feel put upon. But one basic purpose of the hierarchy is to make sure that the pie is unequally cut, to ensure that the superior will have more power than the subordinate so that complex jobs can be done and difficult goals can be reached. To make subordinates feel put upon is *not* a basic purpose, but it is often an unintended by-product of the hierarchy.

Another unplanned psychological by-product is a feeling of dependency on the superior by the subordinate, as children feel dependent on their parents. Relationships of this sort, like all other dependency relationships, are characterized by *ambivalence,* by simultaneous acceptance and rejection, by a desire to preserve the relationship and by a desire to escape it. In such situations, it is difficult for subordinates to be open and honest with their superiors

Society without Authority

A hierarchy of authority as a way of distributing power among people is not a universal human phenomenon. The Central Algonkian Indians of North America, for example, didn't seem to have a hierarchy of authority, nor did they seem to want one. Here are two reports about the delegation of authority among American Indians during the seventeenth century.

The first is from Nicholas Perrot, a French fur trader:

> Subordination is not a maxim among these savages; the savage does not know what it is to obey. . . . It is more necessary to entreat him than to command him. . . . The father does not venture to exercise authority over his son, nor does the chief dare give commands to his soldier. . . . if anyone is stubborn in regard to some proposed movement, it is necessary to flatter him in order to dissuade him, otherwise he will go further in his opposition. . . .

About ten years later a French aristocrat, Baron de La Hontan, commented on conditions among the tribes he dealt with as a military officer:

> . . . Each village hath its . . . Head of Warriors, who in consideration of his valor, capacity and experience is proclaimed such by an unanimous consent. But after all, this title invests him with no power over the warriors, for these people are strangers to military as well as civil subordination. Nay—they are so far from it, that if the . . . leader should order the silliest and most pitiful fellow in his [war party] to do so and so, why truly, this shadow of a captain would receive this answer . . . *that what he orders another to do he ought to do himself.* But it is such an uncommon thing for the leader to act so indiscreetly that I question if there be one instance of it.
>
> . . . The savages . . . think it unaccountable that one man should have more than another, and that the rich should have more respect than the poor; they value themselves above anything you can imagine, and this is the reason they always give for it—*that one man's as much master as another, and since all men are made of the same clay, there should be no distinction or superiority among them.*

—From W. B. Miller, "Two Concepts of Authority," *The American Anthropologist (April 1955).*

about their feelings. They know that any expression of anger or hostility may lead to punishment. So they tend to say nothing, or to say one thing and mean another. Thus systems of formal authority frequently generate a constriction or a distortion of communication between subordinate and superior. Naive supervisors make light of this problem, saying, "My people don't have any trouble telling me

> ### Alone at the Top
>
> Some of the loneliness of authority is reflected in Robert Kennedy's description of President Kennedy's deepest concerns during the Cuban missile crisis:
>
>> Again and again [the President] emphasized that we must understand the implications of every step. What response could we anticipate? What were the implications for us? He stressed again our responsibility to consider the effect our actions would have on others. NATO was supporting the United States, but were these countries truly and completely aware of the danger for them? These hourly decisions, necessarily made with such rapidity, could be made only by the President of the United States, but any one of them might close and lock doors for peoples and governments in many other lands. We had to be aware of this responsibility at all times, he said, aware that we were deciding, the President was deciding, for the U.S., the Soviet Union, Turkey, NATO, and really for all mankind. . . .
>
> —*Reprinted from* Thirteen Days, A Memoir of the Cuban Missile Crisis, *by Robert F. Kennedy. By permission of W. W. Norton & Company, Inc. Copyright ©1969 by W. W. Norton & Company, Inc. Copyright ©1968 by McCall Corporation.*

what's on their mind!" But more sophisticated supervisors know better.

If we look down along the lines of authority from above, a different picture emerges. Why have we, the general, given authority to that lieutenant down there? Why have we commissioned him? The answer is that we expect him to do things for us that he couldn't or wouldn't do before. We expect him to work within the confines of the role we have set for him. Now that we have commissioned him we can talk about his "duty." We expect him to *feel* responsible, and to obey.

Finally, what does the person who holds authority think about it? Besides a boost of pride and salary, what does it mean to be promoted into a position of higher authority? Certainly, it means that we have been given both new freedom and new power. Now we can tell others what to do. But that's not the whole story. Even as increased authority seems to make us freer, it also loads us with a new burden. We know that our hierarchical superiors now expect us to measure up to the job, to do our duty, to fulfill the role they have assigned to us. And the role carries with it, very often, the responsibility for making difficult and painful decisions as well as the freedom to make them. So though authority may mean we can tell other people what to do, it also means that we must be prepared for that red telephone to ring. For the cop on the beat, authority may mean that he can push other people around, but it also means he has to step forward and act in the face of real physical danger.

Authority is also a form of isolation; it demands that we must sometimes act alone, especially in moments of crisis. Formal authority rests on the *individual.* It is a sentence to solitary confinement. Father's authority includes not only the power to withhold the car on Saturday nights but the responsibility for saying "yes" or "no" to his child's emergency surgery after an accident.

In some organizations, as in some families, authority is more widely shared than in others. But even in such organizations the advisers are seldom the final decision-makers. At some critical point, having given their counsel, the cabinet members and staff assistants depart and leave the president to make his lonely decision.

Hierarchies Serve Functions Unrelated to Authority

Organizational hierarchy usually is a system of authority, an arrangement of roles according to which some people have power over others. But authority is not the only basis for a hierarchical structure in organizations.

Consider, for example, an organization without people. Imagine an automated automobile assembly plant. If it isn't designed hierarchically, it probably isn't very efficient. To be efficient it requires an arrangement of several independent subassemblies—motors, axles, wheels, transmissions—followed by intermediate assemblies of wheels with axles, motors with exhausts, and on up to a master assembly of all the subassemblies into a whole unit. This is not just a serial process but a hierarchical one, in which smaller building blocks are assembled into larger ones.

Thinking in terms of subassemblies makes it possible, to a large degree, to work independently on each. If one goes faster than the others, the completed subunits can be stockpiled. If another is creating problems, it can be tinkered with and fixed without disturbing the other subassemblies which are going well.

Consider an elaborate jigsaw puzzle. Do you work from one piece, serially, to all the others? Or do you work a series of subassemblies of pieces and then put them together, and then put those together, and so on? If you follow the second course, your procedure is hierarchical. It is usually faster, and an easier way for several people to work on the puzzle without fighting. But this type of hierarchy has nothing to do with authority.

Is it possible in human organizations to divorce the problem-solving hierarchy from the hierarchy of authority? To design a hier-

On Men and Hierarchies

Here are portions of a parable in an essay called "The Architecture of Complexity," written by Herbert A. Simon. He speaks of functions of hierarchical design that are unrelated to authority, functions often forgotten or misunderstood. The function of the hierarchy in this case is to simplify and order the performance of a complicated task.

> There once were two watchmakers, named Hora and Tempus, who manufactured very fine watches. Both of them were highly regarded, and the phones in their workshops rang frequently—new customers were constantly calling them. However, Hora prospered, while Tempus became poorer and poorer and finally lost his shop. What was the reason?
>
> The watches the men made consisted of about 1,000 parts each. Tempus had so constructed his that if he had one partly assembled and had to put it down—to answer the phone, say—it immediately fell to pieces and had to be reassembled from the elements. The better the customers liked his watches, the more they phoned him and the more difficult it became for him to find enough uninterrupted time to finish a watch.
>
> The watches that Hora made were no less complex than those of Tempus. But he had designed them so that he could put together subassemblies of about ten elements each. Ten of these subassemblies, again, could be put together into a larger subassembly; and a system of ten of the latter subassemblies constituted the whole watch. Hence, when Hora had to put down a partly assembled watch in order to answer the phone, he lost only a small part of his work, and he assembled his watches in only a fraction of the man-hours it took Tempus.
>
> It is rather easy to make a quantitative analysis of the relative difficulty of the tasks of Tempus and Hora: Suppose the probability that an interruption will occur while a part is being added to an incomplete assembly is p. . . .
>
> Now if p is about 0.01—that is, there is one chance in a hundred that either watchmaker will be interrupted while adding any one part to an assembly—then a straightforward calculation shows that it will take Tempus, on the average, about four thousand times as long to assemble a watch as Hora.
>
> —*Reprinted from* The Sciences of the Artificial, *pp. 91–93, by Herbert A. Simon, by permission of The M.I.T. Press, Cambridge, Mass. Copyright ©1969 by The M.I.T. Press.*

archy of activities without granting people the power to see that they are carried out? Some primitive societies may have been built the other way around, with a hierarchy of power that was relatively unrelated to problem-solving. But can we organize people to perform a set of complex tasks which will enable other people to perform another set of complex tasks and so on up the problem-solving hierarchy in a way that is *not* also hierarchical in authority? We leave that question to you, for a very simple reason: we don't know the answer.

Trends in the Use of Authority

It looks today as if the emphasis on the hierarchy of authority is declining. In most western countries, and even in the Soviet Union, there has clearly been a move away from a reliance on arbitrary personal authority and from the old management principle that there must always be "unity of command." We still talk about authority that derives from impersonal hierarchies of roles (seen by some as a sign of surrender to bureaucracy) or from a careful analysis of the hierarchical structure of tasks. We are also moving in a more personal direction again, but with more of an egalitarian tone and more recognition that there are multiple sources of authority in the organization. We're more concerned with coordinating effort and achieving consensus than with exercising command. We're using more "task force" styles of organization where authority and leadership are transitory. We're more aware that while it pays to listen to the president in order to learn what he thinks, it also pays to obey another man who knows the customers well and a third because he's the best widget-designer in the business. "Pulling rank" in industry has become increasingly rare, and authoritarian supervisors tend to be ridiculed. Even the military has had second thoughts about the need to train recruits in the mindless acceptance of authority.

What accounts for this seeming decline in the emphasis on authority? What alternatives to authority have emerged?

Diffusion of the rights and capabilities to command authority has helped to play down its role. In today's complex world the authority of different kinds of knowledge and experience or of affiliation with different interest groups counts as much as position in the hierarchy.

Affluence, education, and opportunities to change jobs easily encourage egalitarianism. Research suggests that traditional authority really didn't work as well as we thought it did in getting people to perform simple, repetitive tasks. Experience suggests that authority of the old kind is hardly even relevant for getting many new kinds of tasks done. One can order a weaver to turn out a specified number of yards every day, but one cannot order professionally trained researchers to come up with a creative idea every day.

But how can we get complex jobs done efficiently if we don't

> ### Knowledge Workers and Authority
>
> Knowledge workers... require that the demands be made on them by knowledge rather than by bosses, that is, by objectives rather than by people. They require a performance-oriented organization rather than an authority-oriented organization.
>
> Knowledge workers still need a superior. The organization structure must clearly identify where final decisions and ultimate responsibility rest.... But knowledge work itself knows no hierarchy, for there are no "higher" and "lower" knowledges. Knowledge is either relevant to a given task or irrelevant to it. The task decides, not the name, the age, or the budget of the discipline, or the rank of the individual plying it. For a disease of the eye the ophthalmologist is relevant; for removal of a gall bladder it is the abdominal surgeon.
>
> —Peter F. Drucker, The Age of Discontinuity (New York: Harper & Row, 1968), p. 289. Reprinted by permission of Harper & Row Publishers, Inc.

resort to the use of direct authority? Apparently we still do get efficiency—more than we used to, in fact.

One substitute for direct, personally implemented authority is extreme institutionalization—a heightened emphasis on impersonal rules. In collective bargaining, for example, we find an elaborate structure of impersonal rules that govern a variety of situations. A supervisor doesn't arbitrarily fire a shop worker; he points out that the worker has violated Clause 27 of the contract. Then he issues the first pink slip in a series of three that must be issued before the worker can be laid off for four days. The structure is tight, but authority now resides more in the book and less in the person who fills the role.

In some cases *nothing* has replaced authority. Authority has simply gone underground, and the silken glove of "human relations" now obscures the same old do-it-or-else reality. The sales manager says, "We haven't called on Customer X for a long time. Don't you think it would be a good idea, Joe, if somebody called on him?" He means: "Get out there and cover Customer X tomorrow morning, or else."

For a long time after the emergence of "human relations" (which we shall discuss later) in the 1930s and 1940s, some observers insisted that it was only an exercise in duplicity. Human-relations techniques, they said, simply taught people to smile while they went right on pushing one another around. According to this view, the major effect of human relations was to reduce the honesty of communication; it led people to play games, to delude one another, to talk at one level while communicating at another.

But the emphasis on human relations has, in our opinion, fostered a real transfer of authority from the formal hierarchy to the peer group, a switch from control from the top to group self-control. More and more, within higher management circles at least, one sees signs of honest discussion. Lower-level executives sit down with higher-level managers to plan programs; management committees come together to work through a decision and then take joint responsibility for it. Power is being distributed more and more widely throughout the organization. The process has been helped along, of course, by such factors as the chronic scarcity of highly skilled people and the rise of unions.

But whatever the causes, the trend seems clear. Large industrial organizations in the United States are moving away from the military model of tight hierarchical authority toward a system of relationships among colleagues who derive their power from knowledge and skill as well as from rank.

Summary

The formal organization is more functional than it may appear to be. Even the hierarchical part of it, which many of us see as the last vestige of an obsolete monster, is useful—perhaps even irreplaceable.

The hierarchy of authority organizes effort so that things get done and goals are reached. It serves to allocate power systematically through the organization, thus providing a tool for maintaining internal law and order. The power that is distributed in the form of authority can be assigned to roles, thus helping to institutionalize the organization. Authority also helps to keep organizational conflict under control by providing a system of higher courts for adjudicating disputes.

On the other hand, the hierarchy of authority imposes constraints on the behavior of subordinates, thereby generating a whole range of human responses. It fosters the feelings of ambivalence which always accompany dependent relationships, but it also evokes feelings of duty and responsibility toward the organization. Hierarchy is a mechanism of socialization.

Alongside the hierarchy of authority (which organizes people) is a problem-solving hierarchy (which organizes tasks). The problem-solving hierarchy permits complex tasks to be broken down into manageable activities. The emphasis on authority seems to be on the decline in the large organizations of the western world, whereas the emphasis on hierarchies for problem-solving does not.

Notes and References

Historically, early arguments in support of hierarchical structure were derived largely from the concept of economic efficiency and systems of social law and order. The design of early structures was developed through logical deduction from "principles" of organization. For some of the classical views on the hierarchy of authority and the principles on which they were based, try reading: Lyndall Urwick, *Elements of Administration* (New York: Harper & Row, 1963); H. Koontz and C. O'Donnell, *Principles of Management* (New York: McGraw-Hill, 1959); Max Weber, "The Essentials of Bureaucratic Organizations: An Ideal-Type Construction," in R. K. Merton *et al.,* eds., *A Reader in Bureaucracy* (New York: The Free Press of Glencoe, 1952).

More emphasis began to be placed on the human and operational aspects of power and authority and less on the legalistic side with the arrival of a pair of books mentioned earlier: Chester Barnard, *The Functions of the Executive* (Cambridge, Mass.: Harvard University Press, 1938); H. A. Simon, *Administrative Behavior* (New York: Macmillan, 1954).

For a more recent discussion and expansion of this "integrative" perspective of organizational structure, look into Bertram M. Gross, *Organizations and Their Managing* (New York: The Free Press, 1968).

For more details on the many games that are played in organizations to beat the hierarchy, see: R. Hofstede, *The Game of Budget Control* (Assen, The Netherlands: Van Gorcum, 1967); R. Townsend, *Up the Organization* (New York: Knopf, 1970).

The reader interested in the basic nature of hierarchies will find a fascinating discussion in H. A. Simon, *The Science of the Artificial* (Cambridge, Mass.: The M.I.T. Press, 1969), especially Chapter 4, "The Architecture of Complexity."

We will be discussing modern human relations in more detail in later chapters. But for a critical summary of the relationship between human relations and power and authority, see G. Strauss, "Notes on Power Equalization," in H. J. Leavitt, ed., *The Social Science of Organizations* (Englewood Cliffs, N.J.: Prentice-Hall, 1963).

4

Organizational Specialization: Little Cogs and Big Wheels

The concept of organizational specialization, like the hierarchy of authority, is a popular target of criticism. It prompts us immediately to think of the Chaplinesque man on the assembly line, robotized, monotonized, dehumanized.

But life is a series of trade-offs. The assembly line *is* a dehumanizing monster. It was when it was invented, it is now, and we ought to be doing our best to get rid of it. It is also an extraordinarily productive monster. So it is unlikely that we will get rid of it entirely at the sacrifice of perhaps the major source of our industrial productivity. We still value productivity. So we try compromises, hoping that higher pay or suggestion systems will make the line a bit more human; or we look forward to the time when we can replace men with real automation, thus solving the problem of dehumanization (and perhaps creating a problem of underemployment).

But if assembly-line specialization is a monster, consider its opposite. Try to build a significant number of cars, or radios, or light bulbs, or toilet seats, or body stockings without *any* specialization of human effort. To discard specialization because it is dehumanizing is like giving up salt because it makes us thirsty. Rather than asking, "Are we for specialization or against it?" we might better ask, "Under what conditions is specialization desirable? At what cost? And in what forms?"

The Scope of Specialization

In most organizations people hold not only ranks but *jobs*. The military officer is not only a lieutenant but a fighter pilot or an artilleryman or a radar specialist.

Such specialization of roles exists in hospitals in the form of physicians, nurses, dieticians, and administrators; in universities in the form of professors of every discipline and many nondisciplines, deans, fund-raisers, specialized students, placement personnel, and many more. We find the same specialization of roles in factories, governments, and clubs.

Job specialization has existed since men first gathered together in groups. In recent years the process has been speeded up by the growth of large economic enterprises. Adam Smith long ago forecast the productive advantages of specialization in his famous prescription for the manufacture of pins. And Henry Ford's introduction of assembly-line specialization in this century spurred major changes in production processes throughout the industrial world.

Though we tend to associate specialization with industrialization, we should remember that many simple, nonindustrial societies have specialized intensively, though not always productively. India's caste system is a form not only of social specialization but of work specialization. And usually where social roles are highly specialized, they are also likely to be very rigid. In such societies, specialties are specified from birth. By contrast, modern industrial specialization seems *relatively* open and flexible. Opportunities to choose and to change specialties are much easier to come by.

The Functions of Specialization

One key function of specialization is to institutionalize an organization—to permit it to endure beyond the lifetime of the men and women who are currently staffing it. What we specialize first are *roles,* or *jobs;* then workers specialize their skills to fit those roles. The whole idea of industrial specialization depends on breaking large tasks down into smaller, interrelated subjobs or subroles.

Specializing the activities of an organization into jobs makes it easier to map the organization so that one can find what one is looking for. Such mapping is important in two ways. First, mapping gives the men at the top a powerful tool for controlling the organization; it enables them to spot the place where control should be exercised. If a customer complains about our product, we can look to the quality-control specialists for an answer. Second, it creates a way to relax and simplify the exercise of authority. When the

Suppose We Didn't Specialize?

It is a curious fact that as we leave the most impoverished peoples of the world, where the human being with his too few calories of energy scratches out for himself a bare subsistence, we find the economic insecurity of the individual many times multiplied. The solitary Eskimo, Bushman, Indonesian, Nigerian, left to his own devices, will survive a considerable time. . . .

When we turn to the New Yorker or the Chicagoan, on the other hand, we are struck by exactly the opposite condition, by a prevailing ease of material life, coupled at the same time by an extreme *dependence* of the individual in his search for the means of existence. . . . The overwhelming majority of Americans have never grown food, caught game, raised meat, ground grain into flour, or even fashioned flour into bread. Faced with the challenge of clothing themselves or building their own homes, they would be hopelessly untrained and unprepared. . . .

We survive in rich nations because the tasks we cannot do ourselves are done for us by an army of others on whom we can call for help. . . . This enormous *division of labor* enhances our capacity a thousand-fold, for it enables us to benefit from other men's skills as well as our own.

Along with this invaluable gain comes a certain risk. . . . Our abundance is assured only insofar as the organized cooperation of huge armies of people is to be counted upon. . . . *We are rich, not as individuals, but as members of a rich society, and our easy assumption of material sufficiency is actually only as reliable as the bonds which forge us into a social whole.*

—Robert L. Heilbroner, The Making of Economic Society. © 1962, pp. 3–4. Reprinted by permission of Prentice-Hall, Inc., Englewood Cliffs, New Jersey.

boundaries of a particular role are clearly established, men have freedom to act *within* those boundaries. The shoemaker can be left to his last, the teenager to his chores. Control is needed only when boundaries are crossed.

Specialization also simplifies communication within the organization. It provides mailboxes and street numbers. Where positions are identified by function in a large organization, people can tell where to get information and where to send it. If you wanted to write a letter of complaint to the maker of your new camera, it wouldn't do you much good to have a list of the names of all the company's employees. But if you had a list of *job titles,* you could easily pick the one or two to whom you would want to address your letter.

Specialization is useful in other ways. It deepens knowledge and skill because it means that an employee has to learn only a limited number of specialized activities and how those activities

On the Advantages of Specialization

Adam Smith, writing in 1776, described the advantages of specialization:

> To take an example... from a very trifling manufacture; but one in which the division of labour has very often been taken notice of, the trade of the pin-maker; a workman not educated to this business (which the division of labour has rendered a distinct trade), nor acquainted with the use of the machinery employed in it (to the invention of which the same division of labour has probably given occasion), could scarce, perhaps, with his utmost industry, make one pin in a day, and certainly could not make twenty. But in the way in which this business is now carried on, not only the whole work is a peculiar trade, but it is divided into a number of branches, of which the greater part are likewise peculiar trades. One man draws out the wire, another straights it, a third cuts it, a fourth points it, a fifth grinds it at the top for receiving the head; to make the head requires two or three distinct operations; to put it on, is a peculiar business, to whiten the pins is another; it is even a trade by itself to put them into the paper; and the important business of making a pin is, in this manner, divided into about eighteen distinct operations, which, in some manufactories, are all performed by distinct hands, though in others the same man will sometimes perform two or three of them. I have seen a small manufactory of this kind where ten men only were employed, and where some of them consequently performed two or three distinct operations. But though they were very poor, and therefore but indifferently accommodated with the necessary machinery, they could, when they exerted themselves, make among them about twelve pounds of pins in a day. There are in a pound upwards of four thousand pins of a middling size. Those ten persons, therefore, could make among them upwards of forty-eight thousand pins in a day. Each person, therefore, making a tenth part of forty-eight thousand pins, might be considered as making four thousand eight hundred pins in a day. But if they had all wrought separately and independently, and without any of them having been educated to this peculiar business, they certainly could not each of them have made twenty, perhaps not one pin in a day....

—Adam Smith, The Wealth of Nations (*New York: Modern Library, 1937*), pp. 4–5.

are related to a few other jobs. We may regret the passing of the general practitioner, but we are grateful for the services of the narrowly but deeply trained neurosurgeon.

We must remember too that as our knowledge of the world around us grows greater and greater, the need to specialize becomes imperative. The more we learn about any set of phenomena, the more difficult it becomes for any one person to master all that is known. So we specialize. And we are not necessarily dehumanized as a

Informed Skill and Specialization Replace Craft Skill

However,
man unconcernedly sorting mail on an express train
with unuttered faith that
the engineer is competent,
that the switchmen are not asleep,
that the track walkers are doing their job,
that the technologists
who designed the train and the rails
know their stuff,
that thousands of others
whom he may never know by face or name
are collecting tariffs,
paying for repairs,
and so handling assets
that he will be paid a week from today
and again the week after that,
and that all the time
his family is safe and in well being
without his personal protection
constitutes a whole new era of evolution—
the first really "new"
since the beginning of the spoken word.

—R. Buckminster Fuller, Untitled Epic Poem on the History of Industrialization (New York: Simon and Schuster, 1970), p. 61.

result. It is "assembly-line" specialization that disturbs us, not the idea of specialization itself. We do not decry the highly skilled, highly specialized woodcarver, or ceramist, or silversmith. We do not object to the specialized styles of sculptors or painters or musicians. We do not argue that the latest rock group is dehumanized because they can't—or don't—play Mussorgsky. Our most valid objections to specialization come when it is imposed by others rather than chosen by ourselves, and when it brings with it the end of challenge. It is not the specialized nature of assembly-line work but its shallowness and its denial of free choice that seem abhorrent.

Forms of Specialization

Planned specialization in an organization serves to define the boundaries between jobs so clearly that the need for coordination between jobs is reduced to a minimum. However, that isn't an easy objective to achieve. It's easy enough to coordinate activities that are all performed by a single individual; it's a little harder to coordinate activities that are performed by different individuals within a closely knit group. The most difficult activities to coordinate are those that are performed by different groups, each with its own identity and with its own commitment to particular objectives.

Role specialization sometimes comes naturally, because it is so appropriate to a given situation. Father drives the car while mother tends the children and reads the map. It would make no sense for father to work the steering wheel and the brakes and read the map while mother pressed the accelerator and fed the baby, even though the total activity load might be the same in both cases.

Often, however, "appropriate" specialization is less apparent. In a university, for example, should the department of economics be organized as part of the school of liberal arts, or should it be part of the school of business? The answer depends in part on what direction the university wants the department to take. For it is almost inevitable that if the economics department is made part of the business school, its orientation and emphasis will move toward applied business economics rather than toward theoretical or macroeconomics.

Decisions about structural specialization that are made early in the life of an organization have a profound effect on its subsequent development. Once made, such decisions are hard to reverse. An obvious illustration is the federal government of the United States. The specialization of judicial, executive, and legislative roles was consciously intended to provide a set of counterweighted, balancing forces. And that early decision by the Founding Fathers has determined in large measure the course of our government over almost two centuries.

When no conscious decision about structural specialization is made in the early life of an organization, specialization tends to emerge with growth. In a very small organization run by the founder, for example, there is usually very little specialization of activities. What specialization there is depends on the founder's whims. The pattern is highly personal and, hence, varies from one small company to another, even within the same industry. As the organization grows, however, specialization tends to increase. The organization becomes too complex for one man to handle everything. Specialization typically begins to occur by function, and gradually the functions of marketing, production, and accounting come to be performed by major units, each with its own supervisor.

As the organization continues to grow, *line* people tend to get separated from *staff* people. The line people take direct responsibility for getting things done, for making or supervising the manufacturing of products, and for seeing that they are sold. The staff people provide specialized services to the line people. They search for better ways of doing the job, or conduct market research, or improve the accounting system. Their formal authority is usually very limited. They undertake jobs largely at the request of line people, and they feed results back to the line people. The line people themselves then use those results to make and implement decisions for which they are held responsible.

As the organization grows even larger, coordination among line groups and between staff and line groups becomes extremely difficult. The production and marketing departments may become so big that they have trouble communicating with each other. The people who design a product may become isolated from the people who make it or the people who sell it. Line people may grow too busy with short-run problems to think much about future problems. The staff people become the specialized planners, but they may find that they are planners without power. They often find that they lack authority to initiate activities themselves, that authority "belongs" to the line people; so long-run planning suffers. Consequently, very large companies with many plants, products, and markets try to reduce their operating units to workable size. They reorganize on a *decentralized* product-market basis by setting up smaller companies, each with its own functional line specialists and its own staff specialists. Thus, even in a company like General Motors, whose products are pretty much homogeneous, a separate division manufactures and sells Cadillacs and another manufactures and sells Chevrolets.

Some Costs of Specialization

Long before Charlie Chaplin made his classic movie *Modern Times,* social critics were troubled by the "dehumanizing" effects of tight specialization, particularly on eye-hand jobs. The notion of a man spending something like half his waking life turning bolts was abhorrent to them. And it is abhorrent to many of us today. Such routine jobs appear dull, monotonous, restrictive, almost enslaving. They run counter to our insistence on individual freedom and autonomy. They inhibit mental growth and personal development.

Some critics go further and claim that overspecialization generates dissatisfaction, frustration, and bitterness in the people who perform such jobs. This argument is not easy to support. First, it is not at all clear that the more specialized a job is, the more workers dislike it. Culture comes into the picture, so does I.Q., and so does personality. City workers, for example, may hold attitudes different from the older, more traditional attitudes of rural workers. People with high I.Q.s may react more strongly against regimentation than people with low I.Q.s. People with "authoritarian" personalities may

> ### Striking for the Right to Sneeze
>
> "Is it true," an auto worker asked wistfully, "that you get to do fifteen different jobs on a Cadillac?" "I heard," said another, "that with Volvos you follow one car all the way down the line."
>
> Such are the yearnings of young auto workers at the Vega plant in Lordstown, Ohio. Their average age is twenty-four, and they work on the fastest auto assembly line in the world. Their jobs are so subdivided that few workers can feel they are making a car.
>
> The assembly line carries 101 cars past each worker every hour. Most GM lines run under sixty. At 101 cars an hour, a worker has thirty-six seconds to perform his assigned snaps, knocks, twists, or squirts on each car. The line was running at this speed in October when a new management group . . . took over the plant. Within four months they fired 500 to 800 workers. Their jobs were divided among the remaining workers, adding a few more snaps, knocks, twists, or squirts to each man's task. The job had been boring and unbearable before. When it remained boring and became a bit more unbearable there was a 97 per cent vote to strike. More amazing—85 per cent went down to the union hall to vote.
>
> One could give a broad or narrow interpretation of what the Lordstown workers want. Broadly, they want to reorganize industry so that each worker plays a significant role in turning out a fine product, without degrading supervision. Narrowly, they want more time in each thirty-six-second cycle to sneeze or to scratch.
>
> —Barbara Garson, "Luddites in Lordstown," *Harper's (June 1972)*, p. 68. ©1972 by Barbara Garson, courtesy of International Famous Agency.

not mind certain job restrictions as much as other people do, and so on.

Moreover, people are highly adaptive. A person who reluctantly accepts a restrictive job may over time learn to live with its routines and even come to depend on them for security. A sudden enlargement of his job may seem downright threatening.

Of course it is simplistic to argue that narrow specialization is just fine because "those people" don't mind monotony and routine. But it is also simplistic to assume that every worker regards his job exactly as you would if you were doing it.

To argue convincingly against specialization these days, we must base our argument on *value* grounds, and to some extent on *pragmatic* grounds.

The value grounds are humanistic. The job a man does for eight hours a day five days a week for forty years must surely affect his whole view of life. And some jobs are so remote from the organization's overall activities, let alone from one's personal goals, that even the most compliant worker can find little satisfaction in his work. Often even the pacing of a job is determined more by machines or by other people than by oneself. Some jobs never change, in the slightest detail, over extended periods of time. A young man can start in an automobile factory, for example, and still be doing exactly the same job when he retires. Many factory jobs are designed with no thought of the human need for variety or growth. Instead, designers concentrate on breaking the job down into standardized segments that can be controlled as smoothly and as efficiently as possible. They design jobs for hands, not men.

Pragmatically, the degree of specialization that is common today may prove insupportable in tomorrow's culture, with tomorrow's people. Even now educated people tend to steer clear of narrow jobs. As society moves toward greater individual autonomy and freedom, such jobs will become less and less attractive. And the more deprived groups in our society, whose members have traditionally manned the nation's assembly lines, are also setting new standards for the quality of their life.

But there are some unusual obstacles on the road to reduced specialization of "overspecialized" jobs. Assume that you, as a manager, opt for job enlargement (or, as it is now called, *job enrichment*) in your organization. You may discover that not everyone will applaud your decision. Not only are the brick and mortar and machinery of your organization designed for a high degree of specialization, but over the years your union contract and your work rules have been built upon it. The very workers you are trying to "help" may resist the changes you want to institute, because the tight, highly defined job structure has generated a set of formal agreements about seniority and pay rates and prerogatives that protect them from arbitrary behavior on your part. The specialized little job with its duties clearly defined in the union contract may seem far more desirable than a new system that promises a bigger job but under unknown conditions. And these aren't the only costs that accompany the specializing process, particularly in regard to the specialization of management personnel.

Specialization tends to breed local loyalties, local commitments, local points of view. It prompts people to identify more strongly with their jobs, or with their departments, than with the organization as a whole. In a research organization the scientist may feel more affinity for his own profession than for the company that employs him. Faculty members extend their first loyalty to their discipline; craftsmen, to their craft. Specialization has a socializing influence; it conditions the specialist to embrace the beliefs and the values associated with his work. Specialists tend to become more and more involved in their own activities and to interact primarily among themselves. They build up their own language and their own value

How Do Workers Feel about Highly Specialized and Highly Routinized Jobs?

In a classic study of the 1950s, Walker and Guest came to these conclusions about the attitudes of the man on the assembly line:

> ... If a man was on a strictly paced, highly repetitive job, and belonged to the majority who did not like it, he said so bluntly. If he had been transferred off the line onto a less strictly paced or a less repetitive job, he reported this circumstance with satisfaction. In short, a majority specifically stated that they liked their jobs to the degree to which they lacked repetitiveness, mechanical pacing, or related characteristics. On the other hand, they disliked them to the degree to which they embodied these mass production characteristics....
>
> When the worker discussed his relations with other workers and reported social interaction, such as joking, gossiping, or general conversation, he mentioned them chiefly as a fortunate counterbalance and compensation for the disliked features of immediate job content.
>
> As to the economic aspects of his job, pay and security both were strong like factors. What is here significant is that the worker himself frequently juxtaposed these likes with the strongest of his dislikes, that is, unpleasant features of the immediate job.

—*Charles W. Walker and Robert H. Guest,* The Man of the Assembly Line *(Cambridge, Mass.: Harvard University Press, 1952), p. 142.*

That was back in the early 50s. Do you think attitudes toward such repetitive specialized jobs are more positive or more negative today? Maybe it depends on where in our society you choose to look. Blood and Hulin, in a 1967 study, collected data from more than thirteen hundred blue-collar workers in twenty-one plants all over the eastern United States and found great differences in job satisfaction, *depending on the kind of communities in which the plants were located.* Workers in rural middle-class communities reported higher satisfaction with their jobs, more interest in advancement to higher-skilled jobs, more concern about planning for retirement, and so on. But many workers from poorer urban communities were less interested in getting skilled jobs or in making retirement plans and more interested in just plain take-home pay.

—*M. R. Blood and C. I. Hulin, "Alienation, Environmental Characteristics, and Worker Responses,"* Journal of Applied Psychology, *LI, 3 (1967), 284–90.*

systems. They become insensitive to what is going on in other parts of the organization. To combat such parochialism many organizations change their bases of specialization periodically by rotating their managers and redefining their responsibilities. And yet specialization serves to impair mobility. It's costly to shift highly trained specialists from one position to another and to wait for them to learn new roles and unlearn old ones. Good salesmen do not always make good sales managers.

Finally, specialization promotes rigidity. Specialization specifies — it lays down rules, often in writing, about what a job includes and what it doesn't include. Written programs have a way of becoming a kind of common law to which all arguments are referred. Hence, as we said earlier, unions that once opposed specialization may end up supporting it, because rules, even restrictive rules, protect workers against arbitrary management. Though workers may feel themselves constrained by written rules, they will, on occasion, use those very rules to constrain management from modifying or abandoning jobs. Having a lousy job, after all, is better than having no job at all. Changes within a specialized system are likely to come in the form of small modifications of existing jobs, rather than in revisions of the whole job structure.

Summary

Job specialization provides order and predictability in complex organizations. It allows for economies in training and furnishes opportunities for learning skills in depth. Specialization also permits economies in manufacture and service and provides all members of the society with the services of highly skilled specialists. It makes mapping of the organization possible and helps to localize responsibility, thereby making control easier. Specialization even simplifies communication. All organizations specialize.

Specialization takes many different forms in organizations. Decisions about just how an organization is to be specialized can profoundly affect its whole later development, as in the decision to specialize our federal government into judicial, legislative, and executive roles, or as in the separation of "line" and "staff" roles in industrial organizations.

Finally, though specialization has proved itself an aid to productivity, its costs have been very great. Overspecialization of jobs can be deadening and dehumanizing, even to the extent of alienating many people from the whole industrial way of life. At managerial and professional levels there are costs, too, including narrowness of view and low organizational loyalty. Specialization can rigidify organizations, making change difficult. On both humanistic and pragmatic grounds, the issue of specialization of jobs is undergoing serious reexamination.

Notes and References

Just as hierarchical organizational structures provide order and predictability, so too does specialization of roles. For one rationale for specialization, see Alfred D. Chandler, Jr., *Strategy and Structure* (Cambridge, Mass.: M.I.T. Press, 1962).

While Chandler's argument for specialization rests largely on an economic base, most arguments against "too much" specialization are based on the humanistic view that extensive industrial specialization restricts individual growth. See Chris Argyris, *Integrating the Individual and the Organization* (New York: John Wiley and Sons, 1964).

For some good ideas on how the man on the receiving end, the worker, reacts to specialization, see: Charles R. Walker and Robert H. Guest, *The Man on the Assembly Line* (Cambridge, Mass.: Harvard University Press, 1952); Theodore V. Purcell, *The Worker Speaks His Mind on Company and Union* (Cambridge, Mass.: Harvard University Press, 1953); and William F. Whyte, *Money and Motivation* (New York: Harper & Row, 1955).

These three books describe the situation of the blue-collar worker. A great deal of work has also been done on the values and attitudes of white-collar, technical, and professional workers. See, for example: Donald C. Pelz and Frank M. Andrews, *Scientists in Organizations* (New York: John Wiley and Sons, 1966); and Louis B. Barnes, *Organizational Systems and Engineering Groups* (Boston: Division of Research, Graduate School of Business Administration, Harvard University, 1960).

Cultural and environmental factors also affect workers' reactions to specialization. For empirical evidence and a discussion of culturally induced effects on attitudes, see C. L. Hulin and M. R. Blood, "Job Enlargement, Individual Differences, and Worker Responses," *Psychological Bulletin,* LXIX, 1 (1968). This article is reprinted in L. L. Cummings and W. E. Scott, eds., *Readings in Organizational Behavior and Human Performance* (Homewood, Ill.: Irwin, 1969).

For details on the recent trend toward "job enlargement" and "job enrichment," see: Robert N. Ford, *Motivation Through the Work Itself* (American Management Association, Inc., 1969); and Frederick Herzberg et al., *The Motivation to Work* (New York: John Wiley and Sons, 1966).

5

Information and Control: Maintaining Organizational Law and Order

Organizations as we have described them are busily achieving objectives and turning out products or services. Yet if you step inside one of the operating units of almost any organization you may find it hard to get any sense of its objectives or to spot anyone making anything. Most of the people, most of the time, handle paper, talk on the telephone, or sit in meetings. They spend their time, that is to say, dealing not with things but with *information.* The higher up you go in management, the closer to headquarters, the truer this is.

Organizations do indeed live to do things—to make products, to provide services, to satisfy clients in one way or another. But organizations draw their nourishment from information. They depend for their very life on networks and systems of communication that make it possible for many people to work in concert. It is this flow of information that binds an organization together into a single, coherent unit.

The people who make up an organization may be scattered in many locations, sometimes clear around the world. They need to talk to one another. They need to consult records in order to plan for the future and to evaluate the past. Information provides the raw material of both coordination and control, not only for the president who is concerned with overall performance but for the salesman in Walla Walla who has promised his best customer a green Stutz Bearcat with a special seven-cylinder engine before May 13.

> ### The Long History of Dependence on Records
>
> There is considerable evidence that man's need to keep records for organized enterprise predated his efforts to preserve descriptions of his experiences as history. Six to seven thousand years ago, in the Nile valley, the officials who collected taxes to pay for the construction and maintenance of irrigation canals used pictorial symbols and tally marks to make a record on the wall of each farmer's house, showing how much tax he had paid. By 2000 B.C. the Egyptians were keeping attendance records and making monthly summaries of wage payments.
>
> As the systems evolved, in Egypt and ancient Babylonia, they took forms that are still familiar today: ledger columns for different purposes, differentiation of cash and credit transactions, profit and loss statements, and even crude forms of balance sheets. King Hammurabi of Babylonia spelled out detailed regulations to ensure not only that records were kept, but that they were kept honestly.
>
> By 2500 B.C. the Peruvians, the Chinese, and the Japanese had all invented devices which speeded computations for record systems. The Oriental invention, the abacus, is still widely used in small and large businesses in the Orient and in the Soviet Union.
>
> For more of the history of accounting and information systems, see the selections in Edward C. Bursk, Donald T. Clark, and Ralph W. Hidy, *The World of Business* (New York: Simon and Schuster, 1962), pp. 61–155.

If the flow of information dries up, as some brokerage houses learned in the early 1970s, the organization dies. Some houses simply could not keep track of purchases or sales, or determine who owned particular blocks of stock. They didn't know when they would collect the cash they needed to pay other bills. The partners were there, and the employees and the customers too, but no one was talking to anyone else any more.

Information Systems Are Where the Action Is

Traditionally, the information-handler and the record-keeper haven't seemed like very glamorous fellows. Bookkeepers and accountants have always worked away dutifully, with their green eyeshades, looking like anything but the powerful shapers of organizational destiny.

Yet today the action centers on the very people who are using their wits to revolutionize the ways in which information is gathered

> ### The Communications Challenge
>
> This deep problem of communication is not solved by providing more volume of data for all concerned, or even by faster accumulation and transmittal of conventional data, or by wider distribution of previously existing data, or through holding more conferences. Indeed, the belief that such measures will meet the communications challenge is probably one of the great fallacies in business and managerial thinking.
>
> What is required, instead, is a far more penetrating and orderly study of the business in its entirety to discover what specific information is needed at each particular position in view of the decisions to be made there.
>
> —From New Frontiers for Professional Managers by Ralph J. Cordiner, p. 102. ©1956 by McGraw-Hill Book Company. Used with permission of McGraw-Hill Book Company.

and disseminated throughout the organization. They are coming up with new thoughts about the age-old problems of using information for planning, decision, and control. They are using new mathematical and statistical tools to transform information into powerful advice for decision-makers. And they are continually devising new technology for transmitting and transforming information.

This chapter is about modern information systems and their vital role in organizations. The next chapter discusses the new mathematical and statistical tools, and the following chapter deals with the computer and its impact on organizational information systems and management in general.

Are Elaborate, Formal Information Systems Really Necessary?

Information is the glue that holds organizations together. All organizations are awash with information—everyone seems to be busy either generating, communicating, interpreting, or using it. There's always more than enough information around, it would seem, for the creative manager to use in making decisions.

Unfortunately, experience suggests otherwise. There's a lot of information around, but much of it is trivial or inaccurate. And it comes in so many shapes and sizes that even creative managers can't always fit the pieces together. Too often, in fact, many of the pieces turn out to be missing.

There is also the problem of sheer size. In larger organizations with tens or hundreds of thousands of employees, sometimes millions of customers, and transactions yielding sales in the billions of dollars each year, the amount of information that has to be transmitted, stored, and processed gets mighty large. No amount of experience or intuition, no combination of purely informal information flows, is adequate for handling the complex informational demands of today's large organizations.

In order for an organization to have reliable journals, ledgers, and records of accounts, it must have some formalized, structured system of handling information. Without a formal information system even small organizations have a hard time describing—much less understanding—their own activities and past experiences. Without an information system, even a highly gifted decision-maker may find himself putting off until January what he should have done in June.

Information systems take many forms. Some are simple, such as reading the *New York Times* every morning or filling in check stubs to keep track of our bank balance. Notice, incidentally, that information systems don't have to deal with numbers; consider, for example, the game films that quarterbacks and coaches study so diligently every week, or the highly condensed codes that chessplayers use for recording their victories and defeats. Some information systems, such as an accounting system, do deal with numbers, describing what has already happened within an organization; others, such as a system for sampling voters' or consumers' preferences, help organizations make something happen in the future. Some systems exist in the form of filing cabinets full of records, others in the form of slips of paper impaled on spindles, or magnetic bars on a production scheduling chart-board. Some are very private and personal, like the playboy's little black book. Others can be maintained only if they get round-the-clock attention by thousands of people and a bank of computers.

In this chapter we can only introduce you to some of the ideas and practices involved in information systems. What we have to say won't substitute for a formal course in accounting, but it may help you to appreciate the tremendous influence that the scribblers and purveyors of data have on the affairs of an organization.

What Are the Important Informational Problems?

In recent years some observers have moved into administrators' offices in order to do empirical research on information systems. Suppose you had access to a dean's office and his in-basket. What would you find? Here are some possibilities:

1. A first draft, awaiting his editing, of his annual report to the chancellor, containing among other things a verbal and statistical profile of the current graduating class, a list of faculty publications and services to professional and community groups, a five-year summary of progress in adding members of minority groups and women to the staff, and some financial statements. These statements might include a performance summary showing revenues and expenses for the year and a balance sheet showing assets (cash on hand, value of buildings and endowment, money owed to the school in deferred tuition, etc.), liabilities (bills, loans, and other obligations that the school must pay), and net worth (the residual difference between assets and liabilities).
2. A memo from the admissions director comparing applications and acceptances this year with the last two years.
3. A copy of the latest American Association of University Professors survey of faculty salaries throughout the country.
4. A questionnaire from another school asking for information on courses and research programs offered in business history.
5. The student government's latest publication evaluating teachers and courses.
6. A five-year prediction from the federal government of the likely demand for graduates with various degrees and course credentials.
7. A control sheet from the associate dean detailing expenses for the month just past and comparing actual versus budgeted expenses for that period.
8. Six letters of recommendation from professors at another university about a faculty member who is being considered for tenure.
9. A memo from the president asking what the dean and the department chairmen are doing to improve the development and evaluation of younger faculty members.
10. An extravagant advertisement from a publisher for a new textbook called *The Organizational World*.
11. A proposal from a team of faculty members recommending the use of videotape in teaching human relations.
12. A book of Tagore's essays on education which an Indian student has asked the dean to read.
13. A request for the dean's signature authorizing the placement of an order for a new computer.

Notice that the list contains examples of items in which the dean is giving information (1) and receiving information (2), of internally produced materials (2) and externally produced materials (3), of regularly supplied information (3) and intermittently supplied information (6), of materials for planning (6) and materials for control (5), of solidly factual information (2) and possibly slanted information (10), of a report-based approach (1) and a special-inquiry approach (9), of quantitative information (3) and qualitative information (11), of practical information (8) and speculative information (12).

You could get another insight into the dean's information system by studying his calendar and learning whom he has seen recently, how much time he spent with each person or group, what were the purposes of his conversations, and where his appointments took place. All these clues would help you understand the kinds of problem he is spending time on and the kind of perspective his conversations and meetings are likely to produce.

There might even be a computer terminal in the dean's office that would give you a print-out of class schedules for the next semester; a list of the names and addresses of influential alumni; or, if the dean has time for research, a sampling of data from experiments he has been running.

On the basis of your investigation, you may conclude that the dean is spending too much time getting and giving out information and not enough time using it. Perhaps you're right. Some deans (and some managers) are scared or indecisive. They spend all their time behind the desk or on the phone, afraid to move until they know exactly and certainly what course of action is the right one.

Much of the information you uncover may not be at all what the dean wants or uses. Some of it is there simply because other people think he should have it. Some has been collected and transmitted because the chancellor or the students or the Ford Foundation feel it will be useful. And some is there only because people around the dean have been gathering such information and passing it along for fifteen years, and no one ever told them to stop.

But clearly the dean is looking for guidance in planning for the future of the school and for ways to control the direction in which the school is moving. He can improve the quality of that guidance by demanding that the information systems that serve him are well designed, and he can also influence to some degree the design of the information systems that serve others inside and outside the organization. Let's turn now to this vitally important matter of the *design* of information systems.

Information for Managing a Chemical Company

The flows of information used for goal setting and key management-planning decisions in a large chemical company have been diagramed by one researcher this way:

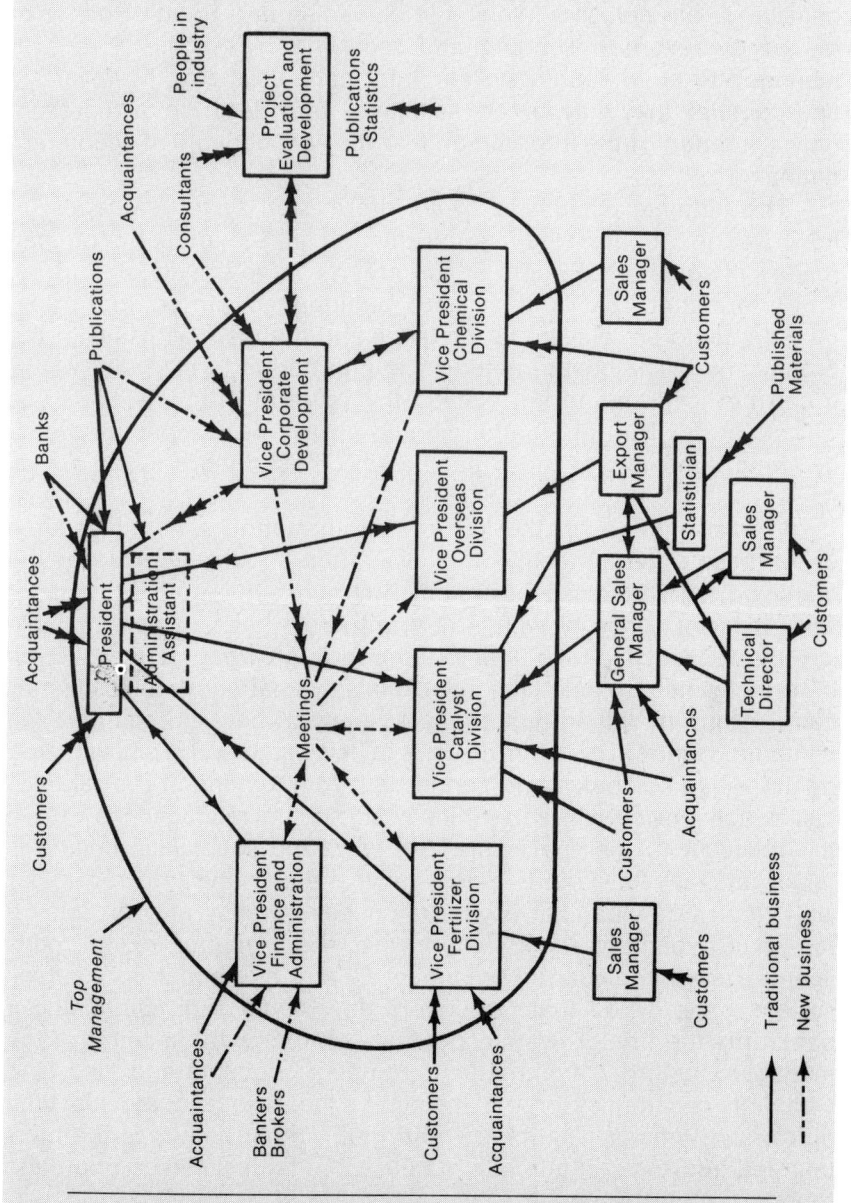

—F. J. Aguilar, Scanning the Business Environment (*New York: Macmillan, 1967*), p. 170. Reprinted by permission of The Trustees of Columbia University.

What Sorts of System Are Needed to Help Solve Problems?

Our understanding of what makes a good information system is still pretty primitive, but we do have some guidelines based on hard experience. Remember that no information system is totally comprehensive or all-inclusive. We would all vanish in a flood of paper or die of overexertion sending and receiving messages if we ever managed to build such a system. Information systems, however big and complex they may be, are selective—they describe or represent only a fraction of the information that they are capable of accommodating.

The ultimate usefulness of an information system depends on how we go about selecting information at the outset. You can readily imagine what some of the criteria of selectivity should be. The information that is generated, manipulated, stored, and transmitted should be relevant to the goals and the main activities of the organization. The cost of getting the information to the point where it can be used should not exceed the value of the benefits its use will generate. The information should always be compact and easily comprehensible to those people who must absorb it and act on it.

Who's to judge whether or not an information system measures up to these criteria? Ideally, this evaluation should be made by the man who is going to use the system. But there's the rub. The manager with the best sense of what's relevant and what's comprehensible is often too busy to take time to think through what he needs. Even if he is willing to take the time, his information specialists may confuse him by telling him about a variety of new devices (like the computer) that will give him all sorts of new services. He's bewildered by the range of choice and cannot tell from looking at the samples just which device will serve him best; so the manager may leave the decision to his specialists. But what the specialists decide is "relevant" may have more to do with what they know and are familiar with than with what the organization needs. They may produce a ten-pound monthly report when what the manager really needs is only a one-page quarterly summary. Or they may construct a supersystem, only to find that the cost of developing and maintaining it bankrupts the firm. They may generate reports with no sense of the manager's ability to comprehend complex concepts and data, and with little awareness of the manager's need to allocate his time efficiently. Winston Churchill wrote multivolume histories to entertain and inform us in our leisure hours, but he insisted on one-page reports from his generals.

*Structure vs. Flexibility: One Major Problem
in the Design of Information Systems*

One big problem confronting the designer of an information system is how to balance the need for stability and sound structure against the need for flexibility and growth potential.

Structure (regular, standardized, repeatable steps) is essential in an accounting system that is responsible for generating the statements that appear at the end of a corporation's annual report. Those statements enable us to make ready comparisons of the corporation's performance between one time period and the next and to compare statements of one organization against those of another. We can look at two pages of figures on the activities of U.S. Steel or General Motors, for example, and make important judgments—as managers, social critics, or stockholders—about their respective performance and potential.

Structure demands that terms be clearly defined and that ways of grouping or valuing items be carefully specified so that readers will understand what a phrase like "depreciation of plant and equipment" means and how it is calculated. Structure determines the way in which information is collected and checked, both through the early stages of "double-entry" bookkeeping and the later stage of "auditing" the accuracy of a completed statement. To be effective for control and planning, an accounting system must be as immune as possible not only from error but from ambiguity. Some of the system's structure must therefore be stylistic so that any knowledgeable reader of accounting reports can know where to look on a page of numbers for the entries that interest him.

Professional accountants are sticklers for structure and standard style because they stake their reputations on the honesty, completeness, and accuracy of those reports. Accountants also have to ensure that their techniques for catching error and fraud remain current and effective as organizations grow and as the technology of accounting changes. The accountant is under an obligation to the government and to the public to demonstrate, after the fact, how over $9 billion in 1970 sales for Sears Roebuck can be traced back to each of millions of individual transactions, such as the sale of a 98-cent package of razor blades in Oshkosh on February 31.

All that emphasis on structure, however, has its costs in reduced flexibility. There is a constant tug of war between the need for the stability guaranteed by structure and the need for the flexibility demanded by growth and change. Some baseball fans, for example, would rather have seen baseball die than have a half-century of record-keeping thrown out of kilter by the lengthening of the season and by the addition of new teams to the American and National

The Hardship of Accounting

>Never ask of money spent
>Where the spender thinks it went.
>Nobody was ever meant
>To remember or invent
>What he did with every cent.

—From The Poetry of Robert Frost, *edited by Edward Connery Lathem. Copyright 1936, ©1969 by Holt, Rinehart and Winston, Inc. Copyright © 1964 by Lesley Frost Ballantine. Reprinted by permission of Holt, Rinehart and Winston, Inc.*

Leagues. They grumble that baseball has become a big business, but in business the record buffs are more resigned to change. Accounting systems and rules must be adapted to new ways and technologies of keeping accounts, to new concepts of financing, such as convertible debentures, to the demand that accounting records include profit-and-loss data by product line as well as for the company as a whole, and to new requirements that accounting systems measure a company's social performance as well as its economic performance. At the same time, though, changes in accounting systems must not obscure real historical trends in an organization's performance.

The Problem of Speed and the Design of a Good Information System

For control purposes, the manager makes still other demands on his information system. He insists that it be able to process information swiftly. Control information must reach the hands of the people who will use it while it still makes sense. By the time a month or six weeks have passed, for example, a manager may find it very hard to reconstruct the situation in which costs first began to get out of control.

Statistical sampling is one technique that helps speed up the processing of information without greatly increasing the cost. Remember that one of the items we found on the dean's desk was an annual report containing a statistical profile of the graduating class. If the school is a large one, and if that summary had to be put together by clerks transcribing information by hand from detailed student folders, probably not every student was included in the profile. Instead of taking data from every single folder, a very reliable profile could be assembled by transcribing data from only every tenth or seventeenth student folder. The accuracy of a sample depends less on its size than on how it is put together. In a good sample design, while not every student is covered, theoretically every student has an equal chance of being included.

Sampling techniques are particularly useful in surveying the behavior of consumers and voters, in evaluating how products are faring in the marketplace, and in checking quality in manufacturing operations. When used for quality control, skillful sampling has another advantage besides speed of analysis and low cost. It doesn't interfere too much in the process it is studying. If, for example, you want to know how well light bulbs are meeting breakage standards, you can't really afford to smash every one. A sampling system lets you selectively evaluate quality without destroying a large percentage of your products.

The Problem of Standards in the Design of a Good Information System

An information system that processes information swiftly may not be very useful unless it is accompanied by standards that permit the manager to make a prompt check on what has actually happened against what ought to have happened. Standards are sometimes treated independently of larger information systems, but we should consider them as one important part of such systems.

Among the papers we found on the dean's desk were a couple of reports that illustrate how standards contribute to the usefulness of an information system. The AAUP survey of faculty salaries reports salaries at different rank levels, school by school. It also gives averages and ranges in salary scales at, for example, small private colleges in the Northeast and large public universities in the Midwest. The report rates each school on the adequacy of its salary scales against the AAUP's own notions of what faculty salaries should be. It thereby arms the dean for his argument about salary with the next faculty member who walks in.

Another report was the dean's control sheet comparing actual expenses with budgeted expenses. The budgeted figures are usually based on experience over recent years and management's sense of what the current year's budget will tolerate. But the basic purpose of a budget, in fact, is really to provide a *standard* for income and expenditures against which actual figures can be compared.

The most elaborate use of standards is in the control of repetitive expenses of the sort one encounters in a factory or a large-scale clerical operation. The technique devised for this use is *cost accounting.*

Suppose you have just taken a job as sales manager in a clothing firm. You have a hunch that you can double sales of long underwear because of the growing popularity of winter sports, but you decide you had better first check on the selling price. The original price of the company's long underwear, you discover, was based on a book of standard costs showing the amount of materials used and the kinds and amount of labor needed to produce each set. But now you also have available detailed records of actual manufacturing costs over a period of time.

At first you had planned to ask for a step-up in underwear production on the assumption that it cost $1.50 to produce a set and that the sets could be sold to wholesalers for $3.00 apiece. When you check actual costs, though, you find that it cost $2,044 to produce the last thousand sets that were made.

What do you do at this point? You look more closely at the standards and the actual results to try to track down the reasons for this *variance* from the standards. You find that the standard cost of $1.50 per set assumed $.50 for materials and $1.00 for labor. Actually, the cost of materials turned out to be only $.46 per set because of a special price break the company had enjoyed on imported wool yarn. Thus the *materials cost variance* for the last 1,000 sets would be:

Standard cost 1,000 sets	Actual cost 1,000 sets	Materials cost variance
$500	$460	$40 in savings

Clearly the answer to the problem lies elsewhere, so you try labor costs. The labor cost standard of $1.00 per set was based on the assumption that a worker could complete four sets an hour. Let's try a *time variance* analysis:

Standard hours to make 1,000 sets	Actual hours to make 1,000 sets	Standard wage rate	Extra cost of time variance
250 hours	360 hours	$4.00/hour	$440

Why the extra labor costs? You find on further investigation that the imported yarn had been harder to handle, so that more hours and more overtime were involved. Therefore the next thing you must do is check the *wage rate variance:*

Standard wage rate	Average actual wage rate with overtime averaged in	Actual hours	Extra cost of wage rate variance
$4.00/hour	$4.40/hour	360	$144

Inside the Organization

Judging from these variance analyses, it looks as though the decision to use a slightly cheaper yarn cost more than it saved, and that either the yarn should be changed or else production methods should be improved before production is expanded. Cost accounting and variance analysis do not always lead to such precise answers, but they can bring problems into the open and suggest alternative solutions.

Using Information Systems for Planning

Standard costs and variance analysis are based on an organization's past experience and on its translation of that experience into an expectation of what ought to happen in the future. These planning tools worked fairly well when the day after tomorrow looked exactly like the day before yesterday. However, in an organization striving to improve costs and sales, or in an organization caught in a shifting, unstable environment, standards cannot be based directly on what has happened in the past. Managers of ambitious or changing organizations — in short, most managers today — have had to learn to look at the future. What do they *want* to have happen? What might happen in the future, regardless of what they would like to see, or perhaps as side-effects of their actions? How can they move most directly toward their goals? The standards for control today, the guidelines for determining what ought to happen, are based less and less on past experience and more and more on future planning.

Let's look at some of the other papers on the dean's desk. The government report on demand for students with various qualifications, the letters of recommendation for a professor being considered for tenure, and the faculty proposal to buy some videotape equipment all seem relevant to the dean's role as planner, and each raises different kinds of dilemmas about how information can be used systematically for planning.

The government report raises one type of planning problem. It provides important information that the dean's school can probably not afford to provide for itself: a broad, comprehensive overview of trends in the demand for different kinds of graduates. But, like most externally produced reports, it doesn't perfectly fit the need of each user.

The dean's dilemma is a little like choosing between a ready-made suit and a custom-made suit. If the dean expects his school to look very much like other schools, he may accept the categories of degrees and students in the government survey. Like the ready-made suit, it's available, it's cheap, and it may fit reasonably well.

But if the dean wants a school with a unique image, the standard government survey may not help much. Custom-made surveys, like custom-made suits, take extra time and money—but they may still be worth it.

The letters of recommendation present another planning problem. They are an example of one kind of future-oriented information —a kind of collective Delphic oracle. Distrusting his own observations of the professor's performance, the dean asks for recommendations from professors at other schools before making a decision on tenure. He knows that at least half of the letters he receives will be useless, either because the writer doesn't really know the man in question or because he can't be trusted to say what he really thinks. The dean is left with the vague, subjective job of interpreting conflicting observations and opinions in order to make his plans for the school's future.

The manager as planner is constantly seeking to divine what the information in the letters of recommendation—or in predictions about the future of nuclear energy or women's fashions—means in terms of the subsequent achievement of specific results. The dean, in other words, wants to convert the favorable comments in the letters of recommendation into specific predictions of how well the professor will be doing in the classroom or the laboratory twenty years hence.

Consider now the informational problems raised by the most interesting item on the dean's desk: the faculty proposal for the purchase of videotape equipment. It raises the problem of planning capital budgets. The faculty argument probably runs this way: By spending $5,000 on the equipment, the school can cut teaching costs and can increase the effectiveness of its human-relations courses. The school has already invested a great deal of effort in building case and problem material that could be used in the new program, and the money spent on the equipment would protect that investment.

This is dangerous reasoning, and the good manager knows it. In the first place, what has already been spent to build case and problem material should have nothing to do with the decision. That money has been spent; those costs—in the economist's jargon —are "sunk." They cannot be used to justify new expenditures. Any new investment must stand on its own merits. Therefore the dean looks at the investment proposal in terms of *incremental* (or marginal) costs and *incremental* (or marginal) benefits. He will have to spend $5,000 for the equipment right away. What about other costs? The faculty forgot to mention $1,200 for an initial suoply of videotapes, $500 per year for a maintenance and service contract for the equipment, $2,300 to transform a classroom into a recording studio and viewing room, and $3,500 per year for a graduate assistant that the department chairman will eventually want to run the equipment and work with the students.

The faculty members say that with the new equipment they can increase class size by 60 percent within three years and still increase teaching effectiveness and the level of student satisfaction. The dean must judge whether these savings in the faculty/student ratio are real and incremental. If he is already overstaffed, particularly with tenured faculty, there may be no real savings at all. If, on the other hand, the equipment will enable him to get along with one less faculty member in the human-relations department three years later, he may, by the time he considers the salary and other costs of supporting and housing a faculty member, save $25,000 per year. Let's assume that he can release one faculty member.

Year	Incremental cash costs	Incremental cash savings	Balance	Cumulative balance
1	$8,500	$ 0	−$8,500	−$8,500
2	4,000	0	−4,000	−12,500
3	4,000	0	−4,000	−16,500
4	4,000	25,000	+21,000	+4,500
5	4,000	25,000	+21,000	+25,500

This extrapolation is called a *cash-flow analysis,* and you can see how rosy it looks. The payback period is less than four years, and by the end of the fourth year the school is making money. Furthermore, starting with the fourth year the school is making a net of $21,000 in incremental revenue every year on an investment of $8,500. The average return on the original investment over a five-year period works out to be over 50 percent per year; over a period of ten years it could average almost 150 percent per year.

Managers rely heavily on estimates of payback period and annual rate of return on investment in planning how to use their organization's time and capital, but they have also learned to be conservative in making those estimates.

In the case of the videotape estimates, what would happen if the cost of maintaining the equipment turned out to be much higher than expected, or if enrollments declined, or if faculty and students lost interest in the equipment, or if course structures were changed so that videotape could no longer be used? Can one really bank on a ten-year return, or might the equipment be scrapped after five years — or even after three? Wouldn't the school be sure to make *some* money just by leaving the $8,500 in its endowment fund?

The professionals who do return-on-investment analysis take such questions seriously. They have developed formal ways of discounting promises of future savings or profits, relying on the old principle that a bird in the hand is worth two in the bush. If they tell the dean that the "present value" of the savings in the fourth year is not $21,000 but $17,000, and in the fifth year not $21,000 but $15,250, they are scaling the distant future savings down to a level that makes the whole investment look less attractive.

Planners still have to add their qualitative assessment to what the numbers tell them. The analysis in our present example might include data about student and faculty attitudes toward the use of videotape. Unfortunately, however, no simple formula can be used to trade off dollars saved against changes in students' attitude or in the educational effectiveness of new media. Therefore, using information to plan for the future remains a very tricky, often subjective business.

Getting It All Together

Almost all efforts to gather information for planning and control have visible, tangible costs: salaries for clerks and analysts, telephone and postal expenses, rentals for copying machines and computers, and a myriad of other items. Many have less visible costs: the time taken from productive work to supply information in four different versions to people who will never use it, or the opportunities that are lost when information is late or wrong.

Thus the information specialist looks at the pile of papers on the dean's desk and throws up his hands in horror, not because of their contents, but because of the sheer wastefulness and inefficiency of the process by which they have been assembled. He knows that there are ways of getting it all together in a simpler and more useful fashion.

To show what can be done, let's take a different example. Suppose you're the president of a company that makes home and farm power tools. You have salesmen and warehouses all over the country, and you have a dozen plants in various locations. Your selling, billing, and shipping activities are conducted in the time-honored fashion: Salesman Jones drops in on the local hardware store in Phillips, Maine. He gets an order for half a dozen of your new heavy-duty chain saws. The hardware dealer thinks those saws should prove very attractive to the farmers in the area. That night Jones gets back to his office in Portland, sits down and writes out the order, and mails it to his company's nearest warehouse, which happens to be in Providence, Rhode Island. Four days later he gets a **letter** back from Providence saying they are out of stock on that item, but they have been reordered from the plant in Chicago. Providence expects the

Cybernetics

... It was apparent during the years immediately preceding the Second World War that the ideas, basic concepts, and methods of communication engineering were of wide applicability to other specialized branches of science. The lead was taken by Norbert Wiener who, with Rosenblueth, called attention to the great generality of the concept of feedback, which had been studied intensively by communication engineers for twenty years, and emphasized that this concept provided a useful relationship between biological and physical sciences. They referred to this general study as cybernetics, from the word "KUBERNETES" (a "steersman"), a word first used by André Ampère in the form *cybernétique,* in his "Essai sur la philosophie des sciences," 1934, to mean the "science of government or control." The simplest feedback systems with which most people are familiar are the Watt steam governor, which regulates the speed of a steam engine, and the thermostat, which controls the temperature of a room. The needs of the war forced attention to feedback theory with the urgency of developing automatic predictors, automatic gun-laying mechanisms, and many other automatic-following, "self-controlling," or "goal-seeking" systems. Wiener and Rosenblueth called attention to the need for a general study that would cover not only these automatic mechanisms but also certain aspects of physiology, the central nervous system, and the operation of the brain, and even certain problems in economics concerning the theory of booms and slumps.

—*Reprinted from* On Human Communication, *by Colin Cherry, p. 561, by permission of The M.I.T. Press, Cambridge, Mass. Copyright ©1968 by The M.I.T. Press.*

saws to arrive within four or five weeks and plans to ship the order to Phillips as soon as they come in.

Meanwhile, back in Chicago, the plant manager has just received instructions from a vice president in New York telling him to stop production of those saws because they aren't selling very well. Production of the saws will now be limited to one plant, in Atlanta. The Chicago plant transfers its order for Jones' saws from Providence to Atlanta. Word goes out to Salesman Jones, who calls the retailer in Phillips to tell him that he won't have his saws for another four or five weeks. The retailer is peeved because by the time the saws arrive the Christmas tree harvesting season in Maine will be over. He cancels the order and calls Jones' competitor to see if he has a comparable saw. Jones writes Providence to cancel, Providence writes to Atlanta, and so on.

Now suppose your favorite genie delivers overnight, fully operational and completely debugged, a whole new substructure for your organization: a large computer with an insatiable capacity for storing information; a network of telephone lines tying the computer to each of your offices, plants, and warehouses; and terminals in each location to provide access to the computer. Jones, if he hasn't quit in frustration, is now about to go "on line" in "real time," which is to say that he is about to become part of an integrated man-machine system.

Now let's start again. Jones gets his order from the retailer in Phillips. He sits down in front of his shiny new console in Portland and teletypes an order directly into the computer center outside New York. The computer searches its memory and finds that the warehouse nearest Phillips is Providence, but it also checks its records on the Providence warehouse inventory and discovers that the last saws of the type in question were sold by Providence three days ago. The computer then proceeds to search for the next closest warehouse. It finds that the Pittsburgh warehouse is as close as any and is carrying twelve of the saws in its inventory. It teletypes an order form and shipping papers directly to the Pittsburgh warehouse and sends a message to Jones' terminal telling him the saws will be shipped immediately from Pittsburgh by air freight. The whole process takes only a few seconds.

Meanwhile the computer program checks to see how many orders have been coming in for those saws from the area served by the Providence warehouse. Discovering that the orders have been heavier than the expected rate (the expected rate is stored in the computer's memory), the computer now teletypes instructions to the Chicago plant to ship three of those saws to Providence for inventory. It also notifies the Providence warehouse of what it has done, and no human hands have gotten into the act, save Jones'. No supervisors have meddled with the arrangements, no clerks have slowed the operation in Providence or Chicago or Atlanta. The adjustments to sales, inventories, costs, and profits represented by all these transactions will be automatically made within the system and will become part of the firm's computerized financial accounting record.

There is, however, still one little bug in the system. Did you notice it? That vice president in New York never told the computer that he had ordered Chicago to stop producing those saws! So even with the new scheme, things can still get fouled up.

Let's add a new level of sophistication to the system. The marketing department wants to know where and how well their new drill bits are selling. The general sales manager, who is looking for a man to promote to a new territory, wants to know how well his salesmen are performing. The computer program can now feed the department managers a wealth of summarized information about sales, prices, performance, and all kinds of things that may help them manage the organization more effectively.

This new kind of information system is quite different from the accounting systems, consumer surveys, sales analyses, teacher evaluation reports, and other kinds of subsystems that we discussed earlier in the chapter. It is vastly more comprehensive and integrated, and is oriented less toward the churning out of periodic reports and more toward the continuous maintenance of files of information. It reduces to a minimum the time needed to transmit information from one location to another and to find out what's going on all through the organization. The system gives management new resources to draw on in its most significant planning and control activities. Also, by making the same information available to salesmen, foremen, and shipping clerks, it minimizes management's need to exercise close supervision and control over the lower levels of the hierarchy.

A few organizations have made remarkable progress in building supersystems to process information, though they have had to overcome formidable design problems to do so. Decisions about what the system will contain and how it will work have far-reaching effects on all the activities within an organization. In our power-saw example, if the new information-system design was a good one, it would have given you a tremendous advantage over your competitors in swiftness of service and economy of operation. But if your newly installed computer began to garble messages—asking Atlanta to send lawn mowers to the retailer who wanted saws, or forgetting the amounts owed by your firm's customers—your competitors would have won the day.

Some highly sophisticated information systems have failed dramatically, but others have proved brilliant successes. The job of putting together an information system based on advanced technology requires highly creative people who are skilled at probing and assessing the needs of real people and who can realize the full capacity of complex computing and communications equipment.

The Whole Man Strikes Again:
Human Problems of Formal Information Systems

The designers of complex, formal information systems have learned that no system is invulnerable to indifference, ignorance, or perversity on the part of people whose job is to keep it going. So before we go on to Chapters 6 and 7, where we describe still more ingenious techniques for handling information, we must remind you that learning to deal with the whole man remains more important than learning to deal with the computer.

Double-entry bookkeeping doesn't keep department stores

from making mistakes in your account, nor does it prevent embezzlers from getting away with purloined fortunes. The best techniques of measuring attitudes, and the most reliable statistical sampling methods, have not outwitted voters who want to conceal their intentions from Gallup and Harris.

We do not always realize how pervasive the people "problem" is. People try to twist the contents and output of information systems to their own ends, and systems break down because key people find it inconvenient to do what the system needs to have them do.

Suppose, for example, you instruct your planning and control system to set standards that prescribe what you expect me to accomplish. You have designed your information system in such a way that it will keep you posted on whether or not I'm doing what I am supposed to do. To top it off, you are going to reward me on the basis of how well I meet your standards. Remember, though, that your information system gets most of its input from people. And those people (including me) know that their lives are being planned and controlled by the output of that same system. They also know that they can make it or break it.

For these reasons, three nearly inevitable and unintended accompaniments ride along with your system. Two of them are negative accompaniments: (1) some people won't like certain parts of the system, and (2) you're going to have a very tough time making those disliked parts of it stick. The third factor, happily, is a positive one: those same people will often rescue a faulty information system and keep the organization operating despite the system's stupidities.

Even a pigeon can learn to manipulate the input levers of a feeding machine to get what he wants on the output side. Likewise, people soon learn to manipulate an organizational information system. They concoct elaborate games in which the systems men are involuntarily teamed up on one side with almost everybody else on the other. Often those games are an expression of resentment against the restrictions imposed by the system, but sometimes they serve to correct for the system's inflexibilities.

Consider, for instance, the Venetian Glass Bulb Company. A young systems engineer named Andy has the notion that the purpose of information systems is to inform. He studies the available data about the process being used to manufacture the company's bulbs and discovers that the variance in bulb thickness is quite low. He is excited by this discovery and deduces that the company can produce a pretty good bulb by a much simpler process than the present one. He designs his new process, and for weeks he tries to make it work. It doesn't. Finally he quits, convinced that his new process is sound but that someone is sabotaging it.

If we run a post-mortem investigation, we discover that Andy's

> *Not Everyone Is Enthusiastic
> about Orderly Business Practice*
>
> A Turk responded to the inquiry of a nineteenth-century English merchant in this fashion:
>
> My Illustrious Friend, and Joy of My Liver!
>
> > The thing you ask of me is both difficult and useless. Although I have passed all my days in this place, I have neither counted the houses nor inquired into the number of the inhabitants; and as to what one person loads on his mules and the other stows away in the bottom of his ship, that is no business of mine. But above all, as to the previous history of this city, God only knows the amount of dirt and confusion that the infidels may have eaten before the coming of the Sword of Islam. It were unprofitable for us to inquire into it.
> > Oh my soul! Oh my lamb! seek not after the things which concern thee not. Thou camest unto us and we welcome thee: go in peace.

scheme was doomed from the start because his "discovery" that the variance was low was a phony discovery. His findings were based on other people's readings of bulb thicknesses. The accuracy of those readings was not very important to the people who made them, so they had "smoothed" out the facts a little because their work went faster that way, and besides, they weren't being evaluated on the accuracy of their reports. The falsified data then showed the narrow distribution of thickness measurements that set Andy trying to accomplish something he couldn't accomplish.

Jim is a foreman in the same glass bulb plant. The control system judges his performance on the basis of the average cost of reinspecting defective lots of bulbs. Jim is in charge of reinspection, among other things. It costs him $3.50 in labor to inspect a thousand bulbs. One day a defective batch of 2,500 bulbs is produced, much to Jim's chagrin. It would cost $5.00 to replace the whole lot with new bulbs. Simple arithmetic tells Jim that he would be a fool to spend $8.75 to reinspect bulbs worth only $5 in the first place. But the system expects him to carry out the reinspection, so he does.

The system is asking him to reinspect those bulbs because it doesn't know that his true labor cost is $3.50 per thousand. Why not? Simply because of the way Jim himself has been doing his own job. Often he has held out bulbs that were defective, but not so defective that a customer would notice. Then, when his boss pushed him for more production, he would simply release some of those stored-up bulbs, as if they had passed inspection. Everyone in the plant knew his game; he had been playing it for years. Everyone except, of course, the bright new MBA who was running the information system.

In neither of these instances were the people trying intentionally to foul up the company. Rather, they were reacting in a perfectly human way to the effect the information and control system was having on them. They did not and could not know the ramifications of their behavior up and down the total system. People who provide inputs to information systems often hold just such local views of the organization and act in response to their own local motives. Seldom do those views lead them to report exactly the information management needs. In extreme cases, people may even produce "information" intentionally designed to mislead others in the organization.

The design engineers in one organization did exactly that. Management installed a new planning and control system. Under the new system the engineers were expected to report (1) each activity they intended to accomplish and (2) whether or not they had actually accomplished it. Then they were to report the next activity and its accomplishment and so on. In effect, the system required them to behave serially, with each task completed before another one could begin. But that wasn't the way they really went about solving their engineering problems. They actually worked on several problems simultaneously, moving back and forth from one problem to another. What they learned while working on one problem, they would transfer to another. Many of them, in a private interview, declared that doing these tasks in sequence would really hurt the company, but they feared that top management might insist that they work according to the new plan.

At first they had tried to talk management out of the new system. When they found that they couldn't, they decided to play the game according to their own rules. The engineers carefully constructed the system's information inputs so that management couldn't know what the key tasks really were. They didn't lie—they just provided management with information about trivial tasks and buried the important tasks in large overhead accounts, thereby winning the freedom to work on the tasks they thought were truly important. None of the engineers, of course, had any intention of defrauding or hurting the company. They simply felt that top management, well intentioned but ignorant of engineering problems, had to be helped along.

For more familiar examples of the games played in coping with control systems, have a chat with someone who is responsible for developing organization budgets—a department head in a company, a school principal, or the director of a government agency. Ask him how he figures out what to ask for, and whether the formal budget request he sends up is in fact an unpadded, exact match to his true requirements. If he answers that he always tells the truth, the whole truth, and nothing but the truth, he's either a novice at the budgeting game or else the budget director.

Summary

The term "information system" is a label used to encompass a whole range of means for distributing, processing, storing, and monitoring organizationally relevant information—it covers accounting systems, feedback and control systems, record-keeping systems, and future-planning systems.

Particularly since the advent of the computer, information systems— which have always been with us—have undergone exciting and innovative developments. The biggest problems the developers of such formal systems face are these: How does one build an orderly, structured system and still leave it flexible enough to adjust to ever-changing requirements? How does one get information to the right places fast enough so that the right decisions can be made in time? How does one set the standards against which to evaluate information from the world outside? How can information be turned toward the future to make it useful for planning ahead? What are the human problems generated by such systems?

Notes and References

For an example of what happens when information networks are not strong enough to hold organizations together, see Alfred Sloan's accounts of the problems faced by General Motors before he took over, in his *My Years with General Motors* (New York: Doubleday, 1964), Chapters 1 and 2. Or see how a railroad merger got off the tracks, in Joseph R. Daughen and Peter Binzen, *The Wreck of the Penn Central* (Boston: Little, Brown, 1971), particularly Chapter 9.

Strong argument for knowledge and "knowledge workers" as keystones in modern organizational functioning can be found in Peter F. Drucker, *The Age of Discontinuity* (New York: Harper & Row, 1969), Chapters 12–17.

The rudiments of accounting can be learned from any of a variety of accounting texts, or even from self-study manuals such as Robert Anthony, *Management Accounting* (Homewood, Ill.: Learning Systems Company, 1970). In another book, *Planning and Control Systems: A Framework for Analysis* (Boston: Division of Research, Harvard Business School, 1965), Anthony moves away from details to talk about how accounting helps managers in their roles as planners, doers, and controllers. John Deardon provides a systems view of the goals and methods of cost accounting in *Cost and Budget Analysis* (Englewood Cliffs, N.J.: Prentice-Hall, 1962).

The links between accounting and management information systems are explored in these two articles: Peter A. Firman and James J. Linn, "Information Systems and Managerial Accounting," *Accounting Review,*

XLIII, 1 (Jan. 1968); Bruce H. Joplin, "The Accountant's Role in Management Information Systems," Journal of Accounting, CXXI, 3 (Mar. 1966).

For discussion of information systems *per se,* in the modern computer-based sense, the following articles and books will take you well beyond the general concepts outlined in this chapter: Robert Beyer, "A Positive Look at Management Information Systems," in Leonard W. Hein, ed., *Contemporary Accounting and the Computer* (Belmont, Calif.: Dickenson Publishing Company, 1969); Evan G. Birks, "The Computer in a Management Information System," in William C. House, ed., *The Impact of Information Technology on Management Operation* (New York: Auerback Publishers, 1971); Sherman C. Blumenthal, *Management Information Systems* (Englewood Cliffs, N.J.: Prentice-Hall, 1969), particularly Chapters 1–3; John Deardon and F. Warren McFarlan, *Management Information Systems* (Homewood, Ill.: Irwin, 1966).

Deardon, more than some of the other writers mentioned, is skeptical of how fast computerized information systems can be developed to meet management needs. On the other hand, among the men who have taken Norbert Wiener most seriously in looking toward closed-loop, cybernetic models of management and society is Stafford Beer, a British executive and author of *Cybernetics and Management* (New York: John Wiley and Sons, 1964). Another proponent of cybernetic models is Jay Forrester, who has steadily enlarged the scope of his world view in three books, all published by the M.I.T. Press in Cambridge, Massachusetts: *Industrial Dynamics* (1961), *Urban Dynamics* (1969), and *World Dynamics* (1971). You can get some idea of Forrester's approach and message from William Bowen's review of *World Dynamics* in *Fortune,* LXXXIV, 3 (Sept. 1971), pp. 131–32.

6

Technical Tools for Decision Making: Systems Analysis, Model Building, and Their Relatives

Suppose we're sailing in a race and the wind suddenly shifts. We have several choices: trim the sails, move the rudder, shift our weight in the boat. For each alternative action we consider, we try to think through what may happen next. Then we choose. What we do depends on our idea, our "model," of how wind, boat, crew, and water will react. That "model" exists even if we cannot explain it to another sailor. Models of how the world works and reacts lie behind all our hunches and choices—they are the hidden foundation of the manager's decisions.

In modern business practice models are moving out of the manager's subconscious, however, and are becoming more explicit and visible. Models are being fashioned into useful tools to help managers think more wisely and deeply about complicated real-world processes. This chapter tells how and why.

Some models are physical: we can refine our racing tactics by experimenting with cardboard cutouts of sailboats on the dining room table or with scale models in a testing tank. Other models are symbolic: we can represent the effects of wind and waves by numbers and equations. All models are simpler than the real-world situation they try to describe. Yet by playing around in purposeful ways with a model and with alternative decisions, we can make predictions about how those decisions will work in real life. If our predictions turn out well, the model is good; if not, then it's back to the drawing board for a new or improved version.

The manager's models are most often symbolic, and they are usually intended to represent very complicated situations. Therefore we have had to develop new ways of symbolizing things and new kinds of mathematical and statistical language in which to state the model and to trace effects. These new tools of analysis are variously called systems analysis, management science, and operations research. The field is young; the names have not quite shaken down yet. But the labels don't matter. Our concern is for the commonalities.

Systems analysis (let's use that name for now) provides tools that enable us to talk to one another about models designed to handle complex and messy problems. These tools discipline our efforts to describe, to analyze, and to speculate, and they are designed to add precision and depth to managerial judgment.

An Early Example of Systems Analysis

Since World War I, naval officers have been concerned about how to spot enemy submarines. Whether one searches for a submarine with a ship or a balloon or an airplane, the basic problem remains much the same: what's the best way to go about it?

Common sense and experience have led to some pretty good answers. One scheme, for instance, used balloons or other aircraft moving slowly over the sea at low altitudes. That method yielded a high likelihood of sighting a submarine if there was one down there, and of not claiming to have detected one when there wasn't. But the trouble with that method was that one couldn't sweep a very large area unless he had a very large supply of balloons. So one could easily miss a submarine even if it was in relatively close range. On the other hand, a very fast airplane, though it could cover a much larger area, was even more likely either to miss a sub or to turn in false alarms.

So unless we have an unlimited number of balloons and airplanes, we have to work out a trade-off. But just how do we find the best trade-off between coverage and speed of search?

During the Second World War a group of physical scientists, though inexperienced in such problems, were asked to work on them. They were not called systems analysts then. They applied their analytic, hard-science modes of thought and did what came mathematically: they built a mathematical model of the problem. The model was no more than an algebraic expression of the relationship between the probability of finding a submarine in a given area and the speed of the search vehicle. Then, by using the model, an officer could specify the most appropriate speed of search for a given number of aircraft in a given situation.

No one, least of all the developers of that simple model, believed that their equations described reality exactly. The best they could come up with was an approximation. And yet, though the model simplified reality, it still gave the user a better tool for making his decision than the bare judgment he had before.

Some Current Examples

The same kind of model-building approach was extended after the war to complex decision-making problems in many other areas. Models were developed to improve the scheduling of paint production, to blend different grades of gasoline in a refinery at low cost, and to signal to management when product quality in a manufacturing process was slipping below standard. The advent of the computer speeded up those developments enormously, making very complex models computationally feasible.

Since much of the early work focused on specific operations (like hunting submarines), the new techniques came to be called "operations research." But that turned out to be an inadequate description, since the same analytic modeling approach proved applicable to a wide range of nonoperating problems in management. So two other names (and more) evolved for elaborations of the process. "Management science" conveyed the sense of broader applications, and "systems analysis" stressed the interrelations between seemingly separate parts of the world. Despite the different labels, all three have one element in common: they aim to provide decision-makers with quantitative representations of the probable effects of alternative choices.

Since quantitative representations almost always simplify real situations and wash out some of the complexities of the real world, they also share a common vulnerability: the danger that they will miss a key element of the real world and, therefore, make entirely wrong predictions. That danger continues even with today's highly complex models. Systems analysts have constructed models consisting of thousands of equations in order to describe complex operational and policy-decision situations, ranging from alternative weapons systems to the styling of shoes and the introduction of new deodorants. Sometimes these models, too, turn out to have missed a vital parameter—like the unforeseen emotional response of investors to bad political news.

Complicated models, though, often do work well. Consider this example: A lumber company built a set of models for the production-

The Stewardess as Finished Product

Many basic operations research models developed in one context can be used in others. Consider what one group of analysts, experienced in scheduling factory production, did for an airline:

> The problem involved the training of stewardesses, of whom the company employed approximately one thousand. Most of these girls left the airline before they had given two years of service, primarily to get married. . . . Because of the high rate of attrition, the airline had a continuous need to recruit and train additional stewardesses.
>
> The company had set up a stewardess training school. It was capable of conducting three classes of fifty girls each. Actual training took five and a half weeks. An additional half-week was required for outfitting; a week was required to bring the girls from their homes to school and another was required to get them to their bases after training. This made for a total of eight weeks "lead time."
>
> The company wanted to know how often it should run a class and how large the classes should be. On examination it became apparent that this was a familiar problem in production and inventory control. The conversion of a young lady (the raw material) into a stewardess (the finished product) by training (the production process) has associated with it an inventory carrying cost (the salary paid to excess girls whose available time for work is not completely used), shortage costs (those associated with emergency measures or cancellations of flights arising out of shortage of stewardesses), and setup costs associated with preparing the school for a class. The problem, then, was one of determining the size and frequency of "production runs" so as to minimize the sum of these costs, that is, to find the economic "lot sizes."
>
> The appropriate mathematical analysis was applied to this familiar problem and it was solved, yielding a set of tables which the school administrator could use to conduct his operation in an optimal way. The savings indicated were impressive.

—*Russell L. Ackoff and Patrick Rivett,* A Manager's Guide to Operations Research *(New York: John Wiley and Sons, 1963), p. 13.*

planning decisions of its plywood mills. Some of the individual equations dealt with things as small as the number of panels a single machine could process in an hour. But the total model described many plants, each of which had many such machines.

The original intention of the model was to help the individual mill manager to make his production decisions. And at the outset that is how it was used. The mill manager, standing there in his red plaid shirt, examined the computer printout from the model and made his daily decisions for scheduling the mill. Even the first mill manager to use it did so with great success. The model showed him that a particular product not now being manufactured could be highly profitable for his mill. He tried it, and it was. Within six months he moved the mill from a loss to a profit position. The company's systems analysis group thereupon received national acclaim from their profession. And the mill manager began to back up almost every argument with, "The model says. . . ."

Another example: Models are now used widely to help factories, stores, wholesalers, and other organizations to make more efficient decisions about inventories: when to restock, how much to buy at a time, how much of each kind of thing to keep on hand. Because so many groups use inventory models so well, economists now believe we have reduced the effect of what used to be a primary cause of swings in the business cycle. Equations are helping to combat recession.

Can Systems Analysis Really Deliver?

There is no such thing as a free lunch. Many models have not paid off so handsomely. A lot of people in a lot of organizations have gotten irritated and raised objections to systems analysis, and not just because they felt threatened by unfamiliar technology. The objections run something like this: The central claim of systems analysis is, after all, that quantitative models can help managers make substantially more effective decisions. But have they really helped? At best, some critics argue, they have made little difference; sometimes they have actually misled the manager. Moreover, many models cost more than they are worth, sometimes in human terms as well as in dollars.

The first problem, then, in using models in an organization is to find models that really describe and predict very well relative to their costs. In astronomy and in space programs, even though Einstein improved on Newton and men are still trying to improve on Einstein, Newton's laws still serve well enough over a wide range of problems. But when we build models of consumer or voter behavior, or models to hunt submarines or to manage inventories, we have nothing equivalent to Newton's laws. Predictions are much more approximate, and models too often can answer only one or two narrow kinds of question.

The other big problem is that when a model is intended to change the way people do things (as models usually are in management), the reactions of people to the model can make it invalid. Suppose, for example, that you're the eager young head of the systems analysis department in a steamship company. You're quite sure that the

Sow the Wind, Reap the Whirlwind

> Formal techniques of probability analysis have been used to propose models for deciding whether or not, in specific instances, seeding hurricanes with silver iodide crystals will lessen their destructive force. The model says that generally seeding should help, but the analysts who developed it recognize that the model's output is at best a recommendation to those whom society has empowered to make the final decisions.
>
>> [Decision analysis] conceptually separates the roles of the executive decision-maker, the expert, and the analyst. The analyst's role is to structure a complex problem in a tractable manner so that the uncertain consequences of the alternative actions may be assessed. Various experts provide the technical information from which the analysis is fashioned. The decision-maker acts for society in providing the basis for choosing among the alternatives. The analysis provides a mechanism for integration and communication so that the technical judgments of the experts and the value judgments of the decision-maker may be seen in relation to each other, examined, and debated. Decision analysis makes not only the decision but the decision process a matter of formal record. . . .
>>
>> The decision to seed a hurricane imposes a great responsibility on public officials. This decision cannot be avoided because inaction is equivalent to a decision not to permit seeding. Either the government must accept the responsibility of a seeding that may be perceived by the public as deleterious, or it must accept the responsibility for not seeding and thereby exposing the public to higher probabilities of severe storm damage.
>
> —R. A. Howard, J. E. Matheson, and D. W. North, "The Decision to Seed Hurricanes," Science (June 16, 1972), 1191–1202. ©1972 by the American Association for the Advancement of Science.

company could save a great deal of money and time in handling cargo by switching to large metal containers. You've gathered data about the size of ships and the types of cargo they carry. You go to some container manufacturers and find out how much containers would cost, and what loads could be carried in them. Then you build some simple models describing the costs of loading and unloading a ship with and without containers. The model says: "Go containers."

You're all set to test your model, much as if you were testing a model that would predict the time of an eclipse. Everything's going your way. The board of directors likes the predictions your model gives and approves your plan to give containers a try.

At about this time, however, the public reads about your new plan in the newspapers, and so do the leaders of the longshoremen's union. Now the longshoremen may not be great mathematicians, but they're not dummies either. They can see that this new model hints at a development they don't particularly like: if it works, there will be a lot fewer longshoremen around.

The point is not just that the special interests of the longshoremen introduce uncertainty into the predictions; that is indeed true, and it's a point that is often missed in model building. Your analysis could, in fact, have included the possible costs of a long strike or of worsened employee relations. The real problem is that model-builders often create an impossible situation for themselves by failing either to forecast negative human reactions or to cope with those reactions, even if they are forecast. This element of human reaction doesn't make model building useless, but it makes it more difficult to evaluate the actual utility of models. Many model-builders will argue that it was a good model even if the longshoremen killed it. The model was right. The people were wrong. But is that argument valid for the manager?

Purposive human behavior, of course, sometimes gives positive support to a model. That is, people make it work because they believe in the model—or in the modeler—even if the model itself is pretty crude. Back in that plywood mill, for instance, some observers felt that the major reason for the model's success was that it stimulated people to work at making the model work. The systems analyst, after all, had come on strong and enthusiastic, spurring people to perform more effectively. The model predicted that they would, and they did. Was the *model* effective, or was the systems analyst a good motivator?

Practically speaking, the answer doesn't really matter. From the organization's view the model and its implementation are inseparable. The model is no good if it can't be made to work, no matter how many footnotes it gets in the scholarly journals.

People come into the picture in other ways, too. Consider the experience of a systems analyst working in the bond trading market in New York City: The analyst gathered data about the market and then constructed a model of its operation. The purpose of the model was to predict what the effects of alternative bidding procedures on a bond would be. The builder of the model then compared the predictions with what people actually did. The traders in the bond market neither knew nor cared anything about modeling. They had simply developed their own rules of thumb about how to bid on bonds, based on years of experience in the market. But when the modeler compared the traders' actual behavior with what the model predicted, he found them almost identical. The bond traders had, by muddling through, worked out an optimal solution to a very complex problem without benefit of any quantitative analytic modeling process.

Was it worth building the model? The answer is a qualified "yes." To the experienced bond trader, the model was not very useful. But the model might transform an inexperienced trader into a pro in a matter of months rather than years.

Perhaps we should measure the worth of a model not only by how well it predicts but by how successfully it modifies human behavior. If it makes people more effective than they were, or helps them learn faster, it's a good model.

Is Modeling a Passing Fad?

The evidence for the value of modeling, as you can see, is mixed. And as you may hope from your own skirmishes with mathematics and statistics, not every manager will be expected to build — or even to understand in detail — complex models. Yet new techniques like systems analysis are not just passing fads. The people who devise them and the people who use them will have a growing influence on our society. And as their power grows, the analyst who perceives how to make the world move as a system will compete more and more directly with managers, legislators, consumers, and voters in shaping the actions of organizations and governments.

Models — and what congressmen believed about them — killed the supersonic transport. Economic welfare models argued that greater social benefits would come if public money was not invested in the new plane. Cost-benefit studies predicted that the plane could never be profitable. Speculative ecological analysis suggested that flights in the stratosphere might change ozone levels and increase the incidence of cancer. Theories derived from experience and experiments yielded unfavorable estimates of the nuisance and damage that would be caused by sonic boom.

Statistical studies of consumer behavior now have a direct effect on the kinds of commercial you see on television, on the amount of junk mail you receive, and on whether or not your favorite magazine will try to survive in the face of declining advertising revenues. A modeling technique called *linear programing* helps design hospital menus, determines ingredients for gasoline and dog food, plans school bus routings, and decides what mix of jobs will be assigned to factory workers. Inventory models are used both to limit and to increase the variety of goods offered to consumers. Cost-benefit models in government have helped sharpen decision making on important programs in health care, education, welfare reform, and defense—but they have not yet managed to prevent fiascos like the C-5A or the F-111 military aircraft.

You will be better able to cope with tomorrow's world if you learn something about systems analysis and its related fields. You may even find it exciting and rewarding to learn to play this game, because it can do a great deal of good for organizations and society. But beware the perils of overenthusiasm.

The great contribution of systems analysts and related management technicians is that they *do* analyze. They ask impertinent questions and try to understand complex relationships rather than accept simple and often mistaken dictates from past experience. They make their assumptions and their equations clear; though the models they produce may be hard to understand, they are openly described. To those who do understand them, their structure and details are subject to question, to criticism, to change. If a model is a poor one, it is possible to diagnose why. If it is good, as in the case of the bond trader's model, it can help new managers get smart faster.

A common failing of systems analysts, their cousins, and some of their organizational sponsors is that they tend to value the clarity, explicitness, and manageability of a model over its completeness. In order to create a model within the limits of mathematical and statistical techniques or within the constraints of time and computer technology, they have to simplify. They have to leave factors out and ignore important nuances in the relationships among factors. Implicitly or explicitly, they may assign different weights to, say, human or esthetic factors than psychologists and artists might; they may value economic issues differently from the way in which experienced managers or politicians value them. Some issues may not even enter their ken, for there are sloppy and callous analysts as well as careless and insensitive managers.

It behooves us all, then, to learn more about models and model-building practices, not just so that we can use the tools as managers, but so that we can ensure that they are used in ways consistent with our consensual interests. Models that glorify competitive enterprise and short-term profit have been used to justify destroying forests with bulldozers, even though those old redwoods may yet prove more valuable to us than either profits or bulldozers.

Glue, Spit, and Baling Wire:
Some Tips on Making Models

Suppose you want to try your hand at model building. You don't need to be a certified mathematical genius to succeed—in fact,

> ### What's Really Important in the Model? Just Numbers?
>
> What's in a number? It seems inevitable that corporations will try to assign numerical values to elusive social values, but in so doing they may run a risk of absurdity.
>
> Prof. C. West Churchman, professor of business administration at the University of California, gives an example from the search for a site to build a third airport to serve London. One spot under serious consideration would have required demolishing the 12th Century Norman church of St. Michael's in the village of Stewkley.
>
> It was disclosed that a cost-benefit analysis had calculated in monetary terms just what would be lost by tearing down St. Michael's. The calculations had used the face value of the fire insurance of the church—the equivalent of a few thousand dollars.
>
> When the calculation was made public, an outraged antiquarian wrote to the London Times to urge another, perhaps no less plausible, method of calculation: Take the original cost of St. Michael's (perhaps 100 pounds sterling, or about $240), and assume the property grew in value at a rate of 10% a year for 800 years. That would put the value of St. Michael's at roughly one decillion pounds. A decillion is a one followed by 33 zeroes.
>
> St. Michael's was spared after a public outcry arose. But to Prof. Churchman it was striking how glibly either side could pin a numerical value on the church. "Only a modicum of plausibility is needed to convince people that the numbers represent reality," he says. "I don't think the need is for more numbers at all. The need is for justifying the numbers"—for some rationale that "tells us what difference the numbers make."
>
> —"Fight Over an Old Church Raises a Tough Question." Reprinted with permission from the Wall Street Journal, Dec. 9, 1971.

there is more art and poetry in the process than the systems analyst or management scientist may admit. Let's try a simple example. Suppose you run a factory with a conveyer-belt line for shaping, polishing, lacquering, and inspecting brass button hooks. Demand is growing and labor costs keep moving up. You want a model that will let you test in advance what would happen if you changed things on the line. Here are the steps you might follow:

Step 1—Ask yourself: "What results do I care about?" For this problem perhaps you care most about the total cost of producing each hook, the scrap rate (or the percentage of hooks that the inspector rejects), or something even harder to measure, like the satisfaction level of workers on the line. Write each result on a white file card, label the cards "dependent variables," and put them to one side.

Step 2—Ask yourself: "What factors affect the things I care about?" These factors might be the speed of the conveyor belt, wage rates, and the number of workers on the line. Write these down on blue file cards and label them "independent variables."

Step 3—Now you have to say to yourself: "It's not enough to know *which* actions could affect my results. I must know *how* they might affect my results."

You have now entered quantitative territory. You are considering mathematical or statistical relationships. Take each white card (dependent variable) and ask which blue card (independent variable) has an influence on it. Now set up a bigger sheet of paper for each dependent variable. List the important independent variables one by one and try to describe in words, graphs, or symbols how a change in each might cause the dependent variable to change.

One important part of total cost, for example, is easy to model:

$$\frac{(\text{Number of workers}) \times (\text{Wage rate per hour})}{(\text{Number of good hooks produced per hour})}$$

Building a model to predict the scrap rate is a tougher problem. Suppose the rate is 2 percent now. You know it will increase if the line moves faster, but by how much? Your engineers may be able to come up with some estimates; you may have to guess. Maybe the easiest way to think about how the scrap rate would change is to draw a diagram that will enable you to visualize the possibilities before you try to write an equation:

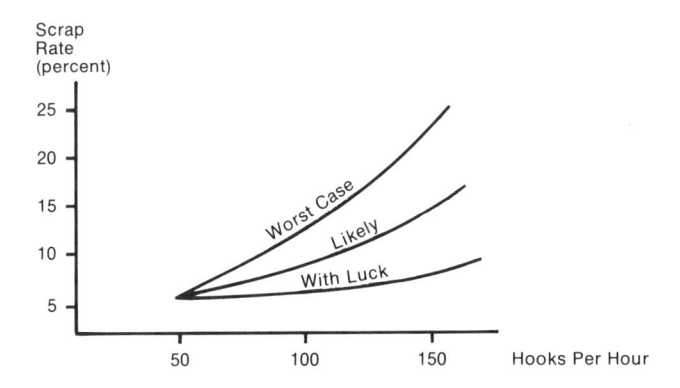

Now comes the really tough problem: predicting the level of workers' satisfaction. Do you measure it by how they answer a questionnaire, by how often they quit, or by how often they strike? However you measure it, how can you know in advance how it will change if line speed or wage rates or anything else changes?

Technical Tools for Decision Making

Now comes the litmus test. If you turn *blue* with frustration at the thought of trying to make things precise and quantitative, you are not likely to be a happy model-builder. If, on the other hand, you turn *pink* with embarrassment but are willing to simplify, to assume, or to guess in ways that you know are only partially right, you are on your way. Your choices should be as good as you can make them, but they may not matter as much as you think. Often when you put a whole model together, with all its variables and relationships, you will find that it works as a whole despite mistakes or bad guesses in individual parts.

Step 4—Now you can ask: "What if?" What if you double the speed of the assembly line but only add 50 percent more workers? Will costs per hook go up or down? What will the scrap rate be? Will workers be so angry over the increased work pace that they will slow down on the job or stage a wildcat strike? Would things be better if you gave them a wage increase?

There you are. You have built a mathematical model and you have seen how it's used.

But what about another *what if?* What if, by speeding up the line, you have to dump twice as much waste acid into the river? . . .

What Gives Models Their Power?

Systematic model building in management has produced three payoffs: new kinds of logical, mathematical, and statistical reasoning; new possibilities for handling high levels of complexity; and new insights into the commonalities of seemingly diverse management problems.

Here are some examples of each of these payoffs. First, the advances in reasoning skills: The first systematic models—like the submarine-tracking analysis described earlier—borrowed heavily from the standard mathematics of engineering and physics. But management problems generally have dimensions that the traditional forms of mathematics do not teach. Businessmen often deal with arrays or tables of data; hence, we have had a growth of interest in the mathematics of sets and of arrays, or matrices. Managers deal with things they can count in units more often than they deal with velocities and flows of a continuous nature; hence there has been new interest in practical mathematical tools to handle the calculus of discrete (or countable), as opposed to continuous (or flowing), functions.

Many problems can be set up as simultaneous equations to be solved, except that managers are often unable to say precisely that $A + B = C$ (where A might be the time a man spends on one task;

B, the time he spends on a second; and C, the number of working hours in a week). Managers can state *inequations* through limits or conditions of the form

A + B must be less than or equal to C
or   D + E + F must be greater than 150

and then state their overall objective: a model to yield maximum profits, for example, or minimum cost.

A whole new field of mathematics called linear, or more broadly, mathematical, programing* has been developed to solve these systems of simultaneous inequations in a way that guarantees the satisfaction of a defined management objective.

Finally, managers, like gamblers, deal with risk and uncertainty. They need to know how to handle erroneous information and how to reduce large volumes of data to simple, but meaningful, summary forms. Their needs have greatly accelerated developments in probability theory and statistics, disciplines that originally served card and dice players more often than executives.

In order to capitalize on these developments in technique, ways had to be found to use them on a large scale. Unlike problems in engineering and physics, few managerial problems worth tackling could be boiled down to a few variables and a handful of relationships. To do a linear programing problem with even ten or twenty inequations to balance, or to calculate a statistical forecast that depended on more than a dozen factors, was so long and tortuous a process by hand—or even by mechanical calculator—that few were tempted to try.

Today, with computers, a problem of that size is done in the blink of an eye (or the blink of a few dozen panel lights). Models involving thousands of variables and relationships among variables can be tried out quickly and cheaply. With less time and energy going into calculations, more time can be spent making sure a model is a good one in the first place and in trying to interpret and understand the results it provides.

But neither the new mathematics nor the new calculating prowess of the computer has contributed as much to the advancement of modeling as the growing skill of systems analysts and managers, working together, in discovering how the same basic model can be applied to many different real-world problems.

Earlier we mentioned that linear programing is used for tasks as varied as routing school buses and planning hospital menus.

* *Not to be confused with computer programing. Linear programing (or mathematical programing) is a very sophisticated and formal brand of mathematics; computer programing is the process of writing sequences of instructions, mathematical or nonmathematical, to direct the operations of a computer.*

Discriminant Analysis: One Approach to Modeling

Models, as conceptual ways of thinking about the world, often develop lives of their own. In the early 1930s, for example, an archeologist named M. M. Barnard wanted to classify ancient skulls according to one of four different historical time periods in which their owners had lived. She had 398 skulls for which the appropriate historical time period was already known, and she took four different measurements on each of these. Let's call these measures: x_1, x_2, x_3, and x_4. To each of the 398 skulls of known origin she gave an arbitrary numerical designation, Z_i, to correspond to the historical time period from which it came. (In one set of calculations on her problem, these values were used: $Z_i = -5$ for the earliest time period, $Z_i = -1$ for the next earliest, $Z_i = +1$ for the third time period, and $Z_i = +5$ for the latest time period.) Then she used a statistical model called *discriminant analysis* to find a set of coefficients that would do the best job of placing the known skulls, on the basis of her four measurements, into the right time period, using a single equation of this form:

$$Z = a_1 x_1 + a_2 x_2 + a_3 x_3 + a_4 x_4$$

The coefficients she got gave this equation:

$$Z = .075 x_1 - .145 x_2 + .145 x_3 - .079 x_4$$

And these average Z values for the skulls from the four time periods:

Earliest time period	Average $Z = -4.57$
Next earliest time period	Average $Z = -.568$
Third time period	Average $Z = 1.43$
Latest time period	Average $Z = 5.43$

This gave a model for classifying other skulls of uncertain historical origins. All she had to do was take the four skull measurements in the proper way, plug the resulting values into the equation, and calculate Z for the new skull. Suppose the resulting value was $x = 1.62$. That value is closest to the average value of Z for skulls from the third time period—hence it is probable that the new skull belongs to that time period.

Discriminant analysis started as a technique to date skulls and later was used to help place samples of goldenrod and iris into appropriate species. But discriminant analysis is not limited to archeology and botany. It is a general method for using what is known about one set of things to make correct classifications or groupings among similar things for which the same measurements can be made but for which the correct classification is not known in advance.

To succeed, the programer must recognize (1) that each of these is a problem in the *allocation* of limited resources (buses to school pick-up points, kinds of food to different meal times); (2) that the allocation must be made within the constraints that exist in the situation (a maximum of ten boys and girls to be picked up at the corner of Dogwood and Maple Lanes, each supper to have between 1,000 and 1,200 calories); and (3) that the solution (allocation plan), in addition to meeting the requirements of the prevailing constraints, should also be the plan that occasions the lowest cost.

We cannot, of course, ignore the real-world nature of the bus-scheduling or the menu-planning problem. But the linear programing model gives us a *way* to think and to ask questions—a *structure* to guide our analysis. Once we understand that structure, we can go beyond routing buses and writing menus and can offer advice on blending gasoline and scheduling factory production.

While the old-time manager had models in his head, they were private models, useful to himself alone. The dominant "language" of each model was specific to the situation—that is, it was the language of bus-routing or menu-planning, but not of both. Because his knowledge was so specific, the old manager tended to live within one kind of organization. The new man—the systems analyst—works with models that are open to public view and that are expressed in a language that allows for powerful acts of manipulation and calculation. He speaks of allocation and minimizing costs, and he moves from school to hospital to refinery to factory.

Systems Analysis and Discontinuities

Most of the early work with mathematical and statistical models was designed to increase the efficiency of more or less routine operations in fields like production and transportation. The operations were stable and repetitive, providing plenty of time to devise and test each model. Yet the real test of a manager's skill is not how well he supervises routine work. The real test—and the real potential of models—lies in how well he can cope with the *discontinuities* in organizations. A discontinuity is what it sounds like—a big break with the past; a situation, therefore, in which past experience isn't likely to help very much.

If, after an agonizing reappraisal, American Motors Corporation decides that it just can't make it any longer in automobiles and begins to think about making houseboats, that's a discontinuity. Modeling is a powerful tool in such wide-open, uncertain situations. Members of the company won't have any "feel" for this new business to help them evaluate its possibilities. But modeling can give them a set of guidelines for doing just that—for estimating the probable outcome of the alternative actions the company might take.

Modeling to cope with discontinuities is now opening up exciting frontiers in systems analysis and operations research. The analyst is beginning to move not only into the territories of the dispatcher, the dietician, and the factory manager, but into the chief executive officer's terrain as well.

But one word of warning: modeling can do little yet to *create* the alternatives that a decision-maker should consider. If it seems to make sense for American Motors to consider building houseboats, a model can help top management decide *how much* sense it makes. But if American Motors really should be thinking about going into the hotel business, someone (whether a manager or a modeler) first has to suggest that alternative. So don't expect a model to save you from asking basic questions about where your organization should be trying to go.

One more warning: don't leave the modeling to the specialists. If you do, two things may go wrong. First, they may not understand what you really want to accomplish and what you are willing to change, so they may model the wrong things. The higher the level of decision making, the greater this danger grows. Second, *they* will learn from the experience of thinking through the situation, but *you* will not. This is especially true when the analysts come in from outside, do their work, and disappear.

Relevant Modeling and the Computer

Most managers, of course, can't spend a great deal of time building models, because their problems are constantly changing. The problem they may confront in the morning, like the day's news, slips out of the headlines by late afternoon. Modeling is too slow and too costly to seem worthwhile. That same fact helps explain the resistance of operating managers to staff people who offer to "help" them by building models. By the time the staff modeler has done his work, the operating manager has moved on to other problems. And even when the problem persists, the circumstances may have changed by the time the model is finished.

This time-lag dilemma has been eased a great deal by the marriage of the model to the computer, and by improvements in computer technology. The computer and systems analysis discovered each other early on. Computers can store hundreds, even thousands, of models. More important, the time-sharing computer allows the manager to play with the model more or less at will, and the play is not only fun but functional. He can try out different models and select the most promising ones. Best of all, the manager can play without being a mathematician.

Summary

Systems analysis (or management science, or operations research) embraces a wide range of analytic methods. It maps the dimensions of a problem and suggests the probable outcomes of alternative solutions. It constructs mathematical or other symbolic models intended to represent the real world and uses those models to reveal, cheaply and quickly, the probable effects of different decisions. The use of models in management has been advanced by new concepts in mathematics, by the power of computers, and by the ingenuity of analysts in applying a few standard models to countless specific problems.

Systems analysis is a powerful new tool in coping with complex uncertainties. It helps us to sharpen our thought processes and enables us to communicate concepts in a standard language. Models do, however, have certain weaknesses. They often oversimplify reality, reflecting the model-builder's limited view of the world rather than the world as it is — or at least the world as it is viewed from some other perspective. Model-builders are limited by what they see and by the techniques they use. Models have often failed at the point of implementation as a result of human distrust or resistance to their real or imagined implications. Finally, old models do not always keep up with new problems, though this lag is being reduced by advances in computer technology.

The potential of systems analysis remains unclear, though it is expanding every day. Governments, universities, and other organizations are turning more and more to the design of analytic models of cities, educational programs, defense systems, and indeed whole nations in their efforts to order and clarify the implications of alternative policy decisions.

Notes and References

For an interesting historical and philosophical perspective on systems analysis and operations research, showing the several different levels at which analysis can be practiced, see C. West Churchman's *Management Sciences, Models and Techniques* (New York: Pergamon Press, 1960).

For a more focused introduction to the ideas that underlie mathematical modeling and to the problems that models can help solve, an excellent short treatment is provided by Russell L. Ackoff and Patrick Fivett, *A Manager's Guide to Operations Research* (New York: John Wiley and Sons, 1963). A more critical view, which also deals with the limits of modeling, is Herbert Simon's *The New Science of Management Decision* (New York: Harper & Row, 1960).

At the next level — understanding concepts and techniques — turn to any of several good texts in systems analysis, among them Van Court Hare, Jr., *Systems Analysis: A Diagnostic Approach* (New York: Harcourt Brace Jovanovich, 1967); David I. Cleland and William R. King, *Systems Analysis and Project Management* (New York: McGraw-Hill, 1968); Claude McMillan and Richard F. Gonzales, *Systems Analysis: A Computer Approach to Decision Models* (Homewood, Ill.: Irwin, 1968).

For a review of management science and operations research, try David W. Miller and Martin K. Starr, *Executive Decisions and Operations Research,* 2nd ed. (Englewood Cliffs, N.J.: Prentice-Hall, 1969); or Harvey M. Wagner, *Principles of Management Science with Applications to Executive Decisions* (Englewood Cliffs, N.J.: Prentice-Hall, 1970).

We pointed out that one of the major problems facing systems analysis as an effective problem-solving technique is the tendency of models to oversimplify reality. To get a feel for the numerous contingencies that must be considered, see John A. Seiler, *Systems Analysis in Organizational Behavior* (Homewood, Ill.: Irwin, 1967).

For deeper consideration of the problem of human distrust and resistance in the use of systems analysis, with some suggested solutions, see Seymour Tilles, "The Manager's Job: A Systems Approach," *Harvard Business Review,* XLI, 1 (Jan.–Feb. 1963); and Jan H. Huysmans, *The Implementation of Operations Research* (New York: Wiley-Interscience, 1970).

Two recent books by C. West Churchman provide thoughtful insights into the problems of making systems thinking work in complex, human, and often recalcitrant organizations: *Challenge to Reason* (New York: McGraw-Hill, 1968), and *The Systems Approach* (New York: Delacorte Press, 1968).

7

*Computers:
Brother? Big Brother? Oh, Brother!*

In the two preceding chapters we credited progress in information systems and in modeling to the availability of computers. This chapter is about those critters. We find them everywhere—flashing their lights in banks and department stores, throwing space capsules out to the planets, even spicing our lives with computerized dating and betting services. Some people are seduced into an almost symbiotic relationship with them; others fight them with everything from mutilated punch cards to bombs. This chapter is not only about computers and how they work, but about why they delight some of us and estrange others, and about how they are changing our lives.

Just One More Machine?

The computer has had good press agents. In less than three decades it has come to be billed as one of the most revolutionary inventions in human history—in the same class as the wheel, the printing press, and the steam engine. The computer stands out in a century that has also brought us the automobile, the airplane, radio, television, and the telephone. What is it about computers as they now exist, or as they may evolve, that has given them such a powerful reputation? The answer lies partly in the functions they perform and partly in the magnitude of their impact on society.

The Mad Scientist and the Poet's Daughter

Many of the most important design concepts and ideas for the use of computers came from an eccentric Englishman, Charles Babbage. His early plans for an *analytical engine* were recorded by one of his collaborators, Ada Augusta, the Countess of Lovelace and daughter of Lord Byron. Both Babbage and the countess hoped that the device could be used not only as an aid to science but to provide an infallible system for betting on horse races. The following remarks are from an Italian report (1842) on Babbage's plan, translated by Lady Lovelace:

> Now, admitting that such an engine can be constructed, it may be inquired: what will be its utility? To recapitulate; it will afford the following advantages: first, rigid accuracy. . . . The engine, by the very nature of its mode of acting, which requires no human intervention during the course of its operations, presents every species of security under the head of correctness; . . . it carries with it its own check. . . . Secondly, economy of time: to convince ourselves of this, we need only recollect that the multiplication of two numbers, consisting each of twenty figures, requires at the utmost three minutes. Likewise, when a long series of identical computations is to be performed, the machine can . . . give several results at the same time. . . . Thirdly, economy of intelligence: a simple arithmetical computation requires to be performed by a person possessing some capacity; and when we pass to more complicated calculations, . . . knowledge must be possessed which pre-supposes preliminary mathematical studies of some extent. Now the engine, from its capability of performing by itself all these purely material operations, spares intellectual labor, which may be more profitably employed. Thus the engine may be considered as a real manufactory of figures, which will lend its aid to those many useful sciences and arts that depend on numbers. Again, who can foresee the consequences of such an invention? . . .

—*Reprinted in B. V. Bowden,* Faster than Thought *(New York: Pitman, 1953), p. 361.*

Most of man's tools have provided an extension of his arms, legs, or voice. From the stone axe to the electric can-opener, tools have augmented man's muscle power. But the computer is not a muscle tool. Its nearest ancestors are devices like the slide rule and the thermostat. The slide rule extends man's mental powers, letting him use limited knowledge (the ability to match numbers in specified ways on two specially calibrated scales) to get quick results on calculations he might otherwise take hours to do (the extraction of logarithms, for example). The thermostat, as a control device, substitutes for man's mental powers by keeping track of temperature variations and, as the temperature moves out of a specified range, by signaling the heating or cooling system to initiate corrective action.

The computer would be impressive enough if it were nothing more than a gigantic calculating engine, performing arithmetical and logical operations in the service of man. What makes it truly awesome, however, is its magnified capacity for self-correcting control and adjustment. Like the human mind, the computer can be "taught" to deal with problems in ways conditioned by other things it knows and senses. Like the human mind, the computer can be guided to learn—to use experience to adjust its mode of operation. The computer is thus blessed with a degree of generality and flexibility that few of man's other inventions can match. The slide rule can multiply and divide, but it can't add and subtract. The thermostat on your home furnace can keep a heating system in balance, but you need a different device to provide noise control in the tuner of your hi-fi system. A single computer, however, can perform a vast variety of tasks. Even small computers can handle arithmetic, do business accounting, sort and switch messages, maintain files, control a production process, and play a little tick-tack-toe on the side. Such versatility neatly complements the flexibility of the human mind.

The Newness of It All

The computer has opened up a whole universe of possibilities that simply didn't exist before. Suppose you are living, for example, in the year 1 A.D. as governor of the great city of Interregnum. A good intelligence network has warned you that in about three months you will be besieged by a barbarian army. You have to decide what preparations to make and how to assign the people of your city to building walls, making armor, bringing in the harvest, and training as soldiers. Thousands of decisions must be made about how best to prepare for the siege and thousands of jobs must be done.

Now suppose it is 1940 and Interregnum is again under threat of siege. Everything has changed—the kind of attack expected and your ways of preparing the city to fight back and survive. The attackers are more likely to arrive by truck and tank than on horse or foot. You have power shovels and bulldozers to help build walls, and combines and tractors to bring in the harvest. The physical appearance of both work and battle would be totally different from what you had known back in the year 1 A.D. But one thing remained unchanged: you would still be comfortable in Interregnum's council chambers as you sat with your lieutenants making decisions about what to do. For in almost two thousand years, the *decision-making* processes had not really changed significantly.

In both eras, you would probably have brought together your leaders and counselors for a series of meetings. By talking, by "analyzing the problem," you would have made estimates of the size and imminence of the threat and how it could best be met. From these estimates, firm decisions would have emerged: you would put so much effort into building walls at the expense of gathering and storing food; you would locate concentrations of defending troops here and there; and so on.

In the year 1 A.D., again in 1940, and indeed probably to a large degree even as late as 1950, all these decisions would have been reached by means of individual study and judgment and by means of group consultation—methods that had not changed much over the centuries. Some men would have done better than others because they were wiser or more observant. Some leaders would have chosen better or worse counselors—philosophers, seers, mad monks, or management consultants. But until recently, no scientist, philosopher, or consultant could have offered clearly more powerful methods for thinking through complex decisions about how to make organizations work and how to help them survive. Decision making wasn't even talked about very much. It was a mysterious activity that went on largely inside people's heads—a process that people did not, perhaps could not and should not, comprehend.

By 1950, though, new kinds of tools for making decisions were beginning to emerge. It became possible to think about setting up large and complex analytic models, models that could lead to better choices, or that could at least sharpen the focus of debate. Still, as many early developers of those modeling tools found out, it was easier to set up a complex model than to put it through its paces. A good yet complex model to evaluate various combinations of attack and defense strategies would have been of no value in Interregnum if the mass of background data had to be hand-copied from thousands of files, or if it had taken four months' work by one hundred clerks to carry out the calculations. By then the barbarians would have been doing your calculations for you.

It was the computer that made it possible to exploit new information-gathering and decision-making tools on a large scale and in practical ways. A computer could store huge amounts of data for immediate, flexible use. It could often do, in seconds, analyses that men had not previously dared to venture because they would have taken months or years. And almost all this change occurred within a single lifetime, not over thousands of years.

How Do Computers Work?

We learned in elementary physics that most labor-saving machines are combinations of a few simpler machines: the lever, the pulley, the wedge, and a few others. What are the equivalents of these components in the computer?

The first is a means of coding and representing information electronically so that it can be stored, changed, and moved within computers or between computers at speeds approaching the speed of light. Most computers use a two-symbol alphabet: a *"1"* to represent the presence of an electrical or magnetic charge; a *"0"* to represent its absence or its opposite. By using the electronic equivalent of strings of such symbols, a computer can represent the numbers and letters we are familiar with, and, by extension, most of the names, words, or symbols we use in our own analysis of problems. Thus, though the computer may prefer to say

010010110101110101
110100111001110110100010
101001010100100101

instead of "See Dick run," it does have an internal language that enables it to do its work fast and effectively, in its own way.

A second component of the computer is an orderly way of storing strings of binary symbols (electronic *1's* and *0's*) representing instructions or data that the computer may need to do its "computing." One of the differences between a computer and an old-time desk calculator is that instructions about what to do as well as the data to be worked on are stored inside the machine. In fact, instructions and data are represented internally by using the same set of electronic symbols; they are stored in the same kinds of memory spaces. In a real sense they are interchangeable, so that the computer can perform arithmetic or logical calculations on instructions as well as on data. The ability to modify instructions is the key to the computer's capacity for self-control and adaptation.

Storage or memory is provided by a variety of physical devices (cores, disks, drums, semiconductors) inside the machine. Some of these devices have only a few thousand locations for holding strings of binary symbols; others have billions of such locations. The principle is much like that of a metropolitan street directory viewed as a "storage unit." In the computer, as in a street directory, each location is known by two characteristics: an *address,* which identifies where it is, and *contents,* which tells who or what "lives" there. In the computer, the "resident" of a given storage location will be an instruction or a unit of data.

However large and complex the memory system is, all the locations are held together by this same organizing principle. Each location has both address and contents, so that the computer's central processing unit knows precisely where to go to find something it needs or to record something it is through with. When we make up file folders, we address generally, providing labels for *large collections* of information. The computer addresses specifically, labeling where to find *each word* or *sentence.* The computer's power depends directly on its capacity for storage (or its number of memory locations) and on its speed of access (the ability of the central processing unit to find one among thousands or millions of locations and to move contents in or out quickly). For the first decade or two of the computer's existence, limited storage capacity and limited speed of access imposed major constraints on the machine's performance.

The third component of the computer is the collection of devices that do the calculating, often called the central processing unit (or CPU). As vital as the CPU is to everything the system does, it is not a superbrain with magical powers. Like the Lorelei, it looks more glamorous at a distance than up close.

The CPU contains several devices: some electronic circuits that can perform a fixed number of simple operations; one or more working registers (or storage locations) to hold the information that is being worked on and to provide temporary storage for results; a register to hold the program step or instruction that is guiding the current operation, along with circuitry to decode its meaning; and an instruction-counter which points to the storage address of the next instruction.

The CPU alternates between doing things (the execution cycle) and checking what is to be done next (the instruction cycle). The things it does are simple, and though a big computer today may have circuitry for a hundred or more basic operations, a dozen or so are really enough. Most of what a CPU does in its "doing" or execution cycle consists of one of the following chores, or some combination of them:

LOAD: Go to a particular address in storage, read the contents of that location, and copy it into the working register of the CPU. (Here and in what follows, assume that there is just one working register.)

ADD: Go to a particular address in storage, read the contents, add it to the contents of the working register, and replace the original contents of the working register with the sum.

SUBTRACT: Go to a particular address in storage, read the contents, subtract it from the contents of the working register, and replace the original contents of the working register with the difference.

COMPARE: Go to a particular address in storage, read the contents, and compare it with what is in the working register. If the contents of the two are equal, continue in sequence for the next instruction. If they are not, go to another specified but out-of-sequence address for the next instruction.

STORE: Record the contents of the working register at a particular address in storage, replacing the contents already at that address.

With these five instructions, the computer can multiply (by successive addition), divide (by successive subtraction), branch to special sets of instructions or recycle to perform a sequence of instructions again (by appropriate use of comparison tests), or simply move vast amounts of data from one place to another (by successive pairings of the load and store operations).

Operations in which the computer compares and branches to other instructions are especially important. Normally the CPU takes instructions one after another in the sequence in which they are stored away in memory. But during the execution cycle logical comparisons can change what happens next by specifying an out-of-sequence number to start a new series of instructions (for example, during a payroll calculation, to make sure that your Blue Cross deduction is calculated if you are a member, but not if you are not a member). "Compare" and "branch" instructions also instruct the computer to return to the starting point and begin all the calculations again (once your payroll calculation has been finished and recorded, the computer starts in on someone else's). The instruction cycle between pairs of execution cycles keeps track of what comes next. If a specific change in sequence is called for, it fetches the contents of the next instruction from the appropriate address in storage and decodes it to guide the next execution cycle.

Through combinations of simple operations like these, and with the ability to compare and branch under the control of the instruction cycle, computers can do more than just move data and do arithmetic. By doing these simple things at blinding speed they can control petroleum refineries, prove mathematical theorems, run an air traffic monitoring system, and play a passable game of chess.

Programs: The Things That Make Computers Go

To orchestrate coding schemes, storage facilities, and a CPU into the totality we call a computer, two more components are needed. The first is a set of machinery for moving data, directly or step-by-step from man to the computer and back again. One of the most fascinating and creative areas of information-processing technology centers around devices for putting data and instructions into the machine and for getting messages back. People can now communicate with the computer by means of punched cards, buttons, typewriter keyboards, light pens, and, in experimental applications, even with the sound of their voice. Some of this communication is input directly to working memory, but much of it goes through intermediate storage media such as magnetic or paper tape. The computer can talk back by punching cards, printing reports, generating words or pictures on a display screen, synthesizing vocal sounds, or driving a typewriter.

The other integrating component is a *set of programs*—the organized instructions that make computers work. When the computer first came onto the scene, programming had to be done in a language the machine could understand; thus the programer had to have a deep understanding of the computer's internal workings. Today, for the kind of programing you are likely to do, the languages and symbols needed are fairly simple to understand. The computer translates these languages into sequences of very simple and structured steps with which the central processing unit can deal. The translating is done by means of other prewritten programs that interpret the ones we write. To change what we write into steps a computer can follow, and to fit the program we want to run with all the other programs that are also calling for the computer's attention, several additional levels of programing are required.

The most basic sets of programs are ones that most users never see. They are there, like the circuits inside the machine, to make it possible for other programs to run efficiently. Called "monitors," "executive systems," or "operating systems," these programs tell the central processing unit how to integrate various memory units with various kinds of input-output equipment. They schedule how various parts of the computer system will perform when the system is working on a dozen or perhaps a hundred problem-solving tasks at the same time. They control how the computer behaves when part of the machinery fails or when deficiencies or errors in a problem-solving program are discovered. Such basic monitor programs sometimes involve hundreds of thousands of instructions. They perform the same function as additional electronic circuitry, but because they can be erased and rewritten they are more flexible than fixed circuits.

The next level of programing consists of translators, or compilers. These are matched to particular kinds of computers and particular versions of monitors or operating systems at one end, but at the other end they respond to a standard language (of symbols, grammar, and formats) in which we can state instructions or present

The Romance of Programing Languages

MAD for SOAP? WATFOR? As common today as a SNOBOL in hell, only a SAP would use IT now. JOVIAL programmers have long since given it the GATE, and other languages are the APL of their eyes.

MAD, SOAP, and the others are all names of programing languages, and few things have been more confusing than the proliferation of names and dialects. Some languages, though, have proved extremely versatile and long-lived:

- FORTRAN: a language which has grown like Topsy as various people have worked with it and improved it, and which has outstripped the systematically designed ALGOL as the main language for scientific and engineering programing.
- COBOL: government-sponsored, systematically planned, and finally widely accepted for business and commercial data-processing applications.
- PL/I: a relatively recent effort to combine, in one master-language, capabilities of FORTRAN, COBOL, and many other languages.
- BASIC: originally designed at Dartmouth to make computers easy to use and now, with the more mathematically oriented APL, one of the most versatile tools for making time-sharing computers solve all sorts of problems.

There are also many important special-purpose languages. Examples would include SIMSCRIPT and GPSS for writing simulation models easily, COURSEWRITER and PLANIT for preparing computer-assisted instruction, and LISP and IPL-V for doing experiments in artificial intelligence. Many, many more languages, with even more whimsical names and more specialized uses, are undoubtedly yet to come.

data to the computers. These compilers make it easier for us to write a program. When we use a BASIC or FORTRAN compiler, for example, we write each step in a form not too different from old ways of writing out steps on mathematics homework problems. Yet each one of the program steps that we write may be translated into eight or ten execution-cycle operations for the CPU that will call on the resources of many different physical components in the computer installation. When we turn the ignition key in our car, we don't have to worry about the firing sequence of the spark plugs; when we write programs in a language like BASIC, we don't have to worry about how the computer will actually do what we ask.

Another set of programs, often called "application packages," consists of specially written standard programs designed to do particular jobs. Back in 1950, in order to run a payroll or do a statistical correlation analysis, you would have had to write a detailed program of instructions from scratch to show the computer what you wanted done. Now, for a great many tasks, "packages" of ready-made programs are available. All you have to do is enter some information identifying the special conditions you want applied to your calculations (in payroll, for example, you may say that you need to include the deduction of a 6 percent state income tax), then enter your basic data (which may already be in the form of magnetic disks or tapes), and "let 'er rip." In this way you can calculate more statistical regressions in one day than the originator of the technique could have calculated in a lifetime. But unless you are sensible about the packaged program you choose and about how you set up the special conditions, the pile of results you get may be worthless.

If you are working with a packaged program, all you may have to do is to push one button to send the system into a frenzy of activity producing a hundred linear feet of computer print-out in six copies. With the poke of a light pen, you can even send the computer into a cycle of self-appraisal that will enable it to do a better job the next time around. But on occasion you (or someone working with you) will need to know enough programing to write your own program in one of the languages the computer system knows. Or you may need to organize and label data that the computer will need in its memory when it tries to run your program.

Writing and running your first program is an exciting experience, but you will discover along the way how stubborn and literal-minded the computer can be. Effective communication with computers, even with help from the best translators and other auxiliary software, still requires precision and care. It is as crucial for the program-writer to keep track of commas and parentheses as it was for King Richard to keep track of horseshoe nails.

How Computers Earn Their Keep:
The Patient Clerk

Now that we have some idea of how computers work, let's look at how they are used. We know that they can play chess and type out patterns of letters and numbers to give a good likeness of John F. Kennedy or Marilyn Monroe. We also know that banks of computers working together can help monitor the nation's air defenses, predict voting results on election night, and guide space capsules to Mars. But most computers, like most people, spend a great deal of their time doing dull jobs, working on bills or payrolls, for example. Many of these dull jobs have also, in the past, been time-consuming, expensive, and repetitive. Programing the computer to take over those jobs may not be easy, but once the program is prepared and tested, it can be used over and over again. Thus whatever the cost of initial preparation, eventual savings can be very large.

On many repetitive jobs, computers simply rearrange or relocate information, updating it or routing it from one place to another. For example, computers at the hub of telephone and telegraph networks receive messages from one source, explore alternative paths to get them to their destination, and then decide what path to use. In mail-order promotion companies computers work with long lists of names and addresses, fitting bits and pieces from each name and address into form letters to make them seem more personal. In organizations where personnel, accounting, or production records have been put into magnetic files that the computer can read, the computer spends a lot of time following instructions to (1) add new information to the files, (2) eliminate or update old information, (3) sort files and keep them in the proper alphabetic or numerical sequence, (4) duplicate records on magnetic tape or in punch-card or printed form so that vital records won't be lost, (5) change file labels and file structures, or (6) display something from the file in response to a user's request.

Because there is so much of this sort of simple or repetitive calculation in business, computers got their start as day laborers in the office. They were cheaper, faster, and, when they were well programed, more accurate than human clerks. This assignment to drudgery, however, did not use the full potential of the machines, any more than it had used the full potential of the clerks the computers replaced.

The Decision-Maker's Assistant

After computers had been around for a while, people began to dream up new uses to put them to. The concepts of operations research and management science, discussed in Chapter 6, could be fully developed only if there were easy ways to do complex things with large amounts of data. The computer offered the answer. After standard package programs were developed for techniques like statistical analysis, linear programing, and inventory control, and after easy-to-use languages were published to help businessmen design simulation programs, the use of advanced analytic techniques began to spread more and more rapidly.

Though the computer does not make these techniques foolproof, it does make them easier to try. Managers can now spend more time defining problems and interpreting the results of their analysis, leaving to the computer the brute-force effort of working from problem formulation to results. Models for production planning and inventory control, once the exclusive province of large and sophisticated organizations, are now available to organizations of all sorts.

But consider also some more unusual problems, like playing chess or balancing jobs on an assembly line. Good analysts have by now traced out several such problems. They have shown that, by exploring every possible combination, one could build a foolproof rule, or *algorithm,* to find optimal schemes for action—in principle. But even with the biggest, highest-speed computers, these and many other problems remain too big to solve completely. Though the algorithm exists, it calls for almost endless calculations and comparisons. Even for a big computer, exploring all the possible moves and countermoves in a game of chess would take not minutes or hours but lifetimes of steady calculation, even though millions of operations were performed every second. And remember that chess is simple compared to the many problems big organizations face.

If a foolproof, optimizing algorithm is not feasible, how can we get at these vastly complex problems? Some bright programers have thought up a different strategy. In effect, they said: "Let's get the computer to work the same way humans do." So they studied the way champions play chess and the way good foremen balance assembly lines. Then they tried to write computer programs that would think and decide as chess players or foremen decided. Once they had good simulations of how humans acted, they tried variations to see if they could improve on the expert's performance.

This approach is called *heuristic programing.* It takes advantage of man's great mental flexibility and his tremendous capacity to simplify complicated matters in a gross, approximating kind of way. Heuristic programs that imitate fallible human beings are, of course, themselves fallible. They are "strategic" programs; they are not *guaranteed* to work, because they do not consider every possible alternative. They use a few fairly straightforward rules, as people do, and then count heavily on extrapolating from their own past experience. Chess players use strategic rules based on their experience; they do not, in fact, play chess by considering *all possible* alternatives.

Heuristic programing is a relatively new art, but it is already providing a basis for using computers realistically to help solve complex, exploratory problems. As computers become more widely used, this type of programing will become increasingly important in direction setting and planning at top levels in organizations.

It is in these more elaborate decision-aiding roles that the computer's powers begin to look truly impressive; they seem almost to rival the mental powers of man. When performing complex algorithmic analysis—like solving a linear programing problem to suggest the "best" manufacturing schedule for a large corporation or the "best" industry development plan for a developing country—the computer can rush out results that men would never have the time or the patience to calculate on their own. In running large simulations of consumer behavior or of the long-range consequences of a decision to build a new factory, the computer helps put some degree of precision into the process of prediction. It shows managers and planners how changes in assumptions and theories about the future change the results their forecasts generate. In the purest heuristic programs, where computers have been programed to learn from their successes and failures, there is good evidence—disquieting as it is for many people—that computers can be taught to think and learn.

Costs and Capacities

The computer has another disquieting power: the power to strip the company treasury bare. The machines themselves are expensive, with rental prices in the thousands of dollars per month and with purchase prices ranging to millions of dollars for a general-purpose system. Even small specialized computers cost tens of thousands of dollars. The people to program, run, and manage the systems are also expensive. Different kinds of computers and different uses impose different sorts of staffing requirements, but a general rule of survival says that for each dollar per year you spend on computer rental, you will have to spend another dollar on people.

Rental and staffing costs, large as they are, are only part of the story. There are other costs, harder to measure, that come from the impact of the computer on an organization's way of doing business and from the rapid changes that keep occurring in computer technology. When a company goes in for computers, many things happen. Departments get restructured, operating procedures get changed, and new kinds of technicians get brought in to put old company jobs onto the machine. The new staff and equipment must be paid for while jobs are being studied, systems designed, and programs written. With a little bit of bad luck—and many organizations have had more than a little bit—the new system won't work the first time round. Records get fouled up, inaccurate bills go out, and customers get mad. Management blows its top because the system isn't working as advertised, and because it's eight months behind schedule. The systems designers apologize but point out (for the first time) that such delays and foul-ups are normal.

Some of these problems develop because many managers sign computer contracts with their wallets open and their eyes shut.

Good planning, good preparation, and sharp questioning of salesmen's claims can help managers to avoid many of the pitfalls. But for the manager who needs the computer in order to modernize his organization, it looks like ulcers if he doesn't go ahead and ulcers if he does.

Even when everything is going well — if that day ever comes — the problem of costs doesn't end. Just as you get things as you want them, a whole new line of equipment comes out. It will do more, do it faster, and cost less — at least that's what the ads and the salesmen claim. The new line will be available in eighteen months, and your competitor has just signed to buy one. Out go the old machines. And you hope that before they have been phased out altogether, the new ones will have arrived and will be working as promised. You rebuild your computer room, hire some new people, put your present staff through anywhere from one to twenty weeks of training, and begin to persuade others in the organization to accept some major changes in their functions that the new computer system will help them to perform.

Computer Speed: The Fastest Gun Is Getting Faster

Detroit has wavered from time to time in its quest for more speed in cars. Not so computer manufacturers. They have been engaged in one long, relentless, and incredibly productive speed race. And it isn't over yet.

Consider one measure of computer speed: the number of instructions a computer can process for one dollar of machine cost. That may not sound like a measure of speed, but by indirection it is. A computer does what it's told to do, and it's told by a set of instructions. Hundreds, even thousands, of instructions can be included in a program. The faster the machine, the lower will be the cost of renting it per instruction run. In 1950 a computer could process about thirty-five thousand machine instructions for one dollar. Now it can process over thirty-five million for a dollar. If we use the cost of a car for comparison, the car that sold for $3,000 in 1950 would be selling for less than $3.00 today. To date, the cost of executing a computer instruction has been dropping about ten times every three to five years.

Similarly dramatic changes have taken place in other elements of the computer's functioning. Working memory for the first computers contained space for a few thousand "bits" of information. (A bit is a binary symbol, either "1" or "0.") Today even small computers have working memories that hold hundreds of thousands of bits; a medium-sized business computer may hold between one and five million bits. Originally, information beyond what the working memory could hold could be shifted in and out only by relatively slow means like punched cards; but now old information can be "dumped" and new information entered from disks and tapes at speeds approaching the speed of access to the central working memory itself. Auxiliary storage on media like disks and tapes is essentially limitless, so long as a good filing system can be established and sufficient numbers of input-output devices are available to handle the exchange of information with the central working storage.

Communication with people has speeded up, too. Formerly, people had to wait for a deck of cards to be punched and then put them onto a separate machine for "listing" or printing. Now the computer can present text or diagrams on cathode-ray display screens as fast as people can read them.

Imagine what it would be like if you had a library with a thousand times more information than the one you now use, and with a thousand times easier access to that information. Suppose your new library could also put together a bibliography, and select and reproduce all the most relevant paragraphs on a particular subject in a very, very short time and feed them all out to you. For the organization, the implications of rapidly increasing computer capacity are at least as great.

The Consequences of Speed

In the early days, computers were relatively easy to understand: someone wrote a program and fed in the data; the computer did the job and produced the results it had been instructed to prepare; and then someone else entered another program and more data. But over the years computers have grown in speed and complexity. The central processing units are faster; storage devices are larger; and instead of one device for input and output, a computer may have dozens or hundreds of such devices. The main computer installation may occupy whole floors of an office building, and the input-output units or terminals may be scattered across the country, even around the world, wherever phone lines or satellite communications will allow. Two or more big computers may be linked together to share the work on large jobs, like running a corporate sales information system; and some of the remote input-output units may themselves have small computers built in, so that certain jobs and functions can be done locally without involving the central processing unit. A large computer requires an operating team of dozens of people each shift to keep all its units loaded and working.

Yet while some programs, like those for weather forecasting or moonshot control, are big enough to choke the largest computer, many programs that a large system has to deal with hardly begin to tax the computer's capacity. The challenge has been to use computer power better.

First, computers and their operating systems were modified so that they could work on several jobs at the same time. This scheme is called "multiprograming." It doesn't affect the way in which a manager writes his programs, but it does affect the way in which those programs are executed. If your program asks the computer to summarize last year's operating results into a balance sheet and an income statement, the central processing unit will go right to work on your job. But from time to time it will break off to answer a request from St. Louis for sales figures, or to work on the weekly payroll. The computer is beginning to look more and more like a superefficient executive, with four telephones on his desk and eight assistants to order around.

Second, the greater speed and capacity of computers has let them undertake assignments on a "real time" basis. Computers used to do their analyses "off-line," like a sportswriter working up his column after watching a football game. But now the computer is like a radio or TV announcer, reporting events as they actually happen. The computer at the heart of a telephone network, the one responding to the salesman's questions about inventories in the Providence warehouse, and the one tied to sensing and control devices in a refinery or steel mill all act and react directly with their surroundings, in "real time."

In the case of a sales information system, real-time operations may simply mean that records are updated as sales are made and that information is available as questions are asked. In the case of a steel mill, where computers regulate speed and pressure much more precisely than the best human operator could, the computer's advantage lies mainly in its speed. It makes better decisions because it can sense something going wrong and can make small corrective adjustments before a human operator could even react. In some situations the computer acts by fairly simple rules to keep a process from drifting outside set limits; in others the computer analyzes fairly complex input signals before sending control signals back.

The capacity to handle many jobs at once and to work and respond in real time have led to a third important development, *time sharing*. Time sharing has done for the computer what electric starters did for the automobile. No longer does the computer user have to get out the crank to get it started. He doesn't have to have his programs punched into cards. No longer does he have to wait for results or let someone else cut in on his program. Nor does he have to experience the agony of punch, watch, and wait, only to find that because there was an error in his third program statement the program didn't run. Time sharing has changed all that.

The time-sharing computer is multiprogramed and operates in real time. But it responds to many human problem-solvers each sitting at his own typewriter or cathode-ray screen terminal. Many users—in some cases hundreds—at different consoles and in different locations can use the machine simultaneously. The machine is so fast and has so much capacity that, so far as the individual user is aware, it is working only for him. More than that, once he has a program worked out he can leave it stored in the computer memory. Then when he wants to rerun the program, all he has to do is sit down at the console again, call for his program, and he's ready to run. All within minutes.

Time sharing has been accompanied by other innovations that make the computer seem friendlier. The languages for programming have been made easier to learn and simpler to use. Some time-sharing systems, in fact, require little more than that you be able to switch on the time-sharing terminal, type your identifying password, and then spell "HELP." The computer then types back the question, "Would you like to learn how to write a program?" or some other equally solicitous line. If you answer "Yes," it presents you with a short course in how to use the system and the available programing language.

With remote terminals and telephone lines, time sharing extends computer power beyond the computer installation itself and into classrooms, offices, and homes. It invites men to use the computer for one-shot problems that once would not have been worth the time required for programing. And on new programs, it means that ideas can be tested and errors found in much less time than ever before.

On Living with the Computer

We emphasize this easier interaction between computers and their users because of its implications for the human encounter with these machines. Even the amateur can now work alone with the computer without embarrassment. He can close his office door and play games at the computer console. Nor does he have to go through a long process of learning strange programing languages. He can use one of the newer languages that are very close to his own natural mode of expression, or he can simply call up a computer program from a whole library of programs.

The nature of the programs available has changed sharply as well. The newer programs are designed to be far more forgiving of human mistakes. Indeed, they sometimes become sickeningly

Man and the Computer

> "This is EPICAC XIV," said Halyard. "It's an electronic computing machine—a brain, if you like. This chamber alone, the smallest of the thirty-one used, contains enough wire to reach from here to the moon four times. There are more vacuum tubes in the entire instrument than there were vacuum tubes in the State of New York before World War II." He had recited these figures so often that he had no need for the descriptive pamphlet that was passed out to visitors.
> Khashdrahr told the Shah.
> The Shah thought it over, snickered shyly, and Khashdrahr joined him in the quiet, Oriental merriment.
> "Shah said," said Khashdrahr, "people in his land sleep with smart women and make good brains cheap. Save enough wire to go to moon a thousand times."
>
> —Kurt Vonnegut, Jr., Player Piano (New York: Delacorte, 1971), pp. 115–16. A Seymour Lawrence Book/Delacorte Press.

chummy. When the user makes a mistake, the program is always cheery and helpful in pointing it out and suggesting what should be done.

The computer is thus approaching the point at which it can become either a full-fledged intellectual companion of man or a full-fledged antagonist. The executive in an organization need no longer view the computer as the property of a specialized staff man. He can deal with it directly and it can deal directly with him.

The information that can be stored and retrieved by computers is becoming almost limitless as computer speeds and memory capacities increase. But the value of these advances depends on whether or not the computer becomes a friend or an enemy of man.

Why should people ever take a dislike to a mere machine—particularly when they don't even know very much about it? The answer lies partly in the way computers have been introduced into organizations, partly in the nature of human beings, and partly in the changing nature of computers themselves.

The prospective user usually hears about computers from computer salesmen or university professors. The salesman offers him a simple argument: "You can use my product to replace workers. It will save you money." The professor argues, "It will let you look smarter and make your business run better." That perceived threat to workers may produce some predictable responses. Here is one example:

In the largest job shop in the world (which covers several acres) there are many, many elaborate and sophisticated metal-working machines. Spare parts for those machines are kept in a warehouse.

In that warehouse there are more than twenty-five thousand different parts stored in little bins. A number of women keep records of every one of those parts on file cards, one card for each of the twenty-five thousand parts. Every time a part is handed to the women's supervisor, she in turn hands it to the woman in charge of the box of cards that includes the record of that part. The appropriate woman then pulls out the appropriate card and enters an appropriate notation to indicate the change in the number of parts in inventory.

Enter the computer salesman. He smells a large commission. He finds his way into the organization and cases the joint. His eyes light up when he discovers the long row of women fiddling with all those cards. It's a natural.

He prepares his proposal carefully, checking out just what the women do and don't do, and just what might be done with one of his computers at a certain cost. Finally, he makes his bid. He calls for support from his troops back at the parent company, and they make a beautiful presentation to the company president and the production vice-president, showing the savings that will result from replacing the women with his blinking new machine. Management is impressed and agrees to a provisional test of the new computerized inventory-control system. End of Act I.

Act II — a few months later. The scene is a bar around the corner from the salesman's office. He has been spending a lot of time there lately. You sit down beside him and ask a few leading questions. He begins to open up. Morosely, he recounts the story of his encounter with the women in the inventory group. He had designed his new system beautifully. It was foolproof. But of course the input to his temporary trial system had to come from the few women who still had jobs. They really clobbered his system! In the final confrontation between the manual system and his machine, women were making the manual system perform better than it had ever performed before. Those who fed the computer fed it poison; those who competed with it were stimulated by its challenge. The women were turned on. Their morale and their productivity rose tremendously. The inventory-control manager decided that computers were great — he didn't have to get one, but they had increased productivity for him. Ms. Henry had licked the new steam drill hands down. Or had she?

In the early years, people resisted the computer for reasons other than the fear that their jobs were threatened. Some didn't like the idea that the computer might be smarter than they were, and for a while IBM even used its corporate advertising program to reassure the public that computers were servants and man still the master. As computers become easier to use and as more people gain familiarity with them, some of the mystery slips away. The mechanical marvel that is very skilled at calculating payrolls or typing out halftones of the Mona Lisa turns out not to be a very good chess player and no good at all yet in recognizing by sight whether the human operator sitting at the console is the same one who sat there the night before. Man and woman can still compete about *machismo* vs. *liberation* without fearing that the computer will steal the ballgame.

Some people resisted the computer because they simply had bad experiences with it. Each new generation of machine promised great new capabilities and services. Too often these didn't get delivered at the time they had been promised. Early designs and first production runs left room for mistakes. Old programers had to learn new tricks before they could get new machines to do anything but grind out garbage. Capabilities which the professors said would rise, too often dipped down. Costs which the salesmen promised would go down, went up. It took courage—some say foolhardiness—to be the first to try a complex new application on a new machine.

Summary

Computers are resources that have made it possible for managers to organize, analyze, and use information in more powerful ways. Through its input-output stations, a computing system acts as a fast and flexible controller for the routing, labeling, and transmission of information and instructions. In its memories it can keep—and can also find and change as instructed—thousands or millions of pieces of information that would take acres to store and years to locate and use if kept on paper. With its central processing unit, it can literally do millions of logical or arithmetic operations per second.

We guide computers to do what we want them to do by entering programs, or sequences of instructions, into their memories. But we write those programs so that the computer will test the instructions and data it is working with and match its actions to specific situations and requirements. We can, in some significant ways, even program or instruct computers so that they "learn"—or improve the instructions—on the basis of experience.

Computers handle large "number-crunching" jobs like calculating payrolls quickly and accurately. Without grunting or swearing, they solve the complex equations that operations research people use. Through multiprograming and time sharing, they can do many jobs and serve many users at the same time. By operating in real time, they can respond to events as they happen and can continuously control and adjust large machines or systems.

Computers are still expensive as tools or as toys; but in an era when the cost of most things has risen, they will do a thousand times more for the money now than they did in 1950. The rapid increase in speed, capacity, and power to serve the user has been of great benefit. At the same time, it has complicated the adjustment of men and organizations to the com-

puter. As fast as we have learned what one generation of machines and programs can do, a new set is there to be studied and mastered.

It is taking time to get used to computers. People have resisted them because they were hard to understand and hard to make work. They have, in a few cases, been feared because they seemed to challenge man's role as thinker and decision-maker. But mainly, fear and resistance to computers have come because their introduction threatened established organizational habits, long-hallowed work procedures, or even job security itself. Computers have created many new kinds of jobs and careers, but they have closed out or routinized others. Some workers and some managers have fought to keep computers out.

The computer, though, is here to stay: as the nerve center of information networks in the organization; as the cheerful and speedy executor of all sorts of routine information processing, calculation, and control tasks; and as a partner to the thinking manager in many kinds of problem-solving and decision-making activities. Love it? That's not yet required. But learn it!

Notes and References

Many of the references cited for the two preceding chapters are also relevant to this one. For an overview of computers, see: Frederic G. Withington, *The Real Computer: Its Influence, Uses, and Effects* (Reading, Mass.: Addison-Wesley, 1969); Donald H. Sanders, *Computers and Management* (New York: McGraw-Hill, 1970); and D. S. Halacy, Jr., *Computers—The Machines We Think With* (New York: Harper & Row, 1962), which devotes several chapters to the historical development of the computer.

There are several excellent collections of readings on computers, including the following: William F. Boore and Jerry R. Murphy, eds., *The Computer Sampler: Management Perspectives on the Computer* (New York: McGraw-Hill, 1968); William C. House, ed., *The Impact of Information Technology on Management Operation* (New York: Auerback Publishers, 1971); Charles A. Myers, ed., *The Impact of Computers on Management* (Cambridge, Mass.: M.I.T. Press, 1967); and George P. Shultz and Thomas L. Whisler, eds., *Management, Organization, and the Computer* (Glencoe, Ill.: The Free Press, 1960). The last book presents five detailed real-life cases of organizational experiences with information technology.

To get some feel for the extent to which computers have entrenched themselves in business organizations, see Humphrey Sturt and Ronald Yearsley, eds., *Computers for Management* (London: Heinemann, 1969). This book discusses the role that computers play in production, marketing, financing, personnel, and general corporate management in British industry. When one considers that in 1969 there were approximately sixty-five thousand computers operating in the United States and only thirty-five hundred in Great Britain, it is easy to see that the impact of the computer on U.S. industry has been immense.

Finally, for a discussion of the impact of computers on organizations, try Harold J. Leavitt and Thomas L. Whisler, "Management in the 1980's," *Harvard Business Review* (Nov.–Dec. 1968); and Herbert A. Simon, "The Corporation: Will It Be Managed by Machines?" in M. L. Anshen and G. L. Bach, eds., *Management and Corporations—1985* (New York: McGraw-Hill, 1960). Both articles also appear in Harold J. Leavitt and Louis R. Pondy, eds., *Readings in Managerial Psychology* (Chicago: University of Chicago Press, 1964).

For broad and recent views of the implications of computers for the world in general, see Richard W. Hamming, *Computers and Society* (New York: McGraw-Hill, 1972); and James Martin and Adrian Norman, *The Computerized Society* (Englewood Cliffs, N.J.: Prentice-Hall, 1970).

Finally, for reassurance that there is still a role for man, see Hubert L. Dreyfus, *What Computers Can't Do: A Critique of Artificial Reason* (New York: Harper & Row, 1972).

8

People in Organizations: People as People and People as Resources

In the next several chapters we shall deal with the fourth and most vital element of organizations: the human being. So far we have not put very much emphasis on the people part of the organization. But organizations are still peopled by people. And for a long while yet the fate of most organizations is likely to lie more in the hands of their people than in the memory banks of their computers.

Two Views of Man-in-Organization

Consider two different views of the role of human beings in organizations:

Let's call the first the *humanistic* view. According to this view every man sits at the hub of his own universe, the sun of his personal solar system. Everything in his ken exists only as it relates to *his* needs, *his* growth. Rain means he cannot go to the lake. Snow means he can go skiing. His ego, his self, is the center of all things.

Imagine an organization inhabited by such people. The organization's goals, *its* growth, *its* welfare—lying way out on the edge of each member's personal world—have no meaning, no value, except as they relate to each individual's private world. From such a view, organizations are *for* people. If they should exist at all, it is to provide opportunity for men and women to do their things.

The Human View

> In achieving operations which are more often characterized by ... highly cooperative, well-coordinated activity, the highest-producing managers use all the technical resources of the classical theories of management, such as time-and-motion study, budgeting, and financial controls. They use these resources at least as completely as do the low-producing managers, but in quite different ways. ...
>
> They use these resources in such a manner ... that favorable and cooperative attitudes are created and all members of the organization endeavor to pull concertedly toward commonly accepted goals which they have helped establish. ... Under their leadership, the different motivational forces in each member of the organization have coalesced into a strong force aimed at accomplishing the mutually established objectives of the organization. ...
>
> *The leadership and other processes of the organization must be such as to ensure a maximum probability that in all interactions and all relationships with the organization each member will, in the light of his background, values, and expectations, view the experience as supportive and one which builds and maintains his sense of personal worth and importance.*
>
> —From New Patterns of Management by Rensis Likert, pp. 99–103. © 1961 by McGraw-Hill Book Company. Used with permission of McGraw-Hill Book Company.

Now consider the other perspective: let's call this one the *resource* view. Man in this view is seen quite impersonally as a multipurpose machine. He has arms, eyes, a nervous system. He can do many different kinds of things. He can dig holes and he can write poetry; he can think up TV commercials and he can fire a rifle; he can perform delicate surgery and he can tie hangman's knots. True, some people can do some of these things better than others. But with training and careful planning a large number of people can be made available who can skillfully perform any of these acts and more.

If what we want of a man in our organization is only that he punch a calculator and he happens to be a poet, his poetic abilities now become a potential liability. He may make errors in his calculations because he is thinking up a poem. So if one takes this resource view of man, a problem arises. Unlike other more mechanical resources, it is very hard to turn off all the other purposes of men and leave operating only the ones we want. With a multipurpose pocket knife we can fold up all the blades except the nail file. And while we use the nail file, everything else will stay passively in its proper out-of-the-way place. But when we hire a human pocket knife, we never

The Resource View

> A typical industrial incentive system is installed in the following way. A work-study investigation of the process is carried out, and this results in . . . a model of the dynamic system. That is, proper times are measured for each element of the work done, and suitable allowances are made for incidental factors. An assessment is made of the rate at which the operatives work, so that the answers can be adjusted against standard human effort. Fatigue should also be assessed, and a factor which allows for this incorporated. In this way the model is completed, and its predictions compared with actual results on the job. This finishes the work study. Management then uses this study to devise an incentive scheme in which bonus payments are set out which are calculated to induce operatives progressively to raise their present performance, until the optimum output assessed from the work study is achieved at a wage level that the management regards as of maximum attractiveness to the operatives and of economic benefit to the company. This is an open-sequence servo-control. . . .
>
> In this typical incentive scheme, the bonus adjustment to the input is calibrated according to the calibration required at the output, the work-study model being used to determine the permanent scale of collaboration. The system exactly resembles Porter's open-sequence control for a steam-turbine driving a generator, in which the valve (payment) is adjusted by a calibration depending on the speed required (output) of the generator. . . .
>
> —*Stafford Beer,* Cybernetics and Management *(London: The English Universities Press, Ltd., 1959), pp. 167–68.*

know when the blades will pop out all over the place, perhaps cutting up a few things they weren't supposed to.

Most people tend to take the humanistic view of themselves. Managers tend to take the resource view of the people they manage. Sometimes even the manager takes the humanistic view, sensing his own centrality in his personal universe and recognizing the centrality of every other person in his. But the manager must also direct and constrain and utilize the behavior of particular people, because those people are his organization's most critical resources.

In some organizations the resource view clearly prevails. Consider the newsreels of Hitler's legions goose-stepping down the Wilhelmstrasse. They seem to be automata, flowing along in absolute precision. The mass unity is so great that it seems impossible to imagine any *individual* soldier. Yet obviously the individual was there. Even as he marched, he was tied in knots of anxiety about his pregnant wife, or he was consumed by his aspiration to become a corporal. But in such organizations he was so much a machine, so constrained into conformity, that he seemed almost a perfect model of man as a dehumanized resource.

In contrast, some organizations allow every member to remain pretty close to the center of his own universe. Consider, for example, a modern company of actors. No goose-stepping here. No problem of distinguishing one personality from another. No question but that every member is unique, unreproducible, individual. And yet it is a *company* of actors, disciplined enough to carry off the complex, coordinated task that is a play. To that extent—for a few hours each evening—the members abandon their own centrality in favor of some kind of coordinated, indeed almost machinelike repetition of the same play they performed the night before. And for those few hours the actor is not *so* different from the German infantryman, goose-stepping through his lines, even though, as Hollywood has told us, he is hurting inside because his lover has run off with another resource.

Our next several chapters—about people in organizations—are, to a great extent, concerned with the dilemma generated by these two views of man: man as individual and man as resource. In the first view, man is free and independent. In the second view, man is a constrained, albeit flexible, multipurpose machine. If we were asked to choose between the two views, few of us would hesitate. But *choice* is not the primary issue; interaction, blending, is. Men utilize one another's work in organizations, toward goals that are often not even held in common. And organizations, we insist, are inescapable in our world.

The issue here, obviously, is not only one of effective management but of values and ideology. So some of the problems we shall consider in succeeding chapters are problems of individuality versus conformity, freedom versus membership, humanness versus machineness.

Men, Groups, and Organizations

In approaching such problems, it is useful to recognize three different levels of discourse: to follow the military analogue, one can look at the army, at the platoon, or at the individual soldier. At each level the issues are different, but all are relevant.

The larger human organization—the whole army of people—can be viewed as a unit, with standards of its own. Sailors used to say that there was a right way, a wrong way, and a navy way of doing things. This is really to say that some things are shared by all members of the navy—certain attitudes toward one another, loyalties, likes and dislikes, and, certainly, uniforms; things characteristic of the navy "culture." And many of those things persist even through a generational change of the organization's human membership. But sailors are, clearly enough, individuals too.

Business organizations are also human institutions that live beyond the lives of their individual members, as do families and universities. The individuals in an organization at any given time are thus not the organization but its carriers. The organization will go on even when they are gone, so long as other carriers replace them. It is possible, therefore, to talk about "organizational personalities," "organizational memories," "organizational attitudes," all of which extend beyond the individuals who right now make up the organization.

But while a man may be a member of an organization, such as an old aristocratic family, and while both his membership in that institution *and* his individuality may be important to him, he also lives in a third, middle world: he is a member of that branch of the family that has a house on Acorn Street. He lives in that house with his wife, his father, his two daughters, and his son. In other words, within the large institution there exists a set of *viable subunits* that are intermediate between the individual and the larger organization — there is the whole world of *face-to-face groups*.

Though we can understand something of a person if we know his larger family background, we can understand that person's behavior even better if we also know his immediate face-to-face family — the group in which he has a much more active membership. Similarly, the individual soldier's behavior seems to be much more responsive to his platoon than to the whole army. It is to his buddies that he is truly loyal; it is to his buddies' standards and beliefs that he pays attention. And yet buried in the army, and buried even deeper in his platoon, the soldier remains a person, a self, an ego. And the father of a household is not only a member of his immediate family and his extended family, he is also himself, independent even of his wife and of his children.

The young person in a business organization is in all these positions too. He or she is a member of the firm, a member of an immediate group, and a person unto himself. Such a triple life is both possible and necessary. As a member of the firm, one may feel competitive with other firms and loyal to one's own; as a member of the group, one may feel a stranger in other groups within the firm but loyal and at home in one's own; as an individual, one may feel cautious and careful with other individuals and be self-consciously oneself. These three roles may come into trivial or serious conflict with one another. Group loyalty may conflict with loyalty to the organization as a whole; self-needs may conflict with loyalty to the group. But humans are flexible. They can live simultaneously in much more complex mazes than these, and they can find pathways through those mazes.

In the next few chapters, as we talk about individuals and about the problem of eyeball-to-eyeball relationships among unique personalities, our context will always be the organization in which men and women are necessarily resources as well as people. Then in succeeding chapters we shall talk about groups, about the lives of groups within organizations and vis-à-vis one another, again in the context of humans as resources as well as humans as humans. And we shall also talk about politics within organizations. We shall look at how organizations differ from one another along human dimensions—in their values, their attitudes, their beliefs, their norms and mores. And in each chapter we shall ask, "How does the functioning individual or group or organizational culture mesh with the other dimensions of organization? With task? With technology? With non-human resources? And with the organization's structure?"

We shall not try to give you a course in psychology or sociology. We shall look at people only as participants in organizations. We shall not be primarily concerned here with men as men; or women as women; nor even with men or women as resources; but with men and women as members.

Summary

People see themselves as people—individual, unique, irreplaceable. Organizations see people more as resources—substitutable, trainable, usable for many very different purposes. A major problem, perhaps the *major human problem, of organizations, lies at that interface. Can humans be humans and* resources?

In succeeding chapters we will explore that problem, considering people's behavior as individuals, as members of face-to-face groups, and as members of large organizations. We shall consider that problem, however, always in the organizational context, asking both how and whether several alternative forms of relationships between human beings and organizations make sense.

Notes and References

For some clear impressions of the humanistic people-as-people view, try Douglas McGregor, *The Human Side of Enterprise* (New York: McGraw-Hill, 1960).

For some insightful variations, extensions, and innovations on this view, see: Chris Argyris, *Personality and Organization* (New York: John Wiley and Sons, 1964); Warren Bennis, *Changing Organizations* (New York:

McGraw-Hill, 1966); and Carl R. Rogers and F. J. Roethlisberger, "Barriers and Gateways to Communication," *Harvard Business Review* (July–Aug. 1952).

For empirical support for the humanistic view, see Rensis Likert, *The Human Organization: Its Management and Value* (New York: McGraw-Hill, 1967).

The notion of people as resources extends at least as far back as the time of the economist Adam Smith and the classical economic idea of labor as a "factor of production." To get a sense of that early view of man, see Arthur H. Jenkins, *Adam Smith Today* (Port Washington, N.Y.: Keninkat Press, 1969).

A recent variant of the resource view is the view of man as a flexible, information-processing device. See, for example: Herbert A. Simon, *Models of Man* (New York: John Wiley and Sons, 1957); and C. C. Holt, F. Modigliani, J. Muth, and H. Simon, *Planning Production, Inventories and Work Force* (Englewood Cliffs, N.J.: Prentice-Hall, 1960).

These resource views in no way, of themselves, degrade or dehumanize man. They simply treat man as a potentially analyzable and understandable factor in a highly complex system, thus permitting the development of integrative models of complex human organizations.

Though we do not, in this book, focus on the nature of the individual, you may want to look at a readable book on personality, such as Abraham H. Maslow, *Motivation and Personality* (New York: Harper & Row, 1969). For a highly readable overview of contemporary personality theory, try Kenneth J. Gergen and David Marlowe, eds., *Personality and Social Behavior* (Reading, Mass.: Addison-Wesley, 1970). For a more formal treatment, see Calvin S. Hall and Gardner Lindzey, *Theories of Personality* (New York: John Wiley and Sons, 1965).

9

Work and Motivation: You Can't Hire a Hand, and You Can't Motivate One

There is one critical fact about the multipurpose resource called man: you can't hire just a piece of him. You can't hire just the machinist's skill. You must hire the whole machinist, with all the accessories attached—his ethnic background, his high-school education, his violin-playing son, his love of singing, his political activism, and all the rest of him. You can't hire a hand.

And yet industrial organizations have been traditionally designed to use *hands,* not whole men. We even used to call people "hands." Hence a problem: what to do with all those extra parts—the memories, the aspirations, the attitudes, the feelings that insist on accompanying the hands to work? Like children accompanying mama to the dentist, are they just to sit quietly and wait around?

This chapter is about the historical evolution of approaches to this organizational dilemma, and about current thinking on work and motivation.

The Hand-Hiring Period

For a long time managers treated the people problem of organizations almost exclusively as hand-hiring. That was one effect of the practice of designing organizations from the larger tasks backward to individual, hand-sized, specialized jobs. The last step in the process was hiring the hands.

> ### Utopia by Testing
>
> In the early days there were dreams, too. Managers didn't always see themselves as hiring hands but as "matching" people and work. Here is a quote from the first major American book on industrial psychology, describing the outcomes that would follow from the introduction of selection tests into industry:
>
> > ... Still more important than the valued commercial profit on both sides is the cultural gain which will come to the total economic life of the nation, as soon as everyone can be brought to the place where his best energies may be unfolded and his greatest personal satisfaction secured. The economic experimental psychology offers no more inspiring idea than this adjustment of work and psyche by which mental dissatisfaction with the work, mental depression and discouragement, may be replaced in our social community by overflowing joy and perfect inner harmony.
>
> —Hugo Munsterberg, Psychology and Industrial Efficiency (*Boston: Houghton Mifflin, 1913*), p. 309.

Accordingly, the chief function of industrial psychologists in the 1920s and 1930s was to select people with particular aptitudes to fit particular specified jobs. Consider a nice narrow Taylorized job like inspecting floor tiles as they pass along an assembly line. First the manager decided what kinds of human skills would be needed; then he proceeded to set up appropriate tests of color perception, visual acuity, and perhaps manual dexterity; and then he applied those tests to a large number of eager-to-work women waiting in the company's employment office. Finally he selected the women with the highest test scores and put them to work.

Having thus hired the most apt hands available from a large market of hands—because the labor market typically was not very tight—the manager assumed the problem was solved. This assumption seemed safe enough, for surely the women, after contracting to perform these tasks, would perform them dutifully and well. For one thing, they needed the job. The prevailing Puritan ethic of the day reinforced this thinking. In the mercantile tradition, in which people trusted one another and in which laws backed up that trust, each employee was seen as an individual contractor, whose *duty* was to fulfill his hiring contract.

But several unforeseen problems arose from this simplistic assumption. First, the labor market tightened up periodically, so that one couldn't always find the kind of hands one needed. Organizations were forced to do some hand-developing of their own. They had to get into the training and even the education business. Second, people on the receiving end of these "contracts" didn't always perceive the contract in the same way the manager did. They didn't necessarily see it as their contractual *duty* to carry out commitments. After a few months the job looked dull, monotonous, repetitive; physical conditions were lousy; the hours were too long. Workers suffered the situation up to a point. Then they fought it. Trumpet calls about duty and responsibility seemed to have little effect. The whole person got restless and started doing other things—complaining, gossiping, organizing, and dogging it on the job.

Managers then began to look at the problem in a new but equally inappropriate light: how could one keep a woman inspecting tiles and *not* doing all those other things that got in the way?

The manager first did what parents typically do when faced with the same problem. He scolded and disciplined and punished. He wrote rulebooks, and laid people off. He developed work standards. He hired more supervisors. And he grew more frustrated. But he muddled through, and tiles continued to flow along the assembly line. And, as with parents, the emotional cost to the manager was almost as high as it was to the workers.

The "Human-Relations" Period

In the 1940s and 1950s managers began to move into yet another view of the old problem, like parents who have read a little child psychology. They began to try to *cope* with all those other parts of the worker, to understand them, and to keep them from getting in the way—by using "psychology." They became interested in employee morale and motivation, in tranquilizing their employees, in keeping the rest of the person relatively comfortable so the hands could go on about their business. In effect, they took a bagful of cookies along when they took the child to the dentist. Instead of scolding, they would now be modern and sensible. They would distract the kid, and, if necessary, bribe him.

For a while American managers became intrigued with suggestion systems, recreation programs, and rest periods. They held meetings at which they urged employees to make decisions about the color of the walls in their workrooms. With a variety of such gimmicks, they tried to keep the whole person relatively distracted so that the hands could get on with the not-very-interesting work.

And again, like parents, they muddled through. They didn't win a great victory, but they didn't fail miserably either. Work got done.

Then yet another problem began to arise. The world changed. Organizations grew. In many parts of them, efforts to define hand-sized jobs began to break down. Taylor's earlier development of

The Whole Man Strikes Again

Once upon a time an Eastern European government set about trying to increase the efficiency of the waiters in the country's restaurants by exerting tighter controls. Efficiency had declined because tips—which were seen as a form of capitalist decadence—had been abolished.

The relevant government agency instituted a group incentive plan in which all waiters in a restaurant received a bonus whose size depended on the total number of meals served per day. But the waiters squabbled with one another, claiming that some didn't carry a full share of the work and yet were receiving a full share of the bonus.

So the agency shifted to individual incentives, giving a bonus in accordance with the money value of all the meals each waiter served. But the waiters then began to push drinks (which were expensive) and to pay more attention to drinkers, while providing poor service to decent, teetotaling folk who had come in only to eat.

The government agency then changed the system again, this time with pay determined by the actual number of dishes carried by each waiter. Now the waiters began to serve every item on a separate dish—peas on one, potatoes on another.

So, it is said, the government agency gave up, permitting the waiters to accept tips again in the wicked old capitalistic way.

Scientific Management (see pp. 21–22) had moved managers toward the specialization of work, toward cutting jobs down to hand-size. And his efforts had succeeded over a wide range of jobs. But by the 1940s and 1950s more complex technology had begun to move in. New kinds of jobs began to show up, jobs that Taylor's Scientific Management could not easily reduce to hand-size. Some were technical or staff jobs performed by chemists, and market researchers, and economic analysts. Some were jobs that were so intertwined with other jobs that they could not be completely separated out—like technical support to selling, or product management.

The Whole-Man Movement

By the 1960s the idea of hiring a hand had all but disappeared from all levels of *management* (though not from all levels of hourly workers). Indeed, it had been replaced by its antithesis: the active search for whole people.

As a result, in most contemporary organizations things both

And Now the Battle to Get Whole People

The battle for whole people at the managerial level has become very active in recent years. Late in 1972, for example, two major companies, Motorola and Fairchild, were still having at it in a lawsuit that had begun in 1968.

Here are some excerpts from the *Wall Street Journal* that outline the story:

... Six executives of the semiconductor products division of Motorola Inc. left the company following the resignation of C. Lester Hogan to become president of Fairchild Camera & Instrument Corp. At least two of the six will join Mr. Hogan at Fairchild Camera. ...
(8/14/68)

Motorola said it filed suit in Federal district court in Phoenix, seeking relief from alleged wrongdoings and asking an injunction to bar any future hiring of Motorola executives by Fairchild.

... The resignations caused a sharp drop in the price of Motorola stock, and at the same time boosted the price of Fairchild. ... The move bolstered investor expectations for Fairchild at a time when that company, a competitor of Motorola, was beset by management strife and an earnings squeeze. ...
(8/28/68)

... C. Lester Hogan, new president of Fairchild Camera & Instrument Corp., was lured from Motorola Inc. by a $30,000 annual salary increase and other inducements, according to the charges in Motorola's suit against Fairchild.

Mr. Hogan also received from Fairchild $250,000 in "cash payment of immediately realizable stock options," an opportunity to borrow $5.4 million for up to 10 years, and a new house, Motorola contended.

The Motorola complaint ... also charges that Fairchild Camera promised to move its main office from Syosset, N. Y., to Mountain View, Calif., so Mr. Hogan "could live in the Bay Area of California according to his preference."
(8/29/68)

—*Reprinted with permission of the* Wall Street Journal, *August 14, 28, 29, 1968.*

It was whole people, not hands, that were involved in this one. Could it have happened if the people involved were machinists? Secretaries? Production workers?

are and are not like they used to be. Although one still finds waiting rooms full of downcast men from whom a few skilled hands can be selected, organizations now also actively search the universities and one another, trying to seduce unusual, indeed extraordinary, whole human beings—people who can cope with a variety of highly ambiguous, ill-structured tasks for which no clear performance specifications exist.

But this new kind of recruiting has emerged chiefly at technical and managerial levels. Its prime cause has probably been changes in technology, not changes in human values. It has not happened out of humanization, but out of necessity. And it has not happened throughout the organization. Today's is a schizophrenic organizational world.

In some parts of the organization we are still hiring hands and trying to tranquilize the rest of the person attached to them. Now we worry simultaneously about finding motivated people, creative people, innovative people, searching people, and *also* about hiring hands.

The schizophrenia may pass, however. There are good reasons to think that we shall be looking for ways of hiring whole people at *all* levels of organization: first, because we need whole brains; second, because as values change and expectations rise, less than whole people may not be willing to work; and third, because managerial values are changing too. Managers increasingly want—even putting the issue of efficiency aside—to provide an environment for whole people and to build organizations of whole people.

Motivation: Is It a Phony Problem?

Notice that until now we have seldom used the word "motivation." Yet far and away the most common question asked of behavioral scientists by managers is: "How can I motivate my employees to work harder?"

And that question has grown up in response to the history we just reviewed. It has taken us a long time to learn just how untenable that form of that question really is. For the question assumes that employees are not now motivated to work very hard. Indeed, one might almost read into it the implicit assumption that employees are not only unmotivated, they may even be negatively motivated *against* working hard. Certainly our traditional view of work has assumed that work is negative, punishing—something we have to do when we aren't playing.

The question, as we have phrased it, is negative, depressing, and even supercilious. Yet it is perfectly understandable in the context of our hand-hiring history. For the other implicit assumption in the question is that the "employees" we are talking about are the hired hands—they are not ourselves. Managers seldom turn that question back on themselves to ask how they can get themselves to work harder. Obviously they are already highly motivated. Don't they work eighty hours a week?

Next question: Is it all true? Are all those other people really unmotivated? Or are they more motivated to escape from work than to do it? Do people prefer smoking in the restroom to working at their jobs? Do we work to eat? Do students prefer not going to class? Do they go to class, punishing though it is, only to get grades to get the degree to get the job to get two cars?

The answers, of course, are partially affirmative. They may be more affirmative for some people than for others. They may be more true for some kinds of work than for others. They may also constitute a self-fulfilling prophecy: once we hire hands, people learn to act like hands. But to the extent that these answers are true, perhaps we should not conclude that people are no damn good. Perhaps another conclusion is that a good chunk of the world of work must be pretty lousy, especially for affluent Americans in the 1970s. For things can't be in very good shape if, even in this haven of progress, a very large part of our waking life, half of it perhaps, has to be spent doing things we don't like to do in order to gain the wherewithal to do the things we like to do.

But if those conditions are real, we are challenged either to change ourselves back to a stiff-upper-lip, it-is-our-duty-to-suffer attitude or else to change the conditions to make them less painful.

It is certainly true that for a lot of us a large amount of what we call work is unpleasant. And it is also true that large numbers of jobs in organizations seem, from the outsider's perspective (and unfortunately often from the insider's, too) to be so dull, so tight, so restrictive of people's needs for variety and spontaneity, as to be essentially inhuman.

So when the manager asks, "How can I motivate my people to work harder?" one of his underlying assumptions may be correct. His people may not be working nearly so hard as they could. But another implicit normative assumption may be unwarranted, namely that reasonable men *should* be working harder on the jobs he has assigned them.

Who in the Organization Is Insufficiently Motivated?

If the manager ever does turn the question of motivation on himself, he gets conflicting answers. Does he have to worry about motivating himself to work harder? Certainly not. He is more likely to be concerned with precisely the opposite problem. His wife complains continually that he never leaves the office until 8:00, never takes a vacation, never enjoys the kids, never thinks of anything but his job.

Does the manager have to worry about lazy or unmotivated engineers or researchers? Or even about unmotivated new young MBAs? Again the answer is likely to be negative. Somehow in those groups motivation seems a trivial problem. Lots of other problems take precedence over it—problems, for example, of coordination, creativity, loyalty.

It is mostly where we have designed tightly constraining jobs, out of a traditionally structured view of organizations, that we really need to worry about motivating people to do them. It is when we have treated men almost exclusively as a resource and have used only a small part of that resource, that the problem of motivation arises. And even there our worry stems largely from the fact that organizations have already killed whatever motivation their people brought with them when they first arrived, eager and anxious. A more correct form of the question is this: "How can we motivate people to work harder at jobs that are essentially demotivating?" And in that form the question is rather nonsensical.

The Worsening Problem

In our mobile society, notably at professional and technical levels, the whole of one's life leading up to entry onto the job is pointed toward expanding one's behavior. Our educational system—particularly higher education—emphasizes independent inquiry and search, entrepreneurial values, individuality. We encourage people to go to school, to achieve, to explore, to experiment, to become unique. Our professional societies profess to support such expansive personal growth; so does our educational system. All these forces don't shape lazy, undermotivated people, but restlessly searching, seeking, moving people.

The same businessmen who want to know how to increase motivation also criticize MBA students because they want to be president within six months. The manager's true motivational problem in coping with the bright young professional employees seems to be how to hold motivation *down,* not how to increase it; and how to set up an organization that will capture and use that motivation effectively. Nor is it hostile or antiorganizational motivation that we are talking about. It is motivation to solve problems, to achieve, to accomplish.

In those senses, then, the problem of "motivating people" is a phony problem, one that has nothing to do with a great number of people who work in organizations. It is a leftover from the tradition of hiring hands.

Structure First, People Last

Much of the "problem" of motivating workers emerges from the early and widespread view that one must first design jobs, then fit people into them. That view was expressed succinctly by one of the great organization theorists and consultants of the first half of this century, L. F. Urwick, who was willing to generalize the idea to include even executive levels:

> ... In good engineering practice design must come first. Similarly, in good social practice design should come first. Logically it is inconceivable that any individual should be appointed to a position carrying a large salary, without a clear idea of the part which that position is meant to play in the general social pattern of which it is a component, the responsibilities and relationships attached to it and the standard of performance which is expected in return for the expenditure.

—L. F. Urwick, The Elements of Administration (New York: Harper, 1943), p. 38.

On Remotivating the Demotivated

Since tedious jobs still exist, the motivation issue is not *entirely* phony. *After* we have hired a hand, there is indeed a problem of motivation. But *two* alternatives, not one, are available: hold the job constant and motivate the man, *or* change the job to fit the nature of human motivation.

If we decide to hold the job constant, we look for tricks to induce essentially uninterested hands to work harder. It was this conception of motivation that led us down the primrose path of piece work, incentives, and suggestion systems. Not that incentives and suggestion systems are necessarily wrong or ineffective. But relative to the motivation of the whole man, they are only minor attacks on symptoms of the problem. They are sugar pills, somewhat comforting to the person who takes them, but even more comforting to the person who gives them. More important, if they help at all, it is by allaying or tranquilizing the people problem.

The other short-term route toward remotivating the demotivated is by changing the job. In recent years this approach has been implemented through job-enlargement and job-enrichment programs designed to increase the size, scope, and variety of a given job so that it uses more of a man than his hand. Such programs necessarily tend to "deprogram" the job itself and to reduce secondary differences among jobs. Ultimately, this approach will reinforce the tendency to design organizations from *tasks* to *people* to *structure,* instead of from *tasks* to *structure* to *people.*

*Motivation as a Problem
in Coordination and Integration*

So the problem of motivation is being reformulated for today's and tomorrow's world. It need not be seen as a problem of devising clever ways to get people to do things they don't want to. There are much more interesting ways to think of it, and those ways are closely related: first, as a problem of *coordinating* the efforts of already motivated people, each of them doing many different things he wants to do; second, as a problem of behavioral *change,* of influencing motivated people to go in one direction instead of another; and third, as a problem of *setting organizational "climate,"* so that natural motivation will be encouraged.

The problem of coordination is very real. Organizations are made up of many people with many motives which must somehow be oriented toward common ends. The manager's coordination problem is like that of parents with many children, all eager to get up Saturday morning to do all the things they want to do. Most of them prefer to do their important and exciting projects in the middle of the kitchen floor under mother's feet, and in one another's way. Several of them need the same pots or blocks at the same time. So squabbles break out. The older ones smack down the younger ones. Mother screams at them all. A few dishes get broken. And everyone ends the day healthily exhausted.

In many organizations today, especially at white-collar and management levels, motivation is a coordination problem in almost a political sense—a problem of leading, arbitrating, mediating, helping the weak against the powerful, trying to distinguish the truly important from the unimportant and the truly useful from the irrelevant.

Viewed this way, the manager's problem is not only one of coordination but of influence and change. How can one influence the directions of *already highly motivated people?* How, indeed, can one persuade busy people to work together, to delay some of their individual gratifications?

The third view of motivation, as a problem in organizational climate, will emerge again and again throughout this book. It is the problem of setting and maintaining an atmosphere that will encourage, not inhibit, motivated people to get on with the job.

A Hierarchy of Needs

Probably the motivational model best known to managers is Abraham H. Maslow's hierarchical model. Here is an abbreviated version of that model:

> The needs that are usually taken as the starting point for motivation theory are the so-called physiological drives. . . .
>
> Undoubtedly these physiological needs are the most prepotent of all needs. . . . A person who is lacking food, safety, love, and esteem would most probably hunger for food more strongly than for anything else. . . .
>
> Obviously a good way to obscure the higher motivations, and to get a lopsided view of human capacities and human nature, is to make the organism extremely and chronically hungry or thirsty. . . . It is quite true that man lives by bread alone—when there is no bread. But what happens to man's desire when there *is* plenty of bread and when his belly is chronically filled?
>
> *At once other (and higher) needs emerge* and these, rather than physiological hungers, dominate the organism. And when these in turn are satisfied, again new (and still higher) needs emerge, and so on. This is what we mean by saying that the basic human needs are organized into a hierarchy of relative prepotency. . . . If the physiological needs are relatively well gratified, there then emerges a new set of needs, which we may categorize roughly as the safety needs (security; stability; dependency; protection; freedom from fear, from anxiety and chaos; need for structure, order, law, limits; strength in the protector; and so on). . . .

Motivation as Imbalance

In thinking about this whole question of motivation, we must remember that motives aren't *things.* They are states of mind that spring chiefly from deficiencies, from felt lacks, from an imbalance between what people have and what they want. People act when they're off balance, in an effort to regain their balance. Sometimes their acts seem irrational; but if we view them as balancing acts rather than as rational problem-solving acts, they begin to make sense.

The executive goes into action when the results of his promotional campaign reveal that sales are far less than he had predicted. He is motivated by the dissonance, the imbalance, between his expectations and the reported results. He can take at least two courses of action to rebalance himself. He can scrap the campaign, or he can start whipping his salesmen and his ad agency. Though one course may be more rational than the other, they are both comprehensible as psychological balancing acts. If you're trying to under-

> ... If both the physiological and the safety needs are fairly well gratified, there will emerge the love and affection and belongingness needs, and the whole cycle already described will repeat itself with this new center. Now the person will feel keenly, as never before, the absence of friends, or a sweetheart, or a wife, or children. ... Now he will feel sharply the pangs of loneliness, of ostracism, of rejection, of friendlessness, of rootlessness. ...
>
> ... All people in our society (with a few pathological exceptions) have a need or desire for a stable, firmly based, usually high evaluation of themselves, for self-respect, or self-esteem, and for the esteem of others. These needs may therefore be classified into two subsidiary sets. These are, first, the desire for strength, for achievement, for adequacy, for mastery and competence, for confidence in the face of the world, and for independence and freedom. ... Second, we have what we may call the desire for reputation or prestige (defining it as respect or esteem from other people), status, fame or glory, dominance, recognition, attention, importance, dignity, or appreciation. ...
>
> ... Even if all these needs are satisfied, we may still often (if not always) expect that a new discontent and restlessness will soon develop, unless the individual is doing what *he,* individually, is fitted for. A musician must make music, an artist must paint, a poet must write, if he is to be ultimately at peace with himself. What a man *can* be, he *must* be. He must be true to his own nature. This need we may call self-actualization. ...
>
> —Abridged from pp. 35–46 in Motivation and Personality, *2nd Edition, by Abraham H. Maslow. Copyright 1954 by Harper & Row Publishers, Inc. Copyright ©1970 by Abraham H. Maslow.*

stand an odd piece of behavior, like unexpected pressure on salesmen by a manager, or unexpected complaints about the ad agency, look into the discrepancies, the dissonances, that may have occurred for a person whose world has suddenly gone out of balance; and then ask whether the odd behavior may be an effort to get it back into balance.

People are dynamic systems. They are not likely to be exactly the same tomorrow as they are today. So, as we think about motivation—as a problem in coordination, or a problem in persuasion, or a problem in climate-setting—we must not assume that there is any single, permanent, fixed solution. We must expect instead that people's motives will evolve and change with time and experience. And *people* includes *you.* The issues that motivate a young person just out of college will not necessarily be important to the same person ten years later. Nor can we assume that the motives that were important to Americans in the depression environment of the 1930s will dominate the behavior of Americans in the 1970s, nor that the organizational climate that was appropriate then will be appropriate now.

Likewise, we must not assume that each person is being driven by only a *single* motive at any one moment. Human beings, again, are complex systems, and they are transiently motivated, multiply motivated. The behavior that emerges is better thought of as the resultant of a mixture of forces than as a simple response to just one need.

That human motives are multiple and changing does not mean that there is no order in the system. In general, human beings seem to move progressively through several broad levels of motivation. In infancy they are motivated largely by physical and physiological imbalances. As they seek to satisfy those needs — almost invariably through the aid of other human beings — social motives evolve: needs for love, for membership, for relationships. And accompanying those, the "egoistic" motives emerge: the needs for esteem, for recognition, for achievement, for power. And then, the motives for what has been called "self-actualization" seem to arise: the needs to do one's thing, to fulfill one's self.

But the process is not one of A through B through C. Rather, it is a layering process of A, then A *and* B, then A and B *and* C, with the newer additions serving as stronger, more important motivators as long as the others remain pretty well satisfied.

Two important points arise here. First, many motives are not altogether conscious. We cannot expect to understand Harry's motives by simply asking him about them. He may not know, or he may not choose to tell. So the problem of diagnosing other people's motives involves careful listening and observation. Second, among the people who may not be fully conscious of their motives is you. A useful rule of thumb for the motivator of others then emerges: before trying to understand and change the motivation of others, take a little time to reflect on your own motives. Are you trying to change the other guy for "his own good"? Or for yours? Do you want him to shave off his beard because it will help *him*? Or because *your* boss looks a little upset every time he comes into your department? If you know *why* you're trying to motivate that other guy, you may do a better job of it for all concerned.

A Dilemma: Acceptance vs. Evaluation

As we grow up we discover that the world is full of moral and professional dilemmas:

> Henry Ichabod, senior partner in a large consulting firm, is an old acquaintance and sometime client of mine. He called me the other day from Chicago to tell me that Joe Zilch had been in

to see him, looking for a key job with his firm. Zilch told Henry he knew me. Now Henry wants to know what I think of Zilch. I know Joe Zilch very well. He is a close friend, whom both my wife and I like a lot. I also know Ichabod pretty well, and I know he has faith in my judgment. I want to keep it that way. I honestly feel that Zilch is a pretty good candidate for the job in question, but I don't think he's the best man available. On the other hand, I know he's in a tough spot and needs a good new job. This would be a great chance for him. It would solve a lot of personal problems for him, too. Zilch has used my name as a reference. Henry Ichabod wants to know what I think. 'If I even suggest to him that Zilch is probably not the best man for the job, Zilch won't get it. What shall I say?

* * *

I am a young man trying to make my way in this government job. I like my boss, who is also youngish. He has been making his way pretty well, too. Recently he took what I consider a far-out position on an important policy problem. I can see that he's getting himself into a more and more strained relationship with the departmental brass. He's going to have to put up or shut up. And even if he puts up, I think he will be in trouble for a long time. He's becoming increasingly defensive about the position he thinks is right, and privately he keeps saying nastier and nastier things about the brass. I like him. I feel loyal to him. Privately, I really think his position is the right one. But how far shall I back him up? When the matter comes up at the young turks' lunch table, do I defend him and let people know that I support his position?

* * *

I have developed a damn good team here. People work well together; they trust one another; the climate is good. The annual personnel evaluation has just come up. Top management is handing out a bonus, but the rule is that no more than two people in my group—the two who have performed best—can get a piece of it. Up till now I really hadn't worried about who was performing best. The whole group was working day and night to get the job done. If I give the nod to just two of them, what happens to morale? What happens to the team?

* * *

There are three bright young people in the department and only one promotion . . .

* * *

*An Acceptance View vs. An Evaluation View:
Are They Really Different?*

In one way or another this acceptance-evaluation dilemma has concerned many contemporary writers. Professor Chris Argyris, one of the strongest proponents of the acceptance model, offers these comments on the acceptance view:

> ... Giving and receiving non-evaluative feedback ... is acquired by developing a basic philosophy and a set of values for individual growth. The underlying requirement is that the individual be accepting of himself and of others. As his acceptance of self and others increases, his need to make evaluative feedback tends to decrease. The degree of acceptance an individual has at any given moment varies with each individual and in the same individual under different conditions. ...
>
> It is a fundamental hypothesis of this viewpoint that a basic drive of human beings is to experience "success" in living and experiencing their "human condition." By "success" I mean that their interpersonal relationships will tend to lead them to become more aware and accepting of their selves and others. These human relationships are those in which man originates and becomes increasingly genuine in such a way that his fellow man can also become genuine.

—*Chris Argyris,* Interpersonal Competence and Organizational Effectiveness *(Homewood, Ill.: The Dorsey Press, 1962), pp. 18–21.*

Argyris goes on to argue that descriptive, nonevaluative feedback makes it possible for individuals to achieve excellence.

Problems like these are endless. A lot of them paralyze us because we carry around two conflicting sets of standards for our relationships with other people.

One set is based on a model of *acceptance,* of trust, of partnership. What we really want in another person is friendship, and friendship assumes mutual acceptance. This model is both humanistic and highly practical. It is reflected in the television shows that portray close, ultra-loyal pairs of intelligence agents or policemen. It is also a model for the family, in which trust between husband and wife, trust between parent and child, is a cornerstone. It is a model that we value in other organizations too. We talk about the "team approach," about group solidarity, about loyalty. Most of us think this model is right, just, human.

This acceptance model of interpersonal relations in the organization is essentially emotional. The primary bonds are bonds of mutual affection, mutual trust, mutual loyalty—these above all.

But there is another model of organizational relationships that

> John W. Gardner, on the other hand, is also concerned with excellence, but he seems to feel that to *find* it in our society we need to be more evaluative of one another, more ready to sort out the better from the worse:
>
>> Americans believe that ability should be recognized at whatever level in society it occurs.... But as education becomes increasingly effective in pulling the bright youngster to the top it becomes an increasingly rugged sorting out process for everyone concerned. This is true today and it will be very much more so in the future. The schools are the golden avenue of opportunity for able youngsters; but by the same token they are the arena in which less able youngsters discover their limitations. The thought rarely occurred to the generations of Americans who dreamed of universal education. They saw the beauty of a system in which every young person could go as far as his ability and ambition would take him, without obstacles of money, social standing, religion or race. They didn't reflect on the pain involved for those who lacked the necessary ability. Yet pain there is and must be.
>
> —*John W. Gardner,* Excellence, Can We Be Equal and Excellent Too? *(New York: Harper and Bros., 1961), p. 65. Reprinted by permission of Harper & Row Publishers, Inc.*
>
> You may want to read both these books and then ask yourself whether Argyris' proposed solution—which he calls the development of *authentic* relationships—is significantly different from Gardner's proposal for what he calls *self-renewal.* Or does neither solution get us off the horns of the acceptance-evaluation dilemma?

most of us value, especially in the western world. This is a more intellectual model—a model based on *excellence,* on *competence. Ours* is the most competent team. *My* colleagues are capable, solid, professional. Only first-class minds can make it in *this* department.

Though this competence model of interpersonal relationships has some emotional ingredients (feelings of pride and accomplishment), it is colder, more rational, more task-oriented. It evaluates others. It judges. The ideal group, according to this model, is a group of skilled professionals bound together by mutual goals and mutually respected skills. We fire the weak and replace them with the strong. If there is friendship, it emerges from mutual respect; but friendship is of secondary importance for the organization. We are all pros together. Our ideal is solid, task-oriented professionalism. Love is irrelevant—except love of excellence, love of skill.

Which Model for the Organization?
Evaluation or Acceptance?

For the manager, juggling these two models generates all sorts of problems. Which model shall he use in selecting and backing up subordinates? Or can he use both? Which model shall he use in promoting and rewarding people? In firing people? In his relations with his boss and with his organization? In his relations with his peers?

It is clear which model most contemporary American organizations profess to have chosen: the evaluative model. Colleges *select* students on the basis of competitive examinations, and they grade students and flunk them out—or at least they used to. They evaluate faculty members every few years to decide on promotion and raises. The progressive company looks for the *best* young technical Ph.D.s and the *best* young MBAs. And then they use elaborate merit-rating schemes to decide who will get raises and promotions.

But these clear-cut choices seem to have become rather blurred in recent years. A student can't flunk out of Stanford any more—that is, his record can't report a fail. He can stay until he achieves enough units and then he is graduated. The publish-or-perish evaluation system for professors is also giving way, apparently to an alternative basis of evaluation—teaching excellence. But when students evaluate teaching, is it the teacher's excellence that is being evaluated or his acceptance of and by his students?

Organizations seem to be moving in two directions at once: toward higher standards of professional competence (and thereby greater emphasis on evaluation) and toward greater mutual acceptance and trust.

One possible outcome, other than schizophrenia, may be a more open organizational world in which *work* is evaluated but *individuals* are not. Such a world will require secure people who are capable of distinguishing themselves from their positions.

The question of evaluation versus acceptance remains open. Organizations need and value competence. Some of them are learning, however, that they also need, and should value, love.

Summary

People are indivisible. Though we may want only some particular skill, the rest of the individual invariably comes along for the ride. Traditionally, managers identified the organization's tasks first, then designed its structure, and finally picked the people to fit. They hired only parts of people, however, even though they had to deal somehow with whole people.

At first managers tried to handle the rest of the whole man by insisting that it was his duty to suppress the rest of himself and concentrate exclusively on turning the nut he was hired to turn. They scolded or punished him like a bad child if some of the irrepressible other parts broke loose on the job.

Then managers tried an early form of "human relations." They pacified, cajoled, and bribed the worker to sit still while he turned nuts all day.

Then managers began to hire more of the whole man—not because they wanted to, at first, but because exploding technology and growing organizational complexity forced them to. But this happened only in certain places. Most hourly jobs remained "hand" jobs, and they still do.

We seem to be in the early stages of another wave of change, however. This time organizations—at all levels—are beginning to redesign themselves, thinking about people first and structure second, bringing the job to the man rather than the man to the job.

Moreover, concern about "motivating" workers has become more widespread in recent years. At first it meant dangling carrots instead of beating with a stick. Then managers hit on the scheme of "making them think it's their own idea." But both approaches were responses, not so much to the nature of man, as to the demotivating nature of jobs designed for hands, not men.

As organizations redesign themselves—especially at the higher levels—they are reformulating the motivational issue in still another way. The question of how to get lazy people to work has been transformed into the much broader question of how to coordinate and integrate already highly motivated people. And even at the lower levels there are signs that the old carrot-and-stick approach is on the way out.

If we want to motivate people, we must understand the nature of human motives. We must realize that motives are not single things, but parts of a broad, dynamic balancing act. If we accept high motivation as the natural state of affairs, we will recognize that low motivation is a sign that something is out of kilter.

Out of these changing attitudes has emerged the dilemma of acceptance versus evaluation. Can we both judge and love others?

In general, organizations seem to be putting more emphasis on evaluation, while society at large seems to be moving toward greater mutual acceptance. Perhaps one outcome will be a more open organizational structure, in which trust is high and evaluation is used more to improve skills and products than to judge the quality of people.

Notes and References

As you will remember from an earlier chapter, the philosophy of "hand-hiring" was integral to Taylor's Scientific Management. For a good review of Taylor's thinking and of critics of his point of view, see: A. Tillett, T. Kempner, and G. Willis, *Management Thinkers* (London: Penguin Books, 1970).

The early forms of human relations appeared to many observers to include goodly chunks of manipulation. Before the human-relations movement really caught on as a viable management philosophy (in the late 1950s), it met with a great deal of criticism. Three critical statements were: Robert N. McMurray, "The Case for Benevolent Authority," *Harvard Business Review,* XXXVI, 1 (Jan.–Feb. 1958); Malcolm P. McNair, "Thinking Ahead: What Price Human Relations?" *Harvard Business Review,* XXXVI, 2 (Mar.–Apr. 1957); and Donald R. Schoen, "Human Relations: Boon or Boondoggle?" *Harvard Business Review,* XXXV, 6 (Nov.–Dec. 1957). All three articles are reprinted in I. L. Heckmann, Jr., and S. G. Huneryager, eds., *Human Relations in Management* (Cincinnati: South-Western Publishing Co., 1960).

On the other side of the argument stood a host of advocates. Their defenses were numerous and varied. You will find some of them in the following statements: Douglas McGregor, *The Human Side of Enterprise* (New York: McGraw-Hill, 1960); Elizabeth Jennings and Francis Jennings, "Making Human Relations Work," *Harvard Business Review,* XXIX, 1 (Jan.–Feb. 1951); and Robert Tannenbaum, "Dealing with Ourselves Before Dealing with Others," *Office Executive,* XXVIII, 8 (Aug. 1957). These articles, too, are reprinted in the Heckmann and Huneryager book. Another useful statement is F. Roethlisberger, "Contributions of the Behavioral Sciences to a General Theory of Management," originally presented to the Symposium on Management Theory and Research, UCLA, GSBA, November 8–9, l962. This is reprinted in H. Leavitt and L. Pondy, eds., *Readings in Managerial Psychology* (Chicago: University of Chicago Press, 1964).

The literature on motivation in the workplace has undergone tremendous growth in the last decade. For good reviews and analyses of what is known, see Victor Vroom, *Work and Motivation* (New York: Wiley and Sons, 1964); and J. P. Campbell *et al., Managerial Behavior, Performance and Effectiveness* (New York: McGraw-Hill, 1970).

For a good sociological perspective, consult Robert Dubin, *The World of Work* (Englewood Cliffs, N.J.: Prentice-Hall, 1958).

In recent years Frederick Herzberg's "two-factor" theory of motivation has been widely propagated among managers despite strong criticisms by researchers. For a brief description of Herzberg's theory, see his "One More Time: How Do You Motivate Employees?" *Harvard Business Review,* XXXXVI, 1 (Jan.–Feb. 1968). For a strong critique of Herzberg's work, see Robert J. House and Lawrence A. Wigdor, "Herzberg's Dual-Factor Theory of Job Satisfaction and Motivation: A Review of the Evidence and a Criticism," *Personnel Psychology,* XX (1967). This article is reprinted in L. L. Cummings and W. E. Scott, eds., *Readings in Organizational Behavior and Human Performance* (Homewood, Ill.: Irwin, 1969).

Similarly, Abraham H. Maslow's "need hierarchy" has also been widely disseminated among managers and widely criticized by empirical researchers. For a brief discussion and description of Maslow's model, look at his article, "A Theory of Human Motivation," *Psychological Review,* L (1943), 370–96; reprinted in H. Leavitt and L. Pondy, eds., *Readings in Managerial Psychology* (Chicago: University of Chicago Press, 1964).

For a critique of Maslow's theory, see Clayton P. Alderfer, "An Empirical Test of a Hierarchical Theory of Human Needs," *Organizational Behavior and Human Performance,* IV, 2 (May 1969).

For a good overview of the psychological evidence and thinking on the topic of motivation, and for a better understanding of the bases of motivation-to-work theories, you might look at C. L. Stacey and M. F. DeMartino, eds., *Understanding Human Motivation* (Cleveland: The World Publishing Co., 1965). Or Robert C. Bowles, *Theory of Motivation* (New York: Harper & Row, 1967).

The issue of pay as an incentive and as a symbol is considered in the following: E. E. Lawler, *Pay and Organizational Effectiveness* (New York: McGraw-Hill, 1971); articles on compensation by Dunnette, Lawler, Weick, and Opsahl in *Organizational Behavior and Human Performance,* II, 2 (May 1967); and David C. McClelland, "Money as a Motivator: Some Research Insights," in *The McKinsey Quarterly* (Fall 1967).

The evaluation-acceptance dilemma is considered in detail in Chris Argyris, *Integrating the Individual and the Organization* (New York: John Wiley and Sons, 1964).

For the results of a study on the effectiveness of the split role as a management strategy, look at H. H. Meyer and J. R. P. French, Jr., "Split Roles in Performance Appraisal," *Harvard Business Review,* XXXXIII, 1 (Jan.–Feb. 1965).

10

*Groups and the Manager:
Just the Immediate Family*

Organizations are people; organizations are groups; and organizations are organizations. Managers manage people; managers manage groups; and managers manage organizations. Managers *are* people; managers are members of groups; and managers are members of organizations. In this chapter we shall focus on the problems of the manager's relationships with groups: the manager as a member of groups, and the manager as a manager of groups within organizations.

Why should we treat groups as though they were separate, viable organizational units? Why not skip directly from the individual to the overall organization? The reason is that the face-to-face group is a real organizational unit. Many organizational acts can be more readily predicted by reading a "group map" of the organization than by reading either individual people maps or total organization charts. And many individual acts can be predicted more accurately from the group map than from the organizational map. The little community of people with whom one works closely and knowledgeably has a direct effect on the decisions made by individual members of the group. It also affects the decisions of the whole organization and the values, loyalties, and attitudes of its members. Groups are sources of frustration for managers, but they can also make him or break him. For they are significant centers of organizational power.

When Are Groups Useful? And Why?

Groups do a lot of the organization's work. Despite the familiar complaints about the inadequacies of groups—their snail-like progress, their exasperating redundancy, their propensity to compromise decisions into meaninglessness—managers find themselves calling upon groups to perform a wide range of organizational chores. They find themselves setting up yet another committee, or scheduling yet another luncheon meeting, or just calling four or five people together to talk things over.

Why is this? Are we somehow addicted to groups? Possibly. We sometimes use groups for personal protection or comfort or to avoid the burdensome weight of individual responsibility.

But there are other reasons. If you want a letter typed, you aren't likely to turn to a group. But suppose you want to plan a weekend party, or raise funds for a political campaign, or resolve a major organizational crisis; then you will probably turn to a group. Suppose you are the president of an oil company facing a sudden takeover of your holdings in Country X by a new government there; or you are the president of an aircraft company trying to prepare a contract estimate on a major new aircraft; or you are the president of a university confronting a student sit-in at the computer center; or you are directing a major research program into the causes of urban crime. In all those situations, calling groups of people together is a reasonable course of action.

What characterizes those problems that lend themselves to a group approach? One common characteristic is that there are no obvious preknown best solutions to such problems. No one knows exactly how to tackle them. We are likely to call on groups, that is to say, when we don't know what we are doing, when we are dealing with a novel, unprogramed, complex task.

Another characteristic is that problems of this sort depend for their solution on the commitment and support of several people. When we are trying to raise funds, or get a decision implemented, or create a reservoir of experience and wisdom, we simply must turn to others. Most of us know intuitively (and social science research backs us up) that if we bring other people in on the planning of projects, the probability is high that they will support and advance those projects. We aren't likely to get enthusiastic fund-raisers just by ordering them to raise funds.

So groups are especially useful under at least these two conditions: first, when tasks are complex, unprogramed, unusual; second, when we need the active commitment of other people to get the job done.

This is not to say that the group route is the *only* route open

Commitment to Eating Liver!

In the Notes and References at the end of this chapter you will find several books that detail studies of group participation in industry. But the grandfather study was a simple one made early during the Second World War. It wasn't set in industry and didn't even have much effect on policy, but it did trigger a whole chain of research into the role of participation on commitment.

The study concerned the effects of group participation on housewives' food-buying habits. During the war, the government wanted housewives to consume more of the cheaper and less popular cuts of meat—hearts, lungs, kidneys, and so on. A group of psychologists designed an experiment using two groups of housewives. Group I was exposed to lectures by nutritionists and home economists on the nutritional value of such "variety meats." Group II engaged in a group discussion of the pros and cons of using such meats; the discussion was conducted by an expert discussion leader. In Group II the housewives aired their concerns about their families' reactions and their personal dislikes and so on. But they were then brought to a decision point at which they agreed as a group to try out the meats.

Several weeks later, the researchers checked to see how many housewives in Groups I and II had actually purchased the meats in question. About ten times as many (32%) of the Group II women as of the Group I women had actually purchased one of the items.

—Adapted from K. Lewin, "Group Decision and Social Change," in E. E. Maccoby et al., eds., Readings in Social Psychology (New York: Holt, 1958), pp. 197–211.

---

under those conditions. If we are very, very bright, we can solve even novel, complex problems ourselves; but as knowledge proliferates, the likelihood diminishes that one person will be able to hold all of it in his head.

Incidentally, one managerial tool that is *not* very effective in dealing with problems that are complex or that demand commitment is the tool of direct authority. Groups often work where authority won't. For authority is not very useful when the manager's own knowledge is low, or when he needs other people *willingly* to contribute their energies.

There is a third condition under which groups are useful. When we know that the interests of *other* groups or organizations or individuals will be directly affected by the issue at hand, then we must bring representatives of those groups into our deliberations.

Failure to bring other people in on decisions that will seriously affect their interest is a sure route to disaster.

Groups That Work and Groups That Don't

The manager facing a problem often has a choice of whether to make his decisions alone or with the help of a group. If he chooses the group route, how can he manage the group so that it is likely to work well?

The answer to that one, of course, is very complicated, but a few rules of thumb have emerged from research on groups over the last two decades. Let's try these, with some trepidation:

(1) If the task is complex, unprogramed, poorly specified, then open the group up. Encourage free communication. Invite criticism, challenge, and discussion. But try to invite it in a way that will not close off the shyer members of the group.

(2) If the task calls for imaginative, original, unusual solutions, open the group up, but *discourage* criticism and challenge. Encourage offbeat ideas by rewarding the most offbeat. This is the time for brainstorming, for chain reactions in which one idea sets off another.

(3) If the task looks touchy, if some people's toes are likely to be stepped on, or if interpersonal conflicts are smoldering just below the surface, then take the group off for a long weekend in the country and open things up there. It is wiser to relieve emotional conflicts than to close them off. But in order to do so, you will need enough time and an environment that will permit them to be brought to some kind of resolution. There is no guarantee that the opening up of interpersonal conflicts will *necessarily* resolve them. But there is pretty good evidence that closing them off will almost *never* resolve them.

(4) If time is short, keep the group small and keep it structured. Tighten your plans and insist on moving from one topic to another according to some sort of deadline; and hope for the best, for you will be trading off thoroughness and participation for speed. Usually, if the pressure of time is obvious to all concerned, people will tolerate and respect that requirement. But if the manager insists on making *everything* a crisis, the group will soon learn that his keeping his eye on the clock is only a way of exerting his dominance over the group.

(5) Similarly, if the coordination of people in time and space is critical, tighten your control. Require that all decisions and plans for action be spelled out in detail. Require, in effect, that every individual repeat aloud his interpretation of the conclusions and of the steps to be taken next. Again there will be emotional costs and another trade-off problem.

Directing a group that is working on a problem is something like controlling an economy. The manager has available to him tools with which he can tighten up the group's activities and other tools with which he can loosen up and increase the internal activity of the group. His tightening-up tools are imposing deadlines, reducing group size, formalizing procedures and rules of order, maintaining tight records, and so on. His loosening-up tools are inviting discussion, encouraging the expression of feelings, setting the group up in an unpressured environment, avoiding deadlines, and, indeed, spending a good bit of time talking about the group's own processes and relationships rather than about the problem at hand.

Breaking Groups In

Of course, groups vary widely in purpose, personality, size, skillfullness, composition, and in a whole host of other ways.

One critically important respect in which groups vary is *maturity*. New groups are very different from old groups, much as infants are different from adults, and they must be dealt with differently. Indeed, one reason many managers have trouble dealing with groups is that they fail to treat them as developmental, dynamic, learning entities. They think of groups as fixed and static. Not so. New groups are stiff, tight, badly lubricated, superficially polished, much like cheap new shoes. We shouldn't expect them to work well until they have been broken in.

Here are some basic rules of thumb for the development and maintenance of effective groups. They are, as you will see, rather simple to state but difficult to follow. Perhaps the most important rule is to think of the group as an organism, with emotions as well as ideas. Then, as with a person, the most important additional rules turn out to be constraints, don'ts:

(1) If you're after long-run productivity from a group, don't pressure for short-run performance. Don't demand immediate action and set strict deadlines. Recognize instead that one of the things a collection of people needs is time to form themselves into a group, time to feel one another out, to raise their level of trust in one another, to learn to predict one another's behavior and to communicate comfortably with one another. All this is hard enough to achieve even in the absence of tight deadlines.

(2) Don't take the early task decisions made by a new group too seriously. New groups tend to rush into decisions, often poorly thought-out ones. This eagerness to take action is often a device by which group members strive to develop a feeling of solidarity by accomplishing something — anything — together.

(3) Don't cut off the early chatter and small talk of a new group. The tendency of people to chatter before and after a meeting, their tendency to tell stories that seem irrelevant, their tendency to name-drop and to form little coalitions—all these are part of the process of group integration. Don't interpret them as irrelevancies that must be suppressed. The group must find ways in which its members can come to terms with one another, standards according to which they can agree to behave, areas in which they feel free to deviate and areas in which they know they must conform.

This "make-ready" process is crucially important in the creation of a truly effective group. In almost any profession it is the amateur who rushes into the job without thorough preparation. The professional sharpens his tools and lays out his work, sometimes using up a good part of his allotted time before getting down to the work itself. An outsider, ignorant of what that work really consists of, might conclude that he was wasting time. But a professional would not be fooled. He would understand that the make-ready process sometimes requires more time than the work itself.

(4) Another long-range suggestion: Don't try to stick too close to the task. Encourage the members of a group to think in terms of "process." In a sense, groups are machines working on tasks, but they work on those tasks through fairly complicated internal processes. Our car is a tool for getting us where we want to go, but it won't be a very effective tool for too long if we don't maintain it—if we don't pay attention to oil pressure, lubrication, tires, fuel supply. None of those things has any direct relationship with the route to Oshkosh, but we won't get to Oshkosh or anywhere else if we don't worry about them.

This notion of maintenance of mechanical equipment seems obvious. It is not so obvious, but just as important, in relation to human "equipment." Group maintenance is a psychologically indirect concept that is not immediately related to tasks. But to have a group perform effectively in the long run, the manager (and the members of the group) must keep the group tuned up, well lubricated, and preventively maintained.

Group Process

Maintenance is a matter of paying attention to group processes as well as to group goals.

But what are group processes? Intercommunication is one of them. Is the noise level low enough? Are people saying what they think? Is anybody listening? Interpersonal relations can be thought of as a process too. Is mutual trust high or low? Mutual hostility?

How about social structure? Are there cliques and coalitions? Are some people cut out of the group and isolated? How about navigational equipment? Are there devices for knowing where the group is and where it has been, as well as where it's going? What are the decision processes like? And what should they be?

More has been written about these process issues than we can summarize here. The important notion is that managers (and the members of their groups) ought *consciously* to consider and talk about the group's processes, its structure, its maintenance, as well as the group's task. This is especially important in *ongoing* groups.

The Cost of Maintaining a Group

One of the marks of an effective manager is his ability to foresee what is usually unforeseen, especially the consequences of his own actions. In his dealings with groups, a good manager foresees unforeseen (often negative) consequences too, and several such consequences may be associated even with the effective use of groups. For groups, like dynamic human systems, tend to generate new problems even as they resolve old ones. For example, they have a propensity to become ethnocentric, to develop strong "we" feelings and to reject outsiders. As the members begin to work together, they come to value their group more and more and to build a kind of wall around themselves.

Another problem is that groups are great brainwashers; they tend to pressure their members to conform. The price of membership in a group is conformity to the group's standards. We may *obey* authority, perhaps keeping our beliefs to ourselves. But we are more likely to *change* our beliefs in the direction of the norms of a group to which we belong.

And as conformity grows, groups begin to reject the intrusion of new members. They also reject the intrusion of new ideas, especially if those ideas threaten the established norms and mores of the group. Some groups accommodate novelty more readily than others. Some, indeed, set a positive value on new and stimulating ideas. But all groups set boundaries. And there is always the danger that violations of those boundaries — even violations that promise to be productive — will be suppressed.

In the last chapter we spoke about the issue of evaluation versus acceptance. As groups become more cohesive, more loyal, what happens to the evaluation of individual members? Don't groups become more accepting and less evaluative of their own members? And perhaps more evaluative and less accepting of members of other groups?

Once a group has become well established, it may pose a serious threat to the exercise of direct authority. An employee who knows that he can count on the support of a strong group may find himself questioning the wisdom of orders from above. And the reassertion of authority over a solid group may become difficult. Groups, once they are firmly established, are hard to crack open. Clearly, then, an organization that emphasizes the development of groups may be faced with the erosion of authoritarian control. If the organization tries to reverse its policy of nourishing group activity in an effort to break up strongly established groups, it is likely to meet determined resistance.

Finally, there is the *turn-off* problem that occurs at all levels—in individuals, in groups, and in large organizations. Once a group gets started along the road toward completing a task, hardly anything can stop it. Suppose, for example, that Group X started a project last year. Now the organization decides that the project is no longer viable, that the results will be obsolete even before they are produced, and, hence, that the project is not worthy of further investment. Don't expect the members of Group X to give up gracefully! Small groups of committed people are driven to push enthusiastically onward—even into quicksand.

All these warnings about the problem-generating propensities of groups are simply manifestations of the trade-off problem. There is no known organizational scheme that will guarantee a manager endless success at zero cost. And the list of possible developments that we have just sketched may not be "bad" at all; they may be just what Organization X really needs. For what manager doesn't want his group to feel committed, loyal, enthusiastic, ready to take risks? It is only when we view these issues in a particular organizational context that we can judge whether they are injurious or advantageous.

Up the Ladder to Autonomy?

As a manager climbs up the hierarchical ladder, he is likely to assume that he is rising toward freedom, independence, autonomy. He imagines himself as a senior executive sitting at his big desk, all by his big self, making his big decisions. That's the picture suggested by our conception of the pyramidal organization, in which there is room for just one man at the top.

But that conception isn't quite correct. People higher in organizational hierarchies generally do wield more power than people lower down. But the notion of increasingly independent, individual decision making is not at all realistic. On the contrary, managers become more and more *members* of groups as they go up the ladder, sharing their decision-making responsibilities with others (and hence being pressed more and more to conform). If we took a count, we would probably find foremen giving more direct orders than company presidents. The top of an organization, psychologically speaking, looks more like a mushroom than the peak of a pyramid. For as one moves toward the top, one moves not only upward into power but outward into a complicated network of responsibilities, a network in which almost no action can be taken alone by anybody. Division managers, indeed company presidents, spend endless hours "in conference," digging their way through masses of interpersonal and political problems, coordinating, mediating, pressuring, informing, as well as deciding.

Toward the bottom of the organization, at blue-collar and clerical levels, jobs are pretty well defined, often nearly independent of other jobs. Within established limits, the skilled workman makes his own decisions. Not so the manager. He may be lonely, but he is not *independent*.

All this is to say that skill in performing as a member of a group is not a requirement of just the junior members of the organization. On the contrary, membership skills grow increasingly important with each rung the manager climbs up the ladder.

To put it more callously, at lower levels in the organization nearly all one needs to do is please his boss. At higher levels, success (whether defined as glory or as getting the job done) depends on the approval and support of many others. Movement up the ladder is not movement toward independence; it is movement away from dependence on *superiors* but toward *mutual dependence* on others.

Groups and Their Relations with Other Groups

As our group becomes more solid and cohesive, as its internal morale and self-esteem build up, what happens to its relations with other groups in the organization? Groups in organizations don't live autonomous lives. They have to work with, interact with, lots of other groups. And what would you expect? Smooth, cooperative integration among the many groups that make up the organization? Or a certain amount of conflict and pressure politics? The next chapter is about groups interacting within the organization.

Summary

Groups exert a powerful influence on the behavior of their members. Indeed, to predict the behavior of individuals in an organization we must know not only the individual and the organization but his immediate face-to-face work group. And to predict organizational behavior, we must understand the interactions of the groups that comprise it.

Moreover, groups are functional tools for the organization. And like other tools they can be used skillfully or badly. They are especially valuable when tasks are large and complicated, requiring many kinds of inputs, and when commitment to decisions is essential to effective implementation.

In general, for complex, novel tasks, open group structures are likely to be more effective. For time-bound, specifiable tasks, smaller, more structured groups tend to be more effective. But those generalizations must be qualified. Groups need a chance to grow. Maximum effectiveness is not something one should expect on the first day; a good deal of make-ready time and effort is needed before a group begins to live and produce. Its internal processes and self-maintenance equipment must be perfected as well as its capability for solving problems. Though we suggested several "rules" for group development, their limitations are apparent.

Working through groups entails several costs. Groups can be used to hide individual responsibility; they can become internally solid at the expense of the rest of the organization; they may be difficult to control once they become cohesive and feel autonomous; they press individual members to conform even when deviant thinking may be productive; and they tend to protect their members, even incompetent ones. And groups, once started on a project, are apt to pursue it stubbornly. They may be hard to stop.

Finally, group skills are not just for junior members of the organization. Senior executives spend more and more time in groups and become more and more dependent on one another as they move upward in the hierarchy. Indeed, probably more time is spent in groups at top levels than anywhere else in the organization.

Notes and References

Vast quantities have been written on the matters we have touched on in this chapter. Several excellent overviews have appeared recently. B. E. Collins and H. Guetzkow, *A Social Psychology of Group Processes for Decision-Making* (New York: John Wiley and Sons, 1964), is especially valuable on small groups. A. P. Hare, *Handbook of Small Group Research* (New York: Free Press, 1962), is a useful reference work. Marvin E. Shaw, *Group Dynamics: The Psychology of Small Group Behavior* (New York: McGraw-Hill, 1971), is a readable and thorough discussion of small-group behavior. Dorwin Cartwright and Alvin Zander, eds., *Group Dynamics: Research and Theory,* 3rd ed. (New York: Harper & Row, 1968), is a collection of research studies on groups, with heavy emphasis on empirical findings. Clovis R. Shepard, *Small Groups: Some Sociological Perspectives* (San

Francisco: Chandler Publishing Co., 1964), is a concise, readable review and analysis.

For summaries and analyses of group leadership and its impact on group performance, see: Chapter 24 of Cartwright and Zander, *Group Dynamics: Research and Theory*, 3rd ed.; and E. P. Hollander, *Leaders, Groups, and Influence* (New York: Oxford University Press, 1964).

For a widely discussed model of leadership behavior, see Fred E. Fiedler, *A Theory of Leadership Effectiveness* (New York: McGraw-Hill, 1967). Fiedler's is a contingency model, emphasizing that effective leadership must differ for different tasks and different conditions of power and affection in the relationship between leader and led.

For the role of leadership and its effect on group problem solving, consult Norman R. F. Maier, ed., *Problem Solving and Creativity* (Belmont, Calif.: Brooks-Cole Publishing Co., 1970), especially Section 7.

The structure of a group has substantial impact on the group's performance. For a good review of structural research, see: M. Glanzer and R. Glaser, "Techniques for the Study of Team Structure and Behavior," *Psychological Bulletin,* LVIII, 1 (Jan. 1961); and Stanley E. Seashore, *Group Cohesiveness in the Industrial Work Group* (Ann Arbor, Mich.: Survey Research Center, Institute for Social Research, University of Michigan, 1954).

For an idea of the current state of knowledge about conformity and group pressure, try C. A. Kiesler and S. B. Kiesler, *Conformity* (Reading, Mass.: Addison-Wesley, 1969).

11

Groups, Politics, and Conflict: The Many Faces of Organizational Warfare

Organizations, as we have seen, can be thought of as collections of groups—often loyal, cohesive groups. And when such groups come into contact, politics and conflict turn up too.

Politics and conflict—problems of power, control, ascendancy—occur in all organizations. We read much about the organizational rat race, bootlicking, power struggles, the organization man, climbing the pyramid over the bodies of others, empire building, espionage. It would be nonsense to deny the existence of such interpersonal and intergroup conflict in large organizations. It would be an even greater mistake to deny the crucial importance of political skills for anyone making his way in organizations. But it is nonsense to equate, as some novelists and critics do, success in managing an organization with success in power-politicking.

This chapter is about intraorganizational conflict; it is not just about how to prevent or eliminate conflict, but how to manage it. For conflict is a fact of organizational life, and not necessarily a negative, burdensome fact. The politicking and accommodating and battling that go on in organizations need not always be wasteful for the executive, or for the company, or even for society. On the contrary, as in the public world of politics, conflict among individuals and groups can provide checks and balances to the system and can motivate creativity and innovation among members of the organization.

In this chapter we shall first consider some typical varieties of conflict, asking why such conflicts tend to occur. Then we'll describe some alternative ways in which organizations have tried to deal with conflict. And finally we shall offer some suggestions toward the more effective management of certain types of conflict.

Some Varieties of Conflict

Conflicts That Are Primarily Interpersonal. Among the most dramatic of conflicts in organizations are those that develop among powerful individuals in the executive suite. These are the ones that make the newspapers. Board chairmen hassle with presidents and chips begin to fly all over the organization. Senior executives get into battles with one another and sometimes mass resignations result. Almost any issue of the *Wall Street Journal* will provide examples of such conflicts. And so will the history and present political state of any university or almost any department within any university.

Many of these interpersonal conflicts are not very destructive — at first. Often people fight about what they believe to be the right answers, or what they just believe to be right. But the battle can soon turn into a struggle for power. And even what we believe to be right answers to objective problems are inextricably tied up with our values, our professional orientation, and our group memberships. It is not easy to separate interpersonal conflicts into their intellectual and emotional components. And it is at the emotional level that most of the dangers occur.

It may seem incredible that members of an organization can destroy their organization, and often themselves, in battle with one another. But it is no more incredible than the waging of war among nations or the destruction of a family by a battling husband and wife. The wonder is not that large organizations are occasionally torn apart, but that they usually hang together despite the internal battering they take.

Conflicts Between the Man and the "System." As we tour the organizational preserve, we sometimes find the individual specimen doing battle with the whole wolf pack. We see such conflict in almost every type of organization: in voluntary organizations like fraternities, when one member simply doesn't get along with the others; in families, when one child is more or less continuously in trouble with the rest; in industry, when a department head finds that an informal coalition has been formed against him.

These are likely to be emotionally costly conflicts, both for the

*Ousted Chairman of Consolidated Foods
Says He Was Victim of Founder's Vanity*

... Upheavals in the executive suite generally are so candied over with public relations that outsiders rarely catch even a glimpse of the bitter corporate infighting that preceded them. Most times the loser departs the scene showered with compliments for his "vital contribution" to the company and that's the end of that.

Not so in the case of Consolidated Food Corp., the billion-dollar Chicago merchandising conglomerate that unceremoniously dumped its chairman and chief executive officer, 53-year-old William Howlett, a month ago.

"Everybody's just jubilant," Nathan R. Cummings, Consolidated's founder and largest stockholder, told a reporter at the time. "Can't you hear over the phone how everyone is laughing and talking?"

The vote wasn't even close—15 directors to one, Mr. Howlett's own vote. And then the board speedily chose William A. Buzick Jr., Consolidated's president, as Mr. Howlett's successor. With Mr. Cummings owning more than a million Consolidated shares, compared with Mr. Howlett's 12,000 shares, the fight was over almost before it started.

Many of the top brass of Consolidated's complicated corporate structure must feel a bit uneasy at the moment. The company has 32 separate divisions, each with its own president, gathered in a semi-autonomous system reporting to six executive vice presidents. Says one insider: "Bill Buzick probably won't do anything with unseemly haste, but you may see several of the executive vice presidents who are considered Howlett protégés get the axe. . . ."

—*Reprinted with permission from the* Wall Street Journal, *Jan. 14, 1970.*

individual and for the group he is battling. As all of us know from our own experience as members of groups, isolation is painful for the isolate and has a crippling effect on the group that must live with him. Such conflict slows down decisions, distorts plans, and intensifies pain. But such conflict also carries positive effects.

What causes such battles between whole groups and between members of groups? The appearance of a stranger on one's native soil will do it—an outsider moving into an already solid and cohesive group. Groups with clearly established standards and rules usually manage to fend off such interlopers.

A second cause of conflict between individuals and groups is the unwillingness of an individual member to commit himself to the group. Political organizations and fraternities and regiments expect their members to be 100 percent loyal, not 50 percent. The sales manager expects his salesmen to be committed to the company's policies and its products, to *believe* that those products are better than any

> *The Value of Conflict*
>
> This week I also finished the first draft of a speech . . . a vigorous and plain-spoken attack on the policies of Wilkie's companies as respects rural electrification, particularly the fighting of cooperatives. It is responsive to my desire to make TVA a largely active enterprise— and nothing will do that better than controversy and excitement over power issues. There has been too much talk about "peace"; too much peace in a huge organization becomes lethargy, following the quiet paths toward bureaucracy. I have always been impressed by something in Lewis Mumford's *The Culture of Cities* about the value of controversy—that it is not the periods of harmony but rather those of lack of harmony that will be longest remembered for their contribution to human culture.
>
> —David E. Lilienthal, an entry for Nov. 12, 1939, in The Journals of David E. Lilienthal: The TVA Years (*New York: Harper & Row, 1964*), p. 143. Reprinted by permission of Harper & Row Publishers, Inc.

other products in the world—whatever the truth may be. Departments, teams, suborganizations also typically demand an extraordinary degree of commitment from the individual member, even to the subjugation of the individual's personal needs. When the individual is not willing to commit himself as fully as his group expects, trouble starts. The group begins to apply sanctions, and the individual must give in, fight back, or pull out.

A third cause of conflict between individuals and groups, though perfectly obvious, is nevertheless surprisingly rare. It resides in an intellectual difference in beliefs about an issue. One member thinks one solution is right, but the group prefers another. The issue is not emotional, not one of personal acceptance or of membership in the group, but simply a difference in cognitive belief. Since most problems in management are open-ended, one best answer seldom leaps out to be accepted by all. One man believes that the space capsule should be built differently. One man believes that the organization should change its product line, and the rest do not.

Sometimes the dissenter is later proved right (mostly in novels), sometimes wrong. *Usually no clear proof ever emerges.* Most often there is no victory or defeat on the issue itself. There is only victory or defeat on the emotional accompaniments—on the loss of face or status or influence that emerges from the battle.

Are such conflicts ever useful? Or, for that matter, do they ever do any real harm? We know a good deal about such questions, largely as a result of research on the processes of deviation and conformity. We know, for example, that when an individual differs from his group on a substantive issue and will not give in, two almost polar things happen: the deviant behavior blocks agreement and thus slows down decision making and action, but the same behavior also generates creativity and catalyzes thought. At times, decisive action is worth much more than creative or thorough analysis of a problem; when the island is sinking fast, any old raft will do. But sometimes the reverse is true. One of the manager's jobs is to decide which he wants more and then, accordingly, to try either to resolve the conflict or to let it persist.

There is another related, though again rather rare, cause of individual-group conflict: the individual who is chronically antiauthoritarian. We have all known such people—people who feel oppressed and imprisoned by *any* establishment. Some servicemen see the army as an unreasoning, restrictive power, almost as much an enemy as the enemy itself. Some students can't stand the restrictions of *any* impersonal, bureaucratic university. The chronically antiauthoritarian individual probably serves one modest function in the organization: he is something of an irritant and may therefore catalyze some reassessment of organizational problems. But if he is really an extreme personality, his influence is likely to drop to zero and he will be seen as an oddball rather than as an agent of change.

As we encounter such "chronic deviants," however, we must be careful not to dismiss them as either hopeless or insignificant. Often their behavior has been bred by organizations that permit the individual only two extreme choices—full capitulation to the organization's norms, or chronic, noninfluential, but principled deviation. And such individuals, too, can become the convenient rallying point for growing dissatisfaction in others.

Conflicts That Occur Primarily Between Groups. Another source of conflict lies in struggles for power and resources among groups within an organization. Often these struggles can best be understood as arising within the organization. Two departments compete for a budget authorization that only one can win. A research division challenges the values and experience that manufacturing executives want to apply to a product design decision. More shadowy coalitions maneuver against one another to place favorites in top management slots. Other struggles, though, rest on the deep divisions that exist more broadly in society.

Within just the last few years, in the United States, in Belgium, in Northern Ireland, in Canada, in Malaysia, in Jamaica, in Africa, and in other places, too, destructive conflict between religious, racial, political, or tribal groups has broken out. At the last Ecumenical Council of the Catholic Church, the liberal group and the conservative group apparently fought like the devil. Protestant sects have not always been able to resolve their differences either. In many business schools there is a split within the senior faculty between the "researchers" and the "teachers." In many companies battles go on continuously between project groups and staff support groups.

This is simply to say that conflict among groups is commonplace within societies and within organizations. It's a fact of life. One reason may be that such conflict is so easy to start. The moment one group identifies another somewhere within the same territory, conflict tends to begin. Groups identify other groups as competitors at the slightest provocation. People in second-class cabins on a ship perceive themselves as a group only because there are, up there, those supercilious first-class passengers. Color differences will generate the same perceptions; so will age, or religion, or geography, or occupation, or sex, or working on the tenth floor rather than on the eleventh. *Almost any mechanism that allows one group to identify itself as different from another group seems sufficient to generate conflict.* And almost any group can find such a mechanism in almost any environment.

These conditions can easily be intensified. Dictators whip up internal solidarity by creating an "enemy" out there. Two divisions of a company, forced to compete for a limited supply of capital, will compete with vigor. A group leader will exploit the presence of another group in order to solidify his support within his own group. Subunits of organizations, physically isolated from one another, may come to see one another not only as strangers but as competitors.

The process by which groups develop such strong feelings of conflict is not difficult to understand. If one studies intergroup conflict experimentally—say by asking each of two groups to come up with a decision about a problem, with the understanding that representatives of the two groups will then try to decide which of the two decisions to use—some very predictable things happen. For example, as the groups work out their decisions, the morale and solidarity of each group begin to increase. And the members of each group begin to think of the other group as an opponent rather than as another unit of the same team. This happens despite the fact that their purpose is to join with the other group in trying to reach the very best decision.

If each group then gets a chance to see the other group's solution and study it for a while, the effect is almost always the same. Seldom does Group A assess Group B's decision "rationally," deciding whether it is better than its own or worse. Each group almost invariably perceives the other decision as a bad decision—not

Conflict Is Easy to Start, but Hard to Stop

A classic experiment on intergroup conflict was conducted several years ago with children at a boys' camp. A few days after camp opened, the counsellors and researchers were able to get the members of two different bunkhouses into such violent conflict that they wouldn't interact in any even mildly cooperative way. The researchers spent the rest of the summer trying to understand the process and testing alternative mechanisms for reducing the conflict. The device that finally did begin to break down the conflict and to promote cooperation was a "superordinate goal." Such a goal was provided in this case when the water supply to the camp was cut off, leaving *all* the campers thirsty and dry.

Here are some of the study's conclusions:

> Intergroup conflict and its by-products of hostility and negative stereotypes are not *primarily* a result of neurotic tendencies on the part of individuals but occur under given conditions even when the individuals involved are normal, healthy, and socially well adjusted....
>
> Co-operative and democratic procedures *within* groups are not directly transferable to intergroup relations. On the contrary, co-operativeness and solidarity within groups were at their height when intergroup conflict was most severe....
>
> Contact between hostile groups as equals . . . does not, in itself, necessarily reduce conflict between them.
>
> Contact between groups involving interdependent action toward superordinate goals is conducive to co-operation between groups.
>
> Co-operative endeavor between groups toward superordinate goals alters the significance of other measures designed to reduce existing hostility between them. Intergroup *contacts* . . . were then used for developing plans, making decisions and for pleasant exchanges. *Information* about the other group became interesting and sought after rather than something to be ignored or interpreted to fit existing conceptions of the out-group. *Exchange of persons* for the performance of tasks was not seen as "betrayal" of one's own group. Leaders found that the trend toward intergroup co-operation widened the spheres in which they could take positive steps toward working out procedures for joint endeavors and future contacts. In fact, a leader who tried to hold back from intergroup contacts found that his group was ceasing to listen to him.

—See M. Sherif, "Experiments in Group Conflict," *Scientific American*, CXCV (1956), 54–58.

nearly so good as its own. And its own solidarity rises accordingly.

When representatives of the two groups come together to try to decide which of the two decisions should be taken, the discussion soon degenerates into a kind of gladiatorial combat. The representatives attack one another and one another's decisions. Each group tries to prove its decision best. And the final result is almost always failure to reach any decision at all. The failure is even more likely if, in the background, there is a board of judges, a kind of supreme court, that will make the decision if the two groups fail.

But the whole process is quite regular, quite predictable. The conditions for the creation of intergroup conflict are very easy to achieve, not only in the laboratory but in nature. Such conflict seems to occur over a wide range of groups and a wide range of cultures. On the other hand, the conditions for the *resolution* of intergroup conflict are obscure.

How Organizations Handle Conflict

For some people conflict is something to be avoided, almost at any cost. For other people conflict is something to be patched up, smoothed over with gifts and offerings. For others conflict is a game of tactics and strategy. Still other people confront conflict directly—they battle things out.

Organizations show the same variety of response. In some organizations most conflicts are avoided at almost any cost. Members do not argue in meetings. They speak politely and stick to the facts. Sharp differences between groups are never acknowledged. In other organizations conflicts are hastily patched up. Someone always rushes in to make peace, fearful lest the conflict become too "dangerous" or threatening. In still other organizations conflicts are exposed to debate and discussion. Management assumes that conflicts will occur and that they must be dealt with openly. Meetings are likely to be rough-and-tumble sessions with politics aboveboard and known to all.

Obviously, there are costs and benefits to each approach. And obviously, organizations can survive under any of the three approaches. Certainly, dealing with conflict in the first way—by preventing or avoiding its occurrence—would seem to be ideal, if it could be done.

At least three conditions are required for successful conflict avoidance: (1) a high degree of socialization of group members; (2) a stable, well-structured set of tasks; and (3) a steady, nonvolatile environment. By high socialization we mean that all members share many of the same relevant organizational goals and values, as all priests once did in the Catholic Church, and perhaps still do—more than, say, all the employees in the same company. If we all basically agree on where we should go, and if we all have a deep commitment to the organization, the probability of conflict is low; the willingness to accept decisions from those in authority is high. When tasks are clear and well structured, we can probably agree easily on how to do them, and the structure can be designed to cover almost any contingency that may arise. And if the world in which our organization operates is steady and predictable, it won't keep throwing up new and unusual problems that may generate conflict.

These are rare conditions, though, and they are becoming rarer. So some organizations have drifted toward the second approach, not avoiding or preventing, but rather denying or covering up conflict in order to keep peace and avoid emotional disturbance.

Recently, however, the idea of managing conflict by facing it and talking about it, indeed almost exploiting it, has become common. Perhaps our more volatile contemporary environment, our more complex and changing tasks, and our less socialized organizational members are all contributing to this change. And if our assessment of the direction of change is correct, it should not be surprising that the tools managers use when they encounter conflict are becoming different from the ones they formerly used.

Some Old and New Tools for Dealing with Conflict

Managers need tools if they are to gain the rewards and minimize the costs of the conflicts that will surely develop around them. Some of the tools are very old. Others are just now being developed to fit new theories about conflict and its management. Let's look at the most important ones.

Authority. One of the oldest and one of the weakest tools is authority. We can order people to stop fighting. Or we can try to. We can order people to stick to the facts, to "keep personalities out of this." Clearly, authority provides a way to make decisions, especially when our battling subordinates cannot reach agreement. In that sense, authority is useful; a supreme court is useful; a mother or father is useful.

But when we use authority this way, we must have enough of it and we must use it skillfully lest the authority itself be rejected by the warring parties, or lest we create one winning group and a disaffected and frustrated losing group. Wise managers foresee that problem and "cool out" losing groups to make sure they are not too badly hurt. Capital budgeting committees, for instance, after deciding which group's proposal to accept and fund, often turn their attention to the losing groups. They grant the losers part of their request or promise them they will get another chance next year.

But authority is becoming a weaker organizational tool, for the reasons we mentioned earlier. People aren't socialized into the organization as completely as they used to be and are less willing to accept decisions from above. Certainly students are not passively acquiescent these days, and professional employees may be more socialized into their professions than into the organization they happen to work for. They may not accept the authority of either the referee or the coach.

"Political" Tools: Trade-offs, Compromises, Promises. Some organizations handle conflict politically—through direct negotiation and bargaining, or through modifications of the negotiation process. In such organizations, conflicts are seldom allowed to get down to a clear "win-lose" situation. The pie may be made bigger so that everybody can feel he has won. Or else management may compromise by adopting a bit of every group's proposal—a solution, incidentally, that is widely used in national politics. We may deplore such trade-offs and compromises, but they make it possible for diverse groups to live together.

These "political" tools are aimed primarily at finding satisfactory solutions for all the parties concerned, rather than optimal solutions to the task itself. Their great merit is that they acknowledge both the existence of conflict and the need to keep the conflicting parties working within the larger organizational system. They constitute another kind of social glue, a means for keeping things together even at the price of imperfect solutions. They are old tools that continue to permit organizations and societies to muddle through without civil war. They remain extremely useful in contemporary organizations and contemporary environments.

Over the years we have found ways of formalizing some of the political means for settling conflict; we have developed legal codes, organizational rules, rules of order—devices that serve more to keep the organization together than to guarantee optimal solutions. Though such methods often are necessary, they are less than ideal tools for resolving conflict. Indeed, their widespread acceptance can be thought of as an admission of inadequacy, of our inability to reach full and unanimous agreement on the best of all possible solutions.

Superordinate Goals. Clever administrators know that a "superordinate" goal—a goal that is important to *all* parties—can often keep a loose coalition of groups together. For example, the ecologi-

Tactics of Confrontation

Confrontation was an early and frequent choice of one young manager brought in to help keep a small manufacturing firm from going bankrupt. He describes his experience this way:

> A week ago I realized . . . that it just wasn't going to work out itself. The bull had to be taken by the horns. I was forced to this realization by the fact that the company had payrolls to meet, vendors to pay, and things like this. The company has to generate its own cash in here. . . . So I finally decided that I, of necessity, had to go to the floor and talk to the lead men out there working for this foreman and lay it straight on the line—which I did. . . . I told them, "These are basic economics that I want to discuss with you fellows. Before I do, let me tell you that I have not had to walk out on this floor to realize that we're in the middle of a slowdown," and the heads began to nod. I knew I was on the right track; it was tipped. I said, "Frankly, two more weeks of this slowdown will be just as effective in closing this shop down as if you take all of your men and walk out there in the street and parade up and down with signs."
>
> Well, they went back to the shop. By Wednesday morning the reports had come back to me that there's an attitude in this shop that's not been seen here in years, that there's more work going out. People are turning to.

—*William R. Dill, Thomas L. Hilton, and Walter R. Reitman,* The New Managers, ©1962, pp. 181–82. Reprinted by permission of Prentice-Hall, Inc., Englewood Cliffs, New Jersey.

---

cal threat has made bedfellows of many groups that disagree over other issues.

Within the organization, however, it is difficult to establish meaningful, positive superordinate goals. And the larger the organization, the more difficult it is. President Kennedy wanted the frontier of space to serve that purpose, but he did not succeed in gaining the full commitment of all American factions to that goal. Certainly, Vietnam did not provide unity as some other wars have. Indeed, when was the last time that the United States or a large part of it was emotionally united in one common effort? Pearl Harbor? The assassination of Martin Luther King? And when was the last time your university, or your agency, or your company was solidly united in an effort to achieve some clear superordinate goal?

So the development of a meaningful superordinate goal for an organization, while much to be desired, is difficult to bring about. Sometimes nature does it for us, by providing disaster or crisis. Sometimes competitors help us just by being energetic and visible.

But to do it for ourselves usually requires long, hard, participative work.

Confrontation. One important technique for coping with conflict within organizations is simple *confrontation*. A third party, if necessary, brings the conflicting individuals or groups together and encourages them to open up, to talk through their feelings toward each other, and to come finally either to some resolution or at least to some accommodation of each other's interests.

Managers don't use this technique very often, however. They seem to prefer instead—rather foolishly—either to deny the conflict, pretending it isn't there, or to call in the conflicting parties, scold them, tell them this nonsense must stop, and send them away. Usually, the outcome of such efforts is simply to drive the conflict underground so that it is never visible enough to provoke another scolding. The children in the back seat pinch each other quietly so that father won't know it's going on—but they pinch hard.

Confrontation, on the other hand, though it may not lead to love, often leads to understanding and reasonable accommodation. And it usually brings the tension level down.

Nor is confrontation guaranteed to provide an optimal solution, any more than bargaining techniques. But it will often yield a more open discussion of all facets of the problem than will most other methods. Generally, it seems preferable for the manager to confront internal conflict than to ignore it. He must control his timing carefully, however, and map out the power structure before he undertakes such action. But conflict must be regarded as an expected, indeed a useful, part of organizational life and not something to be feared. In practice this means that conflicting parties are brought together, not kept apart; that the issues are talked about, not avoided; that disagreements are expressed, not suppressed.

Summary

Organizations, like political systems, are full of conflict. Conflict may occur at any level—between individuals, between individuals and groups, between groups.

Conflict is often costly, leading to internal war that jeopardizes individual and organizational welfare. But it produces positive results too. Conflict generates a richness of ideas and a thorough examination of issues. Indeed, internal conflict is a normal condition in any large organization.

Some organizations consciously set up an atmosphere of high conflict, thereby gaining the rewards of energetic competition but risking the emergence of power coalitions and distorted communication. Others suppress conflict, denying or avoiding it, and insist that employees be polite and agreeable. They gain conformity and coordination, but they sacrifice vitality. Other organizations confront conflict directly while trying to keep it focused on issues rather than persons.

No one knows the "right" way to resolve conflict. Many tools are available, however. Authority can be used to limit conflict, if not to resolve it. Compromises also can limit conflict, providing room for accommodation, though not necessarily resolution. Impersonal but accepted rulebooks can prevent matters from getting out of hand. The setting up of superordinate goals can solidify warring groups. Direct debate and confrontation are increasingly being used.

Notes and References

For a readable discussion of the pressures the group can bring to bear on individual members, see Charles Kiesler and Sara Kiesler, *Conformity* (Reading, Mass.: Addison-Wesley, 1969). On the question of conflict between the individual and the system, consult Edgar Schein, "Organizational Socialization," in B. L. Hinton and H. J. Reitz, eds., *Groups and Organizations* (Belmont, Calif.: Wadsworth Publishing Co., 1971). The classic study on conflict among groups within an organization is Muzafer Sherif *et al.*, *Intergroup Conflict and Cooperation: The Robbers Cave Experiment* (Norman, Okla.: Institute of Group Relations, University of Oklahoma, 1961).

Robert Blake, Herbert Shepard, and Jane Mouton, *Managing Intergroup Conflict in Industry* (Houston, Texas: Gulf Publishing Co., 1964), is a useful study of approaches to group conflict.

For a discussion of conflict between labor and management and some procedures for its resolution, try R. E. Walton and R. B. McKensie, *A Behavioral Theory of Labor Negotiations: An Analysis of a Social Interaction System* (New York: McGraw-Hill, 1965).

You will find a good theoretical analysis of the nature of conflict in organizations and a discussion of how organizations handle conflict in James March and Herbert Simon, *Organizations* (New York: John Wiley and Sons, 1958), Chapter 5.

Toward the end of this chapter, we discussed several methods of dealing with conflict. For further discussion of methods of conflict resolution, see Robert Kahn and Elise Boulding, eds., *Power and Conflict in Organizations* (New York: Basic Books, 1964). On the topic of confrontation and third-party intervention as a method of dealing with organizational conflict, look at Richard Walton, *Interpersonal Peacemaking: Confrontations and Third-Party Consultations* (Reading, Mass.: Addison-Wesley, 1969); and William G. Scott, *The Management of Conflict: Appeal Systems in Organizations* (Homewood, Ill.: Irwin, 1965).

Another strategy of conflict resolution is protest absorption. For a brief treatment of this technique, try Ruth Leeds, "The Absorption of Protest:

A Working Paper," in Cooper, Leavitt, and Shelly, eds., *New Perspectives in Organization Research* (New York: John Wiley and Sons, 1964).

On the use of superordinate goals as a "unifying" technique, consult Muzafer Sherif, "Superordinate Goals in the Reduction of Intergroup Conflict," *American Journal of Sociology,* LXIII (1958). This article is also reprinted in Hinton and Reitz, eds., *Groups and Organizations* (Belmont, Calif.: Wadsworth Publishing Co., 1971).

12

Organizational Growth: A Reprise

Now that we have considered some of the major dimensions of organizations, let's see what happens when organizations begin to grow. And let's use this discussion of growth as a review of Part I of this book. Like people, some parts of organizations grow faster than others, and organizations suffer from growing pains in the process. What happens to task, structure, technology, and people as the organization grows?

*One Example: Double-Ended,
Grass-Scented Candles, Inc.*

You've just invented a grass-scented candle that burns at both ends. The candles are cheap to make and they're legal and your friends want to buy all you have. So you decide to set up an organization to manufacture a hundred candles a day. You devise some molds and you assemble the raw materials and tools you will need—pots, heaters, scissors, paraffin, wicks, coloring, scent, and so on. You start by making a few candles to figure out the major steps and to determine how long it should take to make each one. Then you estimate how many man-hours it will take to make your quota. You discover that it's more than a one-man job, and so you calculate how many people you will need to help you. Then you set up the work area—a big enough space to work in. And that's it.

So long as the task is clear and precise and the resources are readily available, the whole procedure is quite manageable. You can design an organization for the task, set out work processes, specify schedules, and assign people.

But let's complicate things a bit. You have produced a large number of candles and are holding them in inventory in the hall closet. Now you decide that you want to design an organization to sell 500 candles a week at 59 cents each.

This task is a little harder. What do you do first? You need to define "the market" and perhaps get salesmen out to the potential customers. You do some testing to see if your candles sell well in particular outlets, such as college bookstores. From that experience you try to build up a marketing strategy and a team of people to carry it out. But this selling task is less structured, less clean-cut. The time cycles are different. It takes longer to find out the effect of your sales efforts than it did to test ways of making your candles. The slower feedback means slower learning. And what you learn is more ambiguous and puzzling. But you work at it.

Now suppose you add a third task: you decide to design an organization that will develop other new products to make and sell along with the candles—candlesticks, maybe, or incense, or grass-scented T-shirts. That's a more open-ended problem still, more vague and unspecified, with more possibilities to choose from. You might conclude that you really don't need an *organization* to do that job. What you need is a few good people to look around and talk things over, to decide what special kinds of skills your firm already posesses, and what comparative advantages you have that would make one product more appropriate for you to produce than another.

But all three tasks, though they vary in the degree to which they are structured, are very well structured in comparison to the same kinds of tasks when they are carried out on a much larger scale. Assume that your candle business proves an instant success. You reach the point where you are producing 50,000 units a day. Now you must sell them. You must meet a large payroll every week. You have mortgages to pay off. You must satisfy the watchful bankers and stockholders you have borrowed money from.

Is the solution simply to apply what you learned from running the smaller organization to the larger one? Is it just a matter of getting larger work tables and hiring more people to mold candles? Not quite. Somehow new problems begin to crop up in this enlarged environment. Now you begin to worry about *supervision,* about standards of production, about ways of checking on the performance of the many people now in your employ, about how to inventory

Different Sizes Mean Different Problems

Ernest Dale studied a number of companies, with from three to nearly 500,000 employees, and found that he could associate size with the kinds of organizational problems each company was most concerned with. From the analysis, he identified seven stages of growth:

Size (number of employees) when problem begins	The organizational problem	The probable action or solution
Any size	Formulation of objectives	Decide division of work
10	Assignment of responsibility	Accommodate to personalities
50–100	Delegation of more management functions	Define span of control and set limits
50–300	Reduction of executive's burden	Appoint staff assistants
100–400	Establishment of new functions	Develop staff specialists
100–500	Coordination of management functions	Formalize arrangements for group decision making
500 & up	Balance between control and delegation	Formalize arrangements for decentralization

—Ernest Dale, Planning and Developing the Company Organization (New York: American Management Association, 1952), p. 22.

and distribute all those candles, about how to train employees and schedule their work. You must make sure you don't run out of raw materials.

In short, you now have problems of logistics, supply, support, supervision, and maintenance. You must feed the organization you have created. You can no longer concentrate on making a few candles. Your own personal distance from the rest of the organization has become greater. You have moved pretty far away from the bench, from the "real" work. You are spending your time on comparisons, evaluations, controls, plans. You realize that several levels have developed in the hierarchy. You're paying salaries and you have to trust your subordinates, unless you want to work yourself to death by trying to do everything yourself. You have to operate more by indirection than direction, because there are many people in the organization whom you almost never see.

And there are signs of an emerging bureaucracy. People are vying for status in the organization; they are trying to please you. The sales management people are complaining that the production people have cut quality. Production complains that they are getting lousy raw materials and that the maintenance department isn't cleaning the heaters properly. But your maintenance chief is being wooed by your competitors, so you had better not push him too hard.

These new pressures stem not so much from the candle-making task. They arise from the *organization,* from the difficulties of coordinating and integrating large numbers of disparate acts that must be performed by large numbers of disparate people.

In the old days, when there were only two or three people making candles, all of you thought up ideas for improving your operations. You shared your loose, open lifestyle. You were all in on the act. But now you can't have everybody in on everything. You and a select group of supervisors are now the thinkers, the planners; the rest of the organization does pretty much what it's told.

Suddenly a large greeting-card company comes out with a long-burning, double-ended, grass-scented candle. It's bigger, more colorful, and cheaper than yours. They've put a lot of research money into it and into a new plant, and they're offering dealers much better margins. You have to admit their material and overall quality are better too. That makes you uneasy. You need researchers, too, and chemists, and better quality-control methods. You need market researchers to tell you who is buying your product and who isn't and how to advertise to them. And you need financial advisers who can help you get money for expansion.

Gradually even the planning activities begin to leave your hands and get delegated to specialized subgroups around the organization. At first you think that nothing has really changed. You are still running the show. Those staff people will simply advise you on what is new, what is good, what you might do. And then you will make the decisions. So you are really still in charge. But over time the picture grows fuzzy. Though people respect your authority, you begin to feel a little uncomfortable about how much control you really have over the fate of the organization. You seem to have become something of a cog. You find yourself *implementing* more than planning. Those little subgroups of technologists are doing a good deal of the planning. And you find yourself struggling to carry those plans from the planning desk into the shop and into the marketplace—expediting, persuading, coordinating. And then your workers join the Wax Workers International; and you—liberal, humanistic you—are confronted with a strike.

These are just some of the problems that arise as organizations grow. Many of them are frustrating and disturbing to managers, who wish that such problems would go away so they could concentrate on the job. But in large organizations such problems *are* the manager's job.

How Growth Changes Structure

As an organization grows, what kinds of change occur in each of the components that make it up? What changes in structure are most likely to occur? What changes in people? What changes in technology? What changes should management *try* to bring about?

One structural change that is likely to take place is in the shape of the hierarchy of authority. Organizations are at least three-dimensional. They can grow horizontally fat, and they can grow vertically tall. Typically, as they grow fat they also grow tall. As activities are enlarged, or new ones added, new levels in the hierarchy are also added, though at a slower rate. At first, as we add people to our production force, we need add only *additional* supervisors. We add supervisory fat to cope with the increased hourly worker fat. But if that expansion goes on, we will probably have to add a higher level of supervisors—regional supervisors, perhaps—to cope with our larger number of supervisors.

Why does that happen? One reason is to keep the "span of control" from getting too big. Supervisors find themselves overloaded with functions and subordinates. So we add levels simply to keep each set of superior-subordinate relationships reasonably small. For some jobs, where there is great variety in what subordinates do, we may need additional supervisors for every four or five additional employees—as in highly technical fields. But if most subordinates do about the same thing, one supervisor can usually supervise many workers.

There is another, less obvious, reason. People in organizations tend to stay a long time. And in the United States at least, we reward good and loyal people by *promoting* them. A continuously steepening hierarchy offers opportunities for promotion that a flat one doesn't. So we often make new levels in order to keep good people.

But a steepening hierarchy brings heavy costs. It lengthens vertical communication lines. Whether the structure grows flat or tall, some communication lines must be lengthened. But long *vertical* lines are especially likely to distort information important

The A, B, C's of Growth, and D through H as Well

C. Northcote Parkinson has become famous for his analyses of how managers manage to multiply the number of subordinates:

> ... We must picture a civil servant, called A, who finds himself overworked. Whether this overwork is real or imaginary is immaterial, but ... for this real or imagined overwork there are, broadly speaking, three remedies. He may resign; he may ask to halve the work with a colleague called B; he may demand the assistance of two subordinates, to be called C and D. There is probably no instance in history, however, of A choosing any but the third alternative.... By dividing the work into two categories, between C and D, he will have the merit of being the only man who comprehends them both.... When C complains in turn of being overworked (as he certainly will) A will, with the concurrence of C, advise the appointment of two assistants to help C. But he can then avert internal friction only by advising the appointment of two or more assistants to help D, whose position is much the same. With the recruitment of E, F, G and H, the promotion of A is now practically certain.
>
> Seven officials are now doing what one did before.
>
> For these seven make so much work for each other that all are fully occupied and A is actually working harder than ever. An incoming document may well come before each of them in turn. Official E decides that it falls within the province of F, who places a draft reply before C, who amends it drastically before consulting D, who asks G to deal with it. But G goes on leave at this point, handing the file over to H, who drafts a minute, which is signed by D and returned to C who revises his draft accordingly and lays the new version before A.... He corrects the English ... and finally produces the same reply he would have written if officials C to H had never been born.

—C. Northcote Parkinson, Parkinson's Law (Boston: Houghton Mifflin, 1957), pp. 2–13.

to decision making and also to generate frustration among people in the system.

The distortion effect of long lines of communication is illustrated in the whispered-story game children play in school. A tells B, B tells C, and so on to Z, whose interpretation of the original message is wildly distorted. It's bad enough in a class, where the students are peers. But when the lines run vertically up the hierarchy of authority, the problem gets even worse. People not only make errors, they withhold or distort information out of fear or ambition or embarrassment.

For most people, being close to the decision-makers reassures them that they have some control over their "fate." But as their distance from the center of action increases, so does their concern

A Volley of Vice-Presidents

As organizations grow, the load on the man at the top also grows. One compensatory device is the use of multiple executive vice-presidents:

> The advent of the practice of having multiple executive vice-presidents is of relatively recent occurrence, perhaps a decade or two ago. Despite its comparative newness, this organizational device has had wide acceptance among the companies studied. The application would be universal if the position of group vice-president may be considered as virtually synonymous [with executive vice-president]. . . .
>
> Although the more common use of the title of "executive vice-president" or "group vice-president" pertains to a line position with jurisdiction over two or more product divisions, these same designations are occasionally applied to a position with supervisory responsibility over a number of central staff departments. In both instances, the organizational purpose is the same: viz. to decrease the administrative load of the chief . . . executive officer and the chief operating officer or to reduce the span of control for the two top executives.

—From Top Management by P. E. Holden, C. A. Pedersen, and G. E. Germane, p. 61. ©1968 by McGraw-Hill Book Company. Used with permission of McGraw-Hill Book Company.

about not knowing what the decision-maker is up to. Hence they feel that they are losing control over their environment.

Organizations also tend to grow more *authoritarian* as they grow taller. Tall, multilevel hierarchies try to maintain control by developing elaborate bureaucratic rules governing all sorts of behavior. Standard forms, regularly scheduled procedures, and definitions of "proper" communication channels emerge. Deviation is punished.

Organizations that choose to grow horizontally rather than vertically are likely to put less stress on authority. In those organizations the frustration and distortion emerge not from long lines of communication or from authoritarian constraint but from the *inaccessibility* of upper-level people whose span of control has now become very large. Now busy signals become numerous. One can't get to his boss because the boss is too busy, rather than because the boss is too high up.

If big organizations are so hard to handle, why not keep the organization from growing big? Instead of one huge organization, why not develop a colony of little ones—perhaps through decentralization? Decentralization has been widely and effectively employed in American industry. Smaller units permit closer internal relationships, shorter lines of communication, swifter response times, a greater sense of local control, and so on. But decentralized units occasion some costs, too—like the need to replicate certain facilities at many locations, and the problem of coping with conflicts that arise among small, near-autonomous—but interdependent—empires.

Growth and Its Effects on People

What happens to the individual when the organization grows? That depends on (1) where in the organization he happens to sit, and (2) which way the organization grows, horizontally or vertically. If he sits in the upper reaches of the organization, growth usually means expanded responsibility, more hours on the job, and the challenge of planning and dealing with the growth process.

For the people at the bottom of the hierarchy, duties are likely to become more specialized, more compartmentalized. Though the individual may interact more frequently with other people, the range of his interactions will probably be less. And the areas in which his counsel is sought will be reduced.

At the intermediate levels, employees find themselves spending more time maintaining the organization, oiling the machine. The change that comes with growth is especially resented at these levels by the people with special skills, like engineers and researchers. As the organization grows, they are obliged to take on administrative duties (which really have to do with maintaining the group and the organization), with a consequent feeling of personal loss. As their distance from the "real" work increases, they take on what they typically regard as an inferior role—that of administrator.

Even at higher levels, growth generates discomfort. The president of a small company grows uncomfortable as his company expands. He knows less and less about what is going on. He is less and less closely involved in good hard work. He has less control over his organization's activities.

Indeed, with growth everybody in the organization is likely to feel a little less free to move around, a little less free to do the things he "really" wants to do. The president is hindered by the huge organizational albatross and waxes nostalgic about the old days. Middle managers find that there are more and more fires to put out. And the man on the assembly line feels more tightly chained to it than ever.

But organizational growth has a very important positive side for people too. It provides opportunities for promotion, for more frequent job changes, and for bigger responsibilities.

Would you rather work in a static organization or a growing one?

Growth and Technology

The effects of growth on the technology component are a little less clear. But as an organization grows, longer production runs and cost reduction through mechanization become feasible. One can buy large machines for specialized activities, or even design one's own in a form that would never have been possible when the organization was small. This search for economies of scale to accompany growth pushes organizations toward technological developments of all sorts: new production processes, new marketing methods, new technology for accounting and organizational control. And even more important, size permits the organization to devote resources to the search for such new technologies. The organization begins to set up research groups, planning groups, staff support groups. These groups work not on direct production goals but on indirect supporting activities. Advancing technology forces the organization to *differentiate* ever more sharply between planning people and doing people.

This differentiation in turn creates special problems of implementation. In the small organization, nobody worries very much about turning an idea into action, because the people involved in the action were also involved in the idea. But as the idea people become separated from the action people, the organization needs new mechanisms for moving things from the idea stage to the action stage, from the lab to the shop floor.

These new problems of implementation that arise with growth are largely psychological. People often have trouble accepting ideas thrust upon them by others. Staff people characteristically handle this problem by taking their ideas and plans upstairs, and leaving to top management the job of implementing them through subordinates. This is a dangerous practice, for it further fragments the organization, generates conflict between planners and doers, and leaves top managers in an unenviable middleman position.

Task and Growth

Growth usually calls for increased differentiation in tasks too. The organization begins to do many different things, not just one. It makes contact with more different parts of its environment. The larger tasks begin to split up into subtasks that become operation-

Is Growth Good?

Only large enterprises are able to sink the formidable sums of money required to develop basic new departures; a small corporation is rarely able to risk those large sums, perhaps enough to wreck the company if the gamble fails, on the success or failure of a major new project in such areas as electronics or chemicals, for example. . . . Bigness and research activity are largely synonymous whether in big business or in government.

—David E. Lilienthal, Big Business: A New Era (New York: Harper, 1952), pp. 70–72. Reprinted by permission of Harper & Row Publishers, Inc.

The largest producers within an industry are rarely the sources of major inventions. Of seven major innovations in the aluminum industry, one, the dip brazing process, was originated by a large producer of aluminum in cooperation with an aircraft company. Three were the work of independent inventors. In the petroleum industry, all seven basic major inventions underlying the refining process were the work of independent inventors. Of the 25 major innovations of the DuPont company between 1920 and 1950, ten originated in research conducted by the firm; the other 15 originated outside and were developed by DuPont laboratories. In a recent study . . . of 567 technical innovations named as "most important" by 121 firms in five manufacturing industries, 23 percent were found to be adopted from other companies.

—Reprinted from Behavioral Science, Volume 17, Number 1, 1972, by permission of James G. Miller, M.D., Ph.D., Editor.

The causes of the creative backwardness of bigness are endemic to the large corporations themselves. There should be nothing particularly surprising about their unreceptivity to new technologies that would destroy their existing capital investment; about their indifference to new ideas when their existing technology is operating satisfactorily; about their tendency to underestimate the demand for that which is unproved and untried; about their neglect of inventors whose contributions to the corporation's profits are at best infrequent; about the natural bent of corporate officials to direct research into channels which, to them, appear promising; about the difficulties inherent in trying to fit the creative temperament into a hierarchical organization; or about their cooperation with the military in manufacturing weapons systems that seek to combine the appearance of novelty with the use of proven technologies.

—John M. Blair, Economic Concentration (New York: Harcourt Brace Jovanovich, 1972), p. 251.

ally separate. Those who do long-range planning begin to live in a different world from those doing short-range production tasks. If we now ask individual managers to state the goals of their respective departments, some can give well-structured answers, specifying particular outputs or particular sales targets to be achieved by particular operational processes. Some emphasize deadlines. Others can give only vague, unstructured answers, like "developing new business."

In general, in the parts of an organization where tasks can be structured, where we can specify what we want and when we want it, we will find increasing structure with growth. When we know what we have to do, we can specify roles, schedules, responsibilities, and authority. Structured tasks also thereby lead to a search for people with specialized skills who can live in constraining and controlled environments. And structured tasks also move us toward new forms of technology that will improve task performance by replacing people or by supporting people with machines.

On the other hand, if tasks are unstructured and open-ended, we are wise to keep the organization relatively unstructured too. We shall have to live with flatter hierarchies, multiple communication channels, and loosely specified jobs. We shall have to rely less on direct authority and more on self-control by quasi-autonomous individuals and groups.

*The Differentiated Organization
and Its Integration Problems*

As organizations grow, then, they tend to widen the variety of tasks they do, and to set up new line departments and staff groups. Each of these subunits then designs its own structure-technology-people system. A new problem now begins to emerge: the articulation of these loosely related, differently designed units.

Let's assume that we have developed a strong R&D unit and have moved it out into the suburbs away from the helter-skelter of the plant. We have set up new rules, new salary systems, new management techniques. How do we connect the unit back into the parent system? How do we keep R&D from drifting away from the "real" problems of the company? How do we make sure we get *relevant* research—relevant to the needs of the production people and the sales people and the purchasing people? Of course, we could avoid that issue by fragmenting R&D; we could give production and engineering their own little research teams. But that would mean a costly fragmentation of our research effort, and it might lead to too much short-range development and too little long-range research.

So we are now stuck with several specialized groups, each designed according to its particular task. How can we bind them together?

Committees or committee-like mechanisms are one way of doing it. We set up part-time groups whose members, though primarily identified with subgroups, come together periodically to relate their problems to one another, to resolve common problems. This is a crude mechanism—time-consuming and frustrating. And yet it is one of the most effective mechanisms we know. Even companies that have consciously tried to kill the committee system have ended up resorting to it in one form or another. Face-to-face interaction between members of different groups, formal or informal, is still the best available means of binding a loose set of subgroups together.

Another device is to salt the organization with people who have a foot in two or more camps. This is a device we have probably exploited too little, in part because such people are scarce. But as management education directs itself toward "generalists" as well as specialists, it is beginning to create a population of general practitioners in management. They know enough about both organizational surgery *and* internal medicine to be able to translate and interpret the views of the surgeons for the internists and vice versa. Progressive companies already rotate executives for the same purpose, forcing them to identify with many different roles. University business schools are finally beginning to do the same kind of thing; they are paying less attention to developing specialized majors and more to training students with a wide range of skills and understandings.

In the last decade, other mechanisms have been explored for articulating differentiated parts of organizations, for keeping the lines of communication open, for generating ideas in one place and implementing them somewhere else. In technical industry, the so-called matrix organization provides each person with two group memberships—one in his special field, one on a cross-disciplinary project team.

The old hierarchical arrangement has turned out to be less useful than it once seemed. According to that arrangement, Department A comes up with a recommendation and passes it on to top management. Having approved it, top management simply orders Department B to carry it out. That method often led to hassles. The B people often "proved" that the A idea was unworkable. Top management often found itself enmeshed both in the technical details of the problem and in emotional conflict.

When managers discovered the effectiveness of participation, they tried to shift from authority to the mechanism of joint planning.

Now A and B people can come together to plan change jointly. But as technology marches ahead and as organizations increase in size and scope, even joint planning often becomes infeasible. How joint can joint planning be? What people should be involved? Should everybody get in on everything?

Probably the best answer is that the people who should be involved are the people who have to accept and implement the decisions. The more relevant the people who participate, the better. And "relevant" means people whose behavior will have to change if the new idea is instituted. This approach often leads to lengthy debate, security leaks, and a reduction of top management control. But it enhances the likelihood of true acceptance and conscientious implementation.

In the next few years we will learn much more about this problem of how to articulate the parts of the large organization. Clearly, the classic solution—that of direct authority—has become insufficient. It is now apparent that total reliance on widespread participation is not sufficient either.

The Inaccessible Executive and the Plural Executive

As the organizational pyramid grows, the number of people at the top rarely grows proportionately. So the pressures on the key men increase, and so does the problem of accessibility *to* the key men. How many decisions don't get made, or are wrongly made, or are made too late, because the sales vice-president couldn't reach the president who was off in Frankfurt? How many good young executives have quit because they couldn't get a senior man's attention? Because, literally or figuratively, the upper strata were full of busy signals?

An executive is still a person, a body, as well as a function. Bodies can only be in one place at one time, can talk on only one telephone at one time. Most inaccessible executives aren't hiding out; they're simply overloaded. This problem of the apparently indispensable executive can reach critical proportions in growing organizations, even in noncrisis situations.

The classical mechanism for dealing with this problem was the chain of command. In the colonel's absence, the major took over. In a battle, that works pretty well. But when time constraints are looser, in everyday executive life, the president doesn't usually say to the executive vice-president, "Make all the decisions while I am in Milwaukee." He says, "Call me if anything important happens." Indeed, the big customer won't talk to anyone but the president anyway. And the executive vice-president has his own problems. So

Organizational Growth

what is "important" is often decided by the president's secretary, who feels motherly toward him and doesn't want him overburdened. As a result, the "critical situation" the young manager feels needs immediate action gets tabled for a week—or two weeks—while he tries to fend off an angry supplier.

Many organizations, in response to increasing demands on executives, have tried to "pluralize" the executive, to convert *the* executive into a multiperson office. Again, this is a movement toward *groups* as devices for increasing accessibility, for permitting decisions to be taken even in the absence of individuals. Most organizations, however, have backed into this notion of the plural executive, maintaining traditional titles and job descriptions but adding the vague concept of the "president's office" or the "executive committee," or appointing executive vice-presidents.

Organizational growth is complicating the problem of accessibility a good deal faster than we are improving our techniques for dealing with it. One serious human consequence of growing organizational complexity is the increasingly harried, increasingly burdened upper-level manager. Time is rapidly becoming his scarcest resource.

Why Grow?

You may have noticed throughout this chapter two implicit, but contradictory, underlying themes: One is that growth is good, that organizations should try to grow. The other is that growth is bad, that it causes all kinds of trouble for the organization and for its people.

The first is an expansive, perhaps typically American assumption: that bigger is better; that fighting back against a competitor is the right response; that if new technology is available you have to use it; that growing organizations provide opportunities for people.

But the second says growth is painful, difficult, and materialistic, too. So you may well ask, "Why grow? Why not stay small and happy? Why respond to the competitor with competition? Why not just let him have that market? Why go technologically modern? Why plastic candles? Why not nice old-fashioned wax ones? Why a hectic, climbing career? Why not a peaceful, comfortable job?"

All good questions. And all extremely un-American!

Many organizations answer by saying that it's either grow or perish. Growth is essential to survival in a competitive, resource-scarce environment. Others confess that they simply share the avariciousness of Western man, regarding size as an index of value. Another answer is that man is a growth-needing animal, that whatever he has achieved soon becomes insufficient, be it knowledge or affection or power or things. And man's organizations are created in his image.

And finally, of course, one reason you may want your operation to grow is that you want to get rich.

Summary

As organizations grow, they change profoundly and often painfully. Communication lines grow longer. The hierarchy grows steeper or wider or both. The manager grows more distant from the bench and less knowledgeable about the work. He spends more and more of his time maintaining the organization rather than doing the work. Organizations become more formal as they grow; rule books become thicker; procedures become more specific. But organizations also usually become richer through growth. They carry more money to the bank every night.

In many cases the new problems of growth are "solved" by decentralizing — by breaking up into smaller units in order to regain the advantages of the small, informal, flexible, nonbureaucratic structure.

For people, organizational growth means different things depending on where one sits. At the top, overload and integration problems arise. People must interact more and make fewer individual decisions. At the bottom, life becomes more structured. And the middle manager, especially if he has a technical or managerial specialty, must do more and more "administration," which for him usually means record-keeping.

Technologically, organizations search for means of routinizing and controlling as they grow. They tend to separate the planners from the doers, thereby intensifying the problem of implementing plans.

With growth, tasks tend to multiply and differentiate, too, with more subgroups doing more unique tasks. Each group then tends to develop structures, tools, and people appropriate to its set of tasks. So the whole organization tends to become more and more a complex of differentiated little suborganizations, each designed to do its own thing. And the organization must somehow devise ways of integrating these diverse parts — through committees or matrix structures.

As organizations grow, the pyramid expands, still leaving just one man at the top. The job often becomes literally too big for one man. So we are now seeing many experiments in organizations of all sorts — governments, companies, armies — aimed at that problem; experiments in running organizations by committees, or by "troikas," or by other multiman units.

Recently, even in the growth-oriented United States, the value of organizational growth has begun to be seriously questioned. Some critics are raising broad social questions about the power of gigantic organizations in contemporary society. But smaller questions arise too: What are the costs of organizational growth to the people in the organization? They may get richer, but they may also find fewer opportunities to be themselves. Don't larger organizations become dehumanizingly rigid and inflexible? Young

Americans of the expansive entrepreneurial past did not seem to ask such questions nearly as persistently as they are asking them now.

Notes and References

William H. Starbuck, "Organizational Growth and Development," in James March, ed., *Handbook of Organizations* (Chicago: Rand McNally, 1965), discusses the nature of organizational growth and presents a rather sophisticated mathematical model of growth. See also William H. Starbuck, ed., *Organizational Growth and Development* (London: Penguin Books, 1971), for a useful collection of readings.

For a less mathematically based model of organizational growth, see Mason Haire, "Biological Models and Empirical Histories of the Growth of Organizations," in Mason Haire, ed., *Modern Organization Theory* (New York: John Wiley and Sons, 1959). Or Allan Filley and Robert House, *Managerial Process and Organizational Behavior* (Glenview, Ill.: Scott, Foresman, 1969), Chapter 18.

And for a broad treatment of the problems of growth in business organizations, look at Ronald Edwards and Harry Townsend, *Business Enterprise: Its Growth and Development* (London: Macmillan, 1958). This work describes British corporations, but the nature of organizational growth, its problems, and its solutions are similar for most modern organizations.

One of the most frequently suggested solutions to the ills caused by organizational growth is "differentiation and integration." For a brief discussion of the strategies of differentiation and integration, see Paul Lawrence and Jay Lorsch, "New Management Job: The Integrator," in *Harvard Business Review,* XLV, 6 (Nov.–Dec. 1967). We mentioned matrix organization as one way of improving integration. For a further discussion of methods of integrating organizational components, consult C. J. Middleton, "How to Set Up a Project Organization," in *Harvard Business Review,* XLV, 2 (Mar.–Apr. 1967); and John Mee, "Matrix Organization," in *Business Horizons,* VII, 2 (Summer 1964). These three articles are reprinted in David Hampton, ed., *Modern Management: Issues and Ideas* (Belmont, Calif.: Dickenson Publishing Co., 1969).

For a discussion of the "overworked" top executive, read Peter Drucker, *The Effective Executive* (New York: Harper & Row, 1967); or Philip Selznick, "Critical Decisions in Organization Development," in A. Etzioni, ed., *Complex Organizations: A Sociological Reader* (New York: Holt, Rinehart and Winston, 1961).

In response to the problems created by organizational growth and change, a new "field" has appeared: "organizational development" or "OD." The primary purpose of OD is to develop systematic strategies for organizational change and to map out predetermined routes for growth. To get a sense of this approach, see Richard Beckhard, *Organization Development:*

Strategies and Models (Reading, Mass.: Addison-Wesley, 1969). The entire Addison-Wesley series on Organization Development is informative, as is N. Margulies and A. Raia, *Organizational Development* (New York: McGraw-Hill, 1972).

Our approach to organizational growth has been primarily socio-psychological. For an economist's perspective on the growth phenomenon in organizations, see Edith Penrose, *The Theory of the Growth of the Firm* (New York: John Wiley and Sons, 1959).

PART 2

OUTSIDE THE ORGANIZATION

A NOTE ON DESIGN

Part 2 is about pressures. Pressures by the organization on the world around it, and vice versa. Pressures on the consumer by advertisers, and on advertisers by consumers; by big business on government, and by government on business; by managers on stockholders, and by stockholders and bankers on managers. But this section is also about love and marriage; about how organizations woo and cherish consumers and governments and bankers. And the other way around.

But how to order an examination of such difficult and complicated issues?

We finally answered our own question this way:

Let's walk around these complex love-hate, competitive-cooperative relationships and photograph them from different angles. There will be some redundancy, but maybe we can see them best that way. So we have taken six sets of pictures, from the six perspectives that seem to us to be most important.

The first chapter in Part 2 (Chapter 13) is made up of a pair of pictures, one shot from inside the organization looking out, and the other from outside looking in. They're wide-angle shots, showing broadly how the state of the inside of the organization affects its relationships with the world outside, and vice versa.

But we need several more detailed shots. Chapter 14, therefore, is more of a close-up on the critical front end of the organization's relationships with the world: the market and customer end. Chapter 15 moves to the other end, for a closer look at the relationships that provide money and resources for the organization. Then we move the camera off to the flanks to look in more detail at a third critical facet, the organization's relationships with government and the more special problem of its relationships in foreign lands.

In the last two chapters we switch to a movie camera. We look at the evolution of organizational strategies for survival in different kinds of worlds, and finally we run the camera on into a speculative picture of the future.

So Part 2 goes like this:
From inside looking out
From outside looking in
From the front end (where the customer is)
From the other end (where the banker is)
From the flanks (where government and the rest of us are)
And, with a movie camera, through time

13

The Organization and Its Environment: from the Inside Looking Out and from the Outside Looking In

This overview chapter, in which we consider both sides of the organization-environment relationship, is about changes that are generated primarily from inside the organization and those that are generated primarily from outside. We must use the adverb "primarily" because, as is always the case with relationships, one can never be quite sure about just how to separate cause from effect.

First, let's talk about the *kinds* of change in the relationship between the organization and its environment that may be generated by internal and external forces.

The relationship may change at the front end, where the products and markets are. For example, a company may decide to make new or modified products to offer to the world, or it may abandon old ones. Dupont comes out with Nylon. Syntex develops a birth-control pill. Boeing builds the 747. Or an industrial products company may introduce its first consumer product, bringing it into a new set of relationships. Or a company may open markets in a country where it has never sold its products before. All these change the organization's relationships with the world out there.

Organizations may change at the back end, too. A privately held company goes public, bringing it into a new relationship with large numbers of stockholders. Or it borrows from banks to finance expansion.

But there are other, more subtle ways in which an organization can modify or shift its relationships with the world. A company brings in a public relations firm to change its image. One company merges with, or devours, another.

The relationship can be changed by the actions of others as well as by the organization itself. A predatory investor buys up a controlling interest and invades the company. The government orders one of the company's products off the market. Ralph Nader goes after an automobile manufacturer for inadequate safety features. The Chilean government expropriates an oil company's holdings. Someone invents the steamboat, and the company that produces four-masted schooners decides to make buggy whips. Earthquakes, wars, irate students. . . .

Of course, the changes brought by external forces aren't always bad for a company. Government support of population-control programs helps the maker of contraceptives. Rising crime rates benefit the company that provides security service. The antilitter kick creates new kinds of companies to recycle cans and bottles.

Let's begin our overview by looking at the internal forces that bring about changes between the organization and the outside world.

INTERNAL SOURCES OF CHANGE

People Inside the Organization

An organization is changed by the unique, individual people who make it up. New people—and old ones too—steer the organization in new directions and make new demands upon it. The son who inherits the business from his father has new expectations, new needs, new relationships to society—new guilts too, and new values. If Father built the business from scratch, his satisfactions probably lay in making it grow. But for Junior, running the business may not be enough. While earning his degree from Yale, he may have been a young socialist or a budding politician or an art collector or a student radical. And just tending the store doesn't nourish him the way it nourished Dad. He may want to take the business into new relationships with society—perhaps by helping the underprivileged or by supporting social reform.

Or the organization may bring in more highly trained people— professionals or technicians—people who are not simply struggling for survival but who have higher aspirations than their predecessors. Such people force the organization into new relationships with the

> ### An Old View of the Importance of the Young View
>
> Back in the sixth century, St. Benedict prepared a manual for the management of the great, highly organized abbeys of his day. In *The Rule of St. Benedict* he wrote:
>
>> Chapter 3. *Of Calling the Brethren to Council.* As often as any important business has to be done in the monastery, let the abbot call together the whole community and himself set forth the matter. And, having heard the counsel of the brethren, let him think it over by himself and then do what he shall judge to be most expedient. Now the reason why we have said that all should be called to council, is that God often reveals what is better to the younger. Let the brethren give their advice with all deference and humility, nor venture to defend their opinions obstinately; but let the decision depend rather on the abbot's judgment, so that when he has decided what is the better course, all may obey. . . . But if the business to be done in the interests of the monastery be of lesser importance, let him use the advice of the seniors only.
>
> —St. Benedict, The Rule of St. Benedict, *translated by Abbot Justin McCann (Westminster, Md.: 1952), p. 25.*

outside world. Young people, new people, have always been major catalysts of change.

And yet, though bright young new people inside the organization can bring about change, they don't ordinarily bring it about very fast. They must earn their influence. And there's the rub. How does a young woman or a young man win the power to change an organization? One route is by conforming, by convincing the establishment that one is trustworthy and respectable, by submitting to a kind of brainwashing into the organizational culture. But brainwashing has a way of dulling one's appetite for change. The outcome, of course, is gradualism, incrementalism, in organizational change. It has been said that the curse of the poor is their poverty. The curse of new administrators is their newness. The administrator who can remain eager even when he is no longer new has the best chance of changing the organization.

Success and Failure

When a business organization succeeds, when it grows rich and fat and happy, we might expect it to sit back and do nothing. But that's not likely to be the case. It is precisely when an organization has accomplished what it wanted to that it starts searching for new things to do. When the little company has had a few successful years, it begins to look for other companies to gobble up, or new products to make, or new ventures to undertake. When the little college has succeeded in attracting students and raising money, it begins to think about setting up a graduate school.

The taste of success sends organizations out hunting. But so does the taste of failure. After the young businessman has built a successful company, he turns to diversification—or politics or social welfare. But if his company goes into a decline, he will also start searching for something new to ease the crisis.

There are differences, of course, in the *kinds* of change we make as a consequence of success and as a consequence of failure. Failure tends to turn our attention inward. We think about cutting expenses, selling the car, reassessing ourselves. The external effects of failure, if there are any, are likely to be heightened aggressiveness or hostility. We place the blame on the government or the community or our wife or our boss.

The same is true of organizations. When they're in trouble they tend first to tighten their belts, to reexamine themselves, and to reorganize. But when they are affluent and successful, they are more likely to leave their internal structure alone and to launch new ventures in the world around them. They may *add* to their structure, but they probably won't change what is already there.

Organizational Sensors

An organization that has good sensors, reliable means of contact with the outside world, is constantly responsive to its environment and swift to make adjustments in its relationship to that environment. The more sensitive the members of the organization are to the changing environment, the more likely they will be to insist that something be done about those new developments out there. The degree of internal pressure for change is thus partially dependent on how closely the organization's members are attuned to the outside world. Teen-agers in small towns change less from generation to generation than teen-agers in large cities. At least that was true before the advent of mass media.

How do organizations obtain information about what is going on in the world around them? They rely on specialized members who have special contacts with special segments of the environment. The salesman is in contact with customers; the researcher is in contact with other members of his professional discipline; the lawyer is alert to developments in the legal world; the financial expert keeps up with money markets.

Some organizations, however, are suspicious of "too much" interaction between their members and the outside world. A loyal railroad man doesn't become too deeply involved with aircraft companies or truckers. A loyal young bank executive doesn't spend much time with people in savings and loan associations. Even a loyal company researcher doesn't become *overly* active in the affairs of his professional society.

There is a fear that multiple membership will erode organizational loyalty. To be loyal means to some extent to be *local,* to have one's closest identification *within* the organization. For a member of the organization to become too cosmopolitan, even though his cosmopolitanism may make him a valuable source of information, may cost him the organization's trust.

Indeed, some organizations are actively defensive against members who produce too much disturbing information. Organizations get set in their ways. They don't want to be confronted with intelligence that disturbs their equilibrium. And so they set up defenses against external reality, especially if the reality requires them to change. For change is costly and disruptive. People in the leather business resist talk about plastics. Petroleum people convince themselves that the fuel cell will never work. Organizations, like other human groups, set up internal defenses against disquieting inputs.

Understandably, organization members who proffer such unwelcome information are not always loved. In the early days of computers the young manager who urged his superiors to try this new technology seldom found support within his organization. He was more often seen as an impractical visionary.

Professional people in organizations are particularly vulnerable to such rejection. In many colleges and professional groups, for example, cosmopolitanism among members is just as suspect as it is in industry. Sometimes the question is simply one of direction. A professional astronomer may be a cosmopolitan among astronomers; but if he gets too interested in religious phenomena, his fellow professionals may raise their eyebrows. And if an academic psychologist develops close relationships with industrialists, his colleagues may question his behavior.

Yet it is precisely by wandering abroad that organizations glean information that may be essential to their growth and survival. It is in this way that they identify new problems before they become critical and discover new opportunities before their competitors do. And in the process they may set up new and useful relationships with other groups.

The organization that is wise enough to welcome newness and strong enough to embrace change provides passports to certain of its members to wander afield. It sets up "outside" men as well as "inside" men. It delegates salesmen to search a particular segment of society—the customer segment—and it takes seriously the information they bring back, even if it is critical of the organization's products or services.

In recent years progressive organizations have encouraged their members to become more cosmopolitan. The researcher is urged to maintain regular contact with fellow professionals. The recruiter is urged to develop relationships with universities. The advertising and public relations people are supported in their wide-ranging exploration of the world at large. Indeed, if we want a quick, reliable indicator of an organization's propensity to change, we will do well to examine its attitudes toward cosmopolitanism among its members.

The problem is how to use cosmopolitanism in the service of the organization—how to ensure that the professor's Washington experience yields a net contribution to the student's education. Indeed, the university provides a good example of this dilemma. "Cosmopolitan" professors may cut classes and spend less time with students. That's bad. But "local," noncosmopolitan professors may have little firsthand experience with important contemporary social problems. And that's bad too. How can my classes be truly relevant if I am not myself involved in the issues I raise with my students? Is the isolated, aloof university appropriate to the time? True, students are more likely to receive the full attention of their professors in such a setting, but will the full attention of isolated scholars provide a relevant education? In some fields, it will. In most, it will not. Nor is the business organization that isolates itself from society free of this dilemma. Business organizations too must face the problem of continued relevance. Though cosmopolitanism may produce diminished organizational loyalty, that is a cost that organizations must accept. For the environment is changing fast, and failure to sense change may cost an organization its life.

The Basic Function of the Organization

If you were the president of a small bank that wasn't doing very well, you might conduct an intensive campaign to bring in new customers. If you were a large car manufacturer having trouble with your steel supply, you might think about getting your own steel mill.

The possible routes that are open to an organization for changing its relationships with society are largely dictated by its role, by its function in society. For some organizations, particularly service organizations like banks or post offices, the direction of change is likely to be *extensive*—that is, they decide to go on performing the same services, but they make those services available to more people, over a wider market. Organizations that are more focused in their relationships with others, organizations like hospitals and universities, usually try to change through *intensive* means—they bring the patient into the hospital so that the whole facility can work on him, or they build a campus and require the students to live there full time.

Still other organizations, like manufacturing companies, that create products through several successive stages, tend to change their relationships by reaching out and acquiring related organizations. They tie up suppliers with exclusive contracts, or they buy them out. They make special arrangements with their dealers, or they finance them, or they set up their own dealerships. They spread vertically to reduce their dependency on others.

EXTERNAL SOURCES OF CHANGE

Let's turn now to some of the external forces that change organizations. And let's start with a little history.

Time and History: Society Fights Back

The relationship between business organizations and society has changed radically over the last century. A hundred years ago robber barons roamed the land. The Goulds and the Carnegies and the Stanfords were building empires in a single-mindedly exploitative way, a way that is at least much rarer today. In a rough-and-tumble conquest of the environment, power group battled power group to the death. The prize was the vast wealth of a new land. But the nation thus deflowered did receive some partial compensation, in the form of railroads, steel mills, hotels, mines—and, indirectly, universities.

But society, in turn, showed strength and resilience of its own. Labor unions emerged to protect workers against exploitation, and to do a little exploiting themselves. Labor legislation was enacted: the trust-busting era began. Graduated income taxes were imposed. The voice of the conservationists began to be heard. In a whole variety of ways the free-swinging giants began to be at least partially hobbled by the Lilliputians.

Attitudes changed too. Society began to look upon these powerful entrepreneurs with a jaundiced eye. At first the giants didn't care whether or not the Lilliputians loved them. But as time passed they realized that they couldn't ignore public attitudes. Those attitudes were beginning to affect all sorts of things that affected them: the legal structure, the willingness of young people to join organizations, the readiness of consumers to buy, and the propensity of government to establish controls.

So the giants learned some new lessons. Through the 1920s and the 1930s they began to show some concern about the reactions of their host societies, not out of altruism, but because it was good business. They began to worry about those who were forever picking at them. They bought public opinion surveys to find out how their communities felt about them. And the giants decided that they ought to try at least to look like nice guys, good citizens. They put ads in magazines telling people how virtuous they really were. John D. Rockefeller hired a public relations consultant to convert his image from one of an old skinflint to a Santa Claus, handing out shiny new dimes to children.

After a while the giants developed a little more sophistication. Still motivated by self-interest, they began to think more seriously about their long-term relationship with society and about their dependence upon it. They began to live with the fact of mutual dependency between their own organizations and other social institutions. As they did so, they lost a little of their raw entrepreneurial flair. But they adapted; they professionalized; and they emerged from their exuberant youth into a kind of upright, conservative middle age.

Symbiosis between organizations and the society at large has marked the history of the United States. Robber barons exploit society, and society develops defenses and counterexploitative devices. The relationship moves slowly from piracy and rapine toward bargaining and salesmanship. The symbiotic relationship becomes more apparent to all parties, and everyone strives to find areas of agreement that will permit mutual survival.

As trade unions developed to counter the power of big business, they became as ruthless as their industrial counterparts, and their leaders apparently just as power-hungry. Fighting their way to power of their own, the unions learned to bargain with the giants, and the giants were obliged to bargain with them. As their bargaining practices became more institutionalized, each side became more and more like the other. It is no surprise that most leaders of labor unions are no longer seen primarily as fighting champions of the working class, nor even as radical riffraff, but rather as just another wing of the establishment, hardly distinguishable from the managers with whom they bargain.

The Early American Railroaders: Exploitation or Development?

Here is one of two historical views of early railroad development, from Keith Davis and Robert L. Blomstrom:

> When Leland Stanford, Collis P. Huntington, Mark Hopkins, and Charles Crocker formed the Pacific Associates, they had no specific intentions of building railroads. Rather, this was a speculative venture pure and simple, formed to take advantage of any opportunities that might arise. . . .
>
> The Associates now had a problem. Before they could collect any money from the government they had to build trackage, and they were embarrassingly short of money. . . . Fortunately, Stanford had recently been elected Governor of California, and he did not hesitate to use his office to further his own affairs. At his "suggestion" the city of Sacramento contributed $400,000, and Placer County generously provided another $500,000. . . . From a long-range point of view the Associates perceived the potential value of these securities and, as directors of the railroad, blandly issued to themselves some 33 million dollars in Central Pacific stock and 49 million dollars in bonds. But for profits in the short run, two relatively simple devices lay close at hand. First, thousands of acres of land belonging to the railroad were transferred to the partners as individuals. Much of this was choice suburban land which became extremely valuable as cities grew. To help in this department, Huntington convinced the government that the original land grant was insufficient and obtained an additional grant of 4,500,000 acres, much of which the partners appropriated to their own use. Second . . . a construction company was formed by the Associates to build the railroad. It was a simple matter for the Associates, who were directors of the railroad, to sign an exclusive construction contract with their own construction company. . . . The actual cost of the railroad, according to the Pacific Railroad Commission, was $27,217,000, but the government was charged in the neighborhood of 80 million dollars. . . .
>
> —From Business and Its Environment by Keith Davis and Robert L. Blomstrom, pp. 67, 68. ©1966 by McGraw-Hill Book Company. Used with permission of McGraw-Hill Book Company.

Social Protest

Protest from outside or inside an organization is often an effective agency of change: consumer protest, racial protest, ecological protest, political protest. Several techniques are available to the organization in responding to such protest. One—a weak one, though it is often used by strong organizations—is plain overpowering *suppression*.

But another historian, Daniel Boorstin, looks at early railroading in America in an entirely different light:

> Take, for example, the American mode of building railroads. In England railroads, as well as most canals, were built by private funds, unaided by government. In the United States, by contrast, every form of government—federal, state, county, and municipal—gave substantial help. . . .
>
> . . . The enterprising men who secured government subsidies, grants and loans for building canals and railroads out into risky unsettled territory should rank high among pioneer builders of the American West. They, like the fur trappers, the river boatmen, the organizers of westward-moving wagon trains, and the boosters of upstart cities had seized peculiarly American opportunities. . . .
>
> During the pioneer age of railroad building, in the decades before the Civil War, Americans showed great ingenuity in devising ways for governments to help them construct their long and expensive new lines. The muck-raking bias of the late 19th century has put these activities in a false perspective. Hardly a textbook of American history fails to reprint the map of "Federal Land Grants for the Construction of Railroads and Wagon Roads, 1823–71," which shows vast stretches, a sizable proportion of the area of western states, granted to railroad builders. The common innuendo is that there was something peculiarly corrupt about these proceedings, otherwise why would so much land have been given away? But railroad companies were only one class of beneficiaries of the nearly universal government assistance.
>
> The government promotion of railroads, and of the canals before them, is a parable of the distinctive roles of governments in America. Communities grew and population expanded as government-aided canals and railroads were built ahead of the traffic. The railroads themselves brought into being the population that used them. . . .

—*Daniel Boorstin*, The Americans: The National Experience, *pp. 250–52.*
©*1965 by Random House, Inc.*

A more subtle technique—one that large organizations have used for centuries—is *protest absorption.* An organization is faced with a group of protesters who demand that it change its ways. (Black students, for example, at a university; or liberal priests in the Church; or a group of players in professional baseball.) Instead of suppressing the protesters, the organization behaves like a great soft cushion, accepting the protest and absorbing the protesters, usually by making them responsible for implementing some modified version of the change they are demanding. If a group within the organization thinks we should market product X more vigorously, we put the leader of the group in charge of an experimental new marketing program—in Guatemala. If he fails, we never hear from him again. If he succeeds, the organization is better off for it. If an outside group attacks us, we hire its leaders.

University administrators have learned a great deal in recent years about how to coopt protesting groups into taking responsibility for change. In skillful hands, this technique for dealing with protest produces impressive results: (1) change occurs (but more slowly than it would through revolution); (2) the revolutionary leaders of the protest group—perhaps in one generation, perhaps in two—end up acting like bureaucrats; and (3) the protesting group and the changes it works are absorbed into the organization. Those things happen, of course, only if the changes demanded by the protesters turn out to be viable. If they turn out, by the tests of community acceptance and feasibility, not to be viable, then the protest group fades into oblivion.

This coopting process, we must remember, is not just a villainous ploy used by parent organizations to emasculate their dissident children. *The process changes the organization as well as the protesting group.* The coopted have also won a victory. Labor unions have become part of the American establishment, but it is a significantly different establishment because of them. And the university establishment, if it is sufficiently changed by the influence of its absorbed protesters, will also become a different establishment.

The absorption process, of course, lengthens communication lines so that the most extreme among the protesting groups—those that are unabsorbed or unabsorbable—eventually may become isolated from the rest of society. Even though they have caused important and useful changes, they may thus die in the process.

And sometimes, on the other side, certain parent organizations have chosen not to absorb the protesters and accept change, but to fight for the old way against the new. Others have been so rigid that they *could not* change. In the resulting wars, some companies, churches, and governments have won their battles and have pushed the protesters out. Others have perished.

Technology

With the advent of the computer (as with other new technologies), the relationships of some organizations with others have changed significantly. The computer can bring an organization into contact with new kinds of customers or suppliers, with all the new problems and challenges that accompany such a process. The computer has put banks into the credit-card business and food companies into the time-sharing business.

Such changes necessarily alter an organization's relationships with the world, often in unforeseen ways. New information-processing technology raises new problems of privacy, places new strains on telephone and other communication services, generates new alliances of organizations and other institutions with or against one another.

Certainly the explosion of technology has changed the university's relationship with other organizations and with society as a whole. The obscure little physics department of the years before the Second World War found itself advising presidents and negotiating with Soviet counterparts after the war. And later still, it found itself dealing with students politically incensed by the department's behavior. Engineering and business and medical schools have also been thrust by the technological explosion into consulting and research activities no one dreamed of forty years ago.

The general direction of change has been toward more complicated interactions and interrelationships and away from isolation. The old isolated, monastic model of the university has probably been permanently abandoned, and technological progress has been the primary cause.

Indeed, can you think of any organization that technology has *not* changed away from isolation and toward greater interaction with other parts of society? The Church? The professional football club? The fried-chicken stand? The Department of Agriculture? The Navajo Indians?

The Bright Side?

Some of the changes taking place in the relationships between the organization and society are painful and disruptive. Universities are torn by internal conflict in their effort to work out a new relationship with government, industry, and the community at large. Auto companies search for ways to shake off the consumerists nipping at their heels. Kodak goes through a great deal of stress as it is pressured simultaneously by a coalition of the local council of churches, black groups, and Saul Alinsky organizers.

At first organizations react defensively to such new kinds of flank attacks, and often their reactions are not very effective. But organizations, like the rest of us, learn. Initially they may learn only better defensive tactics, still regarding the new pressures only as minor irritants to their well-being.

But some organizations learn to perceive pressures very differently, not just as attacks and threats, but as new and potentially enriching experiences. An active life in a richly varied environment is, in the long run, likely to be just as healthy for the organization as it is for the individual. It helps to keep the organization alert, vital, adaptive, and relevant to the world in which it lives.

Summary

The relationship between an organization and the society in which it lives may be changed by both internal and external forces. First among the internal forces are the people *who make up the organization. Creative, innovative people push the organization toward new friends, new products, new relationships.*

Second, success *and* failure *induce change. When organizations are rich and affluent, they search for new challenges, new tasks. When they are in trouble, they search for ways to change themselves.*

Change depends on the quality of the organization's sensors and the level of cosmopolitanism among its members. An organization that is in regular contact with the marketplace, with other organizations, with colleges and universities, and with social agencies, is likely to modify its relationships with society quickly and often. An organization that has few contacts with the world, that discourages its people from communicating with others, and that tries to insulate its members from outside influences will have a poor sense of what is happening around it and hence will resist change.

The direction of change *depends on the organization's general function. Banks may change by establishing new relationships over a wide sector. Hospitals may intensify existing relationships. Manufacturers may incorporate the groups they are related to.*

Among the external forces that lead to change are countervailing responses to the organization's own behavior, pressures arising from new technology, and the demands of protest groups seeking their own ends.

Historically, countervailing forces arose in reaction to unbridled and often unprincipled exploitation of both people and the physical environment by expanding organizations. The result was the development of legal controls, trade unionism, and a more suspicious public.

Technology has modified external relationships in a host of ways, generally causing closer relationships among government, knowledge-producing universities, industry, and many other institutions in society.

Protest groups commonly spring up in an effort to control expansionist organizations, or to limit the concentration of organizational power, or simply as a means by which minorities can develop enough power to enter the competitive arena in search of their own ends. Organizational responses to such protest groups may range from hostile suppression, through compromise, to the absorption of protesters into the organization.

Notes and References

For a variety of views on the role of people as agents of organizational change, see: G. Dalton, P. Lawrence, and L. Greiner, *Organizational Change and Development* (Homewood, Ill.: Irwin-Dorsey, 1970); D. McClelland and D. Winter, *Motivating Economic Achievement* (New York: Free Press, 1969); E. Ginzberg and E. Reilly, *Effecting Change in Large Organizations* (New York: Columbia University Press, 1957).

For some thoughtful discussions of how organizations can be changed, see: R. Lippit, J. Watson, and B. Westley, *The Dynamics of Planned Change* (New York: Harcourt Brace Jovanovich, 1958); E. H. Schein, *Process Consultation* (Reading, Mass.: Addison-Wesley, 1969).

On the effects of success and failure, see J. G. March and H. A. Simon, *Organizations* (New York: John Wiley and Sons, 1958). See also the symposium, "The Innovating Organization," in W. G. Bennis, ed., *American Bureaucracy* (New Brunswick, N.J.: Transaction Books, Aldine, 1970).

On the nature of and reasons for organizational growth, consult William H. Starbuck, *Organizational Growth and Development* (London: Penguin Books, 1971).

For a treatment of organizational sense organs, see: Harold L. Wilensky, *Organizational Intelligence — Knowledge and Policy in Government and Industry* (New York: Basic Books, 1967); H. Leavitt, L. Pinfield, and E. Webb, eds., *Organization-Environment Relations in the Future* (New York: Praeger, forthcoming), especially the paper by Pinfield, Watzke, and Webb, "Confederacies and Brokers: Mediators between Organizations and Their Environments."

A good discussion of "cosmopolitanism" among organization members is A. Gouldner, "Cosmopolitans and Locals," *Administrative Science Quarterly* (Dec. 1957 and Mar. 1958).

Much of our material on how particular kinds of organizations tend to grow is based on J. D. Thompson, *Organizations in Action: Social Science Bases of Administrative Theory* (New York: McGraw-Hill, 1967).

For some historical overviews of the organization-environment relationship, look at K. Davis and R. Bloustein, *Business and Its Environment* (New York: McGraw-Hill, 1966).

A broader history that includes much material on business development in early America is D. J. Boorstin, *The Americans: The National Experience* (New York: Vintage Books, 1965).

For more specific historic material on some of the early reactions to organizational exploitation, dig out Upton Sinclair, *The Jungle* (New York: Harper, 1951). This book, first published in 1906, is one of several books by social reformers that led to significant changes in society's image of the corporation.

For the union side of the struggle against the giants, one classic statement is C. Golden and H. J. Ruttenberg, *The Dynamics of Industrial Democracy* (New York: Harper, 1942).

On social protest, and for some good illustrations of "protest absorption" in the church and the military, see R. Leeds, "Protest Absorption," in W. W. Cooper *et al.*, eds., *New Perspectives in Organization Research* (New York: John Wiley and Sons, 1964).

In Tom Wolfe's *Radical Chic and Mau-Mauing the Flak Catchers* (New York: Bantam, 1971), the essay on "Mau-Mauing" and "Flak-Catching" provides an intriguing description of some tactics used by protest groups and some countertactics of absorption and deflection used by the establishment.

On technology and social change, a useful book is E. Ginzberg, ed., *Technology and Social Change* (New York: Columbia University Press, 1964).

A more recent treatment is A. Toffler, *Future Shock* (New York: Random House, 1970).

On the knowledge explosion and organizational change, see Peter Drucker, *The Age of Discontinuity* (New York: Harper & Row, 1968).

14

Customers, Clients, Consumers, Constituents: The Restless Love Life of the Organization

We tend these days to picture consumers the way some mothers picture their teen-age daughters—as helpless innocents, powerless against the wiles of big, muscular organizations. The image has a good deal of validity, but it obscures a more fundamental reality. More readily than anyone else inside or outside organizations, customers can make or break them.

The customer isn't always right, but he can never be disregarded. Right or wrong, his attitudes and decisions matter. If enough customers like what they are offered, businesses flourish; but if enough gang up in dissatisfaction, businesses must redesign their products, change their operating style, and sometimes sacrifice their president and sales manager to regain their customers' love. Sometimes the crisis comes quickly, as with small garment factories that make the wrong guess about women's ideas on skirt length. Sometimes it comes more slowly, as with the gradual switch of automobile buyers from Detroit's products to smaller, cheaper, imported cars. Sometimes customers force business to offer better or safer products, as with shoppers' complaints about wilted produce in supermarkets; and sometimes customers curtail progress, as with mothers unwilling to pay the high price of flame-retardant fabrics for their children's pajamas. Swift or gradual, sensible or foolish, though, the wants of customers are a powerful force.

Because customers matter so much, organizations work hard

to find them, hold them, and shape them as lifelong friends. Companies tinker with the products or services they offer. They advertise and promote. They may shift personnel around, or deal on prices and take credit risks. They tease, plead, entertain, educate, and make extravagant promises. Sometimes they threaten, lie, or cheat. Much of the time it's a pleasant game, like more romantic kinds of wooing, and both parties enjoy it; but it can also become a deceptive and vicious game. Dependency sometimes breeds desperation, and organizations with genuine fears about their own survival can go after customers' dollars and loyalties in very ignoble ways.

The name of the game is marketing. This chapter tries to help you understand why it is so central to the existence of organizations and how it is played. The game is associated in most people's minds with business, but it is played in other places too. How many of the advertisements you have read recently, how many pieces of the "junk mail" you have received, were aimed at winning your interest in churches, political organizations, charities, or even competing consumer-action groups? The same people who persuaded companies to backtrack on midi fashions and automobile tail fins have also helped persuade the Pope to change his mind about eating meat on Fridays, college administrators to relax rules against coeducational dormitories, and congressmen to vote more cautiously on big foreign-aid appropriations. For "customer," read "client"—or constituent, consumer, fan, parishioner, subject, voter, patron, prospect, or any of a dozen other substitute labels.

Marketing is as important a game for schools, churches, governments, and opera companies as it is for toothpaste manufacturers.

The Customer as Final Authority

Never underestimate the power of the customer. Think about a professional football team. If the present owners can't continue to meet the star quarterback's salary demands, other teams will be quite willing to pick him up—so long as they know that fans will scramble to buy tickets to see the star play. The team can even prosper without an expensive quarterback—but only so long as the fans stay loyal. Yet neither the wealthiest of owners nor the best of quarterbacks can keep the team in business if football's paying customers decide that soccer is a more interesting game.

General Motors could withstand isolated criticisms of the Corvair, but they could not keep the car in production when frightened and skeptical customers stopped buying it. IBM has more than once announced computers intended for special limited uses, only to have customer demand force the company to add hardware

> **Who's to Blame?**
>
> Aren't consumers—you and I—a little like the young lady from Kent?
>
> > There was a young lady from Kent
> > Who said that she knew what it meant
> > When men took her to dine
> > Gave her cocktails and wine
> > She knew what it meant—but she went.
>
> —From James A. Perkins, The University in Transition, p. 26. ©1966 by Princeton University Press.

features or programing aids that it did not want to spend money to design.

Take a really extreme example: Adolf Hitler and the Nazi government of Germany. As painful as it may be to remember, they achieved power with a great deal of support and encouragement from German citizens. Even some of Hitler's early moves against the Jewish population and against other countries in Europe were applauded by voters who simply saw Hitler righting old grievances and making Germany strong again.

It took many years before people recognized the enormity of Hitler's actions and ambitions and resolved to fight back. Europeans who did not want to be embraced as subjects of the Third Reich finally led a bloody and determined kind of customer resistance to destroy the Nazis. The battle was a long time building, but it was fought and won by customers who rejected the Third Reich as a government and a social order.

Customers don't always look as powerful as they can be. They often dissipate their influence because they don't agree among themselves or because they don't care. Divided, apathetic feelings can keep low-quality breakfast cereals on grocers' shelves and send weak candidates to Congress. Advocates of low-lead gasoline cannot persuade oil companies to stock it if their neighbors won't demand it at the service station.

Customers also tend to give away much of their potential power. They don't know what they want, and they wait passively for organizations to make proposals. They *expect* drug companies to remind them of ailments they may fall victim to. They expect blenders of canned cocktail mixes to suggest new taste sensations, travel agents to dramatize the pleasures of new resorts, colleges to suggest reasons for buying education, and government agencies to lay out attractive arguments for continuing to supply arms to totalitarian governments. Sometimes, when it appears that an organization is riding roughshod over customers' preferences, it's not really rape at all. It's invited seduction.

At other times we conclude that customers are being victimized only because we disagree with their decisions. We want safer cars, but other people still want horsepower, sex appeal, and the lowest possible monthly payments. Ralph Nader didn't make headway simply by forcing companies to pay more attention to what customers were asking for. He won by playing the same game that companies play. He stimulated people to rethink what they wanted from automobile manufacturers and got them to join with him in collective pressures for new kinds of designs and services.

Indifference, disunity, indecisiveness, and willingness to let organizations "advise" may cut the day-to-day influence of customers, but those characteristics should not be confused with fundamental lack of power. The organization has many ways of making a deal, but in the final analysis it is the customers who cut the cards.

The Organization's Stake in Persuading Customers

The most fundamental motive behind the organization's efforts to influence customers is its ultimate dependence on them for survival. But other motives matter too.

One thing an organization wants to do is simply to gain the attention of prospective clients—to let them know that the organization exists. Examples are all around us: service-station signs on hundred-foot stilts to make them visible from an expressway; scores of unsolicited college flyers mailed to top-ranking high-school students; gaudy displays on crowded supermarket shelves; sedate notices in Saturday's newspaper about Sunday morning church schedules; news releases and public relations handouts about organizations and their products; door-to-door canvassing by charitable organizations. Many organizations fail because they never win recognition for their potential for service.

Beyond the need for basic recognition is the urge to build links to particular kinds of customers. Tiffany's needs wealthy clients to maintain its distinctive image. MacDonald's builds its business around quick hamburgers for the whole family. Civil-rights organizations struggle to keep a balance between supporters in the black community and the white community. Democratic party candidates find it difficult to win office without labor union support, and many Republicans are uncomfortable running with it.

Often the attempt to develop a distinctive clientele reflects a carefully thought-out strategy to win distinctiveness in a world where uniqueness helps assure survival. Sometimes, though, the chosen image turns out to be inconsistent with the organization's long-run interests. A mediocre college, for example, may try to attract an academically elite student body that it doesn't have the funds or the reputation to attract. Sophisticated organizations today also spend a lot of energy asking—in the light of goals, resources, and the competitive situation—which customers they really want to go after. The right kind of customers may be more important than product mix or employee selection in establishing a stable identity and a positive reputation for the organization.

But there are other motives too. Much of any organization's concern with customers is aimed at reducing uncertainty, at assuring security for employees and financial backers, and at stabilizing internal operations. Most organizations find that the demand for any given line of products or services, left to itself, waxes and wanes. So while Sam's Plumbing Service may try to extend its activities geographically or may ask the union to help keep some other fellow from invading his territory, the makers of Toreador Potato Chips do something different. They buy into a jewelry company so that they will have income during the Christmas season, when the demand for picnic foods is light. Even organizations that claim to have a high tolerance for risk and change usually try to minimize the chances for unpleasant surprises.

Surprises, or even well-predicted fluctuations in customer demand, can be costly, particularly if they strain financial resources, involve rapid expansion or contraction of staff, or leave expensive plants or equipment idle. Department stores and electric power companies build their facilities to handle demand when it is at a peak, but they must try all sorts of gambits to seduce customers to use those facilities during off-peak periods. Oil companies have to think about demand for services twenty years ahead when they plan drilling, transshipment, and refining operations for a major new area of exploration, like the North Sea or North Slope of Alaska. Ford would have had a success with the Edsel if the customers whose carefully measured preferences settled the original design concept had not changed their attitudes during the three years it took to bring the car to market.

Few things are envied in the world of organizations more than the organization that has found itself a large, stable clientele. It's fine if the customers are loyal and happy, but it's sufficient that they simply keep coming. The motel owner looks forward to hanging out the "no vacancy" sign every night. Sometimes he gets there by being the most hospitable host in town, sometimes by politicking to make sure that his is the only motel in town.

Organizations also woo customers in order to gain acceptance for innovation. Once a company has saturated the country with hula hoops, it needs to have consumers accept another product just so it can stay in business. Sometimes the innovation comes from the restless creativity of the organization, or, more properly, of individuals within it—from those who believed deeply in electrostatic copying machines or in TV dinners and who worked long and hard to persuade the world that these were just the products it needed.

Social-action groups, with their dynamic sense of mission and urgency, do much the same thing. Against great odds, they seek converts to ecology, abortion reform, gay liberation, or the preservation of Grand Central Terminal.

There is yet another motive for organizational interest in customers. For some organizations it really matters at a very personal level that they make customers happy.

Consider the small, family-owned restaurant or the volunteer agency devoted to helping drug addicts, organizations that derive direct and significant psychic rewards from satisfying their customers' needs. One problem, of course, is that as organizations grow larger, the personal, face-to-face relationship gives way to the distant and impersonal one. The maintenance man on a railroad may do indifferent work because no one he sees seems to care. It's the conductor who gets the praise if things go well and takes the abuse if they don't.

The customer, then, is both mealticket and companion. He is wooed and manipulated because his support is essential to the prosperity and even the survival of the organization. He is also courted, though, because his loyalty lays the groundwork for internal stability, his enthusiasm and curiosity support innovation, and his satisfied responses make the effort of trying to serve him seem worthwhile.

The American Way of Marketing

But there's the other side of the coin. Those big muscular organizations really are trying to seduce your daughter, and they work hard at it.

That determination has encouraged aggressive marketing efforts by organizations from the earliest days of barter and trade. But never before has there been anything like the marketing explosion of the last few decades. Our system encourages enterprising suppliers of goods and services to go looking for clients. Customers—many of them affluent and highly educated—expect to be able to choose among many alternatives. Tradition and technology have created a bewildering variety of channels by which organizations can send their messages to customers.

Marketing Is Not a New Phenomenon

Marketing may be newly conceived as a profession, but it has been alive and well for centuries, even in ancient Greece. Herondas describes the sales pitch of Kerdo, a shoemaker, to some ladies of Greece back in the third century B.C.:

> Look first at this, Metro, this sole, is it not adjusted like the most perfect of soles? Look you also, women, at the heel piece; see how it is held down and how well it is joined to the straps; yet, no part is better than another; all are perfect. And color!—may the Goddess give you every joy of life!—you could find nothing to equal it. The color! Neither saffron nor wax glow like this! Three minae, for the leather, went to Kandas from Kerdo, who made these. And this other color! It was not cheaper. I swear by all that is sacred and venerable, woman, in truth held and maintained—with no more falsehood than a pair of scales—and, if not, may Kerdo know life and pleasure no more!—this almost drove me bankrupt! . . .

And then as he fits a shoe to a woman who is complaining about the price:

> . . . I will give them to you for three darics, those, or these others as you choose. This is because of Metro and for the sake of her lips and yours. . . . For you have, not a tongue, but rather a sieve of voluptuousness. Ah! that one dwells close to the Gods for whom, night and day, you open your lips!
> Give me your foot; slip it into the shoe. Good. There is nothing to be added or cut off. All is beautifully adjusted to beauty. You might say that Athene herself made these.

—*Translated by M. S. Buck, reprinted in Edward C. Bursk et al., The World of Business, pp. 514–17. ©1962 by Simon and Schuster, Inc.*

We're not speaking only about advertising or face-to-face selling but about a much more comprehensive set of activities—design, promotion, pricing, distribution, education, service, public relations, and strategies for competitive infighting.

However strongly an organization may protest its belief in the virtues of free and open competition, all this activity is designed to limit that competition in ways that will give the organization a special advantage. The organization wants to make the customer need it as much as it needs him. The organization would really like, in many cases, to achieve some kind of monopoly position—to be sure of the customer's business, to be able to keep prices at a profitable level, and to be immune to his minor gripes. Companies can—and do—try to invent better mousetraps, though they're often satisfied if they can just create a different mousetrap, if they can call attention to its distinctiveness ("new improved SLAP-TRAP—sure catches, easy disposals"), and better yet if they can protect the concept or the name or the manufacturing process by patent. Then, if they can make you want their mousetrap by advertising or by giving you a free sample to use, they can be sure you won't buy it from anyone else.

The advertising and promotion are important. You just can't know how desperately you need five or six mousetraps. An article planted in one of your favorite magazines tells you how rapidly the mouse population is growing and what terrible harm mice do. Displays in your local hardware or grocery store help keep mice on your mind and help push you toward both the decision to buy and the choice of traps. A really good advertisement or package design for SLAP-TRAP should make you walk past seven other varieties at the store and pay a fifty-cent premium to get the real thing.

Advertising and promotion work, though, only if the product is at the store when you go looking for it. One of the least-known but most challenging parts of the marketing game is "distribution." As thousands of SLAP-TRAPs an hour pour off the assembly lines in Keokuk, somebody has to decide where to ship them. Eventually, through a set of decisions that may involve several organizations—manufacturer, jobber or wholesaler, retail chain, and local store—a display of ten SLAP-TRAPs gets set up next to the cheese counter, or a stack of a hundred is arranged near the checkout counter in a San Diego grocery store. It's a very intricate business, getting everything to fall into line and getting the traps to San Diego, where the demand is, rather than to Erie, where it isn't.

Usually there are conflicts and disagreements along the way. Suppose as the manufacturer you want a particular chain of stores to stock SLAP-TRAPs. It may turn out that the wholesaler you've been using for some of the other products you make already handles another line of traps. You may have to adjust your price to make handling SLAP-TRAPs more profitable for him; or you may, if there are other wholesalers you can use, threaten to take all the rest of your business away unless he goes along with you on SLAP-TRAPs. The wholesaler may also have to juggle prices or twist arms to get retailers to go along, right down to walking through some of the retail outlets and arguing that three square feet of display space on a good aisle for SLAP-TRAPs will be worth more to the retailer's sales and profits than three square feet for chewing gum.

Design, advertising, promotion, and distribution are intellectually challenging games, and decisions on how to play them are backed by increasingly sophisticated kinds of research. Advertisers fund in-depth studies of the human psyche to try to understand how and why people make decisions to buy. Companies interested in knowing

If This Book Doesn't Meet Your Needs . . .

Truth in advertising is not a new problem, and may not even be as severe a problem now as it used to be.

> **Treat Colic, Cramps and Dysentery at Once**
>
> Only a little delay and it may run into cholera-morbus, other ailments, and become a menace to life. Take at once a dose internally, as directed, of
>
> **DILL'S Balm of Life**
>
> (For Internal and External Use)
>
> You'll see its results at once. Your druggist or dealer in medicine has it. Also invaluable as a liniment for rheumatism, neuralgia, lumbago, swelling of all sorts, sprains, soreness. Full directions with bottle.
>
> Made by the Dill Co., Norristown, Pa. Also manufacturers of those reliable
>
> **Dill's Liver Pills**
> **Dill's Cough Syrup**
> **Dill's Worm Syrup**
> **Dill's Kidney Pills**
>
> For sale by good druggists and dealers in medicine.
>
> *The kind mother always kept.*

the market for a product, and political parties interested in knowing the appeal of a candidate, have force-fed the development of polling and survey techniques, techniques that have led to increasingly reliable predictions of how masses of people or special groups of people will respond to what is offered them. Economists have developed an extensive literature on the impact of changing prices and market structures. Systems analysts have built complicated computer models of distribution networks so that a factory in Keokuk has the surest chance of getting the right number of SLAP-TRAPs to San Diego and Erie without running out of stock or leaving excessive inventories on the shelf.

To the extent that these games are treated as an intellectual challenge, they're healthier than some of the old ways of playing. Though rough tactics still are used today, it was much more common in years past for companies to try to protect their market by collusion or by strong-arm methods. In those days I might have agreed to sell SLAP-TRAPs only in my specific territory, and you and the others would agree to stay out of that territory. If a wagonful of competing traps appeared in my territory, I might arrange for that wagon to have an accident. Bad as it may be to mislead customers, deception does seem just a shade better than physical attacks on competitors.

The drive toward a monopoly position and toward absolute customer loyalty doesn't always make sense. Some products are almost impossible to make distinctive. (Do you ever think of brands when you buy nails, string, notebook paper, shoelaces?) Other products (like soap and cigarettes) are so heavily challenged by competition that only a limited amount of brand loyalty can ever be achieved. In still other cases (like restaurant meals or overseas travel) the customer can be expected deliberately to seek variety and to buy from many sources, or (as with encyclopedias or hair transplants) he can be expected to make only one purchase in a lifetime.

In these last cases, the game of marketing becomes one of forever generating a fresh flow of customers. The simplest way is just to knock on doors looking for new prospects, as the encyclopedia salesman does. But pretty soon you have covered the whole town and you must move on, from local to regional or national or international markets—if there aren't too many other local organizations trying the same strategy. Increasingly in recent years, though, companies have tried another route: diversification into new products and services. The soap manufacturer buys a cake-mix company and a paper-products company. The brewery starts to bottle soft drinks. The aircraft manufacturer tries to market aluminum ladders and canoes. The conservation society starts publishing books and selling hiking tours. By diversifying, Studebaker survives even though it is no longer making automobiles, and the National Foundation persists even though the fight against infantile paralysis was won many years ago.

Some organizations find the continuing fight for customer loyalty and the continuing effort to diversify a rather exhausting process. So they may decide to take a rest by getting cozy with a single customer. The weapons specialist does all his business with the Department of Defense, or the tentmaker becomes the exclusive supplier to Sears Roebuck. They solve the marketing problem by eliminating it. Or do they?

Building a cozy relationship with a single customer is comfortable only so long as that customer stays interested. If Uncle Sam cuts the defense budget or Sears decides it suddenly prefers somebody else's tents, you're out of luck.

None of the marketing strategies we have discussed is foolproof. If the aim of your strategy is to win distinctiveness and a monopoly position, the more successful you become, the more you attract imitators, or, failing that, the more you become subject to government challenge and regulation. For the rules of our competitive system outlaw monopoly primarily because, while it offers security and profits to suppliers of goods and services, it also offers too many opportunities to abuse customers. Under present law and court rulings, the company that achieves a near-monopoly position because it produces genuinely superior products is just as illegal as the one that achieves dominance through chicanery. Monopoly power is considered socially dangerous because it can too easily be turned, by the organization's choice, toward bad instead of good ends.

Diversification minimizes the organization's need to press for a monopoly position, but in many cases it also tears the organization apart. The same equipment and processes may be used to build airplanes and aluminum canoes, but building and sustaining markets for them requires very different processes. Often hidden costs and problems emerge because a new product requires unforeseen new images or new skills. Even where diversification succeeds, people may know your products but not the company, so that there will be little transfer of loyalty from one product to the next.

So there ain't no free lunch. Successful distinctiveness gives one dominance, but it also stimulates competition; and dominance brings regulation. Diversification brings in new customers, but it also begets diffuseness and unmanageable commitments. Marriage to one customer provides apparent peace and security, but it also creates vulnerability to sudden divorce.

Does He Really Love Me?

Notice in what we've said so far that no matter what the marketer's posture, no matter how good his product or service, his ultimate purpose is to sell us something at a profit to himself. Even in nonprofit settings, the teacher or the minister is trying to please us partly because he wants his job and his organization to survive. So as customers we can never quite feel safe in the relationship, never fully reassured that the love that is professed is real.

And so we're right to be suspicious. The man who regards us as a prospective customer is out to use us for his own ends. He is trying to score. Though he may treat us in the most personal terms, he is

> ### Caveat Emptor
>
> The world is not the way they tell you it is.
>
> Unconsciously we know this because we have all been immunized by growing up in the United States. The little girl watching television asks will she really get the part in the spring play if she uses Listerine, and her good mother says no, darling, that is just the commercial. It is not long before the moppets figure out the parents have commercials of their own—commercials to keep one quiet, commercials to get one to eat, and so on. But parents—indeed all of us—are in turn being given a whole variety of commercials that do not seem to be commercials. Silver is in short supply, and the Treasury is running out and begins to fear a run. So the Treasury tells the *New York Times* that, what with one thing and another, there is enough silver for twenty years. Those who listened to the commercial sat quietly, expecting to get the part in the spring play, and the cynics went and ran all the silver out of the Treasury and the price went through the roof.
>
> — *From "Adam Smith,"* The Money Game, *p. 3. ©1967 by Random House, Inc.*

really thinking in impersonal ways. He may even happily abandon us after he has won us, particularly if our support isn't helping him or if he sees a better prospect elsewhere. The profit-oriented organization especially will not—cannot—behave altruistically in its relationships with customers.

Sometimes he even hangs out a sign to warn us: *Caveat emptor,* let the buyer beware!

Putting the Shoe on the Other Foot: Caveat Vendor!

Customers have many ways of protecting their interests, and sometimes they get help they haven't asked for from the government or from self-appointed protectors of their welfare.

Sometimes in unity they have found strength. For example, to counter IBM's dominance in the computer industry, and to make the design of machines and programing systems fit user needs better, customers organized and became vociferous questioners and critics of IBM's efforts. In the years immediately following the introduction of System 360, when IBM found it hard to deliver many of the features they had promised, it was a sobering experience for responsible executives to answer invitations to talk over the problems at a convention of one of the big user groups like SHARE or GUIDE.

In many instances dissatisfied customers have teamed together to show their disapproval through boycotts or through calls for government intervention. Government's role as a pressure point is especially important. Government can set standards for the quality of food products or the labeling of tires to ensure a reasonable level of product quality. It can release its own test results on the brands it buys. It can use its antitrust powers to break up near-monopoly situations and to force dominant organizations to a stronger test of competition. The United States government believed, for example, that in the long run customers would have more choice and lower prices in film processing if it stopped Eastman Kodak from pricing a roll of film and its developing as a single package.

The government can also create agencies like the Federal Communications Commission and the Civil Aeronautics Board to keep an eye on a wide range of decisions within a single industry. The argument for such supervision is that the combination of consumer power and competitive forces is insufficient to keep an industry committed to serving the public rather than itself.

Where consumer power, competition, and government supervision all seem inadequate, individuals can step in. A single aroused and persistent individual can have a surprising effect: a reporter evaluating the shady practices of travel agents, a young government lawyer determined to improve automobile safety, a citizen incensed over the continued advertising of cigarettes on television after they were branded a major health hazard. Individual efforts have spawned many consumer-protection organizations, some of which are as busy trying to influence consumers as are the companies they attack.

So one way to go after the company is to persuade congressmen to go after the government to go after the company.

The Morality of Marketing

Because the men who market often seem to hold an unfair advantage, some people would have us cut back on advertising, promotion, packaging, expensive distribution networks, and the other gimmicks that Madison Avenue believes have made America great. Modern marketing methods, this argument runs, have made us want things we don't really need or that may even hurt us: men's colognes, cigarettes, weed-free lawns, and ineffectual medicines. But those same methods, of course, have helped us want Sesame Street, population control, and cleaner cities. They have also stirred demand for color television, snowmobiles, and stereo music systems—things that some people regard as curses but others regard as blessings. The kind of "open season" we permit allows for everyone to use almost every means at his disposal to influence everyone else. The system can be used to elevate as well as degrade human tastes. Restrictions imposed for the good of the public may not square with what people at large view as their own welfare.

Why not insist that marketers give people only what they want? Suppose people want pornography, frivolous electrical appliances that overload our generating systems, and cheap rather than safe automobiles?

The marketing game really is one reason our economic and social systems have stayed afloat. As old products and services die away, new ones are introduced and sold. We may have managed to generate a madly materialistic, even self-destructive, society, too acquisitive and frenetic to provide human satisfaction. But that materialistic activity may also have provided the base for freeing increasing numbers of people to pursue their own version of fulfillment—with vast portions of the population able to afford travel, recreation, and exotic kinds of personal experiments that only the very wealthy could afford a century ago.

Consider advertising. It poses serious social problems precisely because it works. Misleading promises in print and on television have led consumers to waste money and jeopardize their health. We worry when elementary-school children can name more brands of breakfast cereal than countries of the world. We look for ways to protest when we realize how much the cost of advertising contributes to the price of our products.

Advertisers tune their messages carefully, building their ideas from profound knowledge of psychology, and pretesting ideas to be sure they will work before going into full production. They have even worked to exploit approaches that will influence people unknowingly, at a subconscious rather than a conscious level.

Yet the question of what to do about advertising and how to regulate it looks very different if we're talking about advertisements to promote regular cancer checkups than if we're talking about ads to promote smoking. We fuss because the cigarette commercials accentuate the pleasures of smoking and gloss over the dangers. But the ads for cancer checkups do the same: overselling the degree to which sure detection is likely and the degree to which early detection promises a cure.

Perhaps the best way to answer the morality question is by the same means we use in many other situations: by letting the pressures build up around specific situations. Where advertising or other marketing tactics get out of line, we protest to the marketers, newspaper reporters, or government officials who can put pressure on the offending companies.

The wise company expects pressure from customers. It recognizes that strong and seemingly isolated voices, unsettling or unpleasant as they may be, can signal the early signs of massive

Andrea and Goliath

> While there are many cases where individuals and loosely structured groups lose battles against organized interests, individuals can make a difference:
>
> > A land developer recently began construction of a mini-skyscraper apartment building on a tiny parcel of land in an area of single-family cabins in the High Sierras—and that was the last straw for a group of residents from Mammoth Lakes, Calif.
> >
> > Led by Mrs. Andrea Mead Lawrence, a former Olympic skiing gold-medal winner, the residents sued to halt the project on the ground that, even though it was on private land, it harmed the surrounding environment.
> >
> > The case worked its way up to the California supreme court—and in a surprising 6-to-1 decision on Sept. 28, the court ruled in favor of the residents. State and local government agencies now must complete environmental impact reports and make them public before they can approve private construction projects that may have a "significant" impact on the environment, the court declared. Presumably, thus forewarned, upset citizens could sue to stop any project that in their view an agency wrongly approved.
> >
> > It's the first time that the idea of "environmental impact" has been directly applied to private developments, and other states are expected to follow California's lead. Conservationists are hailing the case as the most significant yet in their battle to halt what they consider the rape of the California environment. The decision means that citizens can sue to halt any "significant" private construction that doesn't have an environmental-impact study.
>
> —*Reprinted with permission from the* Wall Street Journal, *Oct. 9, 1972.*

changes in customer preference and decisions. The wise customer, in turn, recognizes the importance of thinking through what he wants and of taking time to make his voice heard. Pressure battles take time and organization. Thus customers, if they are to talk back effectively to tightly organized companies, have to get together and stick together in their resistance. You need to know about organizations even if your main goal in life is to fight organizations.

An Illustration: Population Control and Marketing

Let's consider contraception as an illustration of some of the dilemmas (social, moral, and economic) that may arise around the whole business of marketing; and in this case, since one of us has worked in the area, we'll take a position that you can shoot at if you like.

Many people of many persuasions, many races, and many ages think the world is heading for a major crisis because of too-rapid population growth. If we extrapolate from present figures, the world's 1970 population of 3.6 billion will reach about 7 billion by 2000. (It was 1.6 billion in 1900.) Governments—of the United States, Sweden, India, Egypt, China, Indonesia, Malaysia, and lots more—are trying to do something about the problem, as are many foundations and voluntary groups.

One thing governments usually do is start clinics to provide information and cheap or free contraceptives to local married women. For many years the teams of experts sent out by United States groups to help other governments initiate such public-sector programs usually consisted of gynecologists, public health experts, Planned Parenthood people, and demographers.

Do you notice anything missing? No mention of marketers. Nothing about marketing and distributing contraceptives for profit! Yet in Jamaica, for example, in 1970, while government clinics were distributing about 600,000 condoms per year, rum shops and drug stores and groceries were selling about 6 million (and the public sector didn't know it). In the world as a whole, many more contraceptives are being sold for profit than are being circulated through public agencies. Think of what it costs in time and energy and money to build up a system of government-sponsored clinics all over a nation, even in distant back-country villages!

So why not the obvious? Why not market and promote contraceptives through commercial channels that already exist in almost every society in the world—and noncommercial ones, too. Why not use those channels to get contraceptives out to people widely and cheaply? And why not advertise, with radio and TV spots and all the other paraphernalia of Madison Avenue?

One reason these things weren't done until very recently was that lots of people don't like to advertise anything at all and sell it for profit. Others think selling and advertising contraceptives is especially dirty. Others think of contraceptives as a medicine that must be carefully controlled by physicians.

But some people think the population explosion is a good deal dirtier than the selling problem. So train engines in India these days are carrying big banners on their sides advertising contraceptives, and radio and TV commercials are being used widely in Jamaica. Maybe that way people won't have to walk a mile for contraceptives, or have to be fingerprinted by a civil servant to get them, or pay very much for them either. And with a little point-of-sale display at the checkout counter of your local supermarket. . . .

We think the utilization of such marketing and distribution methods will make a modest contribution to the leveling off of world population growth, and that the use of such methods is not only efficient but socially and morally desirable. What do you think?

Summary

Ours has become a marketing-oriented society, not only for business but for most organizations. That emphasis has developed because organizations depend for survival on the good will and support of clients. In some final sense, the client's wish is the organization's command.

It pays, then, for organizations to attend to customer wishes and to try to bend them to their own advantage. Product design, packaging, advertising, promotion, distribution strategies, and personal salesmanship are all elements in the game of marketing as it is played today. Organizations use these elements to draw attention to themselves, to build a distinctive image and reputation, to secure loyal customers or to keep a flow of new customers coming in, to create demand for new products and services, to keep sales and profits up, and sometimes simply to help themselves feel good.

In the process, as organizations have grown larger and more sophisticated about marketing, they have gained advantages over their clients. Some of their tactics and actions have been questionable—even deceitful and damaging to customers. But those actions have led to reactions—to consumer action and government regulation, and to restraints and controls that ordinary competitive forces have failed to provide.

The values associated with an open and aggressive marketing system are at present up for public debate—and properly so—not for the first time but perhaps on a larger scale than we have known before. The challenge is to find ways to curb excess and to restore balance without destroying the momentum that active attention to marketing has given to American society.

Notes and References

Marketing experts have written very little about the ethics or the social implications of their art. Until recently, at least, their concern has been mostly with how to market well. For what is taught in most marketing courses today, look at a couple of good basic texts like: Philip Kotler, *Marketing Management: Analysis, Planning, Control* (Englewood Cliffs, N.J.: Prentice-Hall, 1967); and H. W. Boyd and W. Massey, *Marketing Management* (New York: Harcourt Brace Jovanovich, 1972).

For some social pros and cons of marketing and advertising, try the following books of readings: Lee E. Preston, ed., *Social Issues in Marketing* (Glenview, Ill.: Scott, Foresman and Company, 1968); and R. R. Gist, *Readings: Marketing and Society* (New York: Holt, Rinehart and Winston, 1971).

For a broad economic critique of the marketing way of life, see K. Galbraith, *The New Industrial State* (Boston: Houghton Mifflin, 1967).

On the consumer's problems, the material available is surprisingly sparse. One good new book of readings is D. A. Aaker and G. Day, eds., *Consumerism: Search for the Consumer Interest* (New York: Free Press, 1971). This book contains articles on a range of issues from Ralph Nader on "The Great American Gyp" to data on food costs in ghetto and nonghetto areas.

For more on population control, see: H. J. Leavitt and J. U. Farley, "Population Control and the Private Sector," *Journal of Social Issues,* XXIII (Oct. 1967), 135; H. J. Leavitt and J. U. Farley, "Marketing and Population Problems," *Journal of Marketing,* XXXV (July 1971), 28–33.

On some of the social and practical questions raised by advertising, try S. A. Greyser, *Advertising in America: The Consumer View* (Boston: Harvard Business School, 1968).

And for a spirited and at least partial defense of advertising practice, see Theodore Levitt, "The Morality (?) of Advertising," *Harvard Business Review* (July–Aug. 1970).

15

The Money-Go-Round

Organizations need customers, but they need money too. And organizations that are trying to make an impression on customers will, on occasion, overspend. They may try to grow too fast, or offer more expensive services than customers are willing to pay for, or build plush headquarters on Park Avenue when they can only afford a loft in Greenwich Village. Then cash runs short, and things begin to fall apart.

The money problem exists for schools and communes as well as for stores and factories. Organizations need both customers and cash — both love and money. This chapter is about the role of money in organizations: what it is, why organizations need it, where it comes from.

Money as Social Glue

Organizations of all kinds focus on money, not just because they are acquisitive and materialistic but because money is a simple, convenient instrument of exchange. A nation's money is much like its language. Both provide a mutually understandable and mutually acceptable kind of social glue.

Coins and currency, like words and sentences, serve as surrogates and common denominators for many things and many services.

Whether the units of money are pebbles, pieces of gold, or entries in a bank balance, they serve as symbols for other "real" things. We can carry money around without carrying goods. We can use money as a basis for determining the relative values of different things and for summarizing the viability of programs and activities within an organization. We can use money to delay gratification, by selling something for money today and holding the money until we find something we want tomorrow or the day after. With money, we can engage in complex interactions and exchanges over extended time periods yet keep relatively simple accounts on the balance of trade among participating parties. Money, like language, helps people and their organizations to reduce confusion and uncertainty and to conquer geography and time. Money permits people to interact across class barriers, occupational barriers, and racial barriers.

Money can, of course, become a divisive and destructive agent in society. Many of us associate money with conflict, jealousy, and deceit. We see it as a symbol of selfishness and greed. People and organizations fight bitterly to keep what they have or to take money away from someone else. People con one another for money, betray one another, kill one another. But even as innocent a device as human language has been put to the same uses. Think of the terrible messages sent, even in recent years, from man to man or nation to nation. Consider the role of language in stirring men to kill or enslave others. Yet most of us think of language in a positive way, as a cohesive force, as a means of bringing people together and making interaction possible. But money, which can and does perform the same functions, has somehow acquired strong negative connotations.

But in this chapter let's accentuate the positive about money. Not many societies have found a way of getting along without it; and many, many societies seem to have invented it independently.

Money as Oxygen

Most organizations depend on a continuous flow of money. If the flow is cut off, even for a short period, the organization will suffocate. Note that the continuous availability is what counts, not the total quantity buried in the backyard.

Organizations, like biological organisms, are exchange and conversion mechanisms. Some take materials or services from outside, coordinate the application of skills and effort within, and produce a product or a service for others to use. Others simply move or transport things from one place to another, as a shipping

Big Owners Sometimes Can't Be Big Spenders

Imagine for a moment that a rich uncle has just left you an entire midtown Manhattan block, five minutes from Times Square. Let's say it's the block between 49th and 50th streets on Eighth Avenue. That's 160,000 square feet, worth roughly $15 million. Are you rich?

No. You are probably hurting bad.

At best, you would be in the same type of fix as the Madison Square Garden Corporation, the actual owner of this parcel where the Garden's old sports arena once stood. For four years, the Garden has failed to induce anyone to either acquire or develop the vacant site. Why? The land seems too expensive for apartments, and the neighborhood is too run-down for offices. Once developed, of course, the land may become a bonanza. But where is the development money? Until it is forthcoming, the Garden must shell out more than $1 million a year to cover existing mortgages and taxes.

—See "Who Owns New York," Forbes (June 1, 1971), pp. 24–25.

company does, or from one time to another, as a magazine subscription agency does. Some, like charities and banks, deal mainly with money as a commodity, collecting it from one set of sources and putting it to specified uses.

But all kinds of organizations rely on a steady flow of money to permit them to do whatever it is they try to do: to buy materials, to induce other people to do things, to maintain equipment, or to prepare to meet new requests. They are obligated to pay money out constantly in return for the things they buy and the services they receive, *often long before they can expect money in return from customers.* That means organizations have to keep looking for money, not just by being paid for in-production services but often in advance, in order to underwrite services they are preparing to perform.

People can't solve their breathing problems by taking and holding one big deep breath. Organizations can't solve their money problems that way either. Relatively few organizations have all the money they need. Even organizations that seem to have accumulated great wealth can use that wealth only if it can be easily transformed into cash. Most organizations operate on the expectation that outsiders will help provide financial support in return for some promise of future profit (in the case of business) or in return for social approval and psychic satisfaction (in the case of many private charities).

Organizations that time the inflows and outflows of money well

> ### Infancy and Bankruptcy
>
> One of the most outstanding and seemingly irrevocable failure statistics is the high propensity on the part of young firms to fail. The longer a company survives, generally other things being equal, the smaller becomes the probability of failure.... The new firm usually has an immediate competitive disadvantage relative to established firms in a particular field of industry. This disadvantage is more than likely highlighted in the marketing activities of the firm, whatever the product may be. A second major factor combines the effects of competitive inferiority with the ability of the firm to withstand financial and economic problems.... The large, well-established corporation [has]... adequate reserves accumulated through the years. These firms have much greater access to the money and capital markets than do young companies. A new firm is also usually a small firm and must rely on sources of capital which typically possess only limited amounts of funds....
>
> ... The above reasons account for the fact that the majority of those firms which fail do so within the first five years of their existence.... It appears that the retail industry has the highest early-age failure rate, with the wholesale and manufacturing industries possessing the highest late failure rate. An interesting observation is that within the manufacturing industry's sector, a relatively high early and late failure rate exists. Perhaps this is due to competitive forces which are most severe to the new firm, due to relative plant size and marketing factors, and to the old firm (over 10 years in existence) due to technology problems.
>
> —Reprinted by permission of the publisher, from Edward I. Altman, Corporate Bankruptcy in America (Lexington, Mass.: Lexington Books, D. C. Heath and Company, 1971), p. 21.

can get along with less money than organizations that schedule those flows carelessly. It's always a tricky process, though, because once things get out of balance recovery can be difficult. If an organization begins to run short of funds, suppliers may refuse to supply and workers may refuse to work. Customers may begin to doubt the organization's chances for survival, and they may drift away. Sources of funding—like banks, foundations, or wealthy individual backers—may refuse to keep up their contributions. When such things happen, either the organization is absorbed by outsiders who may drastically change its goals and programs, or else it gasps its last breath.

New organizations are particularly vulnerable to cash-flow crises. They aren't nearly so well equipped for life as are human infants. They are always in danger of running out of the money they've got before they can replenish enough of it to survive. Infant mortality among organizations is strikingly high.

Old organizations are vulnerable too. Consider Rolls Royce,

with an unexcelled reputation for its motor cars and an equally impressive history of accomplishment in providing engines for the world's aircraft industry. Rolls Royce trusted too much in the potential of new technologies, in predictions of growth for airline traffic, in its own ability to forecast and control costs, and in the willingness of the British government to provide subsidies if it got into financial trouble. In full view of some astounded bankers and of incredulous widows and families who could hardly have imagined a safer investment, Rolls Royce misjudged its cash flows and suffocated for lack of money.

Money does, however, have one advantage over oxygen. Organizations have many ways of storing it. Even in a day of heavy reliance on external financing, a foresighted organization looks for ways to fill its coffers when times are good and to save funds in usable, or *liquid,* form for a rainy day. Ben Franklin may be somewhat out of fashion today, but there are still virtues in organizational thrift.

But once again, even that advantage is counterbalanced by serious dangers. Money, though it can be stored, is volatile. Its value changes with time, for reasons that the organization cannot control. Money has different values in different countries, and sometimes severe discounts in value have to be made in transactions that cross national borders. Even more important, money safely stored but lying idle does you a good deal of harm. Organizations don't get high ratings for having a great deal of "cash on hand." High ratings come from having cash that is accessible and that is also being used to earn interest, or to generate other kinds of short-term income, until the time comes to make a big long-term expenditure.

Das Kapital: Fixed and Working

Before we look at ways in which organizations try to get hold of money, let's nail down one important distinction between the kinds of money they need. The most obvious need is for what is usually called *working capital.* Suppose your uncle has just died and left you, at no cost, his hamburger stand on Lake Wippinack. You don't need a building; you don't need equipment; but you do need money to buy hamburgers, buns, napkins, and ketchup. Not being sure how large or how steady your business will be, you will want enough cash on hand to make sure that you can pay your bills, pay your help, buy advertising, and keep up with taxes. You may even want to plan on setting aside some money to have your equipment cleaned and repaired at the end of the summer and to have the stand painted before you open next spring.

All these things will require an initial stock of money to get you going, a stock that can also be replenished by some of the sixty cents you take in every time you sell a hamburger. That stock of money is called working capital, and it represents what you need to cover your expenses while you are waiting for revenues to come in. How much working capital you will need depends of course on the size of the business. But even relative to the size of the business, the amount you need will be either small or large depending on several other factors: for example, whether revenues follow expenses quickly or slowly, whether or not revenues fluctuate while expenses stay steady, and whether you're planning to expand your business or keep it as it is.

But suppose you're designing and building jet engines. In that case several years may go by between the time you start paying design engineers and building test designs and the time a customer pays you for a finished engine. Or suppose you're in the toy business; you run your factory year round, but most of your sales revenues arrive during the Christmas season. Suppose further that you see growth possibilities in the jet-engine business or the toy or the hamburger business, and you want to keep buying more supplies and adding more employees in anticipation of bigger future sales. All these factors mean you will need larger amounts of working capital to reach your goal.

Nonprofit organizations need working capital too. The church in a resort town has to husband summer collections carefully so that it will have enough to pay the minister and run the building and Sunday School programs during the winter months after the tourists have gone home. Colleges get most of their revenues twice a year when tuition payments come in, but they have to pay most of their expenses on schedules that have nothing to do with the timing of tuition receipts. Organizations put together for special purposes like climbing Mt. Everest or searching for a sunken pirate ship have often failed because bad weather or accidents delayed progress and the money ran out before the goal could be reached.

Growth poses some difficult working-capital problems. New expenses for building and expanded business can accumulate at a very rapid rate. Even successful businesses often fail to calculate how much their original nest egg and their present flow of profits have to be supplemented with outside funds. Rapid multiplication requires very careful addition and subtraction.

Working capital, though, is only half the story. Most people who try to make a living selling hamburgers don't inherit a going business from their relatives. They have to build the business for themselves or buy it from someone else. So besides working capital, which helps them meet short-term expenses, long-term expenses have to be covered even before they get started. Land has to be bought, and a stand must be built and furnished with cooking equipment, refrigerators, a cash register, and tables and chairs. The need for each of these things is only indirectly related to the number of hamburgers the entrepreneur plans to sell. All of them, furthermore, represent investments that should last for several years. The tables and stoves will eventually have to be replaced, but the land may turn out to be worth more later than it is now.

Long-term purchases are called fixed assets, and the money required to make them is called *fixed capital*. The fixed capital needed to get into the hamburger business is relatively modest, but the fixed capital needed to get started in the automobile or steel business is rather large. It is the fixed capital, rather than the working capital, that makes so many kinds of organizations difficult to start. The go-ahead depends not only on the idea and your level of enthusiasm but on your ability to get other people who have money to invest some of it.

Again, needs for fixed capital challenge nonprofit organizations as well as businesses. One of the first major problems for a religious group that wants to establish a new local church is to see whether their own ability to make special contributions, the denomination's willingness to give or lend money, and the bank's willingness to provide a mortgage will together yield enough cash to buy some land and build a building. Similarly, though a few colleges have capitalized on the opportunity to live in tents, most have to find a way to build at least some classrooms and dormitories before they start admitting students.

It's as important to anticipate and to chart fixed-capital requirements as it is to anticipate working-capital requirements, especially for those assets which gradually wear out or become obsolete and need to be replaced. Hence, if the stove in our hamburger stand can be expected to last five years, one-fifth of its cost might be charged as an expense every year. We call this process *depreciating* the value of the stove in our accounting of fixed assets, and the amount that we charge each year is called *depreciation*. As you can doubtless guess, business and government play some interesting games in figuring depreciation. Playing by some rules will make profits seem bigger; by others, smaller. Some encourage speedier or slower replacement of assets. "Depreciation" entries in a list of expenses, after all, do reflect money that has been spent just as "wage payments" and "purchase of ground beef" do; but they usually reflect money spent at another time.

Nevertheless, using the money language to reflect declining value in a depreciation account helps firms to understate profits each year in recognition of money paid out earlier, when the stove was bought, and in anticipation of the eventual need to replace it.

There isn't any absolute distinction between fixed and working capital. Fixed capital relates to expenses that have long-term implications and that, within broad limits, have to be covered whatever the volume of business. Working capital relates to short-term expenses that must be covered in advance of receiving sales revenues, and to expenses that are directly connected with the volume of goods sold. Sometimes, if one kind of money is easier to get than another, you can translate a need for fixed to a need for working capital. For instance, instead of seeking $30,000 in fixed capital for building a hamburger stand, you might lease one that someone else has built. That will, of course, increase your working-capital needs by a few hundred dollars a month to cover the rent. Sometimes an expense can be considered in either category. It may be safer to treat the cash register as a repetitive kind of cost to be covered with working capital, rather than as a fixed and nonrecurring investment. You may not need to buy another cash register next year, but by treating that expense as a recurring need you may be able to afford some litter baskets or an ice-cream machine later on.

The capital requirements for an organization can range from near zero to astronomical sums. You can still start many kinds of organizations, many kinds of profitable businesses, with little more than ideas, enthusiasm, and hard work. The ideas, perhaps, should have a price put on them as fixed capital, which is one reason that the inventor of an imaginative new product often is given as much stock in the company that will manufacture it as the people who provide the cash. Hard work, as many people who are in business for themselves can testify, is often donated at less than realistic wages because there isn't enough working capital to pay properly for it. But most organizations, to survive and to grow, need substantial infusions of funds, which can range to levels like the $5 billion that IBM is estimated to have spent in designing and bringing its Series-360 computers to market, or the billions that the United States spent to land a man on the moon.

Clever Accounting and Capital Requirements

Modern accounting practices give companies a great deal of leeway in estimating and reporting their capital needs. If they can pretend, for example, that large expenditures for research and product design are nonrecurring, one-time investments that will be repaid by future sales, they can ignore them in figuring this year's profits and then depreciate them in installments in future years.

That game may get the organization into trouble, though, when

> ### Getting Caught with Your Capital Down
>
> For years now, many small companies that lease out computers or supply peripheral equipment to computer users have been playing a dangerous game. To show a profit while financing huge cash requirements, they have stretched to the limit "normally accepted accounting practices." In essence, they have borrowed from future earnings by bookkeeping legerdemain.
>
> ... The accounting techniques vary, but two perennial favorites are to take excessively long depreciation and to tally long-term leases as immediate sales. Another common ploy: to charge as capital investment a whole string of items that often should be treated as current expenses, including such routine costs as marketing, research and development, and lease acquisitions.
>
> — Reprinted from the August 26, 1972, issue of Business Week (p. 50), by special permission. ©1972 by McGraw-Hill, Inc.

large amounts have to be paid out again the next year for research and design, and the next year after that. Eventually, a day of reckoning comes, as it has, for example, for many small companies in the computer industry that undertook very expensive businesses on very small initial investments.

Looking for Investors

Where does an organization get the capital it needs? In the last chapter, we argued that nothing matters more in the long run than a regular flow of revenue into the organization from willing and satisfied clients: sales dollars for a business, pledge dollars for a church or charity, tuition dollars for a university. But in the beginning—in the short run—the problem of getting capital has to be solved before the revenues start coming in.

To get money in a hurry, you must either buy it or rent it from others who have it. Sometimes the others are individuals, but often they are organizations—organizations whose reason for existence is to collect money from a variety of sources and make it available, for a price, to people who need it.

The idea of charging people money for letting them use your money has been a controversial one for a long time. Witness the vilification of Shylock in *The Merchant of Venice* or the fiery denunciations of usury by John Ruskin and George Bernard Shaw. Yet it remains unusual for most people to part with their money without expecting something in return. The Italian merchants who helped pay for the beauty of the Sistine Chapel probably wanted a little help in arranging accommodations for the afterlife, and university presidents must still contend with donors who care more about where their name will be displayed than about the students' real needs. Even foundations, organizations that exist to give money away for worthy social purposes, worry about what kinds of grants will make them look good. As a result, they seem sometimes to be more interested in starting programs that will get favorable publicity than in quietly continuing to support even the worthiest of going programs.

In many ways, the cold, impersonal banker's calculation of just how much interest he wants in return for a loan is cleaner, fairer, and less subject to whims about how the money should be used than many more nobly motivated grants of aid.

Let's consider some of the many ways of searching for capital. One surprisingly important source even now is reliance on a personal relationship. Many an entrepreneur has got his start (and many others have destroyed good friendships or good marriages) by gathering the money he needs from the people he knows best—from people who would have the hardest time saying no. Charities, churches, and colleges rely heavily on this approach, as every donor knows.

But for the really big money, such personal appeals usually won't serve. So one must go out to the commercial money market, the dangerous land of the money lender. To show what's involved in such a process, consider this example:

You and three friends have just founded a company to make and sell a paper slide rule you have invented. You are convinced that your product will outperform slide rules now selling for ten dollars and more; yet yours will cost only ten cents to make and can be sold profitably, after costs of advertising and distribution, for just one dollar. Your product can be manufactured with inexpensive printing, cutting, and assembly devices available from the local office-supply store. You can operate in almost any kind of building. But to get started, you need more money than you now have, money for modest fixed assets and for enough working capital to support large-scale production and distribution. So out you go to seek your capital.

You're in a state of mild turmoil. How much will each dollar you go after for fixed assets or for working capital generate in sales and profits? How much will you have to pay to get various kinds of money, either in fees and interest or in concessions to share in future profits? When will the money have to be repaid? How much will the money lenders want to control the way in which you run your business? What restrictions will accepting money from one source put on your freedom later on to raise additional money from other sources?

One avenue—but only one—for getting funds is to borrow them. And of course there are many places you can go to seek loans. Banks, insurance companies, pension funds, and other kinds of commercial credit houses live by lending money, and they hope people like you will approach them. They can set up a loan in many ways, under many labels: a note or a mortgage for a fixed amount; a line of credit that allows you to borrow and repay on a continuing basis subject to some kind of maximum limit; a secured loan, which gives them first claim on your equipment or inventory of finished slide rules if the loan goes bad. At a minimum, though, in return for making money available in specified sums at specified time schedules, the lending agency will surely demand at least two things in return: (1) a promise to repay the amount borrowed, again on some timetable, and (2) a commitment to pay interest, figured in many different ways, but almost always reducible to a percentage of the amount borrowed or the amount remaining to be repaid.

They may also demand security, and they may want an extra fee or side payment. They may make you promise not to take on any other obligations that would take priority over your obligation to them, and they may even demand a voice in managing your enterprise. They're worrying about not getting their money back, about how soon you will be in a position to repay, and about other possibly better ways they could use the same money. Since many of these lending agencies are brokers for placing other people's money, their price to you will also reflect the amount they have to offer to get those people to build up their bank deposits or the expense they incur in bringing in insurance premiums.

Organizations borrow to meet both short-term and long-term needs; and while banks and many other lenders are prepared to supply both working and fixed capital, the arrangements and terms will often differ for the two. Another way of borrowing, usually restricted to long-term needs, involves selling bonds or debentures. A debenture is a fancy kind of IOU, sold usually in denominations of $1,000 and up, for which you receive the face value from the buyer (less fees of the bond broker who found the buyers and arranged the sale). In return, you take on an obligation to pay back the face value of the certificate within a fixed number of years, and in the meantime to pay a specified rate of interest.

The bond buyer, in turn, can sell his bond on the open market to someone else who would like to get the interest and, eventually, the repayment. If you seem to have offered a good deal, relative to others selling bonds, that resale may be at a premium price; if your prospects of repaying look poor or if the rate of interest you have offered seems low, the bond will resell at a discount. By watching how your bonds fare in the resale market (and by allowing for the general influence of changes in interest-rate levels), you can get some idea of how the public regards your company.

But borrowing isn't the only way. You might arrange to sell something in return for immediate cash. Suppose, for example, that you already owned a building suitable for handling the manufacture of your slide rules. To get immediate cash for other initial expenses, you might enter into a sale-and-lease-back agreement with someone who would buy the building and agree that for the next ninety-nine years you will have first option to be the tenant at some reasonable rate of rental. This may seem a far-fetched way to get capital for making paper slide rules, but it's commonly used by corporations to get new office space or by financially pressed companies to get cash in a hurry.

And another way is open too, especially if you have already managed to show that there's a good market for your paper slide rules. You can speed up the collection of bills from the college bookstores that distribute your slide rules by finding what's called a factoring company to buy those bills (or "receivables," as the accountant calls them) from you. You may only get eighty or ninety cents on the dollar from the factor, but if you can get that money in five days instead of thirty or sixty days after shipment you can reduce your need to borrow money and pay interest to other sources to meet your payroll. The factor also takes over the task of collecting the bills and the risk that some will never be paid.

If you think you can get away with it, you can also play games on the other end. The fellows who sell you paper and staples may offer a discount if you pay their bills within ten days or they may threaten to impose a penalty if you go past sixty. Many organizations, when pinched, will delay repayment not for lack of the cash but because they have compared the penalty with the cost of borrowing enough more money to make early or on-time payments. A supplier to an organization thereby runs the risk of finding himself an unwitting (even an unwilling) source of some of its working capital.

The big advantage of methods like borrowing money, or selling assets, or leaning on the generosity of suppliers is that they don't require you to give up a share of the ownership of the firm. Depending on how profitable the enterprise will be, and how well you and your friends can stand all the fees and interest payments you have to meet, you may want to keep the business entirely your own. Then, when you strike it rich, the really big returns will go into your pocket, and not to the banks, the factor, or anyone else.

On the other hand, of course, you may decide you would rather get money that will cost you less in the short run but that will oblige you to give others a share of the ownership and the big profits you hope eventually to make. If you choose that route, you can ask for money without making any promise to pay it back, without pledging or selling any assets, and without paying any interest. What you offer as a substitute, though, are some formal rights of ownership (including the right to vote on whether you should stay on as senior partner or president) and a claim on a share of future profits or assets.

You have two ways of bringing in co-owners. If you decide to set up as a partnership, you usually negotiate directly, making the size of the share you grant roughly proportional to the financial contribution (or the talent) that the new partner brings in. One of the risks in a partnership is that you are generally liable for everything you personally own, well beyond what you've put into the business, if the business gets into trouble. And one of the risks of taking in partners is that if one of them decides to pull out, his "stake" is withdrawn directly from the working capital of the firm.

To limit a partner's liability to what he has paid into the enterprise, and to provide a way for him to sell out his investment without taxing the working capital of the firm, most organizations eventually choose another route for bringing in co-owners. They incorporate and issue shares of stock. The number of shares of stock a person has generally reflects, in a proportional way, his share of the ownership interest and his voting rights in managing the company.

One advantage of selling stock over taking in partners is that, while the choice of each partner is a very personal thing and usually implies that the partner will be an active member of management, stock can be sold to many people who care about dividends and capital gains but who have little direct interest in how you run your show. Larger brokerage houses or accounting firms may have hundreds of partners, but it is not uncommon, even for small corporations, to have thousands of stockholders.

Stock can be issued privately, but if it is to be offered to the public at large and traded on one of the major stock exchanges it will be sold through an underwriter. The underwriter advises on how many shares to issue, on how to price them, and on the timing of the sale. He may agree to purchase enough of the stock himself at a set price to guarantee, net of expenses, certain proceeds on the sale for your company. The people or organizations who buy the stock, then, keep watch on your progress. If your sales and profits seem to be going up, they'll raise the price. If your prospects look bad, though, they may have to cut their price to find anyone willing to take the shares.

Once you've got the proceeds of the stock issue, you may think there's no reason to care what happens to the price. You will care, though, and not only because of pride in your organization. The value of your own holdings depends on what the public thinks. They can make you, sometimes overnight, a millionaire or a pauper. Further, if you ever want to sell stock again, you want the price to be as high as possible. Then you'll be able to get any given amount of money by selling fewer additional shares; and the fewer additional shares you have to sell, the more you maintain your ownership interest and your power to control the way the company is run.

The Cost of Capital

If your slide-rule company is like most businesses, over the years you'll seek money from many sources, including both bank loans and the sale of stock. You will pay different prices for that money at different times, and you may be holding loans issued under various conditions at several different interest rates. Your stock price will have fluctuated and, if you have been very lucky, it will have been higher each time you offered shares than it was the time before.

You can at least conceptually combine what you have paid to bring in these extra funds into an aggregate, which is coming to be called *cost of capital*. Cost of capital is the aggregate rate you are paying for money, considering all the ways in which you have acquired it. One of the things we mean when we say that businesses have to make a profit to survive is that they have to fully cover their cost of capital. If the revenues they generate exceed the cost of capital, it will be relatively easy to attract more capital for change and for expansion. But if revenues fall below the cost of capital, sooner or later the people inside and outside the firm who have been providing the capital are going to look for greener fields.

Cost of capital becomes an important consideration in talking about any kind of new investment. Increasingly, companies that carry through the kinds of cash-flow analysis that we illustrated in Chapter 5 are figuring in the costs of finding the money or withholding it from other more profitable uses. Where the projected annual rate of return falls below the cost of capital, the proposed investment—be it a better boiler or a way of reducing the pollutants going into the river—is likely to be rejected.

Companies do, of course, consider intangibles. Expenditures may be made to help clean the air because of an intrinsic weight given to community reaction or the possibilities of eventual government regulation, or even because the managers just think it's right.

But the fact remains that it costs money to get money to do things, and that fact is not fully understood by many people inside and outside business. A business can afford to invest in cleaning up the ghetto if, within a time period tolerable to their stockholders and bankers, it can turn that effort into a profit by creating new customers and new markets. A business can even afford to invest some money for the sake of good will, so long as its overall profits from other sources more than cover expenses and the cost of capital. But sometimes a business, under the rules of the game it is subject to, has to pass up projects of social worth because there is no feasible way to recover the cost of the investment.

Even government faces these limits. It can add beyond current revenue levels to programs of welfare, public education, or military security in one of three ways. It can raise taxes, for which the "cost of capital" may include being booted out of office at the next election. It can borrow, usually by selling bonds, which means adding a long-term commitment to pay interest and, except when the borrowing is carried as debt indefinitely, eventually a commitment to repay the principle out of future tax revenues. Finally, in the case of the federal government, it can create funds by printing more money, thus adding to the money supply. The cost of this last step is borne not just by government but by everyone, because increases in the amount of money in circulation eventually mean a decrease in its value, and that's *inflation.*

Money in Motion: The Concept of Cash Flow

The world we have described in this chapter is one in which money — or capital — is scarce, and in which a great deal of energy must be devoted to keeping track of what's needed, finding new supplies, and getting the most from what you have. In most organizations there is a rapidly and continuously changing balance between money coming in and money going out. Managers want to put to use every bit of money they can, either to earn a return or to forestall the need to pay for borrowing or buying additional funds. One key financial index of this process, and of organizational balance and perform-ance, is called *cash flow.*

This is indeed a critical index. It may say much more about the health of an organization than statements of income and expenses, or profit and loss, since the latter include many kinds of entries that reflect the past or the future more than they do the present. For example, by juggling some special transactions that did not involve an immediate exchange of cash, the Penn Central Railroad was able to report profits for both 1968 and 1969, even at a time when it was heading into bankruptcy. During the same period, in its regular rail-road operations, Penn Central was spending nearly half a million dollars more each day than it was receiving in cash income. By selling off properties at the sacrifice of future income, and by counting as profit income that would not be fully received for several years, the company gave the appearance of maintaining positive earnings while in fact it was bleeding to death as a result of negative cash flow. And many investors were optimistically watching the wrong figures in the railroad's financial reports.

Some of Penn Central's negative cash flow resulted from delays in the marketing cycle. The railroad required that shippers pay their bills within seven days; but because it was slow in sending out bills and settling claims for damages, bills were actually paid in an average of 28 days. This delay tied up $150 million in cash for operating expenses during that longer-than-necessary billing and collection cycle. But nature took a part too. Delays and cancellations during the severe winter storms of January 1970 were estimated to have cost at least $20 million in income.

The negative cash flow also resulted from the shifting of funds from the railroad into diverse new enterprises. From 1963 to 1970, $210 million of railroad funds and borrowed money was spent to buy into a great variety of businesses. During those years, the cash income received in return from those investments was only $200 thousand greater than the $56.4 million in interest that the railroad paid on money borrowed to finance them. So, at a crucial time in Penn Central's history, these enterprises were barely generating enough cash income to pay the interest on money that had been borrowed to buy them.

At the very end, it was the banks that provided Penn Central with working capital who blew the whistle. They forced the company to pay back $40 million in loans in a single month, refusing to support a proposed $100 million bond issue without government guarantees. With cash flowing out at the rate of more than $1 million a day, and with no one willing to put more cash in, there was at last no alternative to bankruptcy.

For a simpler example of the relevance of cash flow, consider your own personal checking account. The flow is positive if inputs exceed expenditures. That's the basic determining force. But you can jiggle the account in a positive direction if the checks you deposit clear promptly and if the checks you issue clear slowly. You can even live well for a while if special gifts provide a cushion to let expenses run at a faster rate than regular income, or if your credit for covering negative balances is good. Cash flow, however, is perhaps the best single way to take an organization's financial pulse, and eventually it tells the story of financial success or failure for an enterprise.

Keeping Your Backers with You

Dependence on outside sources of funds is like dependence on customers. It's a tricky and sometimes whimsical business, particularly in the American financial arena. Though there is close government regulation of banks and financial markets, there is also a great deal of lively and imaginative interchange between those who seek and those who furnish money. If you're looking for money it helps to have a good case, but good contacts and a jazzy presentation don't hurt.

Sometimes, though, getting backers is not nearly so difficult as keeping them. If you choose to go the borrowing route, you don't want to start a fresh set of negotiations every time you need a modest loan. You try to choose your banker originally so that, if you do well, he will be willing to replenish or increase your loans; so that, if you grow, he can help you; and so that, even if you plan to move out geographically, his resources and contacts can help you in other states and other countries.

The ideal situation might be one in which your banker is closely in touch with your cash needs and your changing plans and in which he will be willing to take a few unusual risks to help your business. But the irony is that you may build this relationship best, not by demonstrating how well you can get along without borrowing, but by making sure you give your banker enough business so that he will continue to view you as a profitable customer. The organization that has never borrowed money may have a harder time finding it than the one that borrows and repays regularly.

In dealing with stockholders, there are two problems. The first problem is to keep them persuaded that your stock is worth a high price. Though in the short run a little glitter may fool the investor, there's no long-term substitute for turning in a performance that produces profits and shows potential for future gains. Additionally, companies generally find it worthwhile to pay dividends—even though they may actually have to go out and borrow cash for the purpose. Dividends are not now considered to be as big an influence on stock prices as people used to believe; but they are important for many investors, and they probably help to keep the price of the stock up.

Organizations, of course, are not above feeding publicity to shareholders or trying to obscure bad results in their efforts to build investor confidence. And some company executives spend a whole morning every week trying to get Wall Street security analysts to push their stock, with hopes of raising the stock's *price-earnings ratio* (a measure of price per share in the marketplace divided by the company's most recent annual earnings per share). When people

> ### Building the Price of Your Company's Stock
>
> Many a company has turned the profit corner in 1972, yet the price of its stock hardly reflects it. If your company kept a low profile during the bear market days and still has a low price-earnings ratio, it could be time to tend to your investor relations. Your image could have slipped with security analysts.
>
> "There's no question that the healthy company that is aggressive in dealing with the financial community will enjoy a higher price-earnings ratio than a company which is not," notes William M. Gray, senior analyst for Goldman, Sachs.
>
> "You'll have a lower price-earnings ratio if you don't communicate, and lose potential investors," adds Martin D. Sass, president of his own investment management firm.
>
> The most effective way to improve communications with the Street is through your own full-time investor relations specialist. He should answer analysts' questions, as well as send out earnings reports and other company literature. An outside financial public relations consultant can handle some of these chores, too, but obviously will not know as much about your company.
>
> As a top officer, you will have to spend some time with analysts, of course. Figure on several formal presentations each year before the New York Society of Security Analysts and similar groups. Some companies routinely hold meetings after the quarter's earnings are reported—a move analysts applaud. St. Regis Paper, for example, holds one-hour meetings with 100 or so analysts at the end of each quarter, attended by the board chairman, president, and three executive vice-presidents.
>
> —Reprinted from the Aug. 26, 1972 issue of Business Week (p. 71) by special permission. ©1972 by McGraw-Hill, Inc.

get enthusiastic about a stock, its price may climb to create a P/E ratio of, say, 60 to 1; the stock of an equally solid company that happens to be out of public favor may be priced to produce a P/E ratio of only, say, 15 to 1.

A second problem that managers encounter in dealing with stockholders is keeping them loyal. A manager can get into trouble with his stockholders, just as he can with his bankers. The easiest route to trouble is to do a poor job with the funds they have provided. But he can also get into trouble by doing well and setting a large chunk of cash aside. Then the stockholders may scream for bigger dividends; or, more frightening still, they may join forces with a marauding buccaneer who promises that if they name him to replace the present management he'll take that extra cash and build an even bigger and more profitable business. Sometimes that's what the buccaneer really wants to do; but sometimes he may figure that if he can get the stockholders to vote him into power, he'll be able to clean the till and clear out.

These financial buccaneers are called corporate raiders. They sit in Manhattan and Dallas and Spokane, scanning the financial pages for companies with lots of cash or salable assets, and with a stock price so low that all the shares outstanding will cost very little relative to the real worth of the company. Then they begin quietly to buy up as many shares as they can at the low price. When they have enough to swing a lot of weight, they step out of the underbrush and demand changes in management or seats on the board of directors. More than one dedicated management group has turned up at work one morning to find themselves about to be replaced by new men chosen by the raiders. And usually there's nothing they can do but fume. Sometimes the raider will improve a stodgy, badly managed company. But often the takeover is designed more for the raider's advantage than for the organization's. He is likely to make decisions that will lead to quick payoffs and boost the price of the stock. Then he sells his shares at a fat profit.

But consider for a moment: Are raiders all bad? Or are they, too, a balancing device that keeps managers on their toes, gives stockholders some leverage in management, and clears the system of the slow and the weak?

So when you decide to sell part of your organization to investors in the open and decentralized system of American finance, it's a little like selling your product to customers. You have to convince them that they have something to gain. Financial facts and results matter, but psychological factors—fancy packages and attractive waiting rooms—count as well. Bankers, brokers, and shareholders are people too. Courting them, treating them with tact and sensitivity, and, unfortunately, making sure they don't run off with the silverware—these are all important elements in attracting the support that will keep your organization in cash, and in your hands.

Summary

Money talks in the organizational world. In the form of fixed and working capital, it provides the nourishment by which organizations—both profit and nonprofit—function and grow. You must have capital to survive at all; and if you can attract enough of it, you will have a margin for innovation, experimentation, and even for doing some socially useful things. Money can be an agent for change; it enables groups with better ideas and more desirable goals to challenge old organizations and old ways of doing things.

Money, like language, simplifies communication in a complex society. It provides a medium for arranging and carrying through elaborate kinds of economic and social exchanges across segments of society. It helps to define yardsticks that can be used within and across organizations to assess value and performance.

But money is usually in short supply. Managers in most organizations must spend a great deal of time making sure they always have enough to keep going. If they can build a healthy surplus of income over expenses, they may draw it out of the proceeds of their organization's work. But because many expenses have to be covered before income has been received, other sources of money are needed. The two most common ways of getting extra cash are through borrowing or through selling shares in future growth and profits.

There are no easy choices here. If you borrow, you incur high costs in fees and interest and fixed schedules for repayment. If you sell shares, you surrender to others some of your rights to manage and some of your claims to future profits. You may even find yourself taken over and displaced by disgruntled shareholders.

A good manager of any organization realizes that cash flow is perhaps the best single measure of his organization's financial health. And every time he thinks about buying or building something, he must think about the cost of the capital he will need. In many cases that cost will determine what decision he makes. He must also keep an eye on the many different ways of getting and keeping financial flexibility. He must cultivate his investors as he cultivates his customers, because without the support of both groups he will find himself in deep trouble.

Notes and References

It helps as background in considering the role of money in organizations to learn more about what money is, and what role it plays for society as a whole. A good introduction is Lawrence S. Ritter and William L. Silber, *Money* (New York: Basic Books, 1970).

As introductions to managerial finance and the financial markets which organizations use, the following books are of interest:

G. Scott Hutchison, ed., *The Strategy of Corporate Financing* (New York: Presidents Publishing House, 1971); J. Fred Weston and Eugene F. Brigham, *Managerial Finance,* 4th ed. (New York: Holt, Rinehart and Winston, 1972); and R. W. Goldsmith, *Financial Institutions* (New York: Random House, 1968).

For a more scholarly review of how it's all done, see Simon Kuznets, *Capital in the American Economy: Its Formation and Financing* (Princeton: Princeton University Press, 1961).

Accounting texts such as Myron Gordon and Gordon Shillinglaw, *Accounting: A Management Approach,* 4th ed. (Homewood, Ill.: Richard D. Irwin, 1969), cover topics like financial planning and cash flow analysis.

For more on the meaning of working capital and its effective conservation as an organizational resource, see William Beranek, *Working Capital Management* (Belmont, Calif.: Wadsworth Publishing Co., 1968).

On the question of corporate raids by one organization on another, see Douglas V. Austin, "A Defense of the Corporate Pirate," *Business Horizons* (Winter 1964), pp. 51–58; and Manuel F. Cohen, "Takeover Bids," *Financial Analysts Journal* (Jan.–Feb. 1970), pp. 26–31.

16

Rulemakers and Referees:
To Kibbitz or to Control

In the last two chapters we described the rough-and-tumble world in which organizations seek customers and financial support. We suggested that there is a need for rules and regulators to keep the game fair and honest for all concerned. Government, you say, has that role; but so do lots of other organizations. In the great game of king-on-the-mountain that organizations play in a pluralistic society, there is competition not only among players who want to reach the top of the hill but among those who think they deserve the franchise to referee.

This chapter is about organizations that make and administer rules and about the responses they get from the other organizations they try to regulate. Refereeing organizations are not unique in character or appearance. Internally, they look and behave like all the kinds of organization we have been talking about so far. In fact, we have used some of them as examples. This chapter looks at their *external* dimensions—at their efforts to guide, direct, and limit other organizations. We'll focus on how people communicate, coordinate, and control across organizational boundaries.

Who Owns the Whistles?

Government is the most obvious and important of referees, but many other kinds of organization act as regulators. Consider standard-setting groups such as the Anti-Defamation League and the American Association of Collegiate Schools of Business; testing and evaluation agencies like Consumers Union and the Legion of Decency; certification groups like the Underwriters Laboratories and the American Kennel Club; overseers of local marketing practices like the Better Business Bureau; and futurists like the Sierra Club or the Club of Rome who want to help set the course of public policy in years ahead. Then there are groups like Common Cause, the National Organization of Women, Students for a Democratic Society, and the AFL-CIO —organizations that speak collectively to other organizations on behalf of individuals who feel powerless and aggrieved by themselves.

Some of these organizations work alone and, like Consumers Union, pride themselves on being independent of those they regulate. Others, like the Better Business Bureau, depend for survival on the support of the organizations they police. Still others, like the New York Stock Exchange, depend not only on the backing of member firms but on good working relationships with regulatory agencies of government (such as, for the Exchange, the Securities and Exchange Commission).

None of these private referees has the full powers that a government agency might have. Yet they are all able to inform and educate, to persuade and organize allies to their points of view, to expose and embarrass, to pressure, to bargain, and even, within the scope of their charters, to levy significant penalties. Like clever individuals within organizations who find alternatives to legal authority for exercising influence, these private referees can amass impressive power.

The Many Faces of Government

The rulemakers and referees whose power we most clearly understand are inside the government. Or, really, we ought to say governments—because government is a very diverse and complicated collection of organizations. Even back in the days of small states run by kings or dukes, when the subtleties of power were at levels a poet or playwright could describe, government was not monolithic. Even the most absolute of monarchs had to delegate the regulation of local territories or of specialized activities to members of his court, and he had to adjust to the reality that, by the very act of delegating, he would sacrifice some uniformity and control in what was done. The classic dilemma for an old-time king was to decide how much autonomy a deputy could be allowed to assert before he was charged with treason and lost his head.

Now, though, the world is vastly more complicated. The court—

Pluralism among the Regulated Too

While we stress the fact that government cannot be regarded as a monolith, it is important to remember that companies are not monolithic either. As Robert E. Lane reminds us:

> On the level of the firm, the homogeneity of the concept "businessman" disintegrates and there appears instead a series of specialists: personnel men, marketing experts, industrial engineers, public relations men, and many other varieties. This is useful because the impact of regulation upon these various specialists is often different and this difference may serve the interests of regulators seeking to create a more friendly environment for their measures. The public relations officer of the NLRB [National Labor Relations Board] found lawyers to be a convenient channel through which to work and, in fact, counsel for a large optical firm testified to the value of a conference on labor law attended jointly by government and private lawyers. Evidently, it not only served as a medium for technical communication but also appeared to have taken a step toward the reconstruction of personal attitudes. In other situations personnel men have been found sympathetic to labor laws opposed by management, and the medical profession, allied as advisors and research directors to the drug business, offered a sympathetic channel to the drug industry during and after the protracted struggle for food and drug legislation during the late thirties. These professions . . . occupy middle ground and so, being *persona grata* to business, being members of the appropriate "in group," may serve as agents for the change of group attitudes.

—*Robert E. Lane,* The Regulation of Businessmen *(New Haven: Yale University Press, 1954), pp. 129–30.*

in the form of government agencies—seems to live forever, and it is the king—in the form of elected officials—who at regular intervals risks losing his head to the voters. The court is hard to keep in line, because it no longer consists of individuals. Instead of the Duke of Northumberland, we have the governments of Kansas and Philadelphia. In place of the royal taster, we have the Food and Drug Administration; and now that Rosencrantz and Guildenstern are dead, we have Departments of State and Commerce.

Government organizations coexist in layers—serving villages and towns, districts and counties, states and provinces, nations, and even supernational coalitions such as the European Economic Community. Government also includes some of the largest organizations that man has yet put together. Both layering and size mean that government presents not one but many faces to the organization it regulates.

Think about the corner grocer: when he grumbles about government restrictions, who's to blame? The local zoning board that won't let him hang a lighted sign over the sidewalk? The county health official who has given him a summons for having defective refrigeration equipment? The state agency that forbids him to do business on Sunday? The federal price commission that controls how much he charges? Or the international agencies whose decisions on fishing practices and territorial limits are making seafood scarce? If the small shopkeeper tries to list all the agencies of government that have some right to control the way he does business, he might well find that he has more overseers than customers.

How Regulators Regulate

And yet most regulation has little to do with publicly established rules and laws. Rules and laws are often the last resort, after a variety of other efforts have been made.

Some groups limit their role primarily to informing and educating. The Club of Rome, for example, is a worldwide fellowship of business, public, and intellectual leaders who are deeply concerned about the conditions under which civilization and mankind may survive. They have sponsored the preparation and distribution of studies that call attention to shifts in resource use, population policy, and societal organization that may be necessary to head off catastrophe a century or two hence. The Club of Rome does not have the force of government; it does not even have obvious organizational allies to promote and implement some of the changes its studies recommend. But its members hope by education to stir others to action.

Similarly, the League of Women Voters tries aggressively to influence the quality of government, not by telling people how to vote, but by using several devices to get candidates for office to reveal more to voters about their backgrounds and their views on important issues.

Regulation through education and persuasion is sometimes direct, as it was when Presidents Johnson and Nixon tried to avoid formal wage-price controls by "jawboning" companies and unions to exercise voluntary restraint. But it is often indirect, as with the efforts of Consumers Union to improve design, manufacturing, and marketing standards for a wide variety of consumer products. Consumers Union seldom goes after the manufacturers directly, but over the years it has learned a great deal about how to present ratings of products and companies to its subscribers and to the public in order to influence buying decisions. Manufacturers listen carefully to what Consumers Union thinks when buyers make the ratings a basis for shying away from their products.

While education, persuasion, and efforts to build alliances are mainly weapons for private groups that want to referee the behavior of other organizations, such informal tactics are also widely practiced by government. Educational and persuasive efforts are relatively simple to organize. A president or a mayor can cajole and convince a company to change its ways without having to put a bill through Congress or the City Council. He can get remedial action in one organization without having to develop a general solution for the city or society as a whole. He can relax or change the direction of regulation without having to seek repealing legislation.

Sometimes government efforts are carried on behind the scenes, with elected or appointed officials using their position of authority to suggest things an organization ought to do. Sometimes they are carried out in public. Legislative committees, for example, often act like Consumers Union—drawing out damaging information about an organization's performance, exposing that information to wide newspaper and television coverage, and counting on an aroused public to help force corrective action even when no regulatory legislation follows the committee hearings.

Such informal regulation of one organization by another carries the same hazards as the exercise of authority by one individual over another within an organization. Its effectiveness will depend on what clear thinking, good facts, and smooth talk can persuade the other organization to accept. Response will also depend on what private conversation or public exposure can do to recruit allies whose attitudes and decisions matter to those one wants to regulate. Such informal tactics used on automobile companies helped push the Rambler and American Motors toward success in the fifties and helped kill the Corvair and give General Motors fits in the sixties. Informal tactics are important limiting forces on the behavior of almost any kind of organization, including units of government itself.

Informal regulation has obvious limits. Irrelevant information, shaky arguments, and inadequate resources for the long and costly effort to build the allies one needs all limit its effectiveness. But far more serious are the hidden dependencies that informal referees have to keep to themselves. Consumers Union, for example, has stayed independent of manufacturers, but it does depend on financing provided by subscribers to its publications. This means it deals mainly with products its subscribers care about, and not with others that from the standpoint of society as a whole might be in even more need of regulatory attention. Better Business Bureaus, which depend on local organizations for financing, do a better job of keeping out-of-town charlatans away than penalizing local merchants. Congressional committees that want to use the power of public hearings to change behavior have learned through court challenges that the Constitution limits the kind of questioning they can engage in and the extent to which they can divert their hearings to subjects that are not a focus for potential legislation.

Still, informal systems work well because many people, often including those who are being regulated, prefer them to more formal and legalistic regulatory approaches. They are, however, fragile and vulnerable as alliances shift and as the tolerance of those being regulated hardens into resistance or outright opposition.

Bargaining to Get Your Way

When it makes sense to go after an organization directly, the process of education or persuasion can often be helped along by offering to trade something you can give or control for what you want the organization to provide in return. Organizations that want to function as referees work hard to maneuver themselves into positions where they can bargain or negotiate effectively.

There are many ways to build bases for bargaining. Labor unions bargain by threatening to withhold the services of key groups of employees. Politicians bargain by threatening to enforce old laws more strictly or to enact new laws. Students and civil-rights groups test organizations to see how much they will concede to avoid sit-ins, demonstrations, and other disruptive acts. Philanthropic foundations bargain by hinting that their funds will be available for some kinds of activities and not for others. All these groups, though, get attention and response because they control something that the organizations they deal with would like to have—or would like to avoid.

Some kinds of bargaining are highly entrepreneurial and spontaneous. Student groups and social-action organizations, for example, keep shifting their objectives, membership, and structure—and keep creating new bases for bargaining in effective ways. Other kinds of bargaining, however, like trade union negotiations, are highly institutionalized, with years of tradition and supporting legislation behind them.

Bargaining is consistent with the pluralistic philosophy that we observed in commenting on the manner in which organizations deal with customers and seek financing. As a mechanism for the direct testing of interorganizational power and persistence and as a means for working out highly specific, local agreements, it has real virtues as a refereeing and regulatory process for society. Bargaining is quick, cheap, flexible, and, in most instances, fair when compared with more formal regulatory approaches.

For this reason bargaining is favored not only by organizations like student-action groups that have no other base for asserting power but by units of government that could, if they chose, pass and enforce laws instead. Bargaining, for example, is a strategy often used by the federal government in settling antitrust cases against large corporations. Why should the Antitrust Division of the Department of Justice negotiate terms of settlement with violators rather than fight cases through to definitive court decisions?

It generally is not, as critics of the Division contend, because Antitrust is unwilling, for political reasons, to fight. Rather, it is because the Division has to perform a huge enforcement task with very limited manpower and dollar resources. For each case the Division files, it has to weigh what it might gain by a negotiated "consent" decree and what it would gain by a full trial and perhaps several levels of appeal to higher courts. If the accused company will make the main changes the Division wants short of a full trial, the Division can settle the case swiftly and release manpower to investigate and charge other violators. If the case involves questions about the meaning of "monopoly power" that go beyond what laws passed a half-century ago spell out, negotiation may even permit a more flexible and creative solution than a precedent-minded trial judge could allow. By permitting faster, better settlements, bargaining can benefit society as well as the offending organization.

The antitrust example, though, highlights two features of bargaining relationships that make us uncomfortable at times about how well the process works, especially when we are affected by the results of negotiations but are not parties to them. Bargaining's effectiveness is severely limited by the secrecy that surrounds most negotiations and by the unequal power relationships that often prevail.

Bargaining, under the best of conditions, tends to be a secret process. Our society is supposed to be a society "of laws," not "of men." But bargaining is a process "of men" rather than "of laws." Long historical tradition and modern small-group experiments confirm that negotiating is best done with a fair degree of privacy shrouding the alternatives that are discussed and the concessions that are considered before a final deal is made. We would be much more confident about antitrust "consent" decrees and about many other kinds of bargains struck to give one organization control over another, if we could have a record of what was discussed. Too often, after the fact, we learn that what seemed convenient and good to the parties doing the negotiating had bad side effects on others who have to live with the results of their agreements.

Bargaining also fails if power relationships become unbalanced. We understand that when the Antitrust Division negotiates "consent" decrees it acts as agent for a President who cares about winning the next election. But we do expect the Division and the President, in antitrust actions, to show genuine concern for voters who are victims of monopolistic behavior, rather than for corporations whose campaign contributions may be garnered from monopolistic profits. If potential corporate campaign contributions seem to be producing more generous settlement terms from the Antitrust Division, bargaining has failed as a regulatory process.

Uses of Authority across Organizational Lines

When persuasive and bargaining efforts are not sufficient, other approaches must be taken. These are what we traditionally think of as "regulatory" processes—processes that formally allow one organization to exercise authority over others.

The essential requirement for exercising authority across organizational lines is that there be some sort of contract, written or unwritten, specifying the subordination of one organization to another. The contract may be an informal agreement to respect the expertise of another organization, such as companies accept in establishing an independent testing group to determine and recommend industry standards for product quality and safety. The contract may be a document resulting from negotiations, like a union-management contract that gives the union certain rights to review management's hiring and firing decisions. Or the contract may be a historical agreement like the Constitution of the United States as amended and embellished by congressional action and Supreme Court decisions over the years. Whatever form the contract takes, though, it establishes a range of topics or decisions in which the regulatory organization is assumed to have the primary voice.

That range is usually limited, partly to keep different regulatory groups from stepping on each other's toes, but also to keep any regulatory group from trying to assume open-ended powers. Sometimes the range of powers is clear; other times it is subject to continuing revision and debate. For example, a great deal of the history of federal regulation of business in the United States has hinged upon the interpretation of a clause in the Constitution that gives Congress the power to "regulate commerce with foreign nations, and among the several States, and with the Indian tribes." Courts are still being asked by companies and by government agencies to clarify what does and what does not fall under the heading of interstate commerce.

Sometimes an agreement about range of powers will be accepted and will stand unchallenged until those who granted the power understand that, in fact, it is going to be used. Members of the New York Stock Exchange had over time empowered the Exchange to discipline member firms for defrauding customers or for failing to

> ### What's Good for General Motors Is Not Good for American Locomotive
>
> Why does government need to think through the long-term consequences of regulation? Consider what happened during World War II when the War Production Board tried to maximize production of locomotives by assigning responsibilities for making particular kinds to particular manufacturers. General Motors, a newcomer to the industry, which had built only two diesel freight locomotives in 1940, was "restricted" to building just freight locomotives. American Locomotive, which had built the first diesel in 1924, was restricted to building smaller switching locomotives.
>
> By 1944, GM was building 500 freight locomotives a year, and these big diesels were taking over as the backbone of the railroads. As John M. Blair observes, "Trying to catch up proved an impossible undertaking since railroads, which had already equipped themselves with GM locomotives, understandably did not want to be using two different makes of engines requiring dissimilar repair and maintenance parts. Only 10 years after the end of the war, GM had 83 percent of the market for freight locomotives, 100 percent for passenger diesels, and 53 percent for switchers."
>
> —See John M. Blair, Economic Concentration (*New York: Harcourt Brace Jovanovich, 1972*), pp. 378–80.

maintain adequate supplies of working capital. Those powers were not challenged for many years. Finally, however, after the Exchange used those powers to counter a crisis of public confidence in the securities markets, a few of the firms that were disciplined under the rules went to court to protest the penalties and the procedures by which they were imposed. The issue came down to the question of whether the Stock Exchange exercised its regulatory powers in a way that its members did not intend.

The power of one organization over others is limited by factors other than what the regulatory contract allows. It is often difficult to know what direction regulation should take. Environmental protection laws let government ban sales of DDT or force installation of exhaust-emission devices on automobiles. Yet it isn't enough for government to have that authority. It also needs the expertise to weigh conflicting arguments and evidence about the benefits and dangers of DDT or about the practicality of present emission-control technology. Where both the rule-making authority and the expertise exist, the regulatory process can be emphatic and effective. But where the rule-making authority fails to recognize honest disagreements and conflicting evidence about what the rules should say, rule making and rule enforcement are likely to fail.

Regulation assumes not only the power to make rules but the power to enforce them. Yet making rules is usually easier than enforcing them. Man has a long but not very distinguished history of trying to design controls and penalties that will discourage individuals from lying, cheating, robbing, and killing. At least with crimes committed by individuals, we have centuries of experience to reflect on as we try to devise more effective controls. With organizations, though, there is a dual problem: a problem of responsibility and a problem of shifting size and shape.

To regulate an organization, we must deal not with the fairly predictable components of individual human nature, but with a moving, changing target. If you penalize an organization in totality, say by forcing it out of business or by destroying its good name in the community, you can assume almost as a matter of course that you are creating hardship for many totally innocent and uninvolved employees. If you act instead against individuals, even against the top officers who get paid to be "responsible" in case of trouble, you probably haven't caught the people who really are responsible. In one case, you have cast the net too wide; in the other, not wide enough.

For example, when there is an explosion that takes many lives in a coal mine where there have been numerous violations of federal mine safety regulations, who should go to jail? Who ought to have been penalized for My Lai? In both cases one has to examine the acts of individuals in the context of their roles and powers within an organizational system, and any decision to penalize an individual must be weighed against the question of whether different behavior on his part could have affected others in the system enough to prevent the explosion or avoid the slaughter of Vietnamese civilians.

If you ever get such questions sorted out for a particular kind or class of organization, changes in that organization's size, structure, or mission can invalidate all your efforts. Consider the problems that government has with the regulation of the banking industry. Most of the relevant laws come from an era when banking was largely a local activity; when it seemed reasonable for savings banks, commercial banks, and other kinds of financial institution to pursue quite separate lines of business; and when the primary issue was preserving bank stability during the Great Depression. Since banks today find it less efficient to operate on a local basis, increasingly they want to organize on a regional basis, with some activities extending nationally and internationally. They are involved in new kinds of financial services that blur the lines between kinds of banks and between

> ### Limits to Regulatory Effectiveness
>
> ... There is an urgent need for basing regulation (or the abandonment of regulation) on facts rather than on arbitrary, legalistic determinations of a situation that has existed, whether or not the situation still exists. It would be better if a decision as to airline fares were founded on some knowledge of the elasticity of demand for air transport. It would be better if decisions as to what rate of return American Telephone and Telegraph should be permitted to earn were based on research-based findings as to the needed cost of continuing technological innovation. ... Decisions, dozens of them each month, are made now without the aid of research. Established concepts of competition and legal rituals are rough and obsolete instruments for regulation in a time of rapid change.
>
> ... The assignment of air routes, the issuance of TV franchises, the fixing of quotas for oil imports, the labeling of cigarettes, and the approval of new drug applications all rest on judgments as to what is in the public interest, and these judgments are deeply rooted in scientific considerations. For such judgments there are no generally accepted yardsticks; there is only the increasing reliance that Americans place on the effectiveness of the democratic process and on the disinterested competence of public officials. Stated thus baldly, this thought makes many businessmen tremble.
>
> —From Business in the Humane Society by John J. Corson, pp. 188–89. ©1971 by McGraw-Hill Book Company. Used with permission of McGraw-Hill Book Company.

banks and other financial institutions. They want changes in banking laws so that they can compete more effectively against insurance companies and others who are beginning to do things that only banks used to do. Because banking and financial services have changed so much over the last two decades, greatly changed regulatory structures, rules, and penalties may be needed even though the basic regulatory objectives have not changed.

The constant problem of making regulations fit a variety of organizations and organizational circumstances means that regulation in practice is always more fluid than it looks on paper. It helps to explain why even in situations where regulatory authority is well defined, large amounts of informal persuasion and bargaining back and forth take place to supplement or displace the literal enforcement of rules.

Disunity of Command

The use of authority across organizational lines is made most complicated, though, by competition among regulators. Within organizations, although we have mentioned exceptions, there is a strong tradition that no one should have more than one supervisor. One supervisor is enough, partly because it's easier on the man being supervised and partly because it keeps employees from playing one boss off against another.

This idea of "unity of command," however, often does not apply as a guiding principle in the efforts of private organizations and governments to exercise regulatory powers over other organizations. Think back to the corner grocer we mentioned earlier in the chapter, or to the company that was going to make paper slide rules. You start dealing with regulators when you seek a charter to incorporate from the state or a license to do business in town. Either one sets down conditions about the structure, governance, and responsibilities of your organization. There are many conditions to meet before you can advertise or sell stock to the public. You hire an accountant to keep you out of trouble with the Internal Revenue Service and to help arrange and audit your financial statements so that your reports to stockholders will meet standards set by the Securities and Exchange Commission and by the accounting profession itself. If you prosper, you may eventually get acquainted with the Antitrust Division; if you fail, you will learn that government even has agencies and procedures that will govern the way in which you declare bankruptcy and share what's left with the various people who have claims against you.

Sometimes the confusion becomes monumental, as it is today among the various agencies of government that have an interest in deciding what a student can declare as his "residence" if he is attending a public university in a state other than the one his parents live in. The university and state department of education have one set of rules that have at least a little to do with their desire to continue charging out-of-state students higher tuition. The department of motor vehicles may require students coming from out of state to register their cars locally because it can then collect an excise tax on their cars. The department may not require a local driver's license, though, because the prospective income is not worth the nuisance involved. Voter registration officials are just beginning to wrestle with the criteria that decide where such students "reside." All are beginning to worry about the day when students and the courts get together to forge a single definition of residency that may upset the traditional practices of the separate regulators.

Again, government is multilayered and multifaceted, and its component agencies often work at cross-purposes. Sometimes those being regulated don't care any more about consistency than government does; in fact, they may find it profitable to play off various agencies of government against one another, using rules set by one to defend practices that another agency would ordinarily disallow. If the organization being regulated finds the conflicts oppressive, though, it must bear the responsibility and the cost of getting the regulatory agencies to resolve their differences or of getting the courts to blow the whistle on the referees.

The corner grocer might find that the health commissioner's summons means buying new refrigeration equipment at a time when the price board will not allow him to cover that purchase by increasing prices. It's even conceivable that he could go bankrupt before he finds a way to untangle the conflict that widely separated regulatory groups have forced on him. Particularly when one considers the size and heterogeneity of modern government, the barriers to effective information exchange, coordination, and personalized response that exist within government can make the burden of responding to multiple regulators very difficult.

Dependence as the Counter to Authority

There is a hidden theme in what we have been saying. Just as leaders within organizations need a climate of acceptance for their authority in order to be effective, regulatory agencies of all kinds are dependent on the organizations they try to guide and control. Even the regulatory agency with state or federal legislation to back it up must be sensitive to how organizations and the public at large react to its rulings. It expects cross-pressures on its deliberations and decisions almost as a matter of course.

Dependence can take subtle forms, as with Consumers Union's reliance on the interests of its subscribers in choosing which products to test. Other organizations, like temperance, civil-rights, or social-protest groups, recruit contributions and volunteers by laying out a basic charter for themselves, but then they find themselves prisoners of those same contributors and volunteers when they think about changing direction. Sometimes they get coopted by the organizations they are trying to control. As civil-rights groups like the Urban League and the National Association for the Advancement of Colored People garnered support from rich whites and corporations, they were accused by some blacks of "selling out" to the "Establishment."

The independence of regulatory organizations has been most suspect in cases where they are directly supported by dues or voluntary contributions from the organizations they are supposed to guide and control. This kind of "self-regulation" has ended in many failures, and it always looks a little suspicious. However, the impressive thing is that there have been so many successes.

The motivations to try to make self-regulation work can be very strong. Take the willingness to fund an organization to test and evaluate the quality of an industry's products or services. It can help build markets, as the Underwriters Laboratory did in reassuring consumers that newfangled electric appliances were safe to use. It can help to get an industry working together on new products and uses, as the American Wool Institute did when confronted with the challenge of synthetic fibers. It can help keep suppliers with low standards out of the market, as accrediting agencies try to do with colleges and universities.

Self-regulation also looks attractive against the threat of government intervention and control. Clear signals that Congress and the Securities and Exchange Commission wanted reforms in the securities industry prompted many initiatives from the New York and American Stock Exchanges and from the National Association of Securities Dealers. Member firms would rather have these groups call the shots.

It should be clear, though, that even strongly endowed and supported self-regulatory groups have difficulty from time to time recognizing the difference between the public interest and what their supporters want. They find discipline hard to administer in cases where there may be a clear threat of opposition or withdrawal of financing by influential members. They may back away completely from issues like pollution control because none of the member firms wants to be forced, short of government action, into expenditures that would drastically cut profit margins.

We keep turning to government to exercise authority in areas where private agencies cannot muster sustained support or where self-regulatory efforts don't work. And we keep being surprised when we discover how much government initiatives are subject to the same kinds of cross-pressures and dependencies.

The political dimension should be obvious. A great deal of governmental regulatory action is not far removed from the control of officials or legislators who have to keep an eye on the next election —on where the votes and the campaign dollars are coming from. Politicians talk now and then about the evils of conflicts of interest, but their lives are inextricably tangled in such conflicts. They have a heavy responsiblity to sort those conflicts out, and we all have a continuing duty to see that the effectiveness and fairness of government as referee are not compromised by favors offered by those being refereed.

Because the political world is so volatile and so subject to corruption, much of governmental regulation has been delegated to independent commissions or judicial agencies that are fairly free from worrying about the next election. Those groups are relatively

The Inevitability of Conflict of Interest

A life without potential conflict, in our interrelated business world, is like a business without risk—impossible to legislate, and of doubtful wisdom if possible. Congressmen and presidents live perpetually with conflict—between the public interest and the desire for reelection....

... Newspapers and magazines and television, presumed exquisitely objective in their editorial judgments, are dependent on advertisers for the revenues that enable them to publish and to profit. District attorneys want justice and need convictions....

In short, if the road to hell is paved with good intentions, the road to heaven is paved with bad temptations. We cannot build a wall against every foible, against every unethical act, or we would be forever immobilized. Obviously, we need standards of conduct to govern... the securities industry, as we need standards for politicians and for news media and for education. But to rule on the matter without considering that brokers have always been money managers, that brokers also have a responsibility to give out information and disclose facts and pass judgments, and in short, that life cannot be lived in watertight compartments, is to act naively or from ignorance. An easy platitude says that man cannot serve two masters. I say that, in modern corporate life, a man who cannot serve two is unlikely to be hired by either.

—Donald T. Regan, A View From the Street (New York: New American Library, 1972), pp. 187–88.

hard to sway with talk of money or votes, but organizations controlled by them can strike back in a variety of other ways.

Independent commissions and courts seldom have the staff or resources to monitor, challenge, and regulate well. They rely more heavily than they should on information and services that the regulated organizations themselves provide. In the process they can become so dependent on that kind of cooperation that they begin to think, not like government or the public they supposedly represent, but like the organizations they are supposed to control. A cooperative client may expect bargaining in place of strict enforcement, an understanding that some parts of the law don't apply, and penalties that sting rather than burn. Members of independent commissions may not be concerned about reelection, but their heads may be turned by such things as the promise of high-salaried jobs in the industry they are supposed to control.

Perhaps we should be concerned that so few referees in real life can be trusted to "call 'em as they see 'em" with the integrity and independence of a baseball umpire. But perhaps we shouldn't. There is a great deal of integrity and independence out there, even among those who are obviously faced with temptations to slant their calls. Despite occasional corruption, the cross-pressures on regulators and the competition among those who hold bits and pieces of regulatory power provide important guarantees that no one group can achieve absolute and potentially irresponsible control over other organizations in society. We trust the baseball umpire with arbitrary powers, but we occasionally want the fans or the Commissioner of Baseball to throw the umpire out.

Mixing Regulation with Other Roles

Regulators face other kinds of role conflict. Private regulator groups, such as industry trade associations or educational accrediting groups, often try to mix regulatory with lobbying or promotional functions. Even if they exercise tight discipline and control over their members in some respects, they are often known chiefly to the public or to agencies of government in the role of advocates and defenders of their members' interests. This is one reason for low public confidence in talk of "self-regulation." People find it hard to believe that a boastful parent in public can be a stern one in private.

Government agencies face the same kind of challenge. The Federal Communications Commission, on one hand, is supposed to regulate the radio and television industries; but on the other hand it almost inevitably becomes an advocate for some of the things that the industry wants from Congress or from other agencies of government. The Department of Agriculture has responsibility for seeing that subsidies to corporate farmers are administered responsibly, but it also is expected by the farmers to help lobby for better subsidy arrangements.

With government, there are additional dimensions. For government has become far more than a referee for society; it is a player in many of the games that private organizations are engaged in. Government regulates power companies and universities, but it also competes with them through the public generating plants it has built in many parts of the country and through a network of public colleges and universities that may soon become the dominant group in American higher education. Government regulates the railroads, but it has also underwritten much of their downfall by its investments in highway and airport construction.

Government is a significant source of financing for many of the organizations it regulates. It is partner with the railroads at the local level in strengthening urban commuter services, and at the national level, through Amtrak, in reestablishing intercity passenger schedules. Through loan programs, educational support grants, and research funding, government has in recent years helped finance private as well as public higher education. Government was a major partner through Comsat in the financing of communications satellites for the highly regulated telephone, telegraph, and broadcasting industries.

If the roles of competitor and financier don't complicate things enough, think of government's powers as a customer—not just to purchase huge weapons and computer systems for defense, but as one of the world's biggest buyers of everything from paper clips to hearing aids and consulting services. Especially when various agencies of government get together to set common procurement standards, the design government wants may become the design that the rest of the world has to live with. Government uses this power, in fact, as one of its more effective approaches to regulation. By being fussy as a customer rather than as a formal regulator, it has helped speed the development of automotive safety devices and of interchangeable components and programing languages in the computer industry.

The computer case is an interesting one, because it illustrates how many tools besides such regulatory instruments as antitrust the government can bring to bear. The federal government has been concerned for many years about IBM's dominance of an important and rapidly growing new industry, and IBM has been under more or less continual surveillance by the Antitrust Division for possible restraining action. Well before any antitrust suits were filed, though, government agencies that provided funding to companies and universities for the development of computer resources and applications were cautioned to spread their grants around so that not all the funding would accrue to the users of IBM products. In some cases, government funding on advanced technology projects was channeled in ways that would help other firms match the research and development investments that IBM could afford.

The federal government moved early as a customer to force some centralized planning and review of computer purchase decisions. Various agencies undertook to prepare standards and establish bidding procedures so that they could be met by other than IBM products and services, and large users like the Department of Defense were encouraged to buy from other sources. At the time when work was beginning on machine-independent program languages for business data-processing applications, the government stepped in to keep an IBM-designed language from dominating the field by default. Government groups led the way in developing specifications for COBOL, a language that was as much a challenge for IBM as for any other manufacturer to implement. Government has continued to insist that the specifications for further editions of

COBOL be developed collaboratively by many manufacturers and users, not by a single company. As a customer, government began to resist computer designs that would not permit the attachment of devices built by other companies and began to prod IBM to change pricing policies that made it unattractive for users to mix products and services from two or more sources.

All these steps helped get competitors to IBM established in the computer business; and each, in its own way, contributed to the same goal that an antitrust suit might have pursued. IBM still managed to get a healthy share of government business; but from time to time as IBM managers saw competitive products that got their start in government installations later succeed in the commercial and industrial market, they may have felt only that the government was "giving them the business."

Responding to Regulation

Faced either with massive power or with the more modest kinds of refereeing that a trade association might impose, most organizations normally do not resist regulation and control. Rules are comfortable things to have in business, education, or professional life just as they are in basketball and hockey, because they give a sense of order. They reduce uncertainty, and they also help prevent odd-ball behavior that would be as offensive to the players as to the spectators.

At the same time, organizations don't sit quietly waiting for other people to make the rules, nor do they passively accept whatever government or some other group imposes. The rough-and-tumble of the economic marketplace has its counterpart on the political scene. Housewives try boycotting grocery chains, and large stores get together to limit political activity in parking lots. Students break windows on campus; angered donors ask Congress to pass legislation denying such students access to federal loan funds; and college presidents lobby to have the decision left in their hands. Oil companies in Texas lobby to restrict imports of cheaper oil from overseas, while utility companies in New England lobby to have the restrictions reduced.

All these initiatives are manifestations of the same pluralistic, competitive game we saw in the search for customers and the quest for funds. It's a game in which big organizations can gain advantage by direct access to influential government figures and by their ability to spend money on making their case. But it's also a game in which little individuals can be surprisingly effective. The articulate, persistent antagonist to the big, well-financed organization can find sympathetic listeners. American news media have always liked to play up new versions of the David-Goliath story. Individuals can testify before legislative hearings, just as companies can. Individuals can run for office or try to change the election prospects for others. It pays, then, not to regard regulation as something that happens only when somebody officially passes a law and sets up a supervisory agency, but as an open kind of competition for power over the affairs of organizations, public and private. Anybody can play, and the stakes are high.

Summary

If you expected this chapter to explain and defend a neat and orderly structure for keeping in line the organizations that make up society, we have clearly let you down. We have tried to provide one more piece of evidence on how open and pluralistic our social system is. Regulation is not just a legal process carried out largely by government, but a very complicated network of relationships among organizations, public and private, in which some manage to assert power over others.

Many of these relationships are private and informal, not involving laws or governments at all. Many involve education, persuasion, and bargaining more than they do the exercise of formal authority. Many are complicated because they are not simple relationships between pairs of organizations that concern only an effort by one to guide the other. Any organization has to deal with many kinds of prospective regulators, private and governmental. Some of them are its partners, its customers, its financiers, its competitors as much as they are its mentors or supervisors. And almost none of the relationships are so strong and one-sided that we can look only at the power of the regulator without also considering the ability of the organization being regulated to talk back and to take initiatives that will undermine or change the regulatory effect.

Not only is there no free lunch; it's beginning to look as if there's nothing in sight as simple as a ham sandwich. Everything we have talked about in the last few chapters seems to come up with lettuce, mustard, cheese, pickles, and other trimmings. Perhaps in the next chapter, when we consider the alternative of some more highly organized and centrally structured social systems, we will offer a world-view that's easier to digest.

Notes and References

For three general points of view about government as rulemaker and referee, see Cornelius P. Crotter, *Government and Private Enterprise* (New York: Holt Rinehart and Winston, 1960); John J. Corson, *Business in the Humane Society* (New York: McGraw-Hill, 1971); and Paul W. MacAvoy, *The Crisis of the Regulatory Commissions* (New York: Norton, 1970).

An interesting set of readings is provided by Howard D. Marshall, ed.,

Business and Government: The Problem of Power (Lexington, Mass.: D. C. Heath, 1970). Recent important cases in regulatory policy and practice can be found in Edwin A. Bock, ed., *Government Regulation of Business* (Englewood Cliffs, N.J.: Prentice-Hall, 1965).

For studies with some passion involved, see such products of Ralph Nader's study groups as: James S. Turner, *Chemical Feast: The Report on the Food & Drug Administration* (New York: Grossman, 1970); Robert Fellmeth, *Interstate Commerce Commission: The Report on the Interstate Commerce Commission & Transportation* (New York: Grossman, 1970); *Dead Air: The Report on Air Pollution* (New York: Grossman, 1970); John C. Esposito, *Dry Water: The Report on Water Pollution* (New York: Grossman, 1970).

A useful insight into some of the contending pressures inherent in policy questions of the day is given by Douglass C. North and Roger L. Miller, *The Economics of Public Issues* (New York: Harper & Row, 1971). A more sophisticated analysis is offered by Charles L. Schultze, *The Politics and Economics of Public Spending* (Washington: The Brookings Institution, 1968).

To understand how pressure groups work to achieve political power, try: W. A. Gamson, *Power and Discontent* (Homewood, Ill.: The Dorsey Press, 1968); J. K. Galbraith, *How to Control the Military* (New York: Signet, 1969); and A. Myrick Freeman and Robert H. Haveman, "Clean Rhetoric and Dirty Water," *The Public Interest,* No. 28 (Summer 1972), pp. 51–56.

Finally, for a classic behavioral study of social and personal sources of friction in economic regulation, see Robert E. Lane, *The Regulation of Businessmen* (New Haven: Yale University Press, 1954).

17

*Organizing Society:
Pluralism vs. Hierarchy on a Grand Scale*

In the last three chapters we described the pluralistic, sometimes confusing world in which organizations live. We tried deliberately to put down any illusions that relations with customers, bankers, or government agencies are ever neat and simple. We emphasized the ingenuity with which organizations try to control their relationships with outsiders and with which individuals and groups outside seek to exert control over organizations. We left open the serious question of whether such diverse approaches to marketing, financing, and regulation are good for society at large.

Pluralism is not an accident of history; it is one important concept of how best to serve the public interest. In this chapter we will approach pluralism as a deliberate strategy for social and economic organization and will compare it with some of the alternatives that have been tried. We will raise some questions that should be of compelling interest to readers who may want to redesign society.

Pluralism as a Deliberate Choice

The rationale for pluralism has a variety of historical roots. It has perhaps been best articulated in the philosophical debates of the seventeenth and eighteenth centuries about the nature of man and the requirements for good government; in the Constitution designed

> ### Designing a Government
>
> It is in vain to say that enlightened statesmen will be able to adjust . . . clashing interests and render them all subservient to the public good. Enlightened statesmen will not always be at the helm. Nor, in many cases, can such an adjustment be made at all without taking into view indirect and remote considerations, which will rarely prevail over the immediate interest which one party may find in disregarding the rights of another or the good of the whole.
>
> The inference to which we are brought is, that the *causes* of faction cannot be removed, and that relief is only to be sought in the means of controlling its *effects*.
>
> —From The Federalist Papers, Roy P. Fairfield, ed., p. 19. ©1961 by Doubleday and Company, Inc.

to provide a national government for the United States; and in the efforts of economists like Adam Smith to set conceptual foundations for what we have come to know as the "free enterprise" system.

The advocates of pluralism as a philosophy of social organization set high importance on what individuals want. They see personal, selfish motivations as the main energizing force for human activity. They assume that each person is a better and fairer judge of his or her wants and needs than anyone else, however well intentioned. According to their view, a society is better off to the extent that the actions taken within it make more people happy, on balance, than unhappy.

The assumptions about human nature made by Adam Smith and the framers of our Constitution were not very idealistic. Though they shared the faith of philosophers like Locke that men could be educated to become beneficent and rational decision-makers, they recognized that many people were greedy, combative, unprincipled, and stupid. They did not aspire to bring about any fundamental changes in human nature. Instead, they sought ways of designing a social system that would give people freedom to act in selfish ways but that would set constraints on their choices, thereby ensuring that selfish behavior would often contribute to the overall public welfare.

Hence we find a pervasive emphasis on checks and balances in the American design for government and a reliance on the "invisible hand" of competition in the marketplace to guarantee beneficial social results. On the one hand, the designers encouraged individuals and groups to organize and work hard for personal gain. On the other hand, they believed that social control would emerge from the discipline of the ballot box, the cross-checking of one organiza-

> ### Designing an Economy
>
> As every individual . . . endeavors as much as he can both to employ his capital in the support of domestic industry, and so to direct that industry that its produce may be of the greatest value, every individual necessarily labors to render the annual revenue of the society as great as he can. He generally, indeed, neither intends to promote the public interest, nor knows how much he is promoting it. . . . He intends only his own security; and by directing that industry in such a manner as its produce may be of the greatest value, he intends only his own gain, and he is in this, as in many other cases, led by an invisible hand to promote an end which was no part of his intention. . . . By pursuing his own interest he frequently promotes that of the society more effectually than when he really intends to promote it.
>
> —Adam Smith, An Inquiry into the Nature and Causes of the Wealth of Nations (Homewood, Ill.: Richard D. Irwin, 1963), Vol. 2, pp. 22–23.

tion by others equally powerful, and the decisions of customers to buy or not to buy. On both the political and economic sides they set up arrangements to ensure that selfish persons and organizations who did not serve others would be forced out of power.

What the political and economic designers of the late eighteenth century feared most were patterns of government or economic organization that would give small groups of people inordinate amounts of unrestrained power. Neither the kings and princes nor the monopolistic mercantile combines of the time inspired much confidence that groups possessed of power would serve the public rather than themselves. Pluralism might not make the leaders of society wiser, but it would at least make them fairer and more responsive.

Consider an example of what we must be willing to live with if we truly believe in a pluralistic system: Fred Happenstance wants to get rich. With only that in mind, he opens a night club on a residential street right across from the main entrance to an army base. If the soldiers like Fred's place, for whatever reason, they're happy to part with their money; and Fred is happy to take it. So far, with many people happier and no one less happy, society as a whole is a little better off.

Conversely, if the soldiers don't like Fred's place, they stay away; and Fred is likely to go out of business. Here again, though Fred may be disappointed, society is well served. If Fred still wants to get rich, he'll look for a new way to apply his energies that will be attractive to customers of some kind. The soldiers might get a bowling alley, for example.

Combining the Two

> I believe that competitive enterprise really does possess a dynamism and ability to innovate that bureaucracies divorced from markets do not possess. I believe that profit-seeking enterprise—despite its many faults—does provide the best mechanism we have for spurring efficiency in resource allocation, for encouraging innovation, . . . for securing the transference of resources to new product lines or to play an entirely different role in society. Also private businesses have the great advantage that they can and do disappear when they are not doing a relevant and effective job any longer. . . .
>
> The dynamics of the market and feedback control through profit—not corporate form or management techniques—make private business the most effective innovator and resource allocator man has ever invented. For society to benefit from this much needed ability to fulfill human needs, it is the social responsibility of business to pursue profit. The task of government is to establish incentives and constraints in such a way that profit is made doing what society most needs done, in a manner society finds acceptable.
>
> —John Diebold, "The Social Responsibility of Business" (A speech to the Ministry of Economics and Finance Meeting, Paris, France, June 21, 1972).

Fred has to think about other people's happiness in other ways, too. If he needs money to finance his club, he shops around. He may get a loan from a local bank in return for 8 percent interest and a commitment to keep his checking account there. Or he may borrow from a local mobster at 20 percent interest and a fifty-fifty split of profits. Again, if the soldiers are happy, if Fred is happy, and if the banker or the mobster is happy, more has happened than simply the serving of selfish interests. Enough people are satisfied so that society as a whole is presumably better off.

Now suppose that the neighbors on the street object to having a garish, noisy night club in their midst. As customers of the bank, they can tell the banker they'll take their deposits elsewhere if he doesn't recall Fred's loan. As voters, they can let the mayor know that they'll oppose his reelection unless he finds a way to shut Fred's club down. As neighbors, they can warn the base commander that they'll stop the volunteer services they have previously performed for the base. Or they might threaten to write their congressman about generals who refuse to cooperate with the community.

All these courses of action represent possible approaches, in a pluralistic system, toward accommodation, toward establishing a new balance of individual desires and social benefits. Under such pressures, the banker, the mayor, the base commander, and others will recalculate what constitutes their personal self-interest and will suggest to Fred that he recalculate his. If the accommodation process works, there is no guarantee that everyone will end up happy; but there still is the assumption that the new balance will be better than the old one for the community as a whole. The new balance might leave Fred in business, with his promise to restrict the club's hours or with the city council's ruling that no more clubs will be allowed in that area. Or the new balance might put Fred out of business, with some compensation going to him for agreeing to close the club or to move it.

The point of this example is that a pluralistic system, in a fairly neutral way, allows people like Fred to open up a night club. It leaves Fred free to decide whether he will spend all his profits on ostentatious living for himself or sleep in a bare room over the club's kitchen and donate every cent of the proceeds to help orphans go to college. The system does not prejudge the question of whether Fred deserves customers, financial assistance, or the support of neighbors and the base commander. True, Fred is subject to laws on hours of operation, on minimum ages for buying drinks, and on many other matters. But Fred knows that he can try to get those laws changed by working through trade and community channels.

The system gives Fred opportunity, but it does not guarantee his survival. If he can't build the club into a viable business, if he can't meet his obligations to the bank or the mob, the club will close and Fred may lose every penny he has put into it and be liable for other debts besides. A pluralistic world would regard the club's demise simply as a sign that "it wasn't needed" or "it hadn't proved its worth."

The Failures of Pluralism

By most measures, even to the eyes of detractors, the pluralistic approach to social organization does many things well. It helps keep the level of social tension low because it encourages people to make their own choices. It tries to facilitate individual initiative and stimulate individual motivation without a heavy overlay of social restraints. It keeps the locus and use of power fluid and provides protection and remedies against abusive concentrations of power. To the extent that people know what is good for them now and will be good for them in the future, pluralistic mechanisms give them not only the feeling but the substance of control over their own destinies.

On the other hand, pluralism is not without defects. A number of problems have led even people who believe strongly in individual freedom and in the diffusion of power to propose and try other alternatives.

It is hard, in the first place, to develop and maintain a pluralistic system that really prevents abusive concentrations of power. Superficial developments of democracy and capitalistic free enterprise in many parts of the world have failed miserably, not because the idea was bad, but because power was never distributed widely nor were economic opportunities granted to more than a favored few. Democracy cannot succeed unless those who are asked to accept it feel that their votes count and unless the government changes its behavior as people's preferences change. Capitalism is not truly pluralistic if a few players hold all the marbles and if large segments of the population know that they have no chance to implement their ideas or exercise their talents.

Another difficulty lies in deciding how much each new generation should be allowed to benefit from the accomplishments of the preceding one. Should an Adams, a Roosevelt, or a Kennedy hold any preferential advantage in seeking political office because a father or a brother was a successful officeholder? Should the son of a successful business entrepreneur hold any preferential right to inherit his father's wealth or to take over the management of the business? There is no doubt that the opportunity to build power and status for one's children is a powerful motivation. Nor is there any doubt that the sons and daughters of talented people seem to possess talent as well as money and power. Still, few distortions of power and opportunity in human society have proved more pernicious than the imbalances that result from the unchecked accumulation of hereditary wealth and privilege.

Another concentration of power in a pluralistic society arises from the advantages that size bestows on organizations. A handful of companies in a technology-dependent industry can make it prohibitively expensive for other firms to enter that industry. In 1900, all you needed to get into the automotive business was an idea, a modest amount of capital, access to some skilled metal workers, and a reasonably equipped shop. But now success demands research and engineering laboratories, automatic equipment, complex assembly lines, international marketing organizations, and other necessities that put the price of entry—even on a modest scale—into the hundreds of millions of dollars. The question of whether companies like General Motors or IBM should be allowed to continue in their present form depends not only on how well they have served the public in the past but on estimates of how well the public can be insured against the potentially exploitative behavior that their size makes possible.

Concentration can also result from luck or from skill in winning control over scarce physical resources. Consider Kuwait. A pluralistic, profit-seeking system argues forcefully that riches should come to

> ### The Transformation of Kuwait
>
> In less than thirty years, Kuwait has changed from one of the poorest nations in the world to one of the wealthiest. Before the discovery of oil there, most Kuwaitis worked in pearling and seafaring, and average family income was less than $180 per year. By the mid-sixties, with their country the largest oil producer in the Middle East, revenues to the economy from oil alone amounted to nearly $17,000 per family per year. Social services provided by the state to Kuwaiti citizens were funded at higher levels than in the United Kingdom or Sweden, and Kuwait had put together a fund of nearly a billion dollars to support economic development in other Arab countries.
>
> —See Fakhri Shehab, "Kuwait: A Super-affluent Society," Foreign Affairs, Vol. 42, No. 3 (April 1964), 461–74.

the people willing to take the risks and spend the money and effort needed to explore for oil and develop the wells and transportation facilities to take the oil to market. But the sultan of Kuwait, and his people, have become incredibly rich simply because they happen to be living atop a vast supply of petroleum. In a pluralistic system with a high tolerance for profit seeking and a strongly developed notion of private property, some concentrations of power result not from skill or effort but from blind luck. Whether it's oil, copper, or simply the last remaining unpolluted beach on the lake, questions arise about whether valuable resources should be treated as private or as community property.

Beyond the continuing issue of how to maintain true pluralism in the distribution of power and opportunity, another problem is that pluralism is nearsighted. As individuals, we may be very good in sizing up our short-run interest, but we have a poor record in recognizing and acting on our longer-range interests. Consider pollution control. The villain of the piece, when a history of our times is written, may not turn out to be the greedy corporate manager indifferent to human life and an unspoiled environment. The villain may turn out to be each of us: the citizens who for years have been voting down expenditures to control the discharge of sewage into rivers, the customers who keep buying air conditioners and high-powered automobiles in disregard for the new power plants and offshore oil wells these require, the mining community that would rather have steady work at the risk of lung disease than no work at all.

Another likely villain is the competitive system. While competition encourages efficiency, it also encourages cutting corners—

Alienation from Capitalism

> Writing shortly before the Civil War, George Fitzhugh, the most gifted of Southern apologists for slavery, attacked the capitalist North in these terms:
>
>> In a free society none but the selfish virtues are in repute, because none other help a man in the race of competition. In such a society virtue loses all her loveliness, because of her selfish aims. Good men and bad men have the same end in view—self-promotion and self-elevation. . . .
>
> At the time, this accusation was a half-truth. The North was not yet "a free society," . . . Suffice it to say that, with every passing decade, Fitzhugh's charge . . . became more valid. From having been a *capitalist, republican community*, with shared values and a quite unambiguous claim to the title of a just order, the United States became a *free, democratic society* where the will to success and privilege was severed from its moral moorings.
>
> . . . My reading of history is that, in the same way as men cannot for long tolerate a sense of spiritual meaninglessness in their individual lives, so they cannot for long accept a society in which power, privilege, and property are not distributed according to some morally meaningful criteria. Nor is equality itself any more acceptable than inequality . . . if equality is merely a brute fact rather than a consequence of an ideology or social philosophy. This explains what otherwise seems paradoxical: that small inequalities in capitalist countries can become the source of intense controversy while relatively larger inequalities in socialist or communist countries are blandly overlooked. . . . I would say . . . that people's notions of equality or inequality have extraordinarily little to do with arithmetic and almost everything to do with political philosophy.
>
> I believe that what holds for equality also holds for liberty. People feel free when they subscribe to a prevailing social philosophy; they feel unfree when the prevailing social philosophy is unpersuasive. . . . The average working man in nineteenth-century America had far fewer "rights" than his counterpart today; but he was far more likely to boast about his being a free man.
>
> —Irving Kristol, " 'When virtue loses all her loveliness'—Some Reflections on Capitalism and 'The Free Society'," The Public Interest, 21 (Fall 1970), 7–9.

sometimes on product quality, sometimes on costs. The same people who press an American textile mill to increase its costs by installing pollution-control equipment will also brag about paying less for shirts imported from countries whose mills pollute at will. Efforts to sell shares in mutual funds invested only in the stocks of "socially responsible" companies have failed because those funds have had an indifferent record of achieving capital gains or earning dividends.

> *Freedom and Morality*
>
> Responding to Kristol and Fitzhugh, another author asks why Americans have largely remained enthusiastic about capitalism.
>
>> Not because they looked to it for social justice; . . . They liked capitalism because it was so very suitable to something they valued even higher: namely, personal freedom. For people who wanted above all to decide for themselves the terms on which they made their living, a contract society with all its risks and rigors had obvious advantages over the status societies they or their fathers had left. Capitalism . . . did promise opportunity, and it is for this that Americans have cherished it.
>>   . . . The absence of social justice in capitalism—which Kristol now mourns and I claim was never there—was in any case never a very serious drawback. Believers in opportunity preferred to bet on their own brains, cunning, and energy, but also on their luck. . . . A sane trust in luck has one agreeable social side-effect: the winner can take no moral kudos, the loser need take no moral blame, and his envy of the winner is without bitterness. . . .
>>   [Capitalism] perhaps . . . gave too much scope for greed. If so, it has lost a loveliness it never claimed nor really had. In capitalism's best days, it could rely on other elements in the body politic to point out that greed is not a virtue.
>
> —John K. Jessup, "'Capitalism' and 'The Free Society'," The Public Interest, 22 (Winter 1971), 103.

Success, bargains, profits matter more for the here and now; and in maximizing present rewards and minimizing present costs a pluralistic society may do serious damage to its future.

A third major weakness is that pluralism has at least an amoral, perhaps an immoral, cast to it. It accepts people and their motivations for what they are, and rewards competitive and selfish rather than cooperative and altruistic behavior. One of the most significant contributions to the development of the United States was the construction of a transcontinental network of railroads during the nineteenth century. Yet the men who organized and financed that construction and who reaped financial rewards for their work included some of the greediest businessmen ever to grace the American business scene. And on the political side many of the leaders who have been most effective have been very unattractive men, respected for the services they rendered rather than for the motives that prompted them or for the bribes they accepted.

Competition often looks wasteful and foolish, and indeed at times it can be very inappropriate behavior. Though competition often leads to genuinely better products and services, it can also lead to gross overexpansion of capacity, extravagant expenditures on advertising and promotion, or expensive duplication of effort to achieve separately things that might better have been achieved in less costly ways on an industry-wide or society-wide basis. Often competition produces many organizations that offer identical services, each aimed at the same segment of the market, rather than the development of a variety of differentiated products and services that will satisfy all segments of the market. Competition rooted in slavish imitation sometimes seems to foreclose competition based on creative experimentation and innovation.

Alternatives to Pluralism

Pluralism is not the only answer. There are other ways to run a railroad — and a society. All of them involve concepts of government that make government the principal initiator and controller of organizational activity. Society, in effect, becomes a corporation, organized in good hierarchical form; and government takes over as manager. In ideal forms of socialism or communism, the resources of society and the returns achieved by government belong to the people. The people are owners and stockholders. In fact, however, in the socialized economies of Eastern Europe, government, like the management of many private corporations, develops a momentum of its own. While decisions are taken in the name of the people, the people's voice in planning and decision making may be very faint.

In these societies pluralism is suppressed in favor of order and hierarchy. Government leaders talk of coordinating efforts so that everyone can work together. They orchestrate the society. They operate the organizations of society as units of government. They frown on competition and conflict. Not content to act as referees, they stage and staff the whole shooting match.

At least on a theoretical basis, such a solution corrects the failings of pluralism that we have noted. If government owns the resources of a society — the land, the factories, the accumulated capital — it can allocate and reallocate them in the public interest. It doesn't have to fear that families or churches or corporations will obtain undue power and wealth that they can manipulate for private gain. If an enterprise needs capital, that capital can be budgeted from public resources; and except when the state finds it convenient to exact interest as a way of setting priorities, it can allocate the capital without requiring interest payments. Any profits earned by the enterprise return to the state, either for reinvestment or for the support of other programs.

> *Planning — Pro*
>
> If planned economies, benevolent dictatorships, perfectionistic societies and other utopian ventures have failed, we must remember that unplanned, undictated, and unperfected cultures have failed too. A failure is not always a mistake; it may simply be the best one can do under the circumstances. The real mistake is to stop trying. Perhaps we cannot now design a successful culture as a whole, but we can design better practices in a piecemeal fashion.
>
> —From B. F. Skinner, Beyond Freedom and Dignity, pp. 155–56. ©1971 by Alfred A. Knopf, Inc.

As owner of the resources of society, the government can plan for the future. Instead of leaving to private initiative the decision on whether to start a steel mill or a night club, the state can in principle decide on the relative desirability of each course of action. Government leaders can set priorities and allocate budgets for the economy as a whole much as corporations in the United States do for their internal departments. As custodians of the future of their country, they are in a position to anticipate the need for pollution control and other environmental protection practices.

The government is also in a position to appeal to the best rather than the worst of human motivations. A great deal of the appeal of movements like socialism and communism comes from their emphasis on cooperative effort and sharing rather than on competition and the survival of the fittest. They talk about *from* each, not *to* each, on the basis of his ability. They insist that people are motivated to work hard when they are directly interested in building a better society for all.

Or so these systems are supposed to work. Let's look at what actually seems to be happening in some of the countries that have adopted highly centralized state management of organizations under a socialist or communist system.

Life in a State-Organized Society

Western political ideology has been dominated for many years by the issue of socialism versus capitalism, and many mixtures of the two have been tried. Yet it is hard to see any clear relationship between the mode of economic organization and rates of economic growth. The Soviet Union has built itself into a major industrial power under socialism, and Japan has done the same under capitalism. From 1955 to 1970, Yugoslavia (mostly socialist) had a growth rate of 5.6 percent

> *Planning — Con*
>
> ... History is not governed by reason. ... History grows like a living tree ... reason is an ax: you'll never make it grow better by applying reason to it. ... History is a river; it has its own laws which govern its flow. ... Then along come some clever people who say that it's a stagnant pond and must be diverted into another and better channel: all that's needed is to choose a better place and dig a river bed. But the course of a river can't be interrupted — break it off only an inch and it won't flow any longer. And we're being told that the bed must be forcibly diverted by several thousand yards. The bonds between generations, bonds of institutions, tradition, custom, are what hold the banks of the river bed together and keep the stream flowing.
>
> —*Alexander Solzhenitsyn,* August 1914 *(New York: Farrar Straus & Giroux, 1972), pp. 410–11.*

per year; the Soviet Union had a growth rate of 4.1 percent per year. During the same period, among capitalist countries, some representative rates included West Germany at 4.4 percent, France at 3.8 percent, the United States at 3.1 percent, the United Kingdom at 2.3 percent, and Japan at 10.5 percent.

Many European countries actually operate on a mixed basis. Sweden has brought a number of basic industrial organizations under government ownership, but it lets others operate on an open free-enterprise basis. Yugoslavia sticks for the most part to state ownership, but it has in practice decentralized society in a way that makes each industrial organization autonomous but still responsible to an elected group of its own workers, who control it on behalf of the state.

It's a very different kind of a world in the Soviet Union, where government planners have to decide how much wheat to grow, how many automobiles to make, how many pairs of shoes to produce, and how many new department stores to build — all as part of the comprehensive five-year plan that governs the development of the economy. Once a plan has been made, top government officials work out with the leaders of the various industrial units how the plan is to be achieved, what funding will be granted, how work will be scheduled, what prices will be charged, and how results will be measured. It all gets very complicated.

And because it is so complicated, it doesn't always work well. The state as owner and allocator of capital is in many cases not very effective. Fred Happenstance, in deciding whether or not to open a night club, probably has a good sense of what kind of club will work and what his customers will want. Ben Bureaucrat, sitting hundreds of miles away from the local scene in a ministry of culture and entertainment, might plan a club for the same location Fred chose, but he would have a hard time sensing what would work best in that locale.

For this reason, many socialist countries, including the Soviet Union, have tried to decentralize the planning and allocation function in order to bring planners closer to users. In some countries, restaurants, night clubs, and small stores have been returned to private hands because planning proved too cumbersome and insensitive, even with efforts to decentralize. Plans have been made more contingent on customer response, as they would be in a private American corporation. Gone are the days when a Soviet factory could continue to grind out dresses that no woman would buy, simply because the plan called for 200,000 of that style.

Planners in socialist countries have also begun to use prices and interest rates, or substitutes for them, to help sharpen and control the allocation process. They recognize that when resources are scarce, predetermined prices or promises of capital at no interest cost can lead to the gross misallocation of resources. If the price is right or if capital is free, goods and funds may be used to build thousands of dumptrucks just when the country needs fire engines. Planners in socialist countries are seeking pluralistic ways to respond to what individuals need and want.

Even within state-owned systems, stubborn problems of overconcentration of power and accumulation of privilege emerge. In an open pluralistic system, many such abuses are blocked by the market mechanism, by voters or customers who refuse to support the abuser. The problem in a large state-owned system is that the person who has accumulated excess power and privilege within the bureaucratic hierarchy can be very hard to remove. What should be decided on grounds of economic priority or social need often gets decided on interpersonal, political grounds.

One of the most serious failures of planned economic systems is that they have not proved to be any more farsighted about social needs than the pluralistic, profit-oriented economies of the West. They seem to do less well in anticipating consumer tastes, and they have proved no better in anticipating the long-term consequences of short-term decisions.

The problem is complicated by the monolithic nature of these state systems. In the Soviet Union, for example, public elections are held chiefly for the purpose of ratifying a slate of candidates, not for expressing preferences among different men and programs. State planners and heads of industrial enterprises in the Soviet cannot engage in vigorous public debate, nor can the press be critical of their decisions, because all are part of the same government apparatus. In a pluralistic system, by contrast, many of the best initiatives for change and for long-range decision making are forged in the crucible

Pollution Under Public Management

Marshall I. Goldman has documented the problems that the Soviet Union is having in getting pollution under control. "Any depressing story that can be told about an incident in the United States can be matched by a horror story from the U.S.S.R." He writes of Russian rivers catching fire, like the Cuyahoga in Cleveland; of oil slicks and water level changes in the Caspian Sea; of difficulties that conservationists have had in slowing the discharge of paper mill wastes into Lake Baikal, one of the largest and purest fresh water lakes on earth; of chemical plant fumes that are destroying oak and pine forests near Tolstoy's former summer estate; and of destruction of Black Sea beaches by contractors seeking a cheap source of gravel. He continues:

> Despite the fact that our economies differ, many, if not all, of the usual economic explanations for pollution in the non-Communist world also hold for the Soviet Union. . . .
>
> In addition, . . . there are some reasons for polluting which seem to be peculiar to a socialist country such as the Soviet Union in its present state of economic development. First of all, state officials . . . are judged almost entirely by how much they are able to increase their region's economic growth. . . . There is almost a political as well as an economic imperative to devour idle resources. . . . These officials do not have to face a voting constituency which might reflect the conservation point of view, such as the League of Women Voters or the Sierra Club in this country. It is true that there are outspoken conservationists in the U.S.S.R. who are often supported by the Soviet press, but for the most part they do not have a vote. . . .
>
> It is as hard for the Russians as it is for us to include social costs in factory-pricing calculations. However, not only do they have to worry about social cost accounting, they also are unable to reflect all the private cost considerations. Because there is no private ownership of land, there are no private property owners to protest the abuse of various resources. . . . The lack of such private property holders or resort owners and of such a calculation seems to be the major reason why erosion is destroying the Black Sea coast. There is no one who can lay claim to the pebbles on the shore front, and so they are free to anyone who wants to cart them away. . . .

—Marshall I. Goldman, "The Convergence of Environmental Disruption," Science, 170 (Oct. 2, 1972), 37–42. ©1972 by the American Association for the Advancement of Science.

of open argument among government planners, business leaders, and the press.

Thus the Soviet Union has moved at least as slowly as the capitalist countries in facing the problem of environmental protection. Yet that is an area in which state ownership, farsighted planning,

> ### *Consumer Power in the U.S.S.R.*
>
> ... It was discovered a few years ago that when more than one Russian factory produced supposedly identical television sets, there were wide variations in quality and reliability among the outputs of these factories. This often led to the consumer's refusal to buy any sets since the chance of getting a lemon was high. One way to achieve greater uniformity would have been to set and enforce high in-plant work standards and to back these up with rigid inspection. But this would have been extremely costly. As an alternative each plant was required to place a prominent and distinctive mark on its own output. This clearly identified it as the product of that particular plant. Then when customers experienced quality difficulties, Soviet officials could identify the plant from which it came and take appropriate action. But what happened instead was that the public merely stopped buying that particular "brand" of television sets. When its sales dropped, that particular factory's sales dropped below the volume required under the economic plan. The result was unhappy for the plant manager. Thus the independent action of customers forced the manager to take his own corrective measures rather than requiring a governmental authority to take action. . . . Factory marks became brand labels, and their existence enabled consumers to exercise a particular kind of powerful sovereignty.
>
> —From *The Marketing Mode* by Theodore Levitt, p. 335. ©1969 by McGraw-Hill Book Company. Used with permission of McGraw-Hill Book Company.

and concern for the public good should have led to swift success. It turns out that the Soviet planners have been asleep on this issue. They have given higher priority to the development of industry, viewing expenditures for pollution control as postponable. In some instances deals have been made and bribes paid to avoid the cost and inconvenience of corrective action. All in all, the picture is not much prettier than what we see in capitalist societies.

Socialist countries, finally, have had difficulty making a desire for cooperation and sharing elicit the kind of effort and creativity that is prompted elsewhere by the pursuit of personal wealth and prestige. Self-interest, whatever we might prefer to believe, seems to be a stronger and more reliable source of motivation than concern for others. The cooperative spirit, moreover, is easier to tap in the heat of revolution or in the early stages of a new organization than it is in established industrial or bureaucratic systems. The challenge in the Soviet Union and in the United States as well is to get the factory worker or the middle manager to feel any kind of relationship between doing his job and building a better future for himself or for society.

For a good socialist, it goes against the grain to talk of executive perquisites, monetary incentives, or profits; but even good socialists have had to face up to such matters. One of the most active areas of search in socialist countries today is for ways to build incentives for individuals and organizational units—ways to reward them for producing more, doing better work, suggesting and implementing new ideas, or taking better care of the environment.

Summary

The pluralistic society is not necessarily a pretty one. It involves a lot of pushing and shoving by individuals and organizations. It encourages grubbing for profit, political position, and personal gain. It sometimes seems unmanaged and unmanageable, with no one anticipating or facing the big decisions that eventually may determine society's ability to survive.

Yet pluralism has advantages. It allows for a great deal of individual freedom and organizational autonomy. It permits—in fact, encourages— variety, experimentation, and change. It doesn't prevent the accumulation and abuse of power, but it does help keep the centers of power diffuse and fluid enough so that abuses can be checked before they get badly out of hand.

The alternative to pluralism is centralized planning and control, a step sometimes taken by despots but sometimes by groups sincerely interested in building a better society. Centralized planning may one day deliver on its promises. For the moment, however, whole societies designed like huge corporate hierarchies have not produced clearly better solutions to social problems.

Centralized planners haven't yet discovered how to arrange all the interactions and responses that make pluralistic systems satisfying to individuals. They have had no notable success in looking farther ahead than the managers of organizations in a pluralistic society. And when they make errors in judgment, those errors may do extensive damage and take a long time to reverse.

Centralized systems tend to become bogged down in hierarchical structure and bureaucracy. Efforts are now being made in most state-run economies to borrow from the pluralistic experience some of the incentives and techniques of organization that give pluralism its effectiveness.

The planners in a centralized society often resort to the same simplistic approach that once characterized the managers of private organizations: spell everything out, plan how all the pieces fit together, build a strong system of authority, and make everyone do his part for the good of the company. We have seen how hard that is to do in a factory, a school, or a small service organization; it's many times harder to build such a system for a whole society.

It's well to recognize the potential of planning and systems design, but it's also well to recognize that neatness for its own sake doesn't count. Attention to individual wants and needs, sensitivity to local conditions, and responsiveness to particular problems and opportunities can produce results that put the best planners to shame. Pluralism is not a cop-out. It is a tested philosophy for keeping a large system open, moving, and effective in serving human needs.

Notes and References

For perspectives on various ways of relating government to the organization and control of economic activity, there are many sources. Three that cover a variety of countries and different times in history are: G. Grossman, *Economic Systems* (Englewood Cliffs, N.J.: Prentice-Hall, 1970); Alfred R. Oxenfeldt and Vsevalod Holubnychy, *Economic Systems in Action,* 3rd ed. (New York: Holt, Rinehart and Winston, 1965); and Barbara Ward, *The Lopsided World* (New York: Norton, 1968).

For readings that describe how some particular organizational arrangements work, see Part 2 of M. L. Joseph, N. C. Seeber, and G. L. Bach, eds., *Economic Analysis and Policy,* 3rd ed. (Englewood Cliffs, N.J.: Prentice-Hall, 1971). See also Donald Grunewald and Henry Bass, eds., *Public Policy and the American Corporation* (New York: Appleton-Century-Crofts, 1966).

It helps in viewing the way the world actually runs to read and evaluate some more partisan works, but ones that don't get bogged down in arbitrary distinctions between idealized versions of capitalism and its alternatives. One book that's fun as a "period piece" if you can find it is Bernard Shaw, *The Intelligent Woman's Guide to Socialism and Capitalism* (New York: Brentano's, 1928).

Others, more currently available, include: James Burnham, *The Managerial Revolution* (Bloomington, Ind.: Indiana University Press, 1960); Milton Friedman, *Capitalism and Freedom* (Chicago: University of Chicago Press, 1962); and John K. Galbraith, *The New Industrial State* (New York: Houghton Mifflin, 1971).

See also "Capitalism Today," a special issue of *The Public Interest,* 21 (Fall 1970).

A good, brief review of experience with state ownership of economic enterprises is found in Chapter 25 of John M. Blair, *Economic Concentration* (New York: Harcourt Brace Jovanovich, 1972), pp. 677–706.

18

The Organization Abroad: Good Guy or Bad Guy?

Organizations live in a human, social, political, economic world. And more and more often that world extends well beyond the boundaries of the organization's home country. American automobile-makers go abroad. So does Gillette. So do Brazilian coffee-growers, Norwegian shipping companies, the Lutheran Church, the Ford Foundation, and Coca-Cola. They send parts of themselves into other countries, to other peoples, into other cultures.

The purpose of this short chapter is to raise some moral and social questions associated with organizational tourism, questions that arise for General Electric in Paris, for an oil company on the Arabian Peninsula, and for the Chrysler Corporation in the Union of South Africa. The chapter consists mostly of questions. It gives few answers, simply because we don't have very good answers to offer. But the questions are becoming increasingly compelling, especially for those of us who live in developed countries.

Certainly the problem of American organizations abroad is in the spotlight of public attention. Recently some students at Stanford protested, all in the same breath, against (1) research in biological and chemical warfare, (2) counterinsurgency research, and even (3) research into economic development. The moral issues in number 1 seem clear, in number 2 a little less clear. But is economic development an evil? If so, when and how? When is "economic development" simply a euphemism for exploitation of the have-nots by the haves?

Should the United States government and private organizations keep their economic hands off other countries? And their social and cultural and religious hands, too? Some anthropologists come close to holding that view, arguing that even medical help represents an intervention into the basic cultures of other societies that causes them to lose both their identity and their societal pride.

Morality and Propriety

So the questions we are posing (but not answering) include some mundane ones like whether or not the Coca-Cola Company should try to market its products in Malaysia, and some more transcendent ones like, "Is it our duty to fight against slavery when we see it?"

Let's start with some of the simpler issues. Should Sears Roebuck send its dollars and people to open a store in Rio? Or is that a bad thing to do? Certainly the new store will compete with Brazilian stores. Certainly Sears will take money out of the country sooner or later, probably more than it puts in. If not, Sears would not have been very interested in opening the store in the first place—any more than it would have been interested in opening a nonprofitable store in Kansas City.

Of course, the new store will introduce a wide variety of products into Brazil, many of which were not available to Brazilian consumers before. On the other hand, it will probably stir up materialistic, American-like needs among otherwise (at least in our fantasies) pastoral, idyllic, nonmaterialistic Brazilians. But the store will also provide jobs and training for Brazilians and a market for small Brazilian manufacturing companies and craftsmen. Anyway, shouldn't we leave it to the Brazilian consumer to decide whether he wants to buy a Sears barbecue for his back yard? If the Brazilians don't want Sears' products, the store will fail. So why fuss?

The Graduate School of Business at Stanford University (like many other business schools in the United States) has helped set up counterparts in other countries, including a business school in Peru. Initially, that school was staffed almost exclusively by Americans, but gradually the number of Americans has been reduced and Peruvians educated in Peru, the United States, and elsewhere have now taken over. Peruvian students, who can earn good-quality MBA degrees at the school, thus far have found good jobs in Peru. They go into large companies for the most part, though some go into government.

Most large industries in Peru, however, are not Peruvian. They are either foreign-controlled (mostly by Americans), or else they are locally controlled companies set up by naturalized Peruvians who immigrated from Europe or Asia. The Japanese assemble automobiles in Lima; so do the French, the Germans, and the Americans. And many European and Asian countries hold mining interests in the Peruvian Andes. Many Peruvian MBAs go to work for those firms, or for firms run by German-Peruvians or French-Peruvians.

Question: Is Stanford exploiting Peru? Is it simply producing people to staff foreign firms which thus, even more effectively, can use the Peruvians to their own advantage? Or does a cadre of highly educated, highly skilled young Peruvian executives constitute instead a valuable net asset for Peru?

Recently, Peru was taken over by a military junta that cannot easily be classified as rightist or leftist. Certainly it is not very pro-American. Should Stanford withdraw the slight support it is still giving the school because the government is being nasty to Americans? Or should Stanford have withdrawn that support even if the government had turned out to be pro-American? Indeed perhaps *because* it was pro-American? How far left, or right, must the government go before Stanford pulls out? Or is the nature of the government irrelevant? Or should the Stanford people stay until they're kicked out?

Let's cross over to South Africa. There the regime is avowedly racist, preventing black or "coloured" people or Indians from holding certain classes of jobs and from living or working in, or even visiting, white universities and white neighborhoods. But American firms invest heavily in South Africa, more heavily than they have invested in black African states. Would we help kill racism by pulling our investments out? If our industrial investment should be withdrawn, should other kinds of investment be withdrawn as well? Should American professors, for example, be prevented from teaching in South African universities? Should we refuse to study South African heart-transplant techniques? Should we refuse to admit white South African students to American universities?

If you favor cutting off all contact, would you have favored the same course in Czechoslovakia after the Russians moved in? Would we have helped the Czechs by boycotting them? And if you favor withdrawal, how would you do it? By government decree?

Consider another problem. You are the vice-president for exploration for a large American oil company. You are prospecting for new sources of oil around the world. Your geologists have been permitted to do some exploration in a small state on the Persian Gulf. This state, a small sheikdom with a population of around 75,000, is one of the slowest-changing societies in the world. There are literally no hospitals, no physicians, no schools, no roads, although the sheik is by no means poor. Officially there is no slavery. You might decide not to send your geologists there, to refuse even to explore for oil. You might take the moral position that by going in you would lend support to an oppressive dictatorship that continues to keep its people in serfdom.

Or you might choose to stay out for another moral reason: we have no right to tamper with the traditional ways of another society; what's old is right; oil wells and money and Coca Cola will just ruin those nice simple people.

Or you might seize on the opportunity to do good. If you go in and find oil, then the sheikdom will become really rich. Even though most of the money will go to the sheik, some of it will surely filter down to the people, especially if the sheik has their interests at heart.

Or you might just treat the problem as a short-term economic one. All you're interested in is whether or not there is oil there, and whether or not you can negotiate with the sheik to get it out at an economic price so that you can make some money too. The rest of the problem is the sheikdom's, not yours.

What is the "right" course of action? And if you don't know, to whom should you go for an answer? To the Supreme Court of the United States? To the drug addiction committee of the United Nations? Or to the John Birch Society?

Let's go on without an answer. As an executive in a hard-nosed American oil company, let's suppose you take an old-fashioned view of your duty. You decide that your first job is to make money for your corporation. So you negotiate with the sheik. It just happens in this case that the sheik isn't a very pleasant person. In fact he's a bit of a nut. He sits in a tower in his palace all day with a rifle and a pair of binoculars because he's afraid somebody is going to assassinate him. His fears are not unfounded. Several of his brothers had their heads chopped off by the agent of another brother right in the middle of a big family dinner party. But you sit up in the tower with him and negotiate, and he finally permits you to bring in your tractors, bulldozers, drilling rigs, and two hundred American workers.

Once you're there, you incidentally discover that the drinking water is very brackish. And as long as you have the drilling equipment there anyway, you decide to drill some deep wells for fresh water, at least enough for your own employees. Sure enough, the water comes bubbling up. But the oil does not. So after a year of drilling dry wells you decide to give up. There's no oil to be had. It was a risk. You took it and lost.

Not out of any great altruism, but simply because it won't cost you anything, you go to the sheik before you depart and suggest that you leave the fresh water wells intact so that his people can have some decent water to drink. You also offer to leave several tractors, in part because it's costly to move them and in part because you want to preserve the good will you have built up.

But the sheik flies into a rage. He insists that you cover the water wells with six feet of sand and that you take every piece of your equipment out of the country with you. He doesn't want tractors to plow his sandy fields. He'd rather have the women do it with sticks, as they always have. He doesn't want his people drinking fresh water. They have done just fine with brackish water for 3,000 years.

So you pack your things and get out. Did you do anything wrong? Did the sheik do anything immoral? Should we organize a protest? Against whom?

You go on to the next sheikdom. Here you do hit oil. And you discover, too, that one fellow on your staff has really got through to the sheik. The sheik likes him and listens to his advice and suggestions. Indeed, he will negotiate with no one else. So that executive stays on. But after five years in the desert his wife and children become a little restless. They want to go home to Houston. Do you pull him out? Or do you offer him a fat bonus to stay on?

The sheik's brother-in-law comes around one day and suggests that since things are going so well for your company, and since the country is in bad shape, you might want to contribute to a little charity he has set up for the construction of a hospital. You agree and come up with a generous contribution. Then you discover that the sheik is furious. He doesn't want you dealing with his brother-in-law. He wants you dealing with the sheik, and only the sheik.

After the wells are operating smoothly, the sheik demands a larger cut. Or out you go and he will operate the wells himself. At first you think he can't, but then you realize that a good many of his people have become technically competent by now. The Egyptians, you remember, operated the Suez Canal very well even though the British insisted they couldn't.

On the other hand, you have been in this game for a long time and you know how it's played. Confidentially, you have been *expecting* to be asked to ante up a bigger share. In fact you negotiated at the outset with that in mind. You have already recovered a good part of your investment, and so you agree to accept a smaller share. The sheik permits you to stay on.

Five years later, however, the sheik demands so much that it would no longer be profitable for you to stay. So you get out and look for a new source of oil.

Now the sheik has oil and money, and his people have a hospital, schools, and roads. There is also a growing number of educated, progressive young people in the sheikdom. Some of them are a bit rebellious. Maybe in another ten years they will overthrow the sheik.

Have you done wrong? What should you have done?

Still another problem. Back a few years ago, when the wells were just coming in, the American who is held in such high esteem by the sheik learns that the sheik has been talking to some Russians.

The Organization Abroad

They are offering to start a few local industries and to provide weapons for the sheik's small army. What should your colleague do? Is he an intelligence agent for the State Department? Is your company a flag-carrier?

Or suppose that just when you decide to pull out, the State Department people move in. They "suggest" that your withdrawal at this time would not be in the best interests of the United States. Is your proudly *private* company really an *American* oil company? Is it there to represent *American* national interests? Or should it do what it feels is right for itself? Of course, part of the answer to that one lies in the kind of sanctions the State Department people can impose if you don't want to play their game. Maybe you will have to negotiate with them too.

These are only a few of the dilemmas organizations face abroad. They range from moral dilemmas to ethical dilemmas, to economic dilemmas, to social dilemmas, to cultural dilemmas. From selling contraceptives to manufacturing hand grenades to trying to develop a market for hair coloring. From whether or not to pay bribes when everybody in the society pays bribes, to whether or not to eat sheep's eyes politely when there's a good chance that they will make you throw up.

We said that this would be a short chapter full of questions. Here are a few more questions, and that will be the end of it.

Do you hold any or all of the following convictions (other things being equal, of course)?

—That an economically developed country is better off than an economically undeveloped country?

—That a country with more technology is better off than a country with less technology?

—That a country with more educated people is better off than a country with fewer educated people?

—That a country where per capita income is high is better off than a country where per capita income is low?

—That an economic relationship in which both partners profit is essentially fair and good?

If you don't hold those convictions, what convictions do you rely on for guidance when you encounter issues like the ones we have raised?

Just one more point. Most of the examples we have used here have to do with relationships between rich organizations and poor, underdeveloped countries. How about the other way around? Or how about rich-rich relationships? Is it morally acceptable to set up a business school in England but not in Peru? Is it all right for Chrysler to take over Simca in France but not to build cars in Kenya? Or does that just make the rich richer? Or should we keep out of both places? Or are we doing good in both? When you know all the answers, let us know. We'll revise this chapter.

Summary

When organizations from one nation move into another, a number of ethical and social questions arise. This chapter raises several such questions with a number of examples. The questions are not answered because the answers depend on the personal and social values of the answerer. The intent of the chapter is to suggest that simple, unconditional answers are insufficient, that we must struggle through each case, questioning not only what we find but our own value systems as well. It's comfortable to have pat answers. It may be wiser not to.

Notes and References

The basic ethical issue—under what circumstances, if any, should one people move in on another—is an old and complex one. Before the turn of the century, for example, missionaries brought medicine and education along with their particular version of the truth to East Africa and parts of China. Sometimes troops followed to protect them when the local population saw the truth differently. See, for example: A. J. Hughes, *East Africa* (London: Penguin Books, 1963); and P. A. Varg, *Missionaries, Chinese, and Diplomats* (Princeton, N.J.: Princeton University Press, 1958).

Some anthropologists have argued for leaving simple societies alone. But for one anthropologist's argument for moving in and changing them—if your values are right—see Chapter 8 of Margaret Mead, *Anthropology: A Human Science* (Princeton, N.J.: Van Nostrand, 1964).

And for a broad analysis of the economic implications of these issues, consult C. P. Kindleberger, *Power and Money* (New York: Basic Books, 1970).

An in-depth study of foreign and domestic entrepreneurial activity in Mexico, its costs and its advantages, can be found in F. Derossi, *The Mexican Entrepreneur* (Paris: OECD Development Centre, 1970).

And for another fascinating case study of the "modernization" of a peasant group in Peru by an American team, see the entire issue of *The American Behavioral Scientist,* 8 (Mar. 1965), especially A. R. Holmberg, "The Changing Values and Institutions of Vicos in the Context of National Development."

19

Operating away from Home

From the moral issues raised by organizations abroad, let's go on to more pragmatic ones. Let's assume that our organization has already decided to move into another nation, to do good and to get rich. Now what? How do we go about it? What do we need to know in order to build a viable offshoot in a foreign land?

The Offshoot Squeeze

In the relationship between an organization from culture A and the established organizations in host country B lies one of the central problems of our times. If we are to develop anything like one world, we must develop organizational interactions across national boundaries. But organizations are not culture-free, nor economy-free, nor law-free. They grow up within nations. And when one of them sends representatives abroad to encounter other organizations and other environments, those representatives go as citizens of nation A to live in nation B. When an American firm decides to set up an offshoot to manufacture rubber tires in Jamaica or radio parts in India, or to establish an archeological research station in Greece, and when the host agrees, the squeeze begins.

The new offshoot organization is caught between local environmental demands on the one hand and parental pressures on the other. It must meet parental standards of productivity, innovativeness, efficiency, cost control, even honesty. And those parental demands are insisted on even though the host society may not value efficiency as much as it values family ties, or cost control as much as comfort, or puritanical honesty as much as personal friendship, or innovation as much as tradition.

In short, the manager of an offshoot organization in a foreign environment is subject to a welter of pressures: What does the parent company want? What does the host society want? And what does the manager himself want?

Sometimes, though not often, these demands coincide nicely. Assume that you are the manager of the overseas branch of a highly authoritarian parent company that demands the same high standards from your organization as it demands from its domestic units. And suppose those standards happen to coincide with those valued by your host society. And suppose that you yourself value the same things. Chances are there will be no crisis, no culture shock. A happy three-way marriage!

Or suppose that a strictly controlled offshoot is operating in a very undifferentiated, underdeveloped host environment that offers no internal competition to the offshoot organization and that, in fact, desperately needs what the offshoot has to offer. There again the offshoot may be able to operate like a domestic unit and get away with it. The British managed that in colonial days. British firms and government units regularly behaved in a very British way wherever they happened to be.

But as host environments become more differentiated, as domestic competitors emerge, and as negotiations with the local government and other local organizations become more sophisticated and complex, the offshoot needs increased autonomy and greater flexibility if it is to adjust to the local situation. Can a British organization be very British in Ghana today? If not, must it go native?

Relevant Differences among Cultures

Earlier in this book we saw that in the long run organizations are shaped in part by their tasks and by their technologies. We suggested that modern armies fighting in the desert end up organizationally pretty much alike. But that's in the long run.

In the short and middle runs, organizations are shaped by their cultures as well as by their tasks and tools, by the beliefs and values of people, by religious and political ideologies, and by physical factors like topography and climate. And offshoot organizations must live in those cultures even when the climate is very unfamiliar.

In some communities in southern Mexico men are careful not to grow too rich. A man who does so is obliged to give a grand fiesta in which he spends *all* his wealth.

In Japan employers and employees regard the employment contract as permanent, almost immutable. The contract, in effect, requires the employer to support the employee forever and requires the employee to be faithful and loyal to the organization forever.

In modern Yugoslavia a variation of Marxist ideology has led to an unusual form of organizational decentralization called "self-management." Each firm operates as an independent entity owned by its workers. It is governed by a workers' council which is intended to function much like a board of directors in an American firm. But the board is made up of elected employees who can, officially at least, hire and fire the managing director and approve all major policy decisions.

In some countries in South America, dictating machines are exceedingly popular among executives, even though secretaries are perfectly capable of taking shorthand. The reason, according to one observer, lies in the traditional relationship between men and women. A male dictating to a female secretary may expose his hesitancy and other "inadequacies" in an intolerable way. Making errors or failing to verbalize one's thoughts reduces one's status in the eyes of women. Dictating machines provide a cushion, a buffer, that enables the executive to protect his *machismo*.

Societies also differ in the value they put on entrepreneurial success. Imagine trying to run a business in a place where the more you pay your employees, the less they work and the more time they take off. If people don't treat money as something to be accumulated — and in many societies they don't — then our traditional American payment schemes are inappropriate. If people treat money as a short-run means to achieve a specific, predetermined goal, they may achieve that goal by working only two hours instead of eight. In such a setting, we might think of lowering rather than raising pay, or of finding a very large supply of workers, or of searching for a new set of incentives.

Such examples merely suggest that people in different parts of the world, speaking different languages, accepting different gods, living in different climates, holding to different standards, will organize differently (for a while) to accomplish — or not to accomplish — the same task.

Now let's return to our parent organization worrying about setting up shop in an alien environment. The parent organization has grown up in a culture, too. Indeed, it has a little private culture of its own within the national culture. "In our company," its members say, "we do things this way, not that way. We reward outstanding performance. We expect people to work until the job is done—no clock watching here. We don't care how long a person has been here; if he can't cut the mustard, out he goes. We believe in setting standards and measuring performance. We don't like prima donnas around here. We don't fool around. When we work, we work. That long hair has got to go." And so on.

So the parent organization, with its own firmly held standards and values, sends its offshoot out into another culture with different standards and values. And just because the child has left home doesn't mean that it won't be expected to live up to the parent's standards. Inevitably, there will be a conflict between the cultures. Caught in the crossfire will be the fledgling offshoot. The greater the differences between the parent culture and the host culture, the greater will be the problem of adjustment for that offshoot.

Factors Affecting Adjustment

In the rest of this chapter we shall consider several factors that affect the offshoot's adjustment to both parent and host. Perhaps they will suggest some rules of thumb for offshoot survival.

Cultural Differences in Managerial Style. Though managers seem to be pretty much alike in all cultures, they also reflect their individual cultures. Managers who have grown up in different cultures show somewhat but not radically different aspirations, different attitudes toward one another, different beliefs about authority, and different personal goals. Scandinavians and Germans hold somewhat different attitudes toward supervising, and exhibit different personal needs than Anglo-Americans; both groups differ from managers in France, Spain, and Italy. And all European managers are quite different from Japanese managers. Even the belief of American managers that they must make their organizations more efficient, productive, and creative turns out to be at least partially culture-bound. It is not a belief shared by managers in all other countries.

Given such differences, it is not surprising that head-on collisions occur when an organization from country A tries to establish an organizational beachhead in country B.

When managerial values and styles differ profoundly between the host and the parent cultures, then *training* is in order—either for the host managers who will run the offshoot, or for the managers from home who will have to deal with the host community. Indeed, more than training may be needed. In some cultures, family and social connections may be the major determinants of managerial success, and even the brightest young MBA on your payroll may not be ac-

> ### The Unwelcome Immigrant
>
> An illustration of the difficulties American companies experience in their voyages abroad is G.E.'s venture into the computer business in France in 1964.
>
> > When it gained control of Machines Bull, the big French computer maker, General Electric appeared to be on its way to establishing itself as the computer industry's No. 2. . . . But these high expectations were crashingly disappointed.
> >
> > . . . The troubles of Bull-G.E. . . . illustrate with rending clarity that it takes more than an export of cash and management talent to operate a successful foreign business. Bull-G.E. is the largest segment of G.E.'s international computer complex. Its sales last year, about $120 million, topped General Electric's sales of U.S.-made computers and related equipment. . . . And its losses have displayed an impressive grandeur: reported operating losses add up to $73 million for the first two and a half years, and that figure understates reality. All together—investment, operating losses, and loans—G.E. has sunk into Bull-G.E. something in the vicinity of $200 million.
> >
> > Less tangible but possibly even more costly than the dollar drain has been the loss of prestige and good will abroad. Improbable as it may now sound, shouts of "Vive les Américains!" punctuated the raucous shareholders' meeting at which Bull's management announced that the French Government had consented to G.E.'s investment. "The American flag was paraded up and down the aisles," recalls a participant. But by January of this year G.E. was being reviled in the French press as yet another powerful, callous American corporation come to exploit France and its people. The Bull-G.E. labor force, suspicious and resentful toward the American management, was urging government intervention. . . .
>
> —Gregory Wierzynski, "G.E.'s $200-million Ticket to France." Courtesy of Fortune Magazine, June 1967, pp. 91–95, 157–59, 160–64.

cepted if he is the son of a taxi driver or a plumber. So besides training, *intelligence work* on the social and economic climate of the host society must be undertaken.

But why not hire local managers from the start? After all, they know the territory. They don't know us, of course, but we can always bring them to the home office for a month or two of training. Even then, though, they will still *think* differently from us. We might send our own people out to the host country for a few months of training in the local language and the culture. But they, too, would still think differently from their hosts.

Tasks in Relation to Cultural Differences. Some tasks are independent of the culture in which they're performed. Others are culture-bound. For example, suppose you are a flag-carrying airline from Migrainia. Your country has signed an agreement for weekly nonstop flights to New York. Pan Am will be the reciprocating United States line. You fly two new 707s. You have to set up an operations group at Kennedy Airport and a sales group to sell Americans on the beauties of Migrainian castles and countryside. Should you send Migrainians to New York or try to hire Americans? On the operations and maintenance side, it may not matter very much. A 707 is a 707. Send your own or hire one away from an American airline. But markets differ. Migrainia has no television and only two newspapers. The average annual income is $400 per capita. Women never do any shopping. In the United States, women do lots of shopping; ethnic minorities abound. Indeed, buying habits and attitudes vary a great deal by region, and by degree of urbanization. The number of possible media is very large — radio stations, newspapers, magazines, billboards, and television channels. Advertising agencies vary in size, skill, and coverage. Travel agents serve as important brokers between airline and consumer.

Some tasks are so intimately related to technology that they develop subcultures of their own that transcend differences between national cultures. Airline maintenance people working on Boeing or Douglas jet aircraft share knowledge and skills that are independent of the companies they represent and of the nations behind those companies. Except for relatively minor differences in company standards and routines and languages, their common technical base tends to obscure national boundaries. By contrast, the common technical base in marketing is very small.

A tentative generalization, then: the more technically standardized a task is, the easier it is to transfer it from one culture to another.

Societal Differentiation. Societal differentiation refers to the number and variety of organizations in a given society. A simple, undifferentiated society has just a few organizations per capita. A highly differentiated society has many organizations, and many different *kinds* of organization. If you want to take a quick fix on the level of differentiation in a host city, check its yellow pages (or their local equivalent). How does the number of organizations listed compare with the number listed in other cities of about the same size in different parts of the world? How does the number of categories of organizations compare with other cities of the same size?

An offshoot organization usually has a fairly easy time establishing itself in an undifferentiated society, even if that society differs significantly from the parent society. But if the host society is highly differentiated, trouble sets in. The interests of the established organizations will be affected by the presence of the new offshoot, and yet their interconnections and power positions will be hard to understand.

Communications between Parent and Offshoot. In the old days, when the British Foreign Office sent a young civil servant to India, it had no choice but to let him develop his organization in his own way. It was impossible to keep an eye on him. Distances were great; transport and communication were slow. Nowadays distances are shorter, communication faster and cheaper. Parental control is therefore easier to implement. And when it's easy to interfere, parents find it hard to resist.

The Socialization Dilemma. On the one hand, the parent organization understandably wants to be sure that its offshoot's first loyalty is to the parent. But it also wants the people staffing its offshoot to understand and participate in the local culture. Otherwise they won't be able to operate successfully within it. So how is one to make sure that offshoots become sympathetic to and aware of the local climate without becoming more loyal and committed to the host than to the parent?

Years ago that wasn't much of a problem, especially for organizations from the "have" nations dealing with the "have-not" nations. The haves could run their offshoots in their old parental ways and not worry much about local understanding or participation, either because the host was weak and subservient or because it desperately needed what the offshoot offered. So all the parental organizations had to do to maintain loyalty in distant offshoots was to make sure that the people they sent out were carefully "presocialized" and periodically monitored. "Presocialization" means long and careful training of the people who are to be sent out to offshoots, until the parent organization feels sure that those people are deeply and permanently committed to the parent's values and beliefs. Thus the Jesuits could send their members off to South America without much fear of losing them, because those members had long been socialized into the Society of Jesus. They had taken vows. They had lived by the rules of the Society for many years. They were Jesuits twenty-four hours a day. By the time they went out to proselytize, they were fully socialized; nothing was likely to shake them. And they went out to proselytize, not to understand and involve themselves in the local culture.

But times and needs have changed. Executives are mobile, professional, task-oriented. Loyalty to the organization is limited. And executives who are too socialized into parental values, too well shaped by their own society, do not adapt very well to host cultures. They stand out as foreigners trying to impose their strange ways upon a sovereign people. Presocialization doesn't look as feasible in today's world of proud, autonomous developing nations as it did in colonial days. But notice that it continues to work moderately well for the Mormon Church, and Japanese industry, and the Turkish army.

Some Tentative Rules of Thumb

Some tentative guidelines for setting up offshoot organizations emerge from these considerations:

First, the greater the cultural difference between parent and host, the more autonomy the offshoot needs, and the less it should be forced to behave like a miniature model of its parent.

Second, the more organizationally differentiated and the more complex the host society is, the more autonomy the offshoot needs; again, the less it can behave like a miniature of its parent.

Third, the poorer the technics of communication between parent and offshoot, the more autonomy the offshoot needs. It's hard to control the day-to-day operations of an offshoot organization when messengers emerge from the jungle only once a month.

Fourth, the less technically standardized the task, the more autonomy the offshoot needs. The more local conditions affect the performance of the task, the better it is to let the people on the spot make their own decisions.

Note that the second and third rules are partially contradictory. For in a complicated, differentiated society, the technics of communication are likely to be very good. Telephones and airplanes are easier to come by. It is only in really out-of-the-way places that communication is likely to be a significant technical problem these days. The parent organization, therefore, may find itself in a dilemma. As the host countries in which its offshoots operate become more complex and differentiated, the offshoots need more freedom and autonomy to negotiate and relate. And yet, since communication with the offshoots is more efficient, it becomes easier to control them from the parental base. The happiest solution to this dilemma would seem to be more communication, not so much for the purpose of control but simply for discussion and information sharing. Autonomy need not mean isolation.

*International Offshoots
and Supranationalism*

All the matters we have discussed so far assume *national* parentage. Almost all organizations these days are citizens of a particular country. They may establish offshoots in other countries, but the offshoots normally retain their parent's citizenship. Somehow an organization *is* American or Dutch or French, even though it operates all over the world. But can you imagine a *supranational* organization, one that has no national parentage at all? An organizational world citizen? Some voluntary associations are truly supranational. The International Association for Applied Psychology, for example, and other international scientific and professional groups are, by definition, supranational. And so is the U.N. And in some respects the Common Market is a supranational organization. But there is no commercial organization that we know of that is either legally or in fact a supranational body.

Yet the national boundaries (as far as organizations are concerned) are becoming very fuzzy. It's getting harder to specify national citizenship. Suppose, instead of setting up an American offshoot in Italy, we join with some Italian organizations to set up a new, jointly owned firm that makes our products, some Italian products, and some altogether new products. Suppose we contribute certain expertise and they contribute other expertise. The firm is located in Italy. It pays Italian taxes and obeys Italian laws. Is it an Italian firm? Not quite.

Or suppose our home base is in Amsterdam but most of our operations and markets are outside the Netherlands. We decide that the Indian who is managing our units in Bombay is just the man to take over a new plant we're opening in West Germany. After a while we fall into the practice of choosing our managers from anywhere in the world and dispatching them to anywhere in the world. Even the board of directors meeting in Amsterdam is made up of citizens from all over the world. Are we still Dutch? Should we say that we are? Or would such a claim be meaningless, if not disadvantageous?

What are the social implications of supranationalism among organizations? Would a supranational General Motors represent social progress? A force for peace? Might it not be in the interest of such a supranational organization to prevent conflicts among the nations in which it was doing business? Or, conversely, might it not sometimes be to its advantage to *promote* conflict among nations?

Whatever the implications, the trend seems clear, though very slow. The managerial climate of industrial and commercial organizations is becoming increasingly multinational, less and less ethnocentric. Formerly, an American firm that set up an offshoot in Timbuktu ran it as an American firm, with American management and American standards, under exclusively American control. Today, the operation would probably be managed by a Timbuktuan operating under tight restrictions imposed by the Timbuktu government, and with a good portion of the ownership in Timbuktuan hands. The next manager of the Timbuktu unit might be drawn neither from the United States *nor* from Timbuktu, but from *any* unit in the organization's world structure.

In short, the members of a small, elite group find themselves operating more and more as citizens of the world. Large European firms seem to be moving rapidly in that direction, especially those whose domestic markets make up only a small portion of their total market. Petroleum companies, electrical companies, and pharmaceutical companies are paying comparable wages for the same jobs regardless of location; are promoting people regardless of nationality; and are transferring their managers to posts anywhere in the world.

For cultural, economic, and legal reasons, of course, national boundaries still exert a very real influence. Developing countries want their *own* industries. Developed countries view *their* industries as a military resource as well as an economic one. The United States has to be able to count on Standard Oil to be loyally American in an international crisis. But we are beginning to see a shift in the field of forces. Worldwide company X is daring to say "No" to its home government's request that it move this way instead of that.

We may be entering a time when such international organizations will be cast in a new social role. No longer the cartel villains of the past, they may become a major social mechanism for moving men toward one world. That movement, we must note, is *not* being generated by a conscious one-world ideology. Even conservative nationalists recognize it as inexorable. For its roots lie in new technology, and in the need of growing organizations to reach out beyond national boundaries.

Summary

When a unit from country A is set up in host country B, it finds itself squeezed between parental expectations and local demands. The squeeze is most severe when the cultural differences between A and B are great, and when parent A insists on trying to dictate its offshoot's behavior.

These problems can be exacerbated by factors like these: differences in personal and social values; the absence of precise, standardized tasks; the level of organizational differentiation of the host environment; and the availability of communication channels between home and offshoot.

Organizations used to presocialize their people before sending them abroad to make sure that they would remain loyal to their parent. That practice reduced the danger of their going native or becoming more responsive to the host than to the parent. But in today's mobile executive world, presocialization can't be counted on. Moreover, organizations need executives who can understand and deal with their host environment instead of isolating themselves from it.

Operating away from Home

Supranationalism is beginning to show itself in the world community. We seem to be moving toward large organizations that will "belong" to no single nation but will be true world citizens. Should we move that way? What are the implications for world growth, world unity, and world peace?

Notes and References

There is a massive literature on organization and management in different countries of the world. One good, though somewhat dated, treatment is F. Harbison and C. Myers, *Management in the Industrial World* (New York: McGraw-Hill, 1959).

For a comparative study of styles of management, see M. Haire, E. Ghiselli, and L. Porter, *Managerial Thinking* (New York: Wiley, 1966). This work compares attitudes of managers in the United States, Europe, and some developing countries. You might also try E. B. Lovell, *The Changing Role of the International Executive* (New York: National Industrial Conference Board Business Policy Study #119, 1966).

A good bibliography is available in K. Roberts, *International Research Related to Organizational Behavior* (Stanford, Calif.: Graduate School of Business, Stanford University, 1972).

For the story about dictating machines in South America we are grateful to Dr. Frank Heller of the Tavistock Institute in London. His research is reported in *Managerial Decision Making* (Assen, The Netherlands: Van Gorcum, 1971).

The issue of supranationalism lies just below the surface of much recent interest in international management. For one useful discussion, see H. V. Perlmutter, "Super Giant Firms in the Future," *Wharton Quarterly*, III, 2 (Winter 1968).

20

Strategies for Survival:
How Organizations Cope with Their Worlds

The relationship between an organization and the world is much like the relationship between an individual and the world. We can learn a great deal about an individual without knowing anything at all about his world. We can understand his nervous system, his digestive system, his respiratory system, and the ways in which they articulate. But if we want to extend our understanding, we must find out how he copes with his environment. We must understand not only the structure of his nervous system but how it responds to external stimuli, not only the nature of his respiratory system but how it is affected by the atmosphere in which he breathes. We must understand the environmental limits of survival.

We must also understand how the individual copes with *changes* in his environment. Somehow organisms do manage to adjust to change, and sometimes they even manage to change the world so that it adjusts to them. When the world turns cold, they learn to build igloos, to insulate themselves from unpleasant environments to which they cannot or will not adapt. They even learn to create environments that they positively prefer. They condition and purify the air—usually after they have polluted it.

This complex relationship between the organism and its environment has a counterpart in the exchange between the organization and its environment. Sometimes the adaptation is inadequate; when the organization meets an environment it cannot cope with, it dies.

The Points of Contact

What are the points at which an organization comes into contact with its environment? The list is long, but finite. Consider, for example, a small retail store. It lives at a location, an address. This address, this shop, is in a neighborhood in a town in a nation. It is made of brick and mortar. That means it has been in contact with neighbors and plumbers and carpenters. The shop presumably sells something it has bought from someone else. So there is always the interface with the community of suppliers at one end and customers at the other.

Those are some obvious points of environmental contact, the proximate ones. But there are others. How about municipal services? The policeman on the beat and the fire department? Insurance companies? The PTA that claims the retail shop is selling dirty books to teen-agers? The black community that claims it sells racist books? There are employees, too, who are citizens of the community. They want shorter hours and higher pay.

In a multitude of ways even the small shop finds itself in a complex exchange with its environment, not just passively but in critically active ways. Its survival and growth depend on its ability to maintain and build those relationships in ways that provide the shop with what it needs. If it is a white-owned shop in a black ghetto, or a psychedelic shop in a straight, middle-class town, it may not survive. In certain areas, if it is a shop that refuses to pay off the cops, it may not survive even if it obeys all the laws. So if it *has* survived, it has perforce been shaped, perhaps brainwashed, by the forces that its particular environment exerts upon it.

But the shop can also shape its environment—to some extent. The books it sells—including the dirty ones—may influence the community. The style and design of its storefront may influence the architecture of neighboring stores. Its entrepreneurial activities may bring in all sorts of people from other areas.

Sense Organs and Survival

First, a generalization: the less sensitive an organization is to its environment, the less likely it is to survive. The dress shop that doesn't understand the style preferences or budgets of local women is not likely to flourish. The shop owner cannot assume that the dresses that sell in Istanbul will sell just as well in Fort Wayne.

That generalization seems obvious enough. But the converse does not. It does *not* follow that the greater an organization's capacity to sense its environment, the *more* likely it is to survive. For an organization with good sensors can survive only if it *also* possesses the capacity to modify its behavior in response to the information it receives. Indeed, if it has no mechanism for adapting to that information, its fine sensors may become downright destructive. Suppose, for example, that I am very sensitive to pain but I am paralyzed. If a pin is stuck into me I cannot move away. I would be better off if I weren't sensitive to pain at all.

Consider some recent developments in the Catholic Church. Ritual texts have been translated from Latin into the language of the local community as a means of bringing church and community closer together. Priests have been encouraged to show more awareness of the problems of their communities. The Church, as it were, is trying to improve its capacity to sense what is going on at the interface between its parishes and its parishioners.

But let us suppose—only for the sake of supposition—that no other changes take place within the structure of the Church. Suppose that the new information now entering the system through the parish priest has nowhere to go, that the people "upstairs" either don't listen to it or don't know what to do with it. Is the Church better off than it was before? In one way it is. The local priest can deal with some problems he failed to sense before. But organizationally, the Church may be in trouble. For now it is faced with priests sensitive to urgent problems but frustrated by their inability to prompt responsive action at higher levels.

*Internal Communication,
Muscle, and Survival*

To be effective, then, a sensing mechanism must be tied into an internal mechanism for communicating and processing what is sensed, and a set of "muscles" for responding to what it processes. Without those mechanisms, a good sensing system may make the organization *less* capable of survival than an organization that is sealed off in its own shell, unaware of what is going on around it. The slow, insensitive, hard-shelled turtle can cope with its environment by closing itself off. A sensitive, but still slow, soft-shelled turtle would be vulnerable indeed.

This is another way of saying that an organization needs to be internally coherent to deal with its environment. The system needs to be a full system, with all its parts sensibly related to one another. Good sensors need to be connected to a brain and accompanying muscles. Several different systems may be coherent in their own ways and may work reasonably well, but some work better than others in particular environments.

*Some Alternative Designs
for Survival*

Let's consider four internally coherent ways in which organizations can sense and respond to environments.

Imperviousness: The Withdrawal Model. Some organizations deal with the world by shutting it out—by rolling up into a spiney ball and hoping their unattractive exterior will discourage enemies. Many religious and utopian groups, and some communes, have tried to drop out of the world. To a lesser degree withdrawal has also been the route of some government agencies, and in a less extreme way the route of some American railroads.

They try actively to eliminate any sense of the world around them. Some companies, for example, discourage their people from joining professional groups by suggesting that such activities are disloyal and that the time thus wasted might better be spent within the company. Such organizations are more concerned with sheer survival than with growth or adaptation. Their primary reaction to a changing environment is to find better ways of *not* responding to it— harder shells, tighter restrictions.

Why should any organization want to insulate itself from the world? For much the same reason that ancient cities walled themselves in—to protect what they valued from predators *who valued different things.* For the same reason that many youth communes are hidden in the woods—to permit their members to do their thing without persecution or attack. And for the same reason that the early Mormons settled in Salt Lake City.

Organizations build shells when they want to protect, in their existing forms, their values, their possessions, their beliefs, their people. But there is another reason, too. An organization that is impervious to its environment is not easily shaken from its routines; it is not "distracted" from its objectives, because it does not pay attention to things that might be distracting. It does not push panic buttons, because it does not hear the cries of fire. So an impervious exterior also helps provide for single-minded concentration.

Today, universities are active places, more active than they used to be. Professors are out consulting and carrying on field research. Students, no longer the hub of the university's universe, complain simultaneously of the "irrelevance" of their courses and of the university's multiple connections with other power groups in the environment. Are they asking for a return to isolation? If so, would "relevance" to the current world still be possible?

Or consider the diplomatic services of most nations. Diplomats act as organizational sense organs as well as muscles. One of their functions is to send home relevant intelligence about their host country. To do that, they must really get to know the host country. Yet almost all the world's diplomatic services carefully rotate their people every few years. One reason is the fear that their diplomats will become too sensitive, too understanding, and therefore too sympathetic with the host's problems, and hence may become more representational of the host than reportorial about it. Don't such rotation schemes contribute, in a mild way, to imperviousness from certain types of information?

In many companies salesmen serve as important sense organs. They work outside the organization, spending their time with customers. But they are sometimes reluctant to report back unpleasant information about the company's products or behavior because they know that home-office executives prefer not to hear such news.

And consider the old model of the mental hospital. It was a model of isolation. Get the patients out into the woods, into a walled asylum. Let few visitors in and few patients out. Minimize contact between patient and the world. And how about the model of the convent?

Selective Imperviousness. So far we have considered the organization that closes off *all* environmental inputs. In the long run, especially in a changing environment, such complete imperviousness is disastrous for most organizations in the modern world.

Suppose we are the managers of an organization that foresees the danger of such isolation and wants to avoid it. But we are understandably concerned lest our people be seduced into immorality or disloyalty by exposure to the temptations of the world. And we also want to act upon our environment, to sell our product or to proselytize our religion or to enrich the coffers of our native country. How can we act intelligently upon an environment that we dare not let our people sense too well? We cannot. So we compromise. We sense, but we keep what we sense from penetrating too deeply into our organization. We hold the world at arm's length, in a gingerly fashion, and perhaps distastefully; but at least we look at it, and then act upon it.

Consider English colonialism. The English trained their men in England, in English schools and English universities. They trained them long and well so that their colonial officers would be true Englishmen. Then they sent them off to India with English manners and English dinner jackets to govern the heathen. Those officers carried England with them. They drank tea and dressed for dinner as though they were in London—and to that degree they remained impervious to their environment. They were little concerned about the inappropriateness of English evening dress to the Indian climate.

But they did not *ignore* their environment. They even learned a bit of the local language. They identified local leaders. They trained local people. They set up an intelligence network to learn about local affairs. And, being English, they were polite. They learned local protocol and respected it. Yet never for a moment did they consider going native. Never did they identify with their environment, blend into it, participate in it. No snake charmers for them. They sensed the world they were in, but because they were strongly socialized into their home culture, they remained outside it.

Japanese businessmen working abroad are masters of selective imperviousness. They learn the local ways quickly, designing and marketing their products to fit local practices; but they remain culturally and organizationally Japanese.

For an organization to ensure that its people will sense well and yet not be shaken by what they sense requires a very high level of socialization of its members—high loyalty, high commitment. And the organization must police the whole process, for even strong company men may backslide. One major British company used to check up on its field managers periodically to make sure they were maintaining their British identity. "We know there's a problem," one executive said, "when a manager in Borneo stops dressing for dinner. Then it's time to bring him back to London."

Adaptiveness: The Organizational Chameleon. As the world changes, it becomes more difficult for organizations to sense their environment and still remain independent of it. The British could remain British in India as long as India remained a colony. It is much more difficult for them to remain British and also effective in an economically expanding, independent India, where Indian, American, Japanese, and Russian competitors abound; where the environment is active, turbulent, and differentiated rather than passive and submissive.

One alternative for the organization confronting such an active environment is the opposite of imperviousness. It is to *adapt* to the local environment, to develop good sense organs and to use the information that comes in to make the organization as much a part of the local scene as possible. The adaptive organization, in effect, goes native. It becomes part of the environment. In Rome it is Roman. In Thailand it is Thai. It joins the local clubs, hires local people, and behaves in the approved local way.

There is something seductively attractive about this alternative. It seems to be respectful of local culture, polite, nonintrusive.

But there are many dangers for the organization in such behavior. Your people in Thailand may become so understanding of the Thais' needs and problems that they show more concern for Thai welfare than for your own. Or your people may be rejected by the host for trying to be what they are not. And adaptive behavior is mostly responsive rather than active, forever modifying itself to fit the world. In a volatile, rapidly changing world, an adaptive organization may find itself trying to change its behavior from day to day, blown about by political and social winds.

An ethical danger also arises for the organization that tries too hard to adapt. Should it be adaptive to *any* environment regardless of the conditions that exist there? Should it offer bribes where bribes are commonplace? Should it be racist where the society is racist? Should it treat employees as slaves because that is the societal model? The British colonialists carried not only their tea but their British standards of morality, justice, decency, fair play. Old-fashioned as those standards may now seem, they were high standards around which the organization could stand proud and honorable, whatever the local behavior.

So beware the siren of extreme organizational adaptiveness — your organization may become a chameleon.

Action-Adaptation. The impervious organization shuts itself off, neither permitting change within itself nor creating change in its environment. The selectively impervious organization rejects any stimuli that may induce change in itself but tries actively to modify the environment. The adaptive organization accepts its environment and changes itself to meet it.

But there is still another alternative. An organization may be *both* adaptive *and* active. It may change itself to live with its environment and at the same time alter its environment.

For many organizations, altering the environment is part of their normal work. Public health organizations would be of little use if they did not erase malaria and reduce infantile mortality and thereby significantly alter their environment. Agricultural agencies would be of little use if they did not change the behavior of farmers and the nature of farming.

The prime purpose, after all, of many organizations is to change their worlds. There is a story about two shoe salesmen who were sent to open up a remote African market. The first salesman cabled home: "No one here wears shoes. Sales situation hopeless. Cancel all shipments." The second salesman cabled: "No one here yet wears shoes. Ship all you can."

But a dilemma arises. How can an organization be *of* its environment and still change it? Clearly the first place to look for an answer is in the environment itself. In some environments, like Los Angeles, change is a normal attribute of the environment. A Tibetan organization can move into Los Angeles to sell mothers on the idea of feeding their infants curdled yak's milk, and few will think it very strange. The Tibetan salesmen could easily, if they were sensitive, make themselves quite at home in that turbulent, competitive, shifting environment. The complexity and rapidity of change make almost anything possible. But let the same salesmen try to peddle their yak milk in stable, traditional Charleston, South Carolina, and things will be different.

But can we also adapt to a passive, relatively unchanging environment, and simultaneously change it? That seems almost a logical contradiction.

One possibility, however, may be to try a *sequential* process. First, adapt to the environment, then change it from within. The problem here, of course, is that once the organization has adapted, it may no longer be interested in creating the change it had originally wanted.

One of the great problems for many organizations in the next few years will be to devise some appropriate blend of action with adaptation — a blend that allows the organization to maintain its own identity, to effect change in its environment, and yet to "belong" to that environment. The issues involved in working out such a path are not just issues of efficiency. They are also ethical, ecological, and human issues.

Organizational Tuning

An adult organization, again like an adult person, is not infinitely flexible. It is limited in what it can do, limited by its tasks, its personality, and its history. It may wish to be adaptive and yet be unable to adapt without undertaking major internal redesign. It needs to be "tuned."

Some organizations are appropriately tuned to their environment; some are overtuned; some undertuned. A delicately tuned automobile may be great for the racetrack but not for day-to-day city driving. A highly sensitive organization, alert to every change around it, may do very well in a subtle environment where small news items create large public response and casual remarks portend large changes, where minor shifts in consumer tastes can kill an unresponsive product line. But put such a highly sensitive organization into a stolid, stable, noncompetitive environment and it may be paralyzed by its own sensitivity, overresponding to noise that is fundamentally irrelevant to the organization's activities. Organizations with a strong marketing orientation sometimes get into trouble in foreign environments for that very reason. Marketing people generally are highly sensitive to consumer signals. University faculties sometimes overrespond to local signals, too, even when the cost of responding fully to *all* those signals may be much too great for the university to bear. But organizations dominated by production people or technological people are apt to err in the opposite direction.

Overcentralized and Undercentralized Organizations

Consider, also, the relationship between the degree of centralization in an organization and its ability to cope with its environment. In some settings a high degree of centralization, as in a field army, is a major source of the organization's power. The centralization of control may permit a small force to overcome a larger, loosely organized enemy force with poor internal communication and no central decision points.

But that same centralized organizational design may be a source of weakness in other settings. For one thing, a lucky shot at the brain of a highly centralized organization can kill it. The Norman abbeys in England suffered such a fate. They were excellently, tightly organized communities. But they had single, identifiable heads—the abbots. When Henry VIII decided to get rid of the abbeys, he did so very easily by getting rid of the abbots. And the rest of the organization fell apart.

Conversely, some historical reports indicate that General de Gaulle advocated a *federal* rather than a central form of government for postwar Germany, because—it is said—he believed that decentralized federalism would *prevent* Germany from rapidly regaining its strength. France, after all, had a strong centralist tradition. In fact, Germany came back very fast, probably in large part because of its multiple, relatively loose federal form. It is much harder to chop off the many heads of a federalized government than to chop off the one head of a highly centralized one.

Centralized organizations, as we suggested in the chapter on organizations abroad, have other weaknesses in certain environments. Communication lines are long, for one thing. If issues must go all the way to the top for decision, reaction may be too slow in a rapidly changing environment.

On the other hand, units of highly decentralized organizations may be too adaptive, too ready to take on local color and local loyalty. Such organizations may collapse for lack of controlling bonds from the top.

Strategies for Survival

*The Strategies of Imperviousness,
Adaptation, and Action*

Viewed historically, which of these strategies has worked best, under what conditions?

Imperviousness has tended to work when the goals of the organization either do not require much interaction with the environment, or when the environment is very stable. The scholarly monk can do his work quite well if he is left alone. But as interdependence and change increase, imperviousness becomes less useful. The plumbing-fixture manufacturers of France can go on making obsolete toilets as long as the French maintain their existing attitudes toward toilets. But when tourists start fussing, and Hilton hotels start appearing, and Frenchmen come back from abroad, the pressure for change builds up.

But, since impervious organizations are, by definition, insensitive, we should not expect them to change steadily in response to steadily mounting pressures. It is only when the temperature reaches the boiling point that the turtle may decide to stick its head and feet out of its shell and move. And then it may be too late.

When does selective imperviousness work? First, when the organization succeeds in indoctrinating its members deeply into its organizational beliefs and standards. Selective imperviousness requires a kind of absolute faith, an ardor, a commitment to carry one's message out to the world, to get others to do things our way. And that seems to be getting harder to do each year.

Selective imperviousness also works well in relatively undifferentiated, placid, noncompetitive environments. British colonialists and the early Jesuits had a sort of monopoly over the environments in which they worked. But now there are the Russians and the Cubans and the Chinese, and, oddly enough, the locals, all in the same place.

To take the distant, formal, standoffish role implied by such selective imperviousness becomes very risky in turbulent settings. Not only was that true for the early British; the same is true for the contemporary American company that insists on operating in the American way in Latin America, or in the urban way in a rural setting. It must offer an extraordinary product or service if it expects to remain unsullied in the intricate networks of a briskly moving but foreign environment.

Adaptation, as we have seen, is a fine strategy—for survival. Taking on the local coloring, going native, will usually help an organization to stay locally alive; but it is not likely to produce innovation or to influence the environment. Indeed, it may generate serious *internal* problems for the organization's members. For most of us are not perfectly adaptive. We cannot become one with our environments even if we want to. Our history, our education, our values don't permit it.

Some form of an active-adaptive strategy appears almost a necessity for contemporary organizations, both because of the nature of the modern organization and the nature of the modern environment. G.E. cannot be French, but it must be quasi-French if it is to build and sell computers in France. Certainly France cannot be suborned into the G.E. way; but, on the other hand, G.E. had better not be fully suborned into the French way.

Redesigning Oneself

So what is left? Interaction rather than isolation. Patience rather than precipitousness. Modification rather than conversion. A world, that is to say, of talk and compromise; of incremental changes on the outside accompanied by incremental adaptive changes on the inside; of both sensitivity and identity.

That is a difficult task, but organizations can work at it. To succeed, they need a good sensing apparatus with which to learn about their environment, good action apparatus with which to respond to and influence their environment, and, most of all, good internal communication and decision apparatus with which to do two things: (1) to convert what they sense into appropriate action, and (2) to modify and redesign themselves.

One important difference between man and organization is that man is born with sense organs, brain, and muscles. Organizations must make their own. They can choose to be blind or to see with many eyes, to build lots of action muscle or little, and to devise an effective internal communication and decision mechanism or a faulty one.

Yet most organizations do not treat these problems as a conscious part of their self-design. Their sense organs, especially, tend to develop helter-skelter as an ancillary product of trying to buy or sell or lobby. Their internal mechanisms for processing what they sense are often highly dependent on personalities and prejudices. Organizations hire salesmen to sell, not to listen. And often what the salesman hears, he cannot successfully transmit back into the organization. Sales meetings typically include little listening. The communication is one way, from company to salesman. Similarly, organizations hire scientists to do R&D, not to keep up with their profession. But the scientist who listens to his profession often produces highly useful work for the organization.

Only in recent years has the issue of organizational sensing begun to be examined consciously. Unfortunately, "organizational intelligence" is the phrase often used to describe this process; but that phrase, adapted from the diplomatic and military worlds, connotes spying on an enemy. That is not the central problem. The central problem is knowing one's world.

Summary

Organizations use several different strategies for coping with their environments. All those strategies involve sensing the environment, processing what is sensed, and acting.

Some organizations use a strategy of "imperviousness," sensing little and acting little. This strategy is useful for organizations that want to isolate themselves from change, but it is increasingly difficult to implement in a volatile world.

Other organizations are "selectively impervious." They try to sense the environment and act in response to it, but they also make sure they do not enter into it. Such organizations presocialize their people and require strong commitment and loyalty.

Still other organizations try to sense their environment and to become one with it. That "adaptive" strategy has some limited use for survival, but it does little to foster growth or innovation.

The strategy of "action-adaptation" involves changing both oneself and one's environment interactively. But it is easier to adapt to and to change active, volatile environments than passive ones.

In any strategy, however, one central problem is the tuning of the organization's behavior to the particular state of its particular environment. Appropriate tuning means organizational responsiveness that is neither too strong nor too weak for the organization's environment.

The degree of centralization in an organization affects its tuning. Organizations too centralized for their environment become rigid and slow to respond. Overly decentralized organizations may become too locally adaptive, too hard to control.

Organizations have a distinct advantage over individuals in coping with this problem: they can redesign their own sense organs, brains, and muscles into a system consistent with the strategies they choose.

Notes and References

A good background for this chapter may be found in works on "open systems theory," such as E. Trist and F. E. Emery, "The Causal Texture of Organizational Environments," *Human Relations,* XVIII (1965), pp. 21–32, in which the authors categorize environments into the types we have used in our discussion. This article is also reprinted in F. E. Emery, ed., *Systems Thinking* (London: Penguin Books, 1969).

On the ways in which organizations try to cope, we have borrowed liberally from J. D. Thompson, *Organizations in Action* (New York: McGraw-Hill, 1967).

On the problems of trying to understand foreign environments, we suggest W. J. Lederer and E. Burdick, *The Ugly American* (New York: Norton, 1958).

Tom Wolfe's fascinating piece on the naiveté of white officialdom in understanding black culture is also useful: *Radical Chic and Mau-Mauing the Flak Catchers* (New York: Bantam Books, 1970).

On organizational intelligence, see H. L. Wilensky, *Organizational Intelligence* (New York: Basic Books, 1967).

21

The Future of the Organization-Environment Relationship: Can This Marriage Last?

This last, speculative chapter * — since it *is* last, and since it *is* speculative — is a bit mystical and even sentimental. Indeed, it is built upon three not very well-founded assumptions, and the reader had best be aware of them from the start.

The first is a soap-opera assumption: In the long run, societies, and the organizations that inhabit them, will find harmony and happiness together.

The second assumption is more nearly an observation: What is new in organizations seldom drives out the old. Usually the new pushes the old into a different level of the system, often a lower level; but the old seldom dies. Instead of expecting new organizational forms to drive out old ones, we should expect a *layering effect,* with the new superimposed upon the old. And so we should expect organizations to change from simpler to more complex forms, into patchworks of many forms — old and new.

The third assumption: Though *ideas* must precede social change, ideas are not enough. Only when ideas are converted into viable *techniques* does change begin to take place.

First let's examine our three assumptions more closely. Then we will go on to some wide-open questions: What will our society be

*Portions of this chapter appeared in somewhat different form in Harold J. Leavitt, Managerial Psychology, 3rd Edition (Chicago: University of Chicago Press, 1972), Chapter 30. ©1972 by The University of Chicago Press.

like in the next couple of decades? What kinds of organization will harmonize with it? What new techniques will evolve to make that harmony possible? And what will happen to the old ways as the new ways emerge?

Do Organizations and Societies Blend or Clash?

In the long run, a kind of harmony evolves between the organizations men create and the societies in which they create them. For a while there may be dissonance and conflict, but after a time either organizations begin to adapt to society or society begins to adapt to its organizations. It is not always clear which comes first. Just as the Supreme Court of the United States seems sometimes to reflect current values and at other times to impose values, organizations seem sometimes to reflect and sometimes to create the values of society. This notion of long-term harmony may sound a little soft-headed, but the evidence tends to support it.

Begin by looking backwards. Consider American organizations in the 1900s and consider American society then. It was a melting-pot society, with large numbers of relatively unskilled workers from many cultures, speaking many languages, and bearing little organized power. It was also still something of a frontier society, relatively open, virginal, with lots of possibilities for exploitation. It was a rough-and-tumble society that valued autonomy and individual freedom and abhorred constraint.

It is not surprising then that the organizations of the day were free-wheeling, aggressive organizations that raped the physical environment and exploited the available work force. Nor is it surprising that they embraced the techniques of Taylorism for rationalizing and simplifying work, and for permitting the use of people as muscle rather than as whole men. An elitist group emerged as the designers and controllers of organizations, separate from the mass of laborers. When this owner-manager elite showed any concern at all for the welfare of workers, that concern usually took the form of paternalism. The elite protected the naive and ignorant masses from exploitation by evildoers and from their own presumed child-like impulses. Organizational humanism in those days meant mostly that employees were urged to sing company songs, attend church on Sundays, and avoid temptation. That self-righteousness, however, was accompanied by the exploitation of child labor.

Still, a harmony of sorts existed between the organizations and the society in which they lived. For the goal of the nation was *produc-*

tion. The hungry society needed a diet of material goods. "Efficiency" was the order of the day.

But the frontiers eventually disappeared. Immigration slowed down. The next generation of Americans began to share common values. The educational level of the country rose. Americans became a bit more sophisticated, a little less naive and rough-and-tumble. The children of the immigrants accomplished what their parents wanted them to accomplish. They made their way to college and became physicians, lawyers, chemists. The middle class grew. Then the depression struck and Roosevelt gave the nation a New Deal. The conservatives complained of socialism, of the welfare state. Unions emerged as accepted institutions in the society. And Americans moved toward a concern for social equality.

Initially, most private business organizations fought this constraining trend. But step by step they were driven back. Child labor was abolished; minimum wage laws were passed; conditions of work were improved. Faced with a coalition of unions and government, the unilateral power of management over worker began to shift toward something closer to equality. And the autonomy of the individual—manager, owner, entrepreneur, or worker—was reduced a little. The individual became more and more a group member, an organizational member. He learned to become more careful about the effects of his decisions on others, to protect his flanks, to keep an eye on other groups that might fight back if he swung too freely.

And technology began to move in too. Organizations became more complex; society became technologically more sophisticated. Transportation and communication became more efficient and more readily available. The labor force became better educated, with a larger percentage of professionals and highly skilled workers.

Levels of aspiration rose. Expectations about what constitutes a good life changed. And so, just as Taylorism had emerged in response to environmental conditions, the ideas of *human relations* began to emerge in response to new environmental conditions.

The *ideas* of human relations, of participation, of the more supportive use of human beings, had been around for a long time. Mary Parker Follett, for example, in such works as *Constructive Conflict* and *The Psychology of Consent and Participation,* had been preaching such ideas in the early years of the century. But there had been little development of *techniques* for building up morale and involvement among organizational members. Perhaps the one exception was—of all places—the military organization, which had been morale-conscious for a long time and had developed the twin techniques of identifying a common enemy and building disciplined group membership (in part through consciously stressful initiation ceremonies like boot camp).

So by the 1940s organizations began to show a greater concern for people, in part because they were forced to, in part because they needed resources of human beings to supplement physical resources. They moved from paternalism and despotism toward something like working partnerships in which differences were negotiated. Minds became as important as muscles. But the goal was still *production,* and management was interested in morale mainly because high morale promised high production. The phrases of the day were "incentives" and "cooperation" and "overcoming resistance to change."

But the world did not stand still. The Second World War brought an explosion in technology, indeed in knowledge of all kinds. New frontiers could be attacked as a consequence of innovations in science and technology. And new methods for organizing and controlling massive tasks sprang from those same innovations, particularly in the form of computer technology. The country moved into an era of material affluence, widespread education, and advancing technology. A larger and more powerful middle class evolved—a two-car, television-owning, university-educated class. Mobility was cheaper, easier, and necessary. Society came to take for granted an affluence generated by technological breakthroughs and organizational skills.

And, harmoniously, organizations moved into a *systems-analytic* era manned now by the whiz kids of the Pentagon and the high-salaried young professionals in management, the new MBA's. A new and elitist managerial class began to emerge, one that could be moved quickly into a wide range of new responsibilities. The managerial technocrat was exalted by a society that prided itself on its massive applications of technology. Now people began to talk about "real-time information systems" and "management science." And the goal became *innovation* as much as production.

Change as a Series of Overlays

But note that this harmonious relationship between organizations and their environment did not come about as a series of revolutionary successions, with each movement killing off its predecessors. It occurred rather as a series of overlays. For Taylorism is still with us, and so is much of our unskilled work force, and so is much of our mass-production methodology in manufacturing. Human relations is still with us, and so is social liberalism. And so, obviously, is information technology. Indeed, the whole society has become more complex, more differentiated, with more forces and counterforces, and more levels and more layers.

Organizations have developed in the same way. They have become more complex, more sophisticated, more differentiated. Now there are many kinds of people within organizations, with many entry points, and many submodels to fit different parts of the larger organization. And there are many kinds of organizations, some performing old-fashioned tasks in old-fashioned ways, and others performing constantly changing tasks that were not even dreamed of in years past, using new technologies, new kinds of human relations, and new designs. We are quicker, in our society, at adding than at subtracting.

Techniques Bring Change

Organizations are not *directly* changed either by ideas or by pressures, but by techniques. It was not the *idea* of fair treatment for workers that caused private industry to change its behavior toward workers; it was the *technique* of union organization, and the *technique* of the strike born of frustration. It was not the *idea* of mass production but the *techniques* of Taylor and Ford that generated "rationalized" production organizations. It was not the idea of merger and purchase but specific financial techniques for acquisition and merger that generated the conglomerate organization. These techniques were themselves stimulated in large part, of course, by a tax structure that promised rich rewards to those who could develop them. It was not the idea of participative management that changed American management toward a less authoritarian, more openly communicating posture. It was techniques for improving communication and for utilizing groups, coupled with the social techniques of the New Deal, that effected the change. It was not the idea of quantitative analysis of multivariate problems, nor even the idea of information theory, that generated a new systems approach to management. It was the computer hardware accompanied by the techniques of programing and information management.

This is not to say that ideas are not a basic "cause" of change, but only that changes themselves typically wait upon the evolution of feasible techniques that must intervene between the idea and its fulfillment.

The Age of Aquarius?

Now we shall tell fortunes—about our society and about the organizations within it. But fortune telling is not very hard to engage in these days. Some trends are too obvious to miss.

> ### Sympathy and Trust Abounding—in Organizations?
>
> Here are a few lines from "The Age of Aquarius" from *Hair*. Is this the humanistic organizational milieu of the 1980s?
>
> > When the moon is in the seventh house
> > And Jupiter aligns with Mars
> > Then peace will guide the planet
> > And love will steer the stars.
> > This is the dawning of the Age of Aquarius
> > The Age of Aquarius
> > Aquarius, Aquarius
> > Harmony and understanding
> > Sympathy and trust abounding
> > No more falsehoods or derisions. . . .
>
> —Gerome Ragni, James Rado (*book and lyrics*), and Galt MacDermot (*music*), "The Age of Aquarius," Hair (R.C.A. Victor Dynagroove, LSO1150).

Here are some on the societal side:

Our society is growing uneasy about its physical environment, and with good reason. The technological explosion, coupled with the population explosion and with earlier unbridled autonomy, has generated secondary effects that are more costly than the rewards they bring. So pollution and population begin to emerge as matters of serious social concern.

And that concern, along with others, has begun to generate changes in our society's values. Back in the 1920s the announcement that a new factory was to be built in town was greeted with applause. New jobs, new progress, new growth. The American dream. By 1980, a very large segment of our society may well have organized to fight new factories. For now new factories mean new pollution, new exploitation, new population. Our values seem to be shifting away from material growth, away from technological and scientific gods, indeed away from organizational gods.

But toward what? That is not so clear. Toward humanism, perhaps, toward individualism, toward nature, toward a concern for the quality rather than the quantity of life. Note, however, that though the value changes may seem radical in degree, they do not seem so radical in kind. Individualism is a very old American value, from the Vermont farmer to the Texas cowboy. And the preservation of the natural world is a conservative value. And the brotherhood of man. And the quality of life.

Things turn out to be interconnected. For another major change in the American environment has been the explosion of technological knowledge *and* its application. Technology has generated serious ecological problems and the threat of nuclear holocaust, but it is also causing a reconsideration of values and priorities. And it has also provided opportunities for mankind that must excite even the most blasé and most turned-off among us. For organizations, new technology seems far and away the most powerful agent of change in the foreseeable future. The technological revolution in our society is not finished. It may hardly have begun.

One more aspect of the environment looms large, though scarcely noticed. Not only is our world's human population exploding; so is its organizational population. The organization of the future faces a populous, crowded terrain in which it will bump at every turn into other organizations. No longer can the American company look out upon wide-open untrammeled territory awaiting its productive plow. Industrial (and other) organizations are becoming more like city folk — apartment-dwellers whose noise making arouses the wrath of neighbors, who must share overcrowded transportation and communication facilities, and who are threatened by urban predators. The days of the independent organization are nearly over. The days of the interdependent organization are upon us.

And Aquarian Organizations?

If those are some major directions of social change, what about organizational changes to match them? Let's consider several:

First, the fixed, rigid organization seems to be giving way to the continuously changing organization.

Second, the differentiated, multisystem organization seems to be replacing the simple, undifferentiated one.

Third, the multipurpose organization is more in evidence — one that is not anchored to a specific set of tasks but that has the technology and the professional skills to move anywhere on the playing field.

Fourth, we are seeing the emergence of the participative, democratic organization, one that is literally managed by all its members.

And still one more: we are witnessing the development of the *social* organization, with complex relationships with other organizations and institutions.

Let's take a look at each of these developments and examine the environmental pressures that are giving rise to them. And let's ask what techniques are emerging that may bring some of these ideas to fruition.

The Continuously Changing Organization. Why are many organizations likely to be less fixed, less permanent in the future? Why will organization charts, if we bother with them at all, be changing week by week rather than year by year? Why will people shift more frequently from one part of an organization to another? Why will tasks change more rapidly?

There are probably three big environmental reasons. The first is the skyrocketing growth of technology; the related second reason is the size and complexity of tasks that society has chosen to undertake; the third is the demands of men.

The growth of technology, and the swifter rate of conversion from the discovery of knowledge to its application, mean that many organizations will be continuously changing what they do and how they do it. They can no longer count on making pencils the way they made them last year. New materials, new methods, will require them to reorganize to utilize those materials and methods as they arise.

The growing size of tasks and their rapid change, together with the increasing specialization required by new knowledge, mean that we shall continuously be putting together new combinations of people trained to solve particular new problems. But once a problem is solved, each combination is likely to be disassembled and a new one assembled for some other project. Hence many organizations will be structured on a temporary "project" basis.

But what techniques can we use for putting people together and taking them apart in temporary combinations? What human problems will be thus generated, especially if we have to start with fixed tasks to which people have traditionally been assigned for most of their lives? In the past, after all, managers emphasized the development of solid, cohesive teams whose members learned to live and work closely with one another. How do we move from that form of task-assignment to the assignment of temporary tasks to temporary teams as specialists?

Some moderately satisfactory techniques for working out such problems seem to be close at hand. In the aerospace industry and other high-technology industries, the *matrix* structure has been used experimentally to try to solve part of this problem. In the matrix structure, each individual has dual membership at any given time. He is a member of a permanent group in his specialty and also a member of a project group in which he joins temporarily with people from other specialties to solve a particular problem. He has a home base, but he is almost always on temporary duty somewhere else. This structural model sharply violates certain "principles" of classical organization theory, like the one-man-one-boss principle.

Another set of techniques that can be helpful for such temporary teams derives from the work of social scientists with small groups.

We now have crude but useful means for trying *quickly* to build interpersonal communication and cohesiveness into new teams of men, like the techniques for "team building" in the area now called "organizational development."

It is not only teams within large organizations, but large organizations themselves, that will probably take on a more temporary character. Permanent organizations will form temporary alliances with one another that will last only as long as the common task lasts. And large, but short-lived, organizations may have to be formed (and dissolved), either from scratch or from more permanent modular units. The commission, the task force, the impermanent, transient organization are likely to play a larger role in a technologically complex, highly mobile, rapidly changing society.

Certain social "experiments" may lead to useful new understanding and techniques here. For student groups, the black community, and a whole host of protest movements are learning a great deal firsthand about forming and dissolving temporary organizations for specific tasks. No workable general model has yet emerged from those quarters, but experience and wisdom are building up. And certainly the capacity of the young to tolerate ambiguous, ill-structured organizations seems to be very high relative to the rigid demand for fixed, formal structure that characterizes older generations. Young people may thus be preparing themselves for just the kind of organizational lives that the future will require of them!

Differentiated Organizations. While future organizations and parts of future organizations may be forced by technology and by task and by people to take on more temporary forms, an almost contradictory development may also emerge: the differentiation of large organizations into quasi-independent suborganizations with differing attributes. The temporary organization we have pictured thus far is not rooted in a hierarchy of authority but in the technical skills of its people, jointly aimed at a common, complex, ill-structured task. But while such complex tasks will continue to appear in larger and larger numbers, they will appear as an *overlay,* not as a replacement for the more routine, more ordered, more regular tasks. We will continue to be organized to produce tires and shoes and cans of soup. And while some part of the soup company may be developmental and innovative, and therefore probably temporary and collegial, other parts will still operate assembly lines of some sort, though perhaps with fewer human workers.

For the same technology that promises to create temporary organizations will also tend to eliminate *some* of the need for having humans perform routine tasks. But many tasks, while remaining largely routine, programed, and scheduled, will still require the eyes and muscles of men.

Organizations will thus become more *differentiated,* more like the human body, more like a *set* of different subsystems operating relatively independently of one another to perform independently necessary functions. But the organization must *articulate* one subsystem with another, to make the total system go, just as the human body must articulate its respiratory system with its circulatory, digestive, and nervous subsystems.

We suspect, then, that large organizations will be composed of many relatively independent suborganizations that will be very differently structured from one another. The R&D group will operate by different rules through different time spans with different rewards than the marketing group. And the marketing group will operate by different rules from the production group, or the systems group, or the as-yet-unlabeled new environmental groups. Some parts will take fluid, temporary forms; other parts will remain stolid and unchanging.

Such large, differentiated organizations are likely, on the whole, to be less "democratic" than many existing ones—if by democratic we mean that all members of the organization are treated pretty much the same. On the contrary, people will be treated differently, depending on which subsystems of the organization they work in. Indeed, the same person may find himself tightly controlled in one part of the organization for some period of time and then given lots of freedom in another unit for another period.

Some serious problems are likely to arise as by-products of such changes. People in highly structured organizations with highly specified rules and procedures may not take easily to transfer into much more ambiguous, ill-structured, temporary settings—and vice versa. Organizations will also need flexible, adaptable, and cognitively broad as well as technically skilled people to serve at the interfaces among systems. And yet technical education as we now know it appears, if anything, to reduce rather than increase such flexibility.

The Hungry, Multipurpose, Nomadic Organization. Traditionally, we have tended to label organizations by their primary products or services. General Motors is an automobile manufacturing company. Harvard University is an educational institution. Those primary tasks remain relatively stable and fixed over long periods, usually longer than a human lifetime. And it is around the primary task that the organization develops its structure, its technology, and its people.

That primary task is becoming less and less *the* focal point of the organization, however. Universities are becoming not only educational institutions but centers of research, of consulting, of entrepreneurial activity of one kind or another. General Electric has entered the programed education business, and it sells engineering research data and lots of nonelectrical things. More and more the ads in *Time* and *Fortune* and *Business Week* try to tell the world what the new conglomerates do for a living. These days, you can't tell the players without a program.

New organizational focal points are developing. Instead of basing everything on the task, the product, or the service, the organization looks more and more to its professional people and its technology. Instead of looking for men and machines to perform its fixed tasks, the organization moves toward nomadism, searching the world for new and challenging tasks that can fit its human and technological resources.

This movement toward multiple tasks is a sort of reversion to earlier organizational forms. The old Hudson's Bay Company was a collection of men and resources that could do many things, go many places, exploit many worlds. It was a company in the old sense—a company of men searching for the exploitable.

The techniques for operating multipurpose organizations are still not well defined. No organization we know includes multipurpose departments on its organization charts. Large quasi-public research organizations like Rand perhaps constitute one kind of approximate model, as do some of the conglomerates and some venture-capital companies.

Multinationalism. In the last few decades many organizations have gone international, by choice or by necessity. But they have gone *international* rather than *multinational.* That is, they have maintained a home base, a country of citizenship, and they have operated in other nations as foreigners on native soil. American automobile companies have sent offshoots around the world, but they have remained American offshoots of American companies. Dutch companies explore for oil here and manufacture electrical equipment there, but they too have tended to remain Dutch companies. In the future, national citizenship may gradually give way to *supranational* citizenship for organizations.

The environmental pressures toward such movement look moderately clear. Many complex, highly technical organizations find their national boundaries increasingly limiting and constraining. Smaller countries need highly specialized organizations that simply do not exist within their own boundaries.

But organizational foreigners on one's own soil cause problems. They take physical, financial, and often human resources out of the country. Sometimes they exploit the country in other ways. So host countries, especially developing countries, have been learning to negotiate with incoming visitors to find ways to constrain and control their behavior. And visitors are beginning to find that it is often either wise or necessary to enter joint ventures, to collaborate with nationals rather than to insist on complete autonomy.

A whole variety of alternatives has thus begun to open up, ranging from licensing, to split ownership, to the temporary contract under which the new organization reverts to host ownership after a given period of time. But all of these seem to be transient arrangements not fully satisfactory to anybody.

One future possibility, which looks both promising and threatening, is the emergence of new legal and political techniques and structures for building supranational organizations that will be citizens of the world. Working out the appropriate political, social, and legal environment is a formidable task. But movement in that direction seems inevitable.

The Organization in the Crowded Organizational World. The organization of the future will not do its own thing in a wide-open, passive, and unsullied environment. Like the individual, the organization will inhabit a world densely populated by other, related organizations. The organizational world is becoming crowded, interactive, like the urban world of the individual.

The governmental-industrial-educational complexes of today probably represent only the beginning of such interdependent, interactive arrangements. For in a crowded world, organizations will need to cooperate as well as compete, to set common standards and limits, to form coalitions and combinations of all sorts. The actions of any organization will affect other organizations in much more numerous and complex ways than in the past.

The image of the free entrepreneur felling the forest to build a new world is no longer valid, nor does it any longer seem very heroic. Now he is seen as a tree-killer, an ecological pirate. And plenty of other organizations are going to be around to stop him.

*Some Alternative Ways
of Organizing for the Future*

Authority, as the *primary* mechanism of organizational control and decision making, will surely decline into a secondary, perhaps trivial mechanism in many of the new organizations we envision. And yet classical theories of organization are firmly based on authority. The hierarchy of authority has been the primary basis for orderliness in the organizational affairs of men. In a member's original "contract" with an organization, he was committed to obey orders from "properly constituted authority." From the worker in the hospital to the student in the classroom, our social consensus on the propriety of the supervisor's authority, the officer's authority, the physician's authority, the professor's authority, has kept the organizational world in order.

But the demands of the future will surely further challenge both the legitimacy and the effectiveness of authority. Professional skill and simple negotiation will partially displace authority as the basis for power within organizations. The knowledgeable specialist is not easily controlled by authority, nor is he apt to feel great loyalty to those in positions of authority. Information technology will further displace authority as a means of decision making. Reasonable alternative courses of action and their rationales will become more public; the best decisions will become more frequently knowable before they are made.

The temporary quality of tasks will tend to make the locus of authority transient, because the appropriate source of authority will depend very much on the nature of the task. And social values will change. To be obedient to authority is, to say the least, not high on the priority list of young Americans.

So we shall need alternatives to authority to achieve coordination and continuity in organizations. Such mechanisms will be hard to design. Some student groups have rediscovered the old model of participative democracy and have put it forward as one alternative: "Power to the people," with decisions taken in open public meetings. But it is hard to imagine such processes continuing through extended periods of time and over a wide range of decisions. And though policy decisions can be made this way, the control and coordination and implementation problems of organizations are still left largely untouched by that massive public mechanism.

There will surely be experimental marriages among organizations and experimental new methods of operating complex organizations. The general movement will be toward more *politically* designed organizations. The precise forms are not clear, but many managers of the next few decades are likely to become manager-diplomats, manager-negotiators, manager-arbitrators, rather than manager-rulers. They will deal not only with the highly differentiated groups within their own organization but with highly interdependent external organizations. They will not be just manager-directors, nor manager-technicians, nor manager-psychiatrists.

The wise business executive of the future would do well to look analytically and coolly at the political problems of the college president, for in a very few years his own organization may become very much like a university—more political, more diverse, more power-dispersed.

For the neophyte manager, the organizational world promises to be more exciting and more relevant, but less orderly, less reliable, less anchored, than in the past. He will have to tolerate more ambiguity and more uncertainty, both about his own career and about his work. He will have to share power and live with extended negotiation and debate. He will have to initiate social relationships in his search for new and innovative organizational coalitions. Surely he will have to speak many languages: the language of science and technology, the language of politics, the language of youth. And he might be wise to learn Chinese.

Summary

In this chapter we have reviewed the historical relationship between organizations and the environment, suggesting that there is an evolving harmony between the two. In the long run, organizations are shaped by their environments, and vice versa.

But as environments and organizations change and then exert pressure on one another, the effect is not to wipe out the old and replace it with something brand new. Rather, the new is added to the old. And the total system thereby becomes both more complicated and more differentiated.

In the future, it is likely that we will see the emergence of more temporary organizational forms as parts of more internally differentiated large organizations, more people-anchored, more technology-anchored, and less task-anchored organizations — and more multinationalism. The environment will grow more organizationally crowded and organizations more interdependent, demanding bold innovation in their design.

Notes and References

For some good background material on this whole chapter, refer once again to Daniel Boorstin, *The Americans,* 2 vols. (New York: Vintage Books, 1958 and 1965). Then you may want to look at the attitudes and beliefs of American business as reported in F. X. Sutton *et al., The American Business Creed* (Cambridge, Mass.: Harvard University Press, 1956); and once again at J. Galbraith, *The New Industrial State* (Boston: Houghton Mifflin, 1971).

Some background on the role of technology is in order, too. Try Richard L. Meier, *Science and Economic Development,* 2nd ed. (Cambridge, Mass.: M.I.T. Press, 1956). For a first-class technician's view of organizations, see J. A. Morton, *Organizing for Innovation* (New York; McGraw-Hill, 1971).

And for a sympathetic view of the values of the young, see Henry Malcolm, *Generation of Narcissus* (Boston: Little, Brown and Company, 1971).

On the emergence of human relations, look first at a couple of classics:

Elton Mayo, *The Human Problems of an Industrial Civilization* (New York: Viking, 1960; first published in 1933). And F. Roethlisberger and W. Dickson, *Management and the Worker* (Cambridge, Mass.: Harvard University Press, 1966; first published in 1939). Roethlisberger and Dickson describe the Western Electric researches of the late 1920s. The book is considered by many to be the starting-point of modern human-relations methods.

And then another classic, probably better known and more influential among United States managers than any other work on the human problems of business: D. McGregor, *The Human Side of Enterprise* (New York: McGraw-Hill, 1960).

Even some technologists were aware of the human crisis in organizational life. Norbert Wiener, the creator of cybernetics, also wrote (shortly after he published *Cybernetics*) *The Human Use of Human Beings* (Boston: Houghton Mifflin, 1959).

Back in the early twenties, the ideas of human relations (but without the technology) were being espoused loudly and clearly by Mary Parker Follet, *Dynamic Administration* (New York: Harper, 1940). Though the book was published in 1940, most of the papers first appeared in the 1920s.

An interesting piece on the *temporary* organization is W. Bennis, "A Funny Thing Happened on the Way to the Future," in H. J. Leavitt *et al.,* eds., *Organization-Environment Relations in Organizations of the Future* (New York: Praeger, forthcoming).

A thoughtful study of differentiation (to which we have referred before) is P. R. Lawrence and J. W. Lorsch, *Organization and Environment: Managing Differentiation and Integration* (Boston: Division of Research, Graduate School of Business Administration, Harvard University, 1967).

See also an influential paper by Theodore Levitt, "Marketing Myopia," *Harvard Business Review,* XXXVIII (July–Aug. 1960), pp. 45–56. Here the author urges managers to broaden their view of their own business and to think beyond current products.

For a thoughtful account of the organizational problems of a particular culture, see Michel Crozier, "Why Is France Blocked?" in H. J. Leavitt *et al.,* eds., *Organization-Environment Relations in Organizations of the Future* (New York: Praeger, forthcoming).

Name Index

Aaker, D. A., 226
Ackoff, Russell L., 84, 97
Aguilar, F. J., 63
Alderfer, Clayton P., 147
Altman, Edward I., 230
Andrews, Frank M., 56
Anshen, M. L., 120
Anthony, Robert, 79
Argyris, Chris, 29, 56, 126, 142, 147
Austin, Douglas V., 247

Bach, G. L., 120, 284
Barnard, Chester, 13, 44
Barnard, M. M., 94
Barnes, Louis B., 56
Bass, Henry, 284
Beckhard, Richard, 188
Beer, Stafford, 80, 123
Benedict, St., 196
Bennis, Warren G., 8, 126, 207, 330
Beranek, William, 247
Beyer, Robert, 80
Binzen, Peter, 79
Birks, Evan G., 80
Blair, John M., 182, 256, 284
Blake, Robert, 171
Blomstrom, Robert L., 202
Blood, M. R., 54, 56
Bloustein, R., 207
Blumenthal, Sherman C., 80
Bock, Edwin A., 267
Boore, William F., 119
Boorstin, Daniel J., 203, 207, 329
Boulding, Elise, 171
Bowden, B. V., 100
Bowen, William, 80
Bowles, Robert C., 147
Boyd, H. W., 225
Brigham, Eugene F., 246
Brown, Alvin, 13
Buck, M. S., 215
Burdick, E., 315
Burnham, James, 284
Burns, T., 28
Bursk, Edward C., 58, 215

Campbell, J. P., 146
Cartwright, Dorwin, 157, 158
Chandler, Alfred D., Jr., 56
Cherry, Colin, 73
Churchill, Winston, 29, 64
Churchman, C. West, 97, 98
Clark, Donald T., 58
Cleland, David I., 98
Cohen, Manuel F., 247
Collins, B. E., 157

Collins, V., 29
Cooper, W. W., 172, 208
Cordiner, Ralph J., 59
Corson, John J., 258, 266
Crotter, Cornelius, 266
Crozier, Michel, 330
Cummings, L. L., 56, 146
Cyert, R. M., 14, 29

Dale, Ernest, 175
Dalton, G., 207
Daughen, Joseph R., 79
Davis, Keith, 202, 207
Day, G., 226
Deardon, John, 79, 80
DeMartino, M. F., 147
Derossi, F., 291
Dickson, W. J., 13, 330
Diebold, John, 271
Dill, William R., 169
Dreyfus, Hubert L., 120
Drucker, Peter F., 29, 42, 79, 188, 208
Dubin, Robert, 28, 146

Edwards, Ronald, 188
Einstein, Albert, 85
Emery, F. E., 314
Esposito, John C., 267
Etzioni, A., 188

Fairfield, Roy P., 269
Farley, J. U., 226
Fellmeth, Robert, 267
Fiedler, Fred E., 158
Filley, Allan, 188
Firman, Peter A., 79
Fivett, Patrick, 97
Follett, Mary Parker, 318, 330
Ford, Henry, 46, 320
Ford, Robert N., 56
Forrester, Jay, 80
Freeman, Myrick, 267
French, J. R. P., Jr., 147
Friedman, Milton, 284
Frost, Robert, 66
Fuller, R. Buckminster, 49

Galbraith, John K., 225, 284, 329
Gamson, W. A., 267
Gardner, John W., 143
Garson, Barbara, 52
Gergen, Kenneth J., 127
Germane, G. E., 179
Ghiselli, E., 302
Ginzberg, E., 207, 298
Gist, R. R., 225
Glanzer, M., 158

Glaser, R., 158
Golden, C., 208
Goldman, Marshall I., 281
Goldsmith, R. W., 246
Gonzales, Richard F., 98
Gordon, Myron, 246
Gouldner, A., 207
Greiner, L., 207
Greyser, S. A., 226
Gross, Bertram M., 44
Grossman, G., 284
Grunewald, Donald, 284
Guest, Robert H., 54, 56
Guetzkow, H., 157

Haire, Mason, 188, 302
Halacy, D. S., Jr., 119
Hall, Calvin S., 127
Hamming, Richard W., 120
Hampton, David, 188
Harbison, F., 302
Hare, A. P., 157
Hare, Van Court, Jr., 98
Haveman, Robert H., 267
Heckman, I. L., Jr., 146
Heilbroner, Robert L., 47
Hein, Leonard W., 80
Heller, Frank, 302
Herzberg, Frederick, 56, 146
Hidy, Ralph W., 58
Hilton, Thomas L., 169
Hinton, B. L., 171, 172
Hofstede, R., 44
Holden, P. E., 179
Hollander, E. P., 158
Holmberg, A. R., 291
Holt, C. C., 127
Holubnychy, Vsevalod, 284
House, Robert J., 146, 188
House, William O., 80, 119
Howard, R. A., 86
Hughes, A. J., 291
Hulin, C. I., 54, 56
Huneryager, S. G., 146
Hutchison, G. Scott, 246

Jenkins, Arthur H., 127
Jennings, Elizabeth, 146
Jennings, Francis, 146
Jessup, John K., 276
Johnson, Lyndon B., 251
Joplin, Bruce H., 80
Joseph, M. L., 284

Kahn, Robert, 171
Kempner, T., 145
Kennedy, John F., 169
Kennedy, Robert F., 38
Kiesler, Charles A., 158, 171

331

Kiesler, Sara B., 158, 171
Kindleberger, C. P., 291
Kotler, Philip, 225
Kristol, Irving, 275
Kuznets, Simon, 246

Lane, Robert E., 250, 267
Lawler, E. E., 147
Lawrence, Paul R., 28, 188, 330
Leavitt, Harold J., 13, 28, 44, 120, 146, 172, 226, 316, 330
Lederer, W. J., 315
Leeds, Ruth, 171, 208
Levinson, Harry, 14
Levitt, Theodore, 11, 226, 282, 330
Lewin, K., 150
Likert, Rensis, 122, 127
Lilienthal, David E., 162, 182
Lindzey, Gardner, 127
Linn, James J., 79
Lippit, R., 207
Locke, John, 269
Lorsch, Jay W., 28, 188, 330
Lovell, E. B., 302

MacAvoy, Paul W., 266
McClelland, David C., 147, 207
Maccoby, E. E., 150
MacDermot, Galt, 321
McFarlan, F. Warren, 80
McGregor, Douglas, 13, 126, 146, 330
McKensie, R. B., 171
McMillan, Claude, 98
McMurray, Robert N., 146
McNair, Malcolm P., 146
Maier, Norman R. F., 158
Malcolm, Henry, 329
March, James G., 14, 29, 171, 188, 207
Margulies, N., 189
Marlowe, David, 127
Marshall, Howard D., 266
Martin, James, 120
Maslow, Abraham H., 127, 138–39, 146
Massey, W., 225
Matheson, J. E., 86
Mayo, Elton, 330
Mead, Margaret, 291
Mee, John, 188
Meier, Richard L., 329
Meyer, H. H., 147
Middleton, C. J., 188
Miller, James G., 182
Miller, Roger L., 267
Miller, W. B., 37
Modigliani, F., 127
Moore, D. G., 29
Morton, J. A., 329
Mouton, Jane, 171

Munsterberg, Hugo, 129
Murphy, Jerry R., 119
Muth, J., 127
Myers, C., 302
Myers, Charles A., 119

Nader, Ralph, 25, 195, 212
Newton, Sir Isaac, 85
Nixon, Richard M., 251
Norman, Adrian, 120
North, D. W., 86
North, Douglass C., 267

O'Donnell, C., 44
Oxenfeldt, Alfred R., 284

Parkinson, C. Northcote, 178
Pedersen, C. A., 179
Pelz, Donald C., 56
Penrose, Edith, 189
Perlmutter, H. V., 302
Pinfield, L., 207
Pondy, Louis R., 120, 146
Porter, L., 302
Preston, Lee E., 225
Purcell, Theodore V., 56

Rado, James, 321
Ragni, Gerome, 321
Raia, A., 189
Randall, Clarence, 35
Regan, Donald T., 262
Reilly, E., 207
Reitman, Walter R., 169
Reitz, H. J., 171, 172
Riordan, William L., 34
Ritter, Lawrence S., 246
Rivett, Patrick, 84
Roberts, K., 302
Rockefeller, John D., 201
Roethlisberger, F. J., 13, 127, 146, 330
Rogers, Carl R., 127
Ruskin, John, 235
Ruttenberg, H. J., 208

Sanders, Donald H., 119
Schein, Edgar H., 171, 172, 207
Schoen, Donald R., 146
Schultze, Charles L., 267
Scott, W. E., 56, 146
Scott, William G., 171
Seachore, Stanley E., 158
Seeber, N. C., 284
Seiler, John A., 98
Selznick, Philip, 188
Shaw, George Bernard, 235, 284
Shaw, Marvin E., 157
Shehab, Fakhri, 274
Shepard, Clovis R., 157
Shepard, Herbert, 171

Sherif, Muzafer, 165, 171, 172
Shillinglaw, Gordon, 246
Shultz, George P., 119
Silber, William L., 246
Simon, Herbert A., 13, 29, 40, 44, 97, 120, 127, 171, 207
Sinclair, Upton, 207
Skinner, B. F., 278
Sloan, Alfred P., 29, 79
Smith, Adam, 48, 127, 220, 269, 270
Solzhenitsyn, Alexander, 279
Stacey, C. L., 147
Stalker, G. M., 28
Starbuck, William H., 188, 207
Starr, Martin K., 98
Strauss, G., 44
Sturt, Humphrey, 119
Sutton, F. X., 329

Tannenbaum, Robert, 146
Taylor, F. W., 20–21, 130–31, 145, 320
Thompson, J. D., 29, 207, 315
Tilles, Seymour, 98
Tillett, A., 145
Toffler, Alvin, 208
Townsend, Harry, 188
Townsend, R., 44
Trist, E., 28, 314
Turner, James S., 267

Urwick, Lyndall F., 44, 136

Varg, P. A., 291
Vonnegut, Kurt, Jr., 116
Vroom, Victor H., 29, 146

Wagner, Harvey M., 98
Walker, Charles R., 54, 56
Walton, Richard E., 171
Ward, Barbara, 284
Watson, J., 207
Webb, E., 207
Weber, Max, 44
Westley, B., 207
Weston, J. Fred, 246
Whisler, Thomas L., 119, 120
Whyte, William F., 56
Wiener, Norbert, 80, 330
Wierzynski, Gregory, 296
Wigdor, Lawrence A., 146
Wilensky, Harold L., 207, 315
Willis, G., 145
Winter, D., 207
Withington, Frederic G., 119
Wolfe, Tom, 208, 315
Woodward, Joan, 28

Yearsley, Ronald, 119

Zander, Alvin, 157, 158

Subject Index

Acceptance model, 140–45, 154
Accessibility, problems of, 185–86
Accounting, 58, 65, 234–35
Action-adaptation, strategy of, 309–10, 313, 314
Adaptiveness to environments, 7, 308–09, 312–13, 314
Advertising, 214–16, 222
Agriculture, Department of, 263
Algorithm, 110
Ambivalence, 36–37, 43
American Association of Collegiate Schools of Business, 249
American Federation of Labor – Congress of Industrial Organizations, 249
American Kennel Club, 249
American Motors, 252
American Stock Exchange, 261
American Wool Institute, 261
Amtrak, 263
Anti-Defamation League, 249
Antitrust actions, 254
Assembly line, 45, 49
Auditing, 65
Authority, 32, 327–28: conflict and, 33–35, 167–68; decision-making, 38–39; groups and, 150, 155–56; growth and, 177, 179; managers and, 155–56; psychology, 36–39; trends in use of, 41–43
Automation, 20, 45
Autonomy, 19, 51, 53

Banks, 230, 236, 237, 241–43, 257–58
Bargaining, 253–55
BASIC, 107
Better Business Bureau, 249, 252
Bonds, selling, 237

Capital: fixed, 233–34; working, 231–34
Capitalism, 273, 278, 279
Cash flow, 71, 228–31, 241–42, 246
Caste system, 46
Central processing unit (CPU), 104–05, 118
Centralized planning, 278–83
Change: cosmopolitanism, 197–99, 206; differentiation and, 324–25; external sources of, 200–06; history of, 200–01, 206; internal sources of, 194–200; layering effect, 317–20; multipurpose organizations, 325–26; people, 195–96, 206, 323–25; reaction to, 205–06; sensors, 197–99, 206; social protest, 202–04, 206; success and failure, 196–97, 206; tasks and, 18–19, 323; techniques and, 320; technology, 204–05, 323–24; temporary organizations, 323–24
Checks and balances, 269
Child labor, 317, 318
Civil Aeronautics Board, 221
Civil-rights groups, 260
Classical view of organizations, 3–6, 8–9
Club of Rome, 249, 251
COBOL, 264–65
Collective bargaining, 42
Colonialism, 293, 307–09
Committee system, 184
Common Cause, 249
Communication, 177–79: specialization and, 47
Communism, 277–78
Competence model, 140–45
Competition, 269, 274–77: marketing and, 218, 221
Compromises, 168
Computers, 18, 73–75, 83, 99–120, 204–05, 220, 264–65, 319: central processing unit (CPU), 104–05, 118; coding schemes, 103; components, 103–08; costs, 111–12, 118; flexibility, 101; heuristic programing, 110–11; input-output stations, 106, 118; models and, 96, 109–10; people and, 115–19; possibilities of, 101–02; programing, 93, 106–08, 110–11, 118; speed, 112–15, 118; storage facilities, 103–04, 118; time sharing, 114–15; uses, 108–11
Comsat, 264
Conflict, 159–72: authority and, 33–35, 167–68; avoidance and prevention, 166–67; confrontation, 170; denial and covering up, 167; individual-group, 163–66; intergroup, 163–66; interpersonal, 160; managers and, 170; resolution of, 166–71; superordinate goals, 168–70; trade-offs and compromises, 168; varieties of, 160–66
Conformity, process of, 162

Confrontation, 170
Constitution of the United States, 255, 268–69
Consumers, see Customers
Consumers Union, 249, 251, 252, 260
Control, see Information systems
Coordination, 137, 183–85
Corporate raiders, 245
Cosmopolitanism, 197–99, 206
Cost accounting, 67–69
Cost of capital, 240–41, 246
Cost-benefit models, 88–89
Customers, 209–14: loyalty, 218; organizational interest in, 212–14; power of, 210–12; protection, 220–21; sampling techniques, 67, 88; see also Marketing

Debentures, 237
Decentralization, 179–80, 311, 314
Decision making: authority and, 38–39; computers and, 102; groups and, 151–56; see also Information systems; Model building
Dehumanization, 19–20, 45, 51–53
Depreciation, 233–34
Deviation, process of, 162–63, 179
Differentiation, 19, 320, 324–25: growth and, 181–83
Diplomatic services, 306–07
Discontinuities, systems analysis and, 95–96
Discriminant analysis, 94–95
Distribution, marketing and, 216–17
Diversification, marketing and, 218, 219
Dividends, 243, 244
Double-entry bookkeeping, 65, 75–76

Eastman Kodak Company, 221
Education: motivation and, 135; objectives and goals, 25–27; see also Universities
Egalitarianism, 41
Environmental protection, see Pollution control
Environments, organizations and, see Organization-environment relationship
European Economic Community, 250, 300
Evaluation model, 140–45, 154

333

Face-to-face selling, 215
Factoring company, 238
Failure, change and, 196–97
Federal Communications Commission, 221, 263
Fixed capital, 233–34, 245
Flexibility, in information systems, 65
FORTRAN, 107
Foundations, 236, 253
France, 279, 311, 313

General Electric Company, 313, 326
General Motors Corporation, 51, 210, 273
Germany, 279, 311
Goals, 15–16: constraints and, 24–25, 27; as imaginative process, 25, 28; as political process, 23–24; setting, 22–25; superordinate, 168–70
Government: consumer protection, 220–21; regulation, 248–67
Groups, 148–72: accessibility and, 186; authority and, 150, 155–56; conflict, 159–71; costs of maintaining, 154–55; decision making, 151–56; development and maintenance, 152–53; directing, 151–52; intergroup relations, 156, 163–66; managers and, 148, 151–55; processes, 153–54; usefulness, 149–51
Growth, 173–89: accessibility, problems of, 185–86; authority and, 177, 179; differentiation and integration, 181–85; example of, 173–77; managers and, 174–77, 180; people and, 180–81; specialization and, 50; structure and, 177–80; tasks and, 181, 183; technology and, 181; value of, 186–87; working capital and, 232

Hand-hiring, 128–30, 133, 135, 144–45
Heuristic programing, 110–11
Hierarchy of authority, see Authority
Hospitals: change and, 200; specialization, 46
Hudson's Bay Company, 326
Human relations, 6–8, 42–43, 130–31, 145, 318–19

Imperviousness to environments, 306–07, 312, 314
Incentive schemes, 19, 136, 286
Income taxes, 200
Incremental benefits and costs, 70–71
India, 46
Individual-group conflict, 160–63
Individuals, see People
Inflation, 241
Inflexibility, 11
Information systems, 57–80, 319: design of, 62, 64–69; empirical research, 60–62; human problems, 75–79; managers and, 64, 66–67;

necessity of, 59–60; planning and, 69–72; speed, 66–67; standards, 67–69; structure vs. flexibility, 65–66; see also Computers; Model building
Input-output stations, 106
Institutionalization, 33, 42, 46–47
Integration: growth and, 183–85; motivation and, 137
Intergroup conflict, 163–66
International Association for Applied Psychology, 300
International Business Machines, 25, 117, 210, 220, 234, 264–65
International organizations, 284–302: cultural differences, 293–97; factors affecting adjustment of, 295–301; guidelines for setting up, 299; managers and, 295–96; morality and propriety of, 286–91; socialization problems, 298–99; societal differences, 297–98; supranationalism, 300–02, 327
International Telephone and Telegraph Corporation, 25
Interpersonal conflict, 160
Interstate commerce, 255
Inventory control, 88, 109, 110

Japan, 278, 279
Job specialization, see specialization
Job-enrichment programs, 20, 53, 136
Joint planning, 184–85
Justice, Department of, Antitrust Division, 254, 264

Kuwait, 273–74

Labor unions, 43, 55, 200, 201, 204, 253, 318
Language, role of, 228
League of Women Voters, 251
Legion of Decency, 249
Legislative committees, 252
Linear programing, 88, 93, 95, 109
Loyalty, 198, 199, 218, 298

Management by objective, 20–22, 28
Management science, see Systems analysis
Managers: abroad, 295–96; acceptance vs. evaluation, 144; authority and, 155–56; classical view of organizations, 4, 6, 8; conflict and, 170; in future, 328–29; groups and, 148, 151–55; growth and, 174–77, 180; hand-hiring, 128–30; human-relations, 130–31; information systems, 64, 66–67; motivation of employees, 133–35, 137; organizational goals and, 24, 25; planning, 69–70; stockholders and, 243–44; systems view of organizations, 8–9; see also Model building
Mapping, 46–47

Marketing, 210, 214–26: advertising, 214–16, 222; competition and, 218, 221; distribution, 216–17; diversification, 218, 219; government supervision, 220–21; monopoly, 218, 219; morality of, 221–23; packaging, 216; population control and, 223–25
Materials cost variance, 68
Mathematical programing, see Linear programing
Matrix organizations, 184
Mexico, 294
Military, 30, 32, 33, 36, 46, 318
Model building, 81–98: computers and, 96, 109–10; discriminant analysis, 94–95; linear programing, 88, 93, 95, 109; systems analysis, 82–89, 95–97, 319; tips on, 89–92
Money, 227–47: borrowing, 235–38, 243, 246; cash flow, 71, 228–31, 241–42, 246; cost of capital, 240–41, 246; depreciation, 233–34; fixed capital, 233–34, 245; investors, 235–40; role of, 227–28; stock, 239–40, 243–46; working capital, 231–34, 245
Monopoly, 218, 219
Motivation, 133–45: acceptance vs. evaluation, 140–45; coordination and integration, 137; as imbalance, 138–40; managers and, 133–35, 137; remotivating the demotivated, 136–37
Multinationalism, see Supranationalism
Multiprograming, 114

National Association for the Advancement of Colored People, 260
National Association of Securities Dealers, 261
National Organization of Women, 249
New York Stock Exchange, 249, 255–56, 261
Nonprofit organizations, 232, 233

Objectives, 16, 25–26: management by, 20–22, 28
Operations research, see Systems analysis
Organizational development, 324
Organizational intelligence, 313–14
Organization-environment relationship, 194–208, 303–30: action-adaptation strategy, 309–10, 313, 314; adaptiveness, 7, 308–09, 312–13, 314; centralization, degrees of, 311, 314; in future, 316–30; imperviousness, 306–07, 312, 314; points of contact, 304; selective imperviousness, 307–08, 312, 314; sensing mechanisms, 304–15;

334   Subject Index

tuning, 310–11; see also Change

Packaging, 216
Parochialism, 53, 55
Payroll process, 18, 107–08
Penn Central Railroad, 241–42
People, 4, 9, 121–27: change and, 195–96, 206, 323–25; computers and, 115–19; growth and, 180–81; hand-hiring, 128–30, 133, 135, 144–45; human relations, 6–8, 42–43, 130–31, 145, 318–19; as individuals, 121, 123–24; model building, 87–88; motivation, 133–45; as resources, 122–24; tasks and, 16–20, 27; whole-man movement, 131–33, 145; see also Groups
Peru, 286–87
Piece work, 136
Planned specialization, 49–50
Planning, 23, 28: centralized, 278–83; information systems and, 69–72; joint, 184–85
Plural executive, concept of, 186
Pluralism, 268–84: alternatives to, 277–83; as deliberate choice, 268–72; failures of, 272–77
Politics, see Conflict
Polling, 217
Pollution control, 274–75, 281–82, 321
Population control, 223–25, 321
Presocialization, 298–99
Problem-solving hierarchy, 39–41, 43
Product design, 216
Programing, computer, 93, 106–08, 110–11, 118
Protest absorption, 203–04
Public opinion, 200–01

Quality control, 67

Radio Corporation of America, 25
Rand Corporation, The, 326

Regulation, 248–67: banks, 257–58; bargaining, 253–55; dependence of agencies, 260–63; education, 251–52; persuasion, 251–52; responding to, 265–66; role conflict and, 263–65; self-, 260–61
Return-on-investment analysis, 71–72
Rigidity, specialization and, 55
Robber barons, 200–01
Role specialization, 50
Rolls Royce, 230–31
Roman Catholic Church, 305

Sampling techniques, 66–67, 76, 88
Scientific Management, 131
Securities and Exchange Commission, 249, 261
Selective imperviousness to environments, 307–08, 312, 314
Sensing mechanisms, 197–99, 206, 304–15
Sierra Club, 249
Social protest, 202–04, 206
Social-action groups, 214
Socialism, 277–83
South Africa, 287
Specialization, 23, 45–56: costs of, 51–55; forms of, 49–51; functions of, 46–49; growth and, 50
Speed, information systems and, 66–67
Standards, information systems and, 67–69
Statistical sampling, see Sampling techniques
Stock, 239–40, 243–46
Structural specialization, 50
Structure, 4, 7, 9, 30–44: of authority, 30, 32–39, 41–43; growth and, 177–80; information systems, 65–66; problem-solving hierarchy, 39–41, 43; tasks, 16–18, 27
Student-action groups, 253
Students for a Democratic Society, 249
Success, change and, 196–97
Suggestion systems, 19, 136

Superordinate goals, 168–70
Suppression, social protest and, 202
Supranationalism, 300–02, 326
Survey techniques, 217
Sweden, 279
Systems analysis, 82–89, 97, 319: current examples of, 83–85; discontinuities and, 95–96; early example of, 82–83; effectiveness, 85–88
Systems view of organizations, 3–14

Tasks, 4, 10–12, 15–20: changing, 18–19, 323; differentiation, 19, 27; growth and, 181, 183; management by objective, 21, 28; people and, 16–20, 27; structure and, 16–18, 27; technology and, 16–18, 27
Taylorism, 131, 317, 318, 319
Technology, 9, 318, 321–22: change and, 204–05, 323–24; growth and, 181; tasks and, 16–18, 27
Time sharing, 114–15
Time variance, 68
Trade unions, see Labor unions
Trade-offs, 168

Underwriters Laboratories, 249, 261
Union of Soviet Socialist Republics, 41, 278–82
United Kingdom, 279
United Nations, 300
United States Congress, 255, 261, 263
United States Supreme Court, 255, 317
Universities, 46, 50, 200, 204, 205
Urban League, 260

Variance system, 68–69

Wage rate variance, 68
Working capital, 231–34, 245

Yugoslavia, 278, 279, 294

A	3
B	4
C	5
D	6
E	7
F	8
G	9
H	0
I	1

Subject Index

WITHDRAWN

STAFFORD LIBRARY COLUMBIA
658.4 Lea c.1
Leavitt, Harold J
Organizational ~~world~~

658.4   Leavitt, Harold J.
Lea
        The organization-
     al world

DATE DUE

OCT 27 '82			
DEC 10			
8 '84			
MAY 10 '85			
MAR 23			

DEMCO